The Macintosh Bible guide to Games

Bart Farkas
Christopher Breen

 Peachpit Press

The Macintosh Bible Guide to Games

Bart Farkas and Christopher Breen

Peachpit Press
2414 Sixth Street
Berkeley, CA 94710
510/548-4393
510/548-5991 (fax)

Find us on the World Wide Web at:
http://www.peachpit.com

Peachpit Press is a division of Addison-Wesley Publishing Company
Copyright © 1996 by Bart Farkas and Christopher Breen

Editor: Jeremy Judson
Copyeditor: Joe Curran
Cover design: YO, San Francisco
Cover illustration: John Grimes
Production: David Van Ness

ISBN 0-201-88381-3

9 8 7 6 5 4 3 2 1

Printed and bound in the United States of America

♻ Printed on recycled paper

Acknowledgments

Taking on a project of this scope is impossible without the helping hands and generous nature of many people.

Bart would like to thank Chris McVeigh, Karen Kaye, and especially Craig Farkas for his help in the final assault on the War Games chapter. For Carol Pantella, Bob & Jen Parsons, and family, thanks for the moral support.

Chris would like to thank Chris Lombardi, Johnny Wilson, Graham Nelson, Robert Pelak, Bob LeVitus, and his completely cool *MacUser* editor, Nancy "How-many-ends-do-you-have-on-your-candle-anyway?" Peterson. Thanks too to Eddie, Kevin, Pat, Hobey, Steve, and Steve at System 9, for putting up with all the missed gigs and scatterbrained bookings.

We'd both like to humble ourselves before:

Ted Nace for giving us the chance and Aileen Abernathy for suggesting to Ted that he give us that chance.

Jeremy Judson for shepherding the book through the process (and for believing us when we claimed that the Internet ate our chapters).

Joe Curran for slapping the spelling, punctuation, and grammar into shape and forcing sense into the sentences.

Tuncer Deniz at *Inside Mac Games* for introducing us, putting together the CD-ROM, and helping with all the company contacts.

Every single game company rep who patiently endured our calls, helped line up interviews, and supplied the necessary products. Thanks in particular to Alison Evans at CH Products, Bonnie McDowall at Cyan, and Lisa Nemec at MacPlay for going above and beyond the call of duty—we hope you each get a big fat raise.

Our interview subjects who took time out of their extremely busy lives: Chris Crawford, Rand and Robyn Miller, Eric Parker, Mark Payne, Andrew Welch, Joe Williams, Will Wright, and Keith Zabalaoui.

And finally, the immensely talented software authors who so generously allowed us to include their work on the CD-ROM.

Dedication

This book is dedicated to our wives
—Cori LaCoste and Claire Hamilton Breen—
whose boundless love, patience, and understanding
carried us through the long months.

Table of Contents

Acknowledgments iii

Dedication iv

Table of Contents v

Foreword xiii

Preface xv

PART 1   **MAC GAMING ROOTS**

CHAPTER 1   **In the Beginning ...** 3

Good Things Come in Threes 4

Early Software 9

Interactive Fiction 10

CHAPTER 2   **Classic Games**. 13

Arcade Descendants 14

    Digital Arcade Series featuring
    Defender, Joust, & Robotron 14

Defender Games 17

    Delirium 17

    Sky Shadow. 18

    Glypha III 20

Centipede Games 21

    Firefall Arcade. 21

    Apeiron 23

    Cyclone. 25

    Arashi 1.1. 26

    Swoop 28

Blaze 30
Macman Pro 30
Space Games. 32
Maelstrom 33
HemiRoids 35
Space Madness 36
Lunatic Fringe 38
Video on Tap: the False Promise? 39
Dragon's Lair 40
Mad Dog McCree 41
Pinball 43
Tristan 45
Eight Ball Deluxe 45
Crystal Caliburn. 48
Loony Labyrinth 51
Macintosh Reissues. 54
The Zork Anthology 54
Lode Runner: The Legend Returns 56
Dark Castle 58
Stellar 7. 62
Sub Battle Simulator 64

CHAPTER 3   **Traditional Games** 67
Word Games—Crossword Puzzles 68
Puzzle Master. 69
Take•A•Break! Crosswords 69
Crossword Wizard 69
Word Games—Scrabble Games 73
Scrabble 73
Maven 73
Gambling 76
Caesar's Palace 77
Trump Castle II 77
Casino Buddy. 80
Casino Master Gold. 80
Blackjack for Macintosh. 83
Blackjack Trainer 83
Virtual Vegas Volume 1: Blackjack. 85
Power Poker 87

Traditional Card Games 89
    Anyone for Cards? 89
    Hoyle Classic Card Games 89
    Eric's Ultimate Solitaire 92

Bridge Games 94
    Deluxe Bridge with Omar Sharif 94
    BridgeMaster 95
    Micro•Bridge Companion 96

Board Games. 98
    Risk Deluxe 98
    Monopoly. 100
    Mario's Game Gallery 102
    Jeopardy. 104

Chess Games 106
    Battle Chess 106
    Sargon V 108
    CheckMate 109
    Chessmaster 3000. 110

PART 2 **MODERN MAC GAMING**

CHAPTER 4 **Sports**. 115
Golf. 116
    PGA Tour Golf III 116
    Links Pro. 116

Basketball. 122
    Slam Dunk! 122

Boxing 124
    4D Boxing. 124

Racquetball 126
    Club Racquetball 126

Football. 128
    PlayMaker Football 128
    Tom Landry Strategy Football 130

CHAPTER 5 **Arcade Games**. 133
    The Fable 134
    Running and Jumping. 136
    Prince of Persia I 136

Prince of Persia II, The Shadow & The Flame 136
Deliverance 139
Out of this World 142
Flashback 144
CD-ROM Arcade Games 147
Lunicus 147
Jump Raven 150
More Arcade Action 152
Astro Chase 3D 152
Eat My Photons 156
Crystal Quest with Critter Editor. 157
Crystal Crazy 157
Spaceway 2000 160
Tubular Worlds 162
Zone Warrior 164
Glider Pro 166
Power Pete 168

CHAPTER 6   **Brain Games** 173
Blobbo 174
Ishido 175
Inline Greatest Hits Game Pak
   3 in Three/Cogito/Darwin's Dilemma/
   The Tinies/S.C.Out/Tesseræ. 177
Oxyd 184
Oxyd Magnum! 184
Troubled Souls. 186
Diamonds 188
The Even More Incredible Machine 190
Shanghai II, The Dragon's Eye. 192
Minefield 193
MacMines 193
Super Mines 193
Chiral 196
Tetris Gold
   Tetris/Welltris/Faces/Wordtris/Super Tetris 197
BreakThru 202
Lemmings Oh No! More Lemmings. 204
ClockWerx. 205

CHAPTER 7 **Maxis** 209

SIMply Empowering 210

SimCity Classic 213

SimCity 2000 216

SimTown 219

SimEarth. 221

SimLife 223

A-Train 224

SimTower 228

SimAnt 231

SimFarm. 234

El-Fish 237

Widget Workshop 238

CHAPTER 8 **Adventure Games**. 241

Puzzling Adventures 242

Myst. 242

Jewels of the Oracle 252

Hunting and Gathering. 254

King's Quest VII: The Princeless Bride 254

Return to Zork. 257

Paparazzi! Tales of Tinseltown 259

JauntTrooper Mission: THUNDERBOLT 262

Dark and Scary Places. 265

The 7th Guest. 265

Alone in the Dark 266

Quest Adventures. 269

Ultima III 269

Advanced Dungeons and Dragons Series,
Collectors' Edition 270

Quest For Glory I: So You Want to Be a Hero?. 272

Might & Magic III. 274

Worlds of Xeen 274

Digital Environments 278

Alice. 278

L-Zone 278

Gadget 278

The Madness of Roland 280

Quantum Gate 282

CHAPTER 9   **Science Fiction** 285
Spaceship Warlock. 286
The Journeyman Project 288
The Journeyman Project II: Buries in Time 290
Iron Helix 292
The C.H.A.O.S. Continuum 295
Hell Cab. 295
The Better Dead Ratification. 298
Star Trek: 25th Anniversary 300
Rebel Assault 301
Super Wing Commander 304
The Daedalus Encounter. 307

CHAPTER 10   **First-Person-Perspective Shoot-'Em-Ups** . 311
Wolfenstein 3D 312
Pathways Into Darkness 316
Sensory Overload 319
Marathon 322
Dark Forces 326
DOOM II 330

CHAPTER 11   **Conquest Games**. 335
Ruling the World 336
Empire Deluxe. 336
Civilization. 338
Populous I & II 342
Strategic Conquest 345
Warlords II. 347
Castles: Siege and Conquest 349
Space Conquest Games. 351
Pax Imperia 352
Spaceward Ho! 355
Master of Orion 357

CHAPTER 12   **War Games**. 361
Battlefront Series featuring
Panzer Battles/MacArthur's War/
Rommel/Halls of Montezuma/
Decisive Battles of the American Civil War, Vol. III   . 363
U-BOAT 367

WolfPack 371

Carriers at War I & II. 374

Flight Commander II 378

V for Victory featuring
Utah Beach/Velikiye Luki/
Market Garden/Gold-Juno-Sword. 381

World at War Series featuring
Operation Crusader/Stalingrad 384

Onslaught. 387

CHAPTER 13   **Flight Simulations** 391

The Holy Trinity. 394

Hellcats Over the Pacific. 394

F/A-18 Hornet. 396

A-10 Attack!. 400

The Rest of the Flight Sims 406

Microsoft Flight Simulator 4.0. 406

Chuck Yeager's Air Combat 407

Out of the Sun 410

F-117A Stealth Fighter. 413

Flying Nightmares. 415

Falcon MC. 418

CHAPTER 14   **Hardware** 421

Game Controllers. 422

MouseStick II 422

Mac GamePad. 422

JoyStick 427

Batwing 427

ChoiceStick 430

Jetstick. 432

Flightstick Pro 434

ThrustMaster Flight, Weapons, and
Rudder Control System 436

Other Add-Ons 439

DOS Compatibility Card. 439

Speakers. 443

PART 3   **BRANCHING OUT**

CHAPTER 15   **Network Games** 447
Minotaur (The Labyrinths of Crete) 448
Spectre 451
Spectre Supreme 451
Spectre VR. 451
Super Maze Wars 456
Full Metal Mac 459
Bolo 0.99.6 461
Pararena. 463

CHAPTER 16   **Online Gaming** 467
Commercial Services 468
CompuServe 468
GEnie 469
America Online 471
eWorld 472
Gaming Networks 473
Sim-Net/OMNI Games 473
GameNet 474
Outland 476
MacF.I.B.S. 478
MUDs. 479

Appendix 485
Game Sources 485
Online Services 491
Publications. 492
Shareware 494

Index 499

Foreword

~~~~~~

Hi. Mike Notredame here.

That's right, *the* Nostradamus.

I'm writing this in the Year of our Lord 1564, in a little abbey just a stone's throw from the outskirts of Paris. I've got a couple of years before I shuffle off this mortal plane, my main work is behind me, and frankly, delivering one apocalyptic prediction after another has taken its toll on my spirit.

So today I'm taking a break from the drudgery of star maps and tables, putting my feet up, and inscribing this foreword for Bart and Chris' delightful Mac games book. Why me? Well, I know they could use a big name to kick off their book—and considering that my name will still be known eight centuries from now, who better to handle the job? Besides, I happen to be intimately familiar with the contents of not only this book and CD-ROM but also each successive edition. Gems, each and every one.

You see, since I'm the fella who Knows and Sees All (I can't *tell* you how disappointing this can be around my birthday and Christmas), I know for a fact that you *will* enjoy this book. Append that to my list of predictions: *You will enjoy this book.*

Okay, with one exception. There's a latte-sipping guy perusing this very foreword in the computer section of Kepler's Books in Menlo Park, California, USA—yeah, you in the loafers, blue jeans, and black t-shirt—who won't enjoy this book. He has no sense of humor, and his interest in Mac games is nil. But if he takes the time to buy the book anyway, he'll avoid a nasty accident with a SamTrans bus right there in front of Ken's House of Pancakes in about ten minutes. Word to the wise, my friend … .

Sorry, I'm rambling. Where was I?

Ah, yes. You will enjoy this book for a number of reasons. To begin with, Chris and Bart have played more Macintosh games than is considered healthy for any two individuals who hope to sustain a functioning social life. If you seek guidance on which current commercial and shareware Mac games are worth your time, you couldn't find two more qualified game experts to help you along (well, okay, you will be able to find two others, but not for another 83 years, and you don't have time to wait). Secondly, the bundled CD-ROM is brimming with demos, patches, cheaters, and shareware games. Even if you never crack the book's cover, you've neatly procured hundreds of dollars' worth of software (but pay your shareware fees; I'll know if you don't). Thirdly, the intelligentsia of the Macintosh game business have consented to be interviewed for this book—if you want the real poop on Mac games, read what these folks have to say. And finally, the book's a heck of a good read. Some of the stuff in here still cracks me up.

But I'm afraid it's time to wrap it up. One of the other brothers will appear in exactly two minutes, find my feet on the table, and give me a proper scolding. After that I will consume a stew that has gone past its prime and be up half the night with indigestion.

Sometimes this soothsaying racket isn't all it's cracked up to be.

But enough about my problems. Relax, enjoy Bart and Chris' *Macintosh Bible Guide to Games*, and play a game or two. Despite all the rotten things you've heard about the future, you have plenty of time and everything's going to be just fine.

—Michel de Notredame

Preface

You hold in your hands the product of thousands of wasted man-hours—or so our mothers would claim. We can just hear their plaintive pleas:

"Honey, are you getting outside more often? All those computer games *can't* be good for you!"

"Gee, I'd love to Mom, but I can't right now. I'm going to have to call you back later in the week. I've got a pesky dragon on level 12 that's giving me a world of trouble and my chapter deadline's coming up tomorrow. Say hi to Dad."

Yes, while you slogged away at school, home, or the office, we were sequestered in the back bedrooms we call our offices, being paid to play computer games for months on end.

Try to hold back the tears of sympathy.

But transcribing conversations with our mothers and griping about our recently lonely lives is hardly what prefacing is about. No, our assignment for this page is to present you with an idea of what you'll glean from these pages now that you've been kind enough to open the book. So let's get to it.

Who Needs This Book?

- Consumers confronted with the myriad of Macintosh games—commercial, as well as free- and shareware—on the market.

  This book isn't just an excuse to wrap a few words around a disc full of games. We care about Mac gaming and think it's important for you to know the score about a particular game before laying down your hard earned cash. If we love a game, we let you know. If we loathe it, by gum, you'll hear about that too.

- Parents who routinely find themselves standing in the games aisle of their local Macintosh software outlet muttering, "I know Tommy likes airplanes, but which of these flight simulations would he prefer?"

  Mom, Dad, we've played 'em all. Turn to the appropriate chapter and you're home free.

- Anyone seeking great Mac games at a bargain price.

  Included with this book is a CD-ROM containing hundreds of megabytes of the absolutely best games in the galaxy. You'll also find cheaters, patches, demos, and selected back issues of *Inside Mac Games*, the hottest online Mac magazine going.

- Infomaniacs.

  In addition to reviews and tips, we've packed in loads of information covering such wide-ranging subjects as networking, online gaming services, MUDs, PowerBook gaming, and repetitive stress injuries. We've also included interviews with the most happening cats in the Mac games biz.

- Our families and friends.

  If we come over to your house and don't see the *Macintosh Bible Guide to Games* displayed prominently, there's gonna be trouble.

Why You Should Believe Us

We've been around. Just check out these credentials:

Bart Farkas has written for *Inside Mac Games* magazine since the dawn of time and is currently an associate editor for *MacSense* magazine. Bart resides in Calgary, Canada and spends his days working as a registered nurse while occupying his free time with computer games and various writing endeavors.

Christopher Breen wrote a hefty chunk of the Games and Multimedia chapters for the fifth edition of Peachpit Press' wildly popular *Macintosh Bible*. When not gaming, Chris is designated Tips Czar and partner to Bob LeVitus in *MacUser* magazine's Help Folder column. He also contributes game reviews to *Inside Mac Games* and Ziff-Davis' *Computer Gaming World*.

Rules of the Game

We use certain conventions in this unconventional book of which you should be aware.

Ratings

As Lucretius was so fond of saying, "Ut quod ali cibus est aliis fuat acre venenum" (What is food to one, is to others bitter poison). Taking this as our creed, we would like to remind you that our opinions and ratings are purely subjective. There is no scientific way to measure the qualitative characteristics of a particular game, so we instead rely on our years of experience to determine ratings.

Those ratings are:

5.0 = Great gosh almighty! The cream of the crop.

4.0 = Pretty darned good.

3.0 = Just fine, thank you.

2.0 = Kinda stinky.

1.0 = Execrable.

PARCHEESY DELUXE	
Fun factor	3.0
Look and feel	2.5
Value	4.0
Replayability	1.5
Overall	2.5

The half points give us a small measure of weasel room for those areas where we thought something was a *little* better than this but not quite as good as that.

Although we could have easily rated the individual aspects of each game six ways to Sunday, we managed to hold ourselves to five category divisions. They are:

Fun factor = Any joy to be had from this experience?
Look and feel = Graphics, sound, animation, and smoothness of play.
Value = Is it worth the price you pay?
Replayability = How long will you keep this game on your hard drive?
Overall = General impressions of the game.

The importance of category ratings varies among the game genres. For example, a high Look-and-feel number is obviously much more important for Flight Simulations than it is for Text Adventures. Likewise, an adventure game such as Myst that has a definite ending will have a much lower Replayability rating than an arcade game such as Apeiron. For this reason, we didn't bother devising arcane weighting schemes to arrive at the Overall rating. Rather, the Overall score is based on our general impressions of the game.

And as much as possible, we tried to avoid comparing apples to oranges. Therefore the Overall rating applies to a particular game category only. In other words, a score of 4 for a particular brain game should be used in comparison to other brain games, not to all Mac games.

Icons

Every so often you'll find a small pictogram worth exactly 1,000 words next to one of the paragraphs. These icons indicate points we feel are especially important. They are:

Something you'll find on the included CD-ROM.

This could damage you or your machinery.

A wonderful feature.

We find this appalling and make no bones about it.

Ewww.

A helpful hint.

Interruptions

Once in a great while you may discover short messages from our editor, Jeremy, that appear in this form:

Hi there!—J.

We placed his comments in the book for three reasons:

• We thought it was funny.

• We wanted to make sure that he read the whole book.

• We figured that by making him a modern-day folk hero he would allow us to keep more of the funny stuff in.

I'm cutting this entire section unless you admit that you're kidding.—J.

We're kidding, of course.

Which Games are Discussed

Considering the heft of this tome, you might assume that every Mac game ever spawned is covered in its pages. Regrettably, no. Our intention was to be as comprehensive as possible while staying within the bounds of readily-available software. In all likelihood you will stumble across a few games at your local software outlet that are not mentioned in this book. There are a number of possible explanations for these exclusions:

• The game was released after our deadline.

   We strove to be as up-to-date as possible, but eventually, work must come to an end.

• It's a shareware game that you'll find on our CD-ROM or online.

   We discuss a handful of shareware games, but the sheer number of great games prevented us from mentioning more than a choice few.

• Our pleas for evaluation copies fell on deaf ears and we were unable to obtain the game in the conventional manner.

   Everyone in the world wants free games and a small number of companies were more than a little reluctant to send out evaluation copies just because a couple of shmoes like us asked them to.

• In rare cases a game was so unremarkable that we didn't bother to waste our valuable page count on it.

Prices and Contact Information

One of the realities of the book business is that there's a significant lag between the time we type these words and when they meet your eyes. Because things change very rapidly in the software business, we elected not to include prices for the products we discuss. You may easily obtain this information from one of the mail-order houses (we've included the phone numbers and online addresses for many popular outlets), or by stopping by your local software retailer. And rather than cluttering up each review with contact information for each game publisher, we've piled a long list of them in the Appendix.

Contacting Us

We'd love to hear from you. Drop us an online line (unless, of course, you're an angry game publisher, in which case we'd like you to know that, in reality, we had nothing to do with this book, and you should direct your comments to our ghost writers.

Bart can be reached at: `farkasb@cadvision.com`

Chris' address is: `cbreen@rahul.net`

~~~~~~~~~~~~~~~~~~~~~~~~~~~~~~~~

PART 1

Mac Gaming Roots

Join us as we guide you through a brief chronicle of monochrome Mac gaming—from the putty-colored days of the orignal 128K through the SE. With our historical house in order we'll then examine contemporary Mac games whose lineage trails back to the kind of diversions found at the arcade or played at the dining room table.

CHAPTER 1: In the Beginning ...

CHAPTER 2: Classic Games

CHAPTER 3: Traditional Games

1 In the Beginning ...

Relax. Let your mind drift back through the years.

1995 ... 1990 ... 1989 ... 1988 ... 1987 ... 1986 ... 1985 ...

In 1984, the Apple Macintosh—a self-contained, putty-colored marvel—was introduced to the world as an appliance, the computer for everyone.

Does everyone crunch numbers?

No.

Does everyone create relational databases?

No.

What does everyone do?

Goof off.

Cool. This is the machine we've been waiting for.

Or so we thought. Unfortunately for Macintosh gamers, Apple quickly abandoned the appliance model and adopted the business model. The company seemed to believe that if the Macintosh was to gain wide acceptance business users must be persuaded that it was not a toy but rather a productivity tool. Pursuing this strategy meant that business software developers were actively courted while programmers interested in "lighter" fare were officially ignored.

Although this ensured that the Macintosh would become a viable computing platform, it drove many game designers to the DOS-based PC, which had a larger base of users, many of whom welcomed gaming. Lack of support from Apple dampened its games market but couldn't quite kill it. Demand for entertainment products was high, and developers brave enough to enter the market discovered that it was possible to build impressive sales figures for Mac products simply because of the dearth of available games. That's not to say that everything about those early days was dark and gloomy. During the black-and-white compact Mac years, a number of incredible games, such as Balance of Power, Dark Castle, The Colony, and Lunar Rescue, were produced. With the release of second-generation modular Macs that supported color and stereo sound, and with the wider acceptance of the CD-ROM, the market started to blossom.

Good Things Come in Threes

In recent years, three major factors have contributed to the explosion in Macintosh gaming.

Mac price reductions. Every veteran Mac user has heard these words: "Yeah, the Mac's a nice enough computer, but jeez it's expensive." Deep in their hearts, Mac users knew this was true. If you wanted a Mac, you had no alternative but to buy from Apple and pay Apple's price. The one comfort was that you had the Mac's superior graphical user interface; the poor stiffs working with PCs had to endure DOS's wretched command line interface.

Or they did until the debut of Microsoft Windows. When that occurred, the blinking command line was replaced by something marginally friendly. Unsophisticated users trying to decide between the two platforms took one look nd thought, "Heck, both of 'em have windows and menus. They must be just out the same." They then looked at the price tags, pointed to the PC, and ght, "Nope. That one's cheaper! Cheap enough, in fact, that I could give the kids."

ice from the street became, Apple, bring your prices down and start the needs of the home user. And, quick as a very slow wink, it was ple finally abandoned the Apple II, created the low-priced LC and home-use Performa lines, and opened distribution of their prod-res and warehouselike outlets. Schools stocked classrooms with couraged sales of Macs for home use. Witnessing this growth

INTERVIEW: CHRIS CRAWFORD

Veteran Macintosh game designer Chris Crawford started his programming career back in 1978 with a KIM-1 computer that had 1,024 bytes of RAM and a 6502 processor. After a stint programming games for various Atari systems, Chris adopted the Macintosh, for which he produced such classic titles as Balance of Power, Patton vs. Rommel, and Patton Strikes Back. Mr. Crawford continues to work on the Mac for his current project, Le Morte D'Arthur.

What was it like creating games for the Mac in the early days?

In the early days, there wasn't much software of any kind for the Mac. I had to develop on a Lisa, and its hard drive was slower than the floppy drive on the Mac and only held five megabytes of stuff. Things were rough back then. Compounding problems were the very negative attitudes of the Macintosh community towards games. I can still remember wangling a chance to show my game at *Macworld* magazine back in early 1985. They were polite enough to hear me out, but it was obvious that they regarded games as software scum. *Macworld* magazine never ran a story on Balance of Power, even though it was a huge seller and very strong on the Mac.

Contrast Apple's attitude about Mac games then and now.

Apple felt much the same way about games in the early days. They were, of course, willing to have me as a certified developer, but the official position towards games was none too supportive. However, this was only the company line; within Apple there were plenty of people who understood the worthiness of games. The technical support people were very helpful. Another engineering group invited me over to give a lecture and paid me with a complete fat Mac system. That was a huge lecture fee for those days! Nowadays, of course, Apple is more open to games on the Mac, but I fear it may be too little too late.

Are you satisfied that modern game designers are creating products that are as innovative as they could be?

Innovation in games? I don't think so. We crossed a major divide around 1990. It was around then that games became so snazzy that it was no longer possible for one person working at home to create one. That was when we made the final transition from lone wolf to studio. And in the process it became necessary for game developers to obtain financial support for their products before they were created, rather than after. That made the really innovative stuff almost impossible. The last truly innovative product to come out of the industry was SimCity, created in 1988.

From this point forward, games will be put together by groups. However, there is a bright spot in the future. At some point, we'll develop some institutional respect for the talent of game design, and a few "name brand" game designers will emerge who will, by virtue of their reputations, be able to command financial backing for their efforts. I expect the pendulum to swing towards more innovation when that happens.

Do you think "interactive entertainment" has a future? What will it take to make these games more than high-tech videos containing a few branching plot lines?

Interactive entertainment certainly has a much brighter future than games have. However, we're going to have to do a lot better than we're doing just now. The junk we see now, with branching plots and a bunch of video snippets, will be discarded within a few years in favor of more synthesized approaches.

If you weren't hindered by the limitations of today's technology, what kind of entertainment experience would you create?

I don't need much in the way of technology. For the short term, all I need is a system fast enough to crunch through my AI (artificial intelligence) systems and allow me to properly test them. Right now, this 26-hour test run is a little too slow for my needs. For the medium terms, what I really want is good text-to-speech synthesis. After that,

I'd like to have good synthetic video. *Not* video playback a la QuickTime, but actual synthetic video. For example: "Computer, set up the following scene: it's late afternoon in August; we're standing in a clearing in an oak forest, fairly dry vegetation. The sun is behind us and slightly to the left. First character is Nicholas—you've got his specs in your files—dressed for riding, on his chestnut horse. Second character is Henrietta, in her flowing yellow gown. They come cantering up together and halt in the middle of the clearing, looking upward. Now, draw that."

You have expressed a reluctance to upgrade some of your older software so that it will run on today's machines. Will we ever see Balance of Power again?

Balance of Power? I do believe that the world has changed. I would like to go back and do a simulation reflecting the new geopolitical realities, but I fear that it would not be so exciting as the old superpower showdowns of the 1980s. The real problem, though, is that I have at least five years of work ahead of me in interactive storytelling.

in the home market, entertainment and education developers began devoting more attention to people who owned Macs.

The Mac Games Evangelist. A few years ago, Apple finally got hip to the fact that Mac users like to goof off just as much as their PC counterparts do. Yet most new games were created for PCs. Understanding that great software is sometimes a strong enough incentive for consumers to purchase your hardware, Apple made a concerted effort to encourage game development through the auspices of the newly created position of Mac Games Evangelist.

Any predictions about the future of Mac gaming?

I am not optimistic about gaming on the Mac. I much prefer the Mac, and every time I turn on my PC, I find something new to sneer about. However, the Mac-versus-PC war is pretty well decided: the PC won. It's not a matter of superiority; Windows still can't touch System 6. But market reality beckons. In planning my interactive storytelling studio, I have had to yield to the judgment of my technical director, who wants to get Pentium machines. But I'll be sure to wash my hands after touching one.

Whoa! Chris, what's with the doom and gloom?

I don't want to sound too pessimistic here. The Mac is not going to die any time in the next ten years. It's the best machine out there, its price continues to come down; and there's a huge supply of software and a large community of Macintosh developers. I was at the MacHack conference a few weeks back, and there's still plenty of energy in that group.

I don't think that we need to think in terms of gloom and doom. I don't think

that the Mac will go the way of the Atari 800, the Amiga, or the Next—certainly not in the foreseeable future. But the Intel-based machines are unquestionably the dominant systems, and the Mac will not displace them. The big trick is whether Apple can hammer out a stable niche as the number two system. I think they can do it. In that case, the Mac won't enjoy the very best software, but it will get ports of the big hits on the PC.

Is the PowerPC going to have an impact on the Mac as a games machine?

I don't think that the PPC will do much to change things. I really want one for myself, but the momentum that the Intel-based machines have in the game design community is all but unstoppable now. In order to change things, the PPC will have to reverse the sales ratios, and that isn't going to happen.

What are your favorite early games?

I really liked Lode Runner. Didn't like Ancient Art of War. Liked Dark Castle. Hated Airborne!

This job has been held by two people: first Craig Fryar and currently Eric Klein. We imagine that a list of the responsibilities for the position might look something like this:

- Encourage developers of PC games to port their current products to the Mac. Provide technical assistance for creating reasonable ports.

- Seek out small companies creating cutting edge Mac games and provide them with encouragement and assistance.

- Convince large game publishers to devote more resources to Mac games.

- Solicit advice from game developers on how Mac technology can be improved to create a better gaming environment. The inclusion of MIDI in QuickTime 2.0 was the direct result of the evangelism effort.

- Provide developers with the latest hardware and software.

We enjoy the efforts of these men and their staffs every time we play such PC-based games as Super Wing Commander, DOOM II, Dark Forces, Links Pro, and PGA Tour Golf III.

The Power Macintosh. One of the major reasons PC games were not ported—or were ported so poorly—to the Mac is that the processor overhead required to create the Mac's high-resolution graphics was so high. Mac graphics have four times the resolution of the graphics seen on PC monitors, and their creation requires four times the processing power. After some unfortunate forays into the Mac world, PC game developers realized that the chunky graphics in their games were unacceptable to Mac users. But when they created high-res graphics, their games' performance slowed to a crawl.

In 1994, when Apple released the RISC-based Power Macintosh line of computers, game developers who had invested the majority of their resources in the PC world lost their last technology-based excuse for ignoring the Mac. These babies came with processing power to spare. Whether the developers are convinced that the Mac market is worthy of their attention and effort remains to be seen.

Up to Date

From all outward appearances, the future of Macintosh gaming couldn't be brighter. People are buying Macs in record numbers. Apple has recognized the importance of entertainment software. And the hardware offers high-resolution color graphics, 16-bit stereo audio, built-in networking, and blazing RISC speed. It took a little over a decade, but Apple's initial vision has been realized—the Mac truly is a computer for everyone. The machine we've been waiting for has, at long last, arrived.

Early Software

1984

Little entertainment software was available for the Mac in the first months after its release. One type of game on the shelves in 1984 was the text adventure. At that time, text-only games were available for nearly every computing platform. They emphasized imagination and mental prowess. Companies such as Telarium and Infocom were the forerunners in the field, and although their games did nothing to take advantage of the Mac's special qualities (save for putting a couple of commands in a menu), the games sold well in the absence of other products.

The only game to really make a splash in 1984 was Airborne! from Silicon Beach Software. There wasn't much to it other than shooting planes and paratroopers out of the sky without sustaining mortal injuries. Although Airborne! wasn't complex, it did give us a taste of what the Mac was capable of: great sound, fluid animation, and exceptionally crisp graphics. What made the graphics so special was their resolution. No computer of the day could come close to the detail the Mac's black-and-white 9-inch screen mustered. Airborne! was the precursor to the fabulously popular Dark Castle duo, whose release had a lot to do with rewriting the book on Mac animation.

1985

1985 saw increased porting of software from other platforms and, more importantly, innovative new games designed specifically for the Mac. This was the year Chris Crawford broke onto the scene with the geopolitical thriller Balance of Power, a game that helped bring mouse-driven gaming to the world.

Although Electronic Arts has only recently reintroduced itself to the Mac, in the early days the company gave Mac gamers virtual basketball via One on One with Larry Bird and Dr. J. Epyx software was responsible for another popular sports-related product—Winter Games, a collection of popular Olympic winter sports that proved to be well suited to the Mac's black-and-white screen. Spectrum HoloByte also threw its hat into the Mac arena in 1985 with GATO, a submarine simulation.

1986

Whether DOS gamers want to accept the notion or not, 1986 was a very important year for computer gaming, and all of the kudos go to the Mac. Although many DOS and Windows folk seem to think that network gaming had its genesis in 1991, the truth is that the Mac inaugurated it with two 1986 titles: Strategic Conquest and Maze Wars Plus.

1986 was also the year that many large computer game companies took a quick glance at the Mac and then just as quickly walked away. Origin's Ultima III was little more than a weak attempt at Mac gaming, and Electronic Arts took the midnight train out of town after One on One. Previously strong game companies such as Infocom and Miles Computing fell victim to bankruptcy or takeovers.

Fortunately though, for every company that dropped out of the Mac market, another stepped in to deliver a solid product. Silicon Beach Software released the stunning (and recently rereleased) Dark Castle, a game that dismissed many critics' suggestions that the Mac couldn't handle a lot of graphics and animation.

ICOM released DejaVu in the same year, and although in black and white, it gave computer gaming its first taste of mouse-driven graphic adventures. This series of games included Uninvited and Shadowgate. It used an innovative graphics engine that allowed the user to interact with the surroundings by manipulating objects on the screen through pointing and clicking. This breakthrough is still utilized in many adventure games.

1987

In March of 1987, Apple released the Mac II. It came complete with color, higher memory capacity, and a large screen. The entry of this machine gradually spelled the end for a number of our old favorites and marked the beginning of modern Mac gaming.

Interactive Fiction

In the early days of computer entertainment software, when 3D graphic interfaces and colorful sprites were little more than programmers' fantasies, interactive fiction (IF) ruled the roost. These games, lacking graphics and sound, depended solely on rich storytelling and beguiling puzzles to capture the player's attention. For those who missed these text-based delights, here's the idea:

You played the main character in a story centered on puzzle solving and goodie gathering. To travel around the story's landscape, you used simple direction commands like N for north and D for down. As you entered unexplored areas, you were greeted with such colorful descriptions as:

```
You are standing next to a foul-smelling, weed-choked
drainage ditch. In the ditch is a rusty can, a blue
salamander, and a swarm of horrid insects. To the
north is a cave. To the south is a drinking fountain.
Paths lead to the northwest and southeast.
```

Interaction with this particular scene might have taken the form of:

```
> TAKE THE CAN
Taken.
> TAKE THE INSECTS
The insects swarm angrily up from the ditch.
They are not happy.
> KILL THE INSECTS WITH THE FLY SWATTER
Nothing happens.
Now they're really angry!
> RUN
Which direction?
> RUN EAST
Sorry, you can't go that way.
The insects begin to sting you.
> RUN SE
Forest Path
You run along the path, but the insects follow and
continue to sting.
It appears that you are allergic to the venom of this
particular variety of flying insect.
**** You have died ****
```

Encounters like these quickly taught you that maintaining up-to-date maps and saving early and often were vital to success.

A Short Story

Interactive fiction was first popularized in 1977 with a program called ADVENT (also known as the Colossal Cave Adventure) written by Don Woods and Willie Crowther. This game contained such elements as mazes, inventories, and the shorthand verb/noun parsing (KISS MULE) that the genre became known for.

A group of MIT students followed ADVENT with a game they wrote called Dungeon (better known as Zork). In 1980, these students went on to create Infocom, a company that produced such popular IF titles as those in the Zork series, Planetfall, and a particular favorite of ours, Leather Goddesses of Phobos.

Infocom ran into financial trouble in 1986 and 1987 and was purchased by Activision. Following the sale, many Infocom staff members were laid off and the company became, for all intents and purposes, little more than a fondly remembered brand name.

Still Breathing

With advances in technology, interactive fiction fell out of favor with mainstream computer gamers. Players were drawn away by multimedia adventures that, though visually and sonically impressive, often lacked the quality story lines that made interactive fiction so appealing.

Thankfully, interactive fiction lives on via the Internet. Over the years, a number of programming tools have been created that allow resourceful users to create their own text adventures. Along with such classics as the original Colossal Cave Adventure, Deep Space Drifter, and Unnkulian Unventure, you can find brand-new IF online. Some of it is as compelling as the original Infocom titles.

The big daddy of IF Internet ftp sites is: `ftp.gmd.de/if-archive`

If you lack full Internet access, commercial services such as America Online, CompuServe, eWorld, and GEnie carry a selection of text adventures.

CD-ROM Alert

The creators of three interactive fiction programming tools were generous enough to grant us permission to include their work on our CD-ROM. In addition to a couple of games, the Interactive Fiction folder contains Adventure Simulator by Scott Henderson, Michael Roberts's TADS, and Graham Nelson's Inform (Mac front end courtesy of Robert Pelak; z-code interpreter by Andrew Plotkin). Although we expect only a small percentage of our readers to use these tools, we include them in the hope that they will encourage those with the necessary desire and talent to create enthralling new text adventures. (And when you do, send us copies.)

2 | Classic Games

In the electronic entertainment industry, time doesn't work the way it does in real life. It doesn't plod along through lazy weekends or shift gradually over the seasons. At the end of a long day, it doesn't loosen its belt and put its feet up on the coffee table. In this business, in which time is measured in milli-, micro-, and nanoseconds, things develop and change at blinding speeds, and games that were considered to be on the cutting edge as recently as the second Reagan administration are now thought of as quaint and outdated.

But as any gaming pundit will tell you—and we fit that category as well as anyone else—what makes a game work is the game itself, not the technology surrounding it. So although some of these games and the concepts behind them are as old as the hills, their entertainment value has diminished very little over the years. And why *should* detonating a wicked alien, knocking over a spot target with a well-placed pinball, or hunting and gathering in a classic text-based game be any less enjoyable today than it ever was?

So limber up those arcade muscles, flipper fingers, and text adventure synapses and join us as we take a peek at reissues and enhanced descendants of our oldest and dearest electronic friends.

Arcade Descendants

Since the dawn of video gaming—actually, if we consider Pong to have marked the dawn, the arcade era began at about a quarter to eight in the morning—players have taken special pleasure in eluding or destroying ranks of tiny hostile creatures who flicker across the lengths and breadths of video screens. Millions of quarters and thousands of hours were invested in such classic coin-op machines as Space Invaders, Asteroids, PacMan, Defender, and Centipede.

Although today these games are considered relics, they were the foundation upon which many modern Macintosh arcade games were built. Without Asteroids, could Maelstrom exist? In a Centipedeless world, who would have thought of Apeiron and Firefall Arcade? Lacking PacMan, would Super Maze Wars have found its way to market?

The games we discuss here are the spiritual descendants of these venerable machines. They've been tarted up with vivid color, 3D graphics, and dazzling sound, but at heart they're the same games we fell in love with at the old arcade.

Digital Arcade Series featuring Defender, Joust, & Robotron
Digital Eclipse

You can't get any more traditional than these three classic arcade releases from Digital Eclipse. These aren't revisions of the old Williams coin-op games, they *are* the Williams coin-op games—right down to the hidden bookkeeping and

game adjustment screens. You won't have to plunk a quarter into your floppy drive to get them to run, but the original computer code from the stand-alone machines was directly ported, thanks to emulation trickery, to the Macintosh. When you fire up Defender, Joust, or Robotron, you will hear the same sounds, view the same screens, and go through the same hell that players enjoyed over a decade ago.

Just in case you weren't around for the original experience or through the passage of time have simply forgotten, here's the lowdown.

Defender

You control a space ship that jets up and down and left and right across a scrolling screen. Below are the humble citizens who look upon you as their sole defense against the alien hordes creeping down from the top of the screen. To keep the loving respect and fidelity of the population, all you need do is vaporize the aliens and rescue any citizens who have been carried away by the unfriendly other-worlders. Should the aliens succeed in transporting any townspeople to the top of the screen, these once-friendly folks experience a hideous metamorphosis and become mutants. And guess what? They hold grudges.

Joust

You sit astride a flapping ostrich, lance poised forward, and have at a collection of buzzard-riding bad guys. To dismount the pale riders, you must furiously flap the ostrich's wings and crash down on your opponents from above. As the buzzard dwellers leave their mounts, collect the glowing green spheres that have been left in their stead. Oh, and while you're at it, avoid the "unbeatable" pterodactyl and lava trolls.

Robotron

It's the year 2084, and despite the warnings of movies like *2001* and *Terminator*, humankind has created a race of robots that, wouldn't you just know it, has decided that flesh and blood is passé and all humans must be eliminated. You control a character who possesses the superhuman powers necessary to blast the robots back to the Radio Shack from whence they came. To put thought into action, you can walk and fire in eight directions—a good thing considering that at the opening of each round you are completely surrounded by clanking metal beings who wish you anything but well.

Low Tech

To fully appreciate these games, you have to look at them for what they are: pieces of history. You can't fairly compare these things to modern Mac games

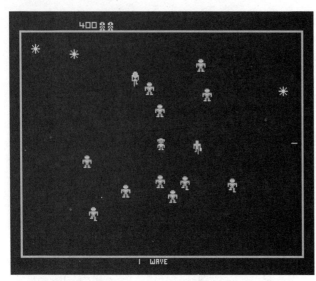

Yup, we used to think those little blocks in Robotron represented terrifying robots.

that feature high-resolution graphics and stereo sound. Technology has advanced tremendously in the last 15 years, and these games look decidedly cheesy by modern standards. Not everyone will find these machines as endearing as we do.

But players who spent any time with coin-op arcade machines in the early '80s will be amazed to see their old friends delivered so faithfully to home computers. And those age-impaired individuals among us who'd like to see what their elders had to grapple with may find that these "old" games still have some life left in them.

Pros: Duplicates of the original Williams arcade machines. Finally we can see how the evil arcade bosses altered these machines to suck down our quarters.

Cons: Blocky graphics and cheap sound may not appeal to everyone. Games haven't gotten any easier.

System Requirements: Color or grayscale monitor, 20MHz-68030 processor or better, 4MB RAM, 2.5MB hard disk space, System 6.07 or higher.

DIGITAL ARCADE SERIES	
Fun factor	4.0
Look and feel	5.0
Value	3.0
Replayability	4.0
Overall	4.0

Tip

• Once the games have gone through the initialization stage, press the Return key to bring up the Bookkeeping and Game Adjustments screens. See, you were right. Some machines *were* harder than others.

Defender Games

Although you can get the real thing in Digital Eclipse's release of Defender, if you want more of this kind of side-scrolling action, you have a couple of alternatives. One is an outstanding shareware program from rising star Tuan Huynh that updates Defender with great sound and graphics. The other is another wacky Casady & Greene vehicle that is only loosely based on the Defender model.

Delirium
Tuan Huynh

Along with Andrew Welch and a few others, Tuan Huynh makes some of the coolest shareware games ever to hit the great electronic wagontrail. Delirium is a fine addition to his other well-known work, Space Junkie.

Delirium Tremendous

Defender players will feel right at home once the game begins. Below are the familiar mountains studded with little blue citizens. Above are the octopusinal aliens bent on carrying off the poor humanoids. And there you are against a 3D starfield in your round little fighter (okay, Delirium's fighter *is* a little less sleek than its ancestor).

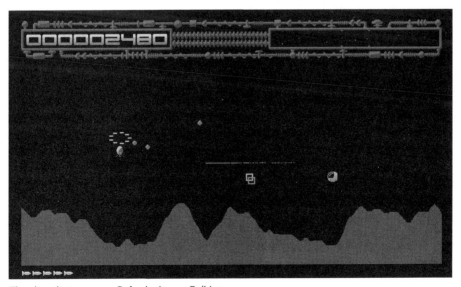

The glory that once was Defender is now Delirium.

Other than graphics and sound, the only obvious difference between the two games is that Delirium makes it unnecessary to push a thrust key to move the fighter; simply pressing the left or right direction key will get the job done. For this omission, we raise a hearty cheer. In a game this fast and frantic, one less thing to worry about is a godsend.

Pros: Great updated version of a classic game. Inexpensive.

Cons: Just as tough as the original.

System Requirements: 13-inch color monitor, 68020 processor or better, 2MB RAM, 450K hard disk space, System 6.07 or higher.

DELIRIUM	
Fun factor	4.0
Look and feel	4.0
Value	5.0
Replayability	4.0
Overall:	4.0

Sky Shadow
Casady & Greene

Chris, the co-author of this book, is the guy responsible for those five mice that adorn the box that Sky Shadow comes in, and his opinions haven't changed much over the years. Yes, the game shows signs of aging; its performance on a Power Mac is a little shaky; the 4-bit color graphics are strictly vintage 1989; and when the game was written, the use of stereo sound in games was still only a dream. But even after all these years, Sky Shadow still cracks him up.

What's So Funny?

Patrick Buckland, the guiding light behind the Crystal Quests, came up with this little gem, and it bears his unmistakable mark. The game is packed with hysterical sounds and the oddest collection of enemies you're likely to find any-where in the galaxy. Rather than Defender's lean and mean fighter, you pilot a funky craft that looks like a battered piece of cookware. The scenery below is completely cartoonish and features such oddities as giant mushrooms and rail-road flatcars carrying enormous chicken carcasses (at least, we think that's what they are).

The dreaded Razoropers have occupied your home town, and only through your courageous efforts can the remaining citizens be saved. You kerchunk your way across the scrolling landscape, blasting whatever outrageous flying things the Razoropers throw your way. When not otherwise engaged destroying your ene-my's air force or picking up the myriad of goodies scattered across the skies, you can drop bombs on the occupied territories below. Once out of bombs, you must

Smarts ▦ ▦ ▦ ▦	7	Bombs		0	Ships ✈ ✈ ✈		3
Shields ▮▮▮▮▮▮	100%		✖	Damage			
Player 2 score	0	Ship score		51300	Player 1 score		51300

Is it a bird? Is it a double-boiler? No, it's Sky Shadow's funky spacecraft.

land your craft at the local air base—no mean feat—where your ship is rearmed and repaired.

Not a Laughing Matter

Although half of us dearly love this game, we must, in good conscience, issue a warning. Back in 1989, people weren't nearly so concerned about repetitive strain injuries as we are today. Because Sky Shadow lets you fire only with the mouse button, because only one shot is fired per press of the mouse button, and because the game is so addicting, we strongly recommend that you play this game only with a game controller that can be configured to repeat-fire. Sky Shadow is a kick in the pants, but it's not nearly entertaining enough to risk the kind of physical injury that could result from hours of nonstop fun.

DANGER

Pros: Extremely funny sounds and graphics. Runs in black and white. Hysterical take on Defender-style game.

Cons: Not Power Mac-friendly. Serious risk of repetitive strain injury.

System Requirements: Mac Plus or better, 1MB RAM, 1.2MB hard disk space, System 6.07 or higher.

SKY SHADOW	
Fun factor	4.0
Look and feel	3.0
Value	3.5
Replayability	4.0
Overall	4.0

Tip

• After you've flipped into double-speed Mega Mode and have obtained the Invulnerability Shield, position your ship to the left-middle of the screen. Scan the right of the screen to pick up any incoming goodies. While in this mode, don't bother picking up Healing Shields; you're already fully healed.

Glypha III

john calhoun

If you liked Joust, you'll love Glypha. Glider author john calhoun—yes, that's the way he writes it—put together this tribute to Joust years ago and has recently upgraded this classic freeware game to version 3. The code for version 3 was written from the ground up, and the program now supports System 7.

Although Glypha sports a colorful Egyptian motif, its basic theme is the same as Joust's. You ride a goose against the fearsome flying sphinxes (try saying that three times fast). If you crash down on them from above, they turn into eggs that can be collected for points. If you fail to collect the eggs, they hatch into stronger sphinxes.

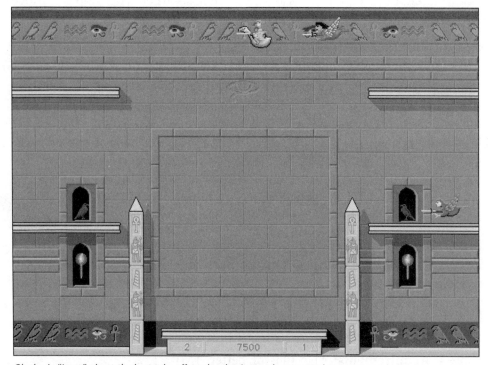

Glypha is "Joust" about the best take-off on the classic arcade game we've ever seen.

Glypha has been one of our favorites for years. The graphics are wonderful, the sounds terrific, the game play just as great—okay, more so, but don't tell Williams—as the original arcade machine, and you can't beat the price—Glypha is freeware.

GREAT FEATURE

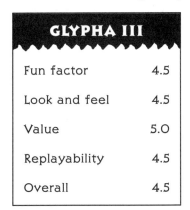

GLYPHA III	
Fun factor	4.5
Look and feel	4.5
Value	5.0
Replayability	4.5
Overall	4.5

Pros: It's cool and it's free.

Cons: We wouldn't dare.

System Requirements: 8-bit color Macintosh, 1.8MB RAM, 600K hard disk space, System 6.05 or higher.

Centipede Games

Centipede was one of the '80s most popular video arcade titles. The idea was simple: You control a moveable gun at the bottom of the screen and attempt to blast to bits a scurrying centipede before it has a chance to bite you. Scattered about the screen are a variety of mushrooms that provide cover for the centipede as it wends its way southward. Although the mushrooms can be destroyed, you must expend several shots to do so. And you can fire another shot only when your last shot has found a target.

As you hit the centipede, it separates into segments, all of which now follow new courses. While you're about the business of hunting down the many segments, you are harassed by a poisonous spider who leaps in from the sides of the screen. In later levels, a scorpion who poisons select mushrooms appears. Once the centipede comes in contact with one of these toxic toadstools, the multiped heads directly down, and unless you're quick on the trigger, you become bug chow.

Two excellent descendants of Centipede are now available for the Mac: Inline's Firefall Arcade and Ambrosia's Apeiron.

Firefall Arcade
Focus Enhancements

CD

Take Centipede, add some beautiful graphic elements and a jazzy New Age sound track, and you've got Firefall Arcade.

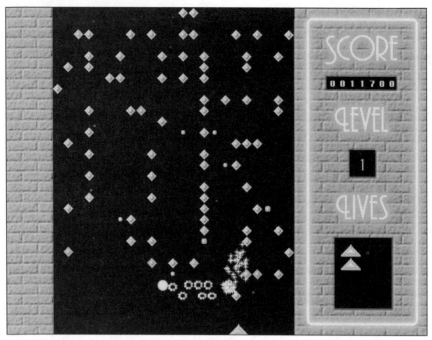

With a shower of sparks, another piece of the fireworm bites the stardust in Firefall Arcade.

Rather than centipedes, you're hunting fireworms that soak up valuable minerals necessary for the survival of the human race. Instead of mushrooms, you must clear the area of crystalline minerals. In place of poisonous spiders, you will encounter Everlasting Barriers that creep along the bottom of the screen. And like Centipede's fleas, little bunched balls that look vaguely like strings of carbon atoms drop from the top of the screen, adding more crystals during their journey.

Extra Segments

GREAT FEATURE

In addition to the neonesque graphics and intriguing soundtrack, Firefall Arcade tosses in a few other goodies. To begin with, some of the crystals carry such bonus PowerUps as three-way shooters, shields, and double shots. To free and collect them, you must first destroy the crystal and then run your shooter over the falling PowerUp. Also, at the end of each round, you are thrust into a bonus round in which you are invincible and need concern yourself only with shooting the swirling fireworms that swoop colorfully by.

Because this is another game from Pangea Software (the same folks responsible for Power Pete), you can rest assured that it's well designed and a treat for the eyes. The main screen, with its cascading shower of colorful sparks and thrumming synthesizer music, is so mesmerizing you'll be tempted to simply stare at the screen for hours on end.

A Few Flames On Firefall Arcade

What would a review be without complaints? To begin with, there are only nine levels of play. Traditionally, arcade games go on and on until the demands made on the player are superhuman. Secondly, each time you lose a life, the game resumes from the point where you left off rather than starting at the beginning of the round. This is challenging, yes, but there are times when you're boxed in by crystals, barriers, and fireworms when you have no hope of escape. At these times, you quickly lose your remaining lives and that's no fun.

LOUSY FEATURE

Pros: Outstanding graphics. Groovy music.

Cons: Only nine playing levels. Game continues from where your last shooter was destroyed.

System Requirements: Color Mac of LC variety or better, 3MB RAM, 3.5MB hard disk space, System 6.07 or higher.

FIREFALL ARCADE	
Fun factor	4.O
Look and feel	4.5
Value	3.5
Replayability	3.O
Overall	3.5

Apeiron
Ambrosia Software

CD

Apeiron comes from the mind of Andrew Welch, one of the preeminent game designers of our time (and we think his shareware utilities are also really cool!). This game is different from Firefall Arcade in that it completely embraces the insect-and-mushroom theme and adds a fair dollop of humorous graphics and sound to the mix.

Big Yucks

Take, for instance, Cheech the Pentipede, who divides, but we're not sure how well; Larry the Scobster, part scorpion, part lobster, who dances a treacherous tarantella across the screen; and Groucho the flick, a tick/flea combination who rains new mushrooms across the screen. Drawn in the style of the Max Fleischer and Warner Brothers cartoons of the '40s, these characters, though deadly, are just as cute as … well, bugs.

GREAT FEATURE

In keeping with this comic theme, the bonuses known as PowerUps in Firefall Arcade are called Yummies in Apeiron, and they bestow such wonders as the Z-145 Mark III Transflogulator tracking device, the QMT-69 Sprinkly Shield, and YummieLock. When you come in contact with Larry, your poor little dilithium crystal shooter explodes "like a grenade in a china shop" and you are consoled by a whimpering, whining voice that says, "Oh no."

Apeiron is a terrific game. Our one suggestion would be to include the kind of keyboard controls found in Firefall Arcade for movement of the shooter. Even though Centipede games depend largely on aiming and squeezing off a single shot rather

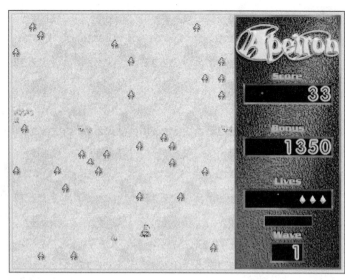

Blast through the mushrooms to try to desegment the Pentipede.

DANGER

than rapidly clicking the mouse button, it's always a temptation to let loose, and a sore wrist can result.

Food of the Gods

If Andrew had a lick of sense, he'd be working for a commercial software concern and driving a Ferrari. We're thankful he doesn't. Apeiron is commercial-quality software at a bargain price. Although we've extolled you to register your shareware elsewhere in this book, consider this a not-so-subtle reminder. People like Andrew Welch are a rare breed. Encourage him. Give him your money. Send him cookies in the mail. We don't want to lose this kind of talent to GameCorp of America.

Pros: Nearly perfect arcade game.

Cons: No keyboard controls.

System Requirements: 13-inch color monitor, 3MB RAM, 3MB hard disk space, System 6 or higher.

APEIRON	
Fun factor	4.5
Look and feel	5.0
Value	5.0
Replayability	4.5
Overall:	4.5

Tip

• At the end of each round, place your shooter below the closest row of mushrooms and hold down the mouse button. This quickly clears away any nearby mushrooms before the Pentipede has descended very far or the Scobster has appeared onscreen. Because the shooter only fires again after the last shot has found a target, don't bother trying this with mushrooms you can't actually touch with the shooter.

Cyclone
High Risk Ventures

It's a time-honored tradition to resurrect classic arcade games from the era when an arcade was the only place a video junkie could play high-quality games. (Back in those days you were a technomaniac if you had an Intellivision system linked to your TV with an RF modulator. Home video games of the day had a long way to go to match the power harbored by dedicated processors in the upright machines.) While we are mulling over the damage to our joints that games like Asteroids and Defender imposed, we shouldn't forget some of the lesser titles that had their 15 minutes of fame, like Star Castle, which has received a quality re-creation in Cyclone from High Risk Ventures.

Spin-o-Rama

Cyclone puts you in a practically defenseless ship face to face with an enemy who is surrounded by several layers of rotating shields. From time to time, honing

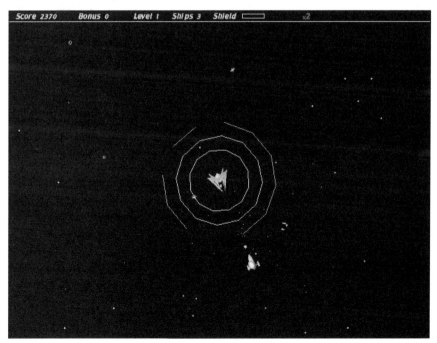

This re-creation of Star Castle incorporates 3D rendered graphics and a few new weapons to make this classic even more endearing.

spark mines fly off the enemy's shields and smash into your own shields, spilling coffee all down the front of your shirt. To get even, you must punch a hole in the three layers of shields and time your shot perfectly to destroy the central foe. If you attempt to shoot out all three layers, the pesky adversary merely builds another, making a war of attrition impossible. In the attempt to foil the shields, it is important to remember that if you can see the enemy ship, he can surely see you and thus blast you into oblivion.

Additions

A classic like this would quickly become rather stale if not for an injection of flashy graphics, sound, and toys to make blasting truly a pleasure. Cyclone does not disappoint; it adds such nuances as triple and auto-shots, extra shields, bonus points, a challenge round, and even a "keep locket" that lets you maintain your weapons status after death. Controls in Cyclone are whatever you want them to be (the opening control screen is an exact copy of the other game these guys developed, Space Madness).

True to Form

Cyclone is an accurate and enjoyable resurrection of one of the lesser classic arcade games, and Mike Kelly and Jon Milnes have done an outstanding job of marrying updated graphics and sound to the feel of the old game. Apparently they accomplished this in part by having an original upright version of Star Castle installed in their office. Just for research, of course. Yeah, sure.

Pros: Online documentation and new features that enliven a faithful re-creation of a classic make this a great value at only $10 shareware.

Cons: Endless loop game with no ending.

System Requirements: 256-color Mac, 68020 or better, 2.5MB RAM, 1.6MB hard disk space.

CYCLONE	
Fun factor	4.0
Look and feel	3.5
Value	4.0
Replayability	3.5
Overall	3.5

Arashi 1.1

Project STORM Team

Atari's Tempest was one of the hottest early vector-style arcade games. This challenge had you operating a small yellow craft around the edge of a geometric shape while enemy craft climbed toward you from below. It could be likened to pouring boiling oil on an enemy who was attempting to scale futuristic castle walls. Once the foe was eliminated, you were literally sucked through the structure and

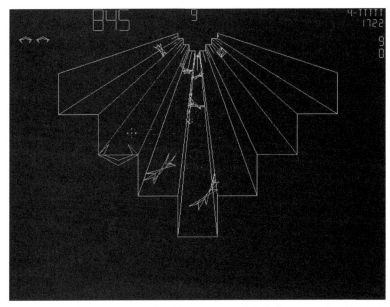

*Arashi is almost an exact clone of Atari's Tempest, and with a freeware price (nothing)
it can't be beat.*

into the next level. Arashi, from the Project STORM Team, is by far the most
accurate arcade reproduction of this game available; it is faithful to the original in
every aspect of play. Apparently the similarities are a little too remarkable, and
rumor has it that Atari would threaten a law suit if Arashi was put on the market.
So, much to our good fortune, this remarkable game is freeware for all to enjoy
without having to think about opening the old pocket books.

GREAT
FEATURE

What Do You Want for Nothing?

Arashi's online instructions are a tad vague, and perusing the Read Me file is fairly critical if you want to know the ancient secret of changing the control keys.
However, once you've oriented yourself to Arashi's ins and outs, the controls
become almost second nature. You can set the keyboard to rotate your ship
around the edge of the chasm, but we found a trackball to be the optimal form
of locomotion. Keep a firm finger on the Super Zapper button for those tricky
situations when the bad guys climb to the top, because unlike Tempest, Arashi
does not allow for an escape once they have fully ascended.

TIP

Credit Due

Full credit goes to the Project STORM Team that devised a Vector animation
toolkit to develop Arashi. With the only cost that of the download, you cannot
surpass the value and fun of this clone of the classic arcade thriller. Its solid
controls, faithful vector graphics, and similar-to-the-original sound assure

Arashi of a place on hard drives wherever Macs are found.

Pros: True arcade-style play. Amazing re-creation of Tempest. Freeware.

Cons: 256-color Macs only. Interface could be more intuitive.

System Requirements: 256-color Mac, 68020 or better, 2MB RAM, 370K hard disk space.

ARASHI 1.1	
Fun factor	3.5
Look and feel	3.5
Value	5.0
Replayability	3.0
Overall	3.5

CD

Swoop
Ambrosia Software

Thank goodness for a fickle public. For just as interest rates and hair styles change, so must a video game evolve in new and exciting directions. The genesis of Swoop can be traced back to the venerable Space Invaders, which had alien ships moving incrementally from side to side while you fired missiles at them from below. From this basic notion evolved the two classics Galaga and Galaxian, which may be directly responsible for an exponential increase in wrist and finger injuries across America. The premise was similar to that of Space Invaders, but the insectoid craft migrating across the phosphorus would occasionally run a dive bomb right down your throat. Add to this some special bonus rounds, along with a variety of naughty enemies, and you've got a video game blockbuster. True to their style, Ambrosia Software took a classic game and made the necessary awesome enhancements to create another champion.

Bombardment of the Bugs

To make a short story long, you have been sent to protect miners on an alien planet from waves of attacking bugs whom the miners unwittingly awakened from a cozy slumber. You are equipped with three ships that are strikingly reminiscent of some space ships seen in B-grade movies in the '50s. Standard armaments issue includes unlimited bullets, one Reagan Shield (orbital defense), and a Dynamic Duo (double shot). The latter are temporary weapons that linger precious few seconds before disappearing. Fear not, brave warrior, for you can earn more interesting goodies, such as "Ollie North-Class Shields," by annihilating an Imperial Flagship. Swoop involves wave after wave of bulbous bugs descending upon you while dropping everything from bullets to proximity mines. They come at you in carefully planned formations of three or four Toady Escorts or as single Kamikaze Blue Grunts making wide sweeping passes designed to lull you into irritability. The carrot dangled in front of your nose is the challenge level, which comes up after the completion of every fourth round. These are swooping bug fests in which careful aim and a quick trigger finger can equal big point totals and maybe extra ships.

Accuracy Is King

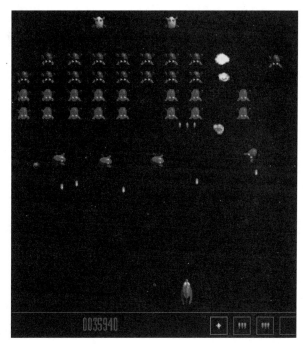

Accuracy is paramount in this high tension shoot-'em-up from Ambrosia.

To make any progress in Swoop, you must be highly accurate. You may think you're hot stuff because you can knock off an entire asteroid in Maelstrom with five shots, but you ain't seen nothing until there are four Shadow Swoopers screaming toward you in formation. Only one shot at a time can be on the screen (unless certain special weapons are in use), making every shot of critical importance. When there's a giant Blue Spider breathing down your neck, you don't want to be waiting for an errant bullet to leave the screen so you can fire your gun again. Swoop's controls are left, right, fire, and weapon selection, which leaves you to concentrate on where you're shooting instead of fumbling with finger placement while a big nasty bug flies into your mouth.

Don't Bug Me

Swoop incorporates its musical score in a manner we have never before witnessed in an arcade game or, for that matter, in any game. The ship's movements are actually tied in with a full-orchestra soundtrack. Musical "hits" are provided when the bugs begin to swoop or when a ship is destroyed. The game is worth a look for this feature alone.

GREAT FEATURE

We've been considering starting a 12-step program to deal with the addictive nature of Swoop, but we can't seem to pull ourselves away from it long enough to organize a meeting. The only gripe we could aim at Swoop is that it's very difficult to play; some people may give up before mastering its basic structure. Ambrosia is on track again with another update on an old theme. Swoop is fun, challenging, and an incredible value.

Pros: High-quality graphics and awesome sound. Easy to learn. Fabulous incorporation of musical score. Great value.

Cons: Highly addictive. High difficulty level.

System Requirements: 256-color Mac, 4MB RAM, 3.5MB hard disk space, System 6.07 or higher.

Blaze
Softstream International

SWOOP	
Fun factor	4.0
Look and feel	5.0
Value	5.0
Replayability	4.0
Overall	4.5

Macman Pro
Varcon Systems

PacMan has gone down in history as one of the biggest smash hit video games ever. We recall watching an ABC news spot about a guy who had spent hundreds of dollars figuring out the patterns made by the ghosts as they chase the PacMan. Although it goes without saying that to produce a comprehensive game book your humble scribes must play many a game, we hope we never deteriorate to the point of drooling, glazed-eyed exhaustion while a news team examines our heroic exploits in the battle against Zontar. However, that is just the kind of power games like PacMan could exert. They were indeed a wonder to behold.

Blaze

Although there are six or seven PacMan-type games lingering in the shareware domain, the best of the breed lies in the commercial sector. Blaze, from Softstream International, gives us a variation on the theme that sees the protagonist as a water droplet being chased by bits of fire. Blaze occupies about two-thirds of your screen. It has decent sound effects, average animation, and is, well, average. It will supply the user with the desired amount of PacManism needed to satisfy a craving. All of the traditional components are present, including the pellets in the corners of the maze that enable you to gobble the fire wicks. You can also configure the control keys to whatever your heart desires. (No doubt many will configure their control keys to play Maelstrom rather than Blaze.)

Macman Pro

Macman is perhaps the most accurate reproduction of the original title. However, to really enjoy its effects you need a magnifying glass mounted on your screen to see the barely one-third size image that appears on a 13-inch monitor.

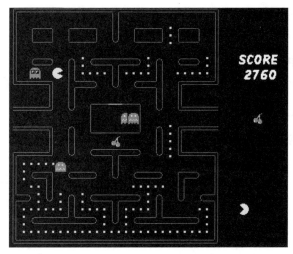

Macman Pro could easily be called "The Incredible Shrinking Game" judging from the miniature playing area.

The sound effects are lame as well, consisting of bleeps and bloops that don't even do the original justice. Although Macman Pro plays alright, its tiny screen size and poor sound put it in second place behind the average-quality Blaze.

Maybe Next Time

Perhaps in the future we will see more exciting variations on the PacMan theme that can stay true to the original but still exploit the Mac's graphics and sound

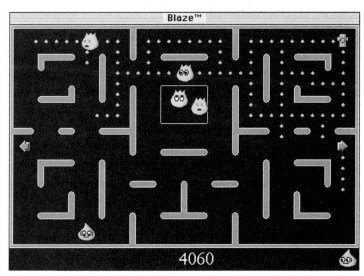

At least the screen size in Blaze is adequate. Note the alteration in theme from a PacMan to a droplet of water.

BLAZE	
Fun factor	2.5
Look and feel	3.0
Value	2.0
Replayability	2.5
Overall	2.5

MACMAN PRO	
Fun factor	1.5
Look and feel	1.5
Value	3.0
Replayability	2.0
Overall	2.0

capabilities. For now, we will have to plod along with a large body of very average material.

Pros: Acceptable screen size. Game play fairly true to form.

Cons: Nothing new. Rather dull game play.

System Requirements: Any Mac with 256 colors, 4MB RAM, System 6.07 or higher.

Pros: Decent value in Arcade Pack.

Cons: Miniature screen. Crummy sound.

System Requirements: 256-color Mac, 4MB RAM, System 6.07 or higher.

Space Games

Atari's Asteroids was the inaugural game in the space shoot-'em-up continuum that captured many a heart (and coin) in the video game parlors of the world. Since those early days, this basic formula has made hundreds of triumphant returns in a wide range of incarnations on all computer game platforms. The teeth-clenching tension produced by this genre has kept dentists flush with cash from broken molars and bifurcated bicuspids. The premise is basic enough. An overhead view shows a triangular ship and globs of asteroids floating softly through space. Using cannon, the task is to blast the rocks into oblivion and get nose to nose with the odd flying saucer. Sounds dull? Well it sure beats playing fetch with your cat. All of the games that have arisen from the asteroids theme share a common thread of shields, weapons, and objects to blast. Many of the newer variations include such enhancements as varied weapons, bonus points, and cool 3D-rendered graphics.

Maelstrom
Ambrosia Software

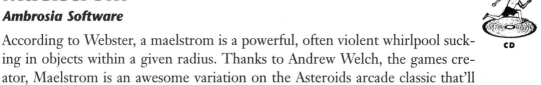

According to Webster, a maelstrom is a powerful, often violent whirlpool sucking in objects within a given radius. Thanks to Andrew Welch, the games creator, Maelstrom is an awesome variation on the Asteroids arcade classic that'll have you damaging your keyboard from pounding the weapon key. This was Andrew's first foray into the Mac gaming world, but after a glance at this captivating game, you will think he'd been a seasoned entertainment programmer. In it, you play a forlorn border guard patrolling the area of space between Alpha Centuri and Beta Carotene. This area forms the boundary between humankind and the Shenobi race of saucer flying cretins. Unfortunately, it is within the Hormel asteroid belt, and you will have to do your best to vaporize any rocks that cross your path. Of course, this isn't the easiest thing in the universe. Your ship will be rubbing elbows with Shenobi ships, vortex fields, and even autonominous mines. The latter are spherical spike-wielding death traps that will hone in on your ship and happily blow it to pieces. Fortunately, there are a variety of canisters floating around that, when grabbed, will supply you with everything from multiple guns to retro-thrusters.

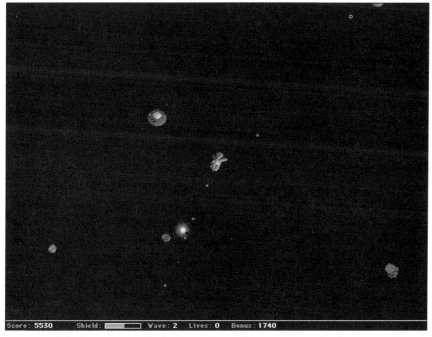

Be sure to grab the canisters marked with a red cross. They contain goodies that will greatly improve your score.

Doctor, My Eyes

The most stunning feature of Maelstrom is the incredible 3D graphics spinning and twisting before your eyes. The asteroids themselves are complex fractal wonders that rotate in an incredibly fluid manner. Your trusty ship is a space shuttle clone with a giant cannon mounted on its roof. As the figure of your ship spins, its shading changes to reflect light from a stationary off-screen source. When something is destroyed, a mesmerizing fire ball bursts on the screen.

GREAT FEATURE

Sound is also spectacular, and sound bites of various pop culture are sent forth during game play. Maelstrom has a unique modular design that enables new sprites and sound packages to be put into the game. For example, right now we have a sound set that has Dr. McCoy declaring, "He's dead, Jim" and Kirk responding, "But that's impossible" every time a ship is annihilated. Different visual aspects of Maelstrom can be similarly altered, and there are many different "modules" available on BBS services and online. This adds markedly to the replay value of the game, and, of course, it prevents innocent bystanders from going insane hearing the same sound bites again and again.

The Dom Pérignon of Asteroids Games

Maelstrom is an awesome example of the Mac's power as a game machine. Fantastically addictive game play, easy controls, and breathtaking sights and sounds make this truly a classic, a trend setter, a must have, and a tremendous value at only $15. Note: You might want to make sure your health care coverage is up to date before you throw your Carpal Tunnels into this one.

Pros: Awesome 3D-rendered graphics. Interesting and humorous sounds. Smooth graphics and animation. Configurable controls. Modular design that allows for new graphics and sound. Low price.

Cons: Will run only on a Mac with 256 colors/grays. Only 40 levels of play. No cash reward for finishing game.

System Requirements: 256-color Mac, 4MB RAM, hard drive, System 6.07 or higher.

MAELSTROM	
Fun factor	4.5
Look and feel	5.0
Value	5.0
Replayability	3.5
Overall	4.5

Tips

TIP

• To start playing on any level you like, press the L key while you are at the main screen.

• Pressing the X key in the High Score screen brings up an interesting poem or song lyric.

HemiRoids
Varcon Systems/MacSoft

CD

Imaginations certainly have been stretched when a game comes along with a plot that has your beautiful home planet of Nausea threatened by a deadly worm hole that is leaking huge hemispherical asteroids. These fragments have been dubbed HemiRoids by the brightest minds Nausea has to offer. Worse yet, naughty aliens are traveling through the worm hole from the vengeful planet Wedgie to destroy you and your homeland. Despite the unbelievable nature of the HemiRoids theme, the game is fun and unpretentious, which is just how it's marketed, as a "simple little diversion."

Shareware Material

HemiRoids plays like a decent shareware game. In fact, one might suspect after a quick glance that Maelstrom was a commercial venture and HemiRoids a pay-as-you-play game. Despite this, HemiRoids represents something more true to the original asteroids concept than any of its contemporaries. You have a shield (which is automatic), a gun (rapid-fire, which should save finger injury), and dual thrusters for propulsion. Throw in a few smart bombs, and you've pretty much summed it up. The HemiRoids themselves break into the obligatory smaller chunks, and of course Wedgie ships taking pot shots occasionally enter the screen. The graphics are 3D and of a similar, although not as stunning, style as Maelstrom.

Get Some Preparation H

HemiRoids supplies a quick asteroids fix for those who want an unsophisticated variation on the theme. It comes as a good value bundled in the Varcon Arcade Pack with four other games and should provide some simple fun and diversion when the boss isn't looking.

Pros: Decent 3D graphics. Configurable controls. Easy to learn. Good value in Arcade Pack.

Cons: Unsophisticated game play. Rapid-fire feature takes away from aiming expertise.

System Requirements: 256-color Mac, 4MB RAM, hard drive, System 6.07 or higher.

HEMIROIDS	
Fun factor	3.0
Look and feel	3.5
Value	3.5
Replayability	3.0
Overall	3.5

Space Madness
Changeling Software

There you are in your long-range DS27-E ship with specially designed auto-mated systems and a blistering top speed of 11,721 km/s. Your craft also has the good fortune of having a transmogrifier that can change any raw material into just the stuff your ship needs to repair itself. All you might wish for now is a pesky menace upon which to unload your ordnance of photon pellets and guid-ed missiles. Not to worry! A science ship has recently come across hostile crea-tures who have decided to place a few ships in your vicinity and clean your clock. Seems they haven't appreciated your space excavation methods and are really peeved that you didn't send them a Christmas card last year. It's time yet again for you to save humanity through cunning and raw courage.

The Gravity of the Situation

Space Madness juggles the asteroids formula by introducing an infinite space arena (you can move beyond the confines of the screen edges) and a wide vari-ety of weapons, bad guys, and miscellaneous goodies. The concept of proximity

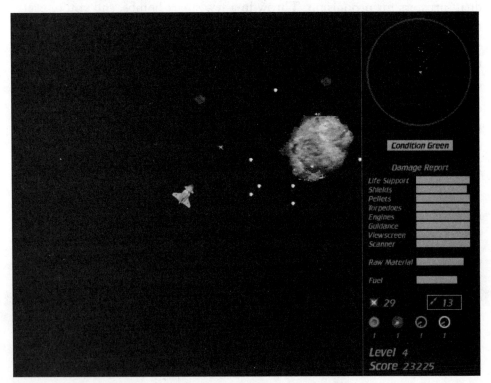

This ship is about to take major damage from being too close to an exploding enemy base.

GREAT FEATURE

damage is a welcome feature. According to it, if you are close enough to an explosion, your craft will feel the shock wave and might suffer considerable damage. Gravity also becomes an important component of game play because even the smallest piece of debris has a gravitational field that will affect your flight path if you wander too close to it. The detestable aliens have six different ships with various capabilities and tendencies, but perhaps their most annoying weapons are the space mines. These do not show up on your conventional radar, but they pack a big punch when set off by your presence. Your goal on every level is to destroy the base ship from which the other ships are born. When you are successful, a vortex appears that will literally suck you into the next level.

Lost in Space This Is Not

Space Madness's controls are completely changeable, and the original layout is more than adequate. Players with configurable joysticks can elect to program the necessary keys for more wrist action than finger bashing. The action is fast and furious, and only skilled pilots will make it through the 20 preset levels of mayhem. After the twentieth level, the game just repeats the last three levels indefinitely, perhaps to annoy you, and perhaps to deny you the thrill of definitive victory. The graphics and sound are excellent, and Mike Kelly (the game's creator) deserves full marks for coming up with a captivating, exciting space game and a commendable addition to this species of game.

Pros: Outstanding 3D graphics and animation. Configurable controls. Excellent variety of enemies. Integrated manual.

Cons: Only 20 levels of play. No end to game. Addictive nature can cause hand injuries.

System Requirements: 256-color Mac, 68020 or better, 2.5MB RAM, 1.5MB hard disk space, System 6.07 or higher.

SPACE MADNESS

Fun factor	4.0
Look and feel	4.5
Value	4.0
Replayability	3.5
Overall	4.0

Tips

• Try to take on the enemies one at a time; stay far enough away from the main base so that it can't shoot at you.

TIP

• If you are very low on raw materials, you can blast an asteroid into smaller chunks and grab them for a full boost of raw material.

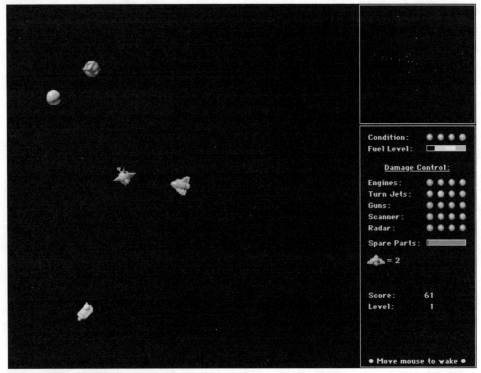

Note the large spiked mace the HammerHead has flung at my ship. Great 3D graphics are the order of the day in Lunatic Fringe.

Lunatic Fringe
Berkeley Systems (More After Dark)

Fortunately, the plot behind Lunatic Fringe does not submit to the same level of absurdity as those of its contemporaries. You are patrolling the borders of the Interstellar Alliance's territory when you're attacked by a marauding band of aliens. It almost makes one wonder if aliens from the different games aren't in cahoots with one another. At any rate, you are set the task of single-handedly repelling these outsiders before all hope for the human race's future is lost.

Save the Earth ... and Your Screen

The Fringe actually comes as a screen saver on the Berkeley Systems "More After Dark" disk. It represents an early example of entertainment software creeping into a program that was originally designed merely to blacken your screen, prevent screen burn-in, and decrease troublesome tartar build-up. You enter the game by selecting it as the active module in your After Dark control panel and clicking the Caps Lock key when prompted. Immediately you are transported into a beautiful 3D world that includes brilliant color and the now familiar space shuttle-like craft. The sound in Lunatic Fringe is hilarious and is comprised of nifty little bites that will have even the most stoic chuckling.

The directions are online, and as is the standard with this breed of game, the controls can be set to just about whatever your little heart desires. The *real* fun of the Fringe is the super cool bad guys, who, despite their penchant for vaporizing people like you, have a cartoonlike quality. You must fight such bad guys as the MultiBlaster, the Puffer, the HammerHead, and, of course, the venerable Cosmic Chicken. Fortunately for you, Ben Haller, the game's creator, has randomly incorporated spare parts, better weapons, invulnerability pods, and Turbo Thrusters throughout the game. This will not only help you fry those chickens, it'll also let you convincingly smoke the Puffers into oblivion.

The Ultimate "Boss" Key

Perhaps the most endearing feature of this great little diversion is the fact that as a screen saver, only the nudge of your mouse instantly transports you back to that innocuous spreadsheet that makes the Big Cheese so happy. Lunatic Fringe is a superb addition to any After Dark library, and although there is essentially no end to the game, it will ensure thousands of hours of lost productivity in business offices throughout the world.

Pros: Outstanding 3D graphics and animation. Fun sounds. Cool cartoonlike enemies. Fastest "boss" key in the West.

Cons: No end to game. Enemy base cannot be destroyed. Sometimes a nudge of the mouse will end a game accidentally.

System Requirements: 256-color Mac, 68020 or better, 2.5MB RAM, After Dark Screensaver.

LUNATIC FRINGE	
Fun factor	4.0
Look and feel	4.5
Value	4.5
Replayability	3.5
Overall	4.0

Video on Tap: the False Promise?

Back in 1983, something extraordinary happened in the video gaming universe. A talented Disney animator named Don Bluth set out to change the way computer-based games were made. Mr. Bluth wanted to give gamers something for which so many children had been longing: the ability to participate in a cartoon and control the action of the protagonist. Recent advances in video disk technology enabled Bluth to open the curtain on an entirely new category of video entertainment and to start a trend that would lead to such contemporary arcade favorites as Mad Dog McCree. A revolution of the multimedia kind has allowed these games to creep onto the CD-ROM drives of home computers. But is the current horsepower of today's machines capable of reproducing cartoon classics? The answer is a definite maybe.

Dragon's Lair
ReadySoft

You are Dirk the Daring, a fine example of what a cartoon medieval knight should be. Handsome, dexterous, fearless, and willing to fight through 27 rooms of fabulous mayhem to face off against Singe, the Evil Dragon who has kidnapped the fair Princess Daphne. The game has hundreds of different outcomes to the various situations Dirk is dropped into. If you move a joystick in the right direction at the right time, the cartoon continues to the next segment. It may sound dull, but this game really packed 'em in back in 1984, when it cost 50 cents to play, twice the going rate. At the time, there was nothing else like it, and it gave every quarter-slogging gamer the chance to live in a cartoon world—at least until the green goo dissolved your legs or you were pulled into the moat by the purple one-eyed tentacle beast.

Hard Times at Hardware High

GREAT
FEATURE

These games are not much fun if you're playing them at the crawl rate of three frames per second and are having to endure video jumping, audio blackouts, or general control problems. ReadySoft has done an excellent job of ensuring that your gaming experience is dramatically similar to the original arcade versions. There is a built-in fine-tuning system that Dragon's Lair goes through to optimize game play and quality. Thankfully this has to be done only once; you could digest a turkey dinner while it's doing its stuff. "They're exaggerating" you're thinking. But the fine tuning of your system takes anywhere from 30 to 60 minutes. However, if you have an 040 Mac, a double-speed CD-ROM drive, and a color monitor, you are going to be very impressed with Dragon's Lair and will be drawn back into the 27 separate tricky situations you learned to love a decade ago. Folks with slower machines will probably be in decent shape, and the ReadySoft folks stress that what's key is a double-speed 300 K/s CD-ROM drive, not the speed of your processor.

The Real McCoy

We found Dragon's Lair to be a great example of a video-based game done right on the Mac. The digitized sound comes right from the pioneer game, and the "demo" mode is just as much fun to watch as it ever was. By the time you read this, ReadySoft will have released Don Bluth's sequel to Dragon's Lair, Space Ace (Borf's Revenge). Due to the similarities in technology between the two games, it is reasonable to expect that Space Ace will also hit the mark and provide an authentic re-creation of Borf's Revenge, the story of a Space Cadet whose body is continually mutating between that of a child and that of a macho hero.

DRAGON'S LAIR	
Fun factor	3.0
Look and feel	4.0
Value	3.0
Replayability	3.0
Overall	3.5

Pros: High-quality graphics and sound. True to the original; very similar game play.

Cons: Game play can become frustrating. Little replay value. High hardware requirements.

System Requirements: 256-color Mac, 4MB RAM, 150K/s CD-ROM drive or better, System 7 or later.

Tip

• Watch carefully for the built-in clues. Doorways, ropes, and other items will flash to hint at what to do next. Although this advice is not always sound, it's a great starting place.

Mad Dog McCree

American Laser Games

Sometimes we wish we had a real gun when playing Mad Dog McCree. Not with the idea of lending more realism to this Old West shoot-'em-up by putting a bullet through the monitor, mind you. But rather to take the CD-ROM disc outside and put the poor game out of its misery.

Mad Dog McCree is a QuickTime-based version of the live-action game that appeared in the arcades a few years back. American Laser Games, realizing that the original was a pretty big hit with the quarter-dropping crowd, ported the game over to DOS and Macintosh CD-ROM. They may be sorry they did.

This Ain't the Arcade, Pardner

You play a gunslinger who's just made his way into a new town. Mad Dog McCree and his band of hooligans have taken over, kidnapped the mayor and his beautiful daughter, and locked the sheriff in the jail house. Ostensibly your job is to wander around town, blow the bad cowpokes away by pointing your

This old cowpoke from Mad Dog McCree pleads with you, "Please, get me out of this game!"

mouse/gun and clicking at the perfect moment, and rescue the mayor's daughter in anticipation of a smoochy reward.

Of course, your real job will be to pull your hair out as you try to determine exactly when the game expects you to fire your weapon. Now? Oops. How about now? Dang! Okay, it must be now! Dad blast it!!! And so on and so on.

LOUSY FEATURE

In addition to the general frustration of trying to form a psychic link with the game, Mad Dog McCree includes the very specific frustration of trying to get the video to run smoothly on your Mac. You can install three flavors of the game, each intended for a different screen resolution. Well, we checked it out.

We tried the large install on a large screen. Unh uh. We tried all of them on a Power Mac. No way. We tried it on a 68040 with medium resolution. Fergit it. Finally we found the winning combination: the small install on a small screen running 256 colors. Anything else we tried resulted in wretchedly choppy QuickTime performance.

Sing Along!

Oh, give me a game,
Not so terribly lame,
Like a shoot-'em-up made just for me.
Believe what I say,
No, this game's not okay
Stay away from this Mad Dog McCree.

Pros: When you can actually hear and see the actors between the QuickTime blips, their performances are pretty good.

Cons: Poor implementation of QuickTime. Hard to tell when you can shoot successfully.

System Requirements: 12-inch or larger 8-bit color display, LC III or better, 4MB RAM, 2.6 to 4.5MB hard disk space, System 7 or later, double-speed CD-ROM drive.

MAD DOG MCCREE	
Fun factor	1.5
Look and feel	1.5
Value	1.5
Replayability	1.5
Overall	1.5

Tip

• Although it may seem that you can't save the old cowpoke at the beginning of the game, give it a try. If you work out the timing just right, he might thank you for saving his life by letting you in on a little secret.

TIP

Pinball

A moment of reflection from Chris:

When I was a kid, my parents used to take the family to a burger and beer joint called the Oasis. Even though the place served food, there was a large sign at the door proclaiming that patrons under the age of 21 would not be admitted. The sign was apparently intended for the intimidation of nearby Stanford students—parents with young children were jake as far as the "O" was concerned. The O was a pretty freewheeling place in those days, and customers were encouraged to toss peanut shells on the floor, carve their initials into the tables and walls, and drink as much beer as they could reasonably hold. As minors, we were banned from taking part in the last activity and were saddled with one additional prohibition: no pinball.

PINBALL TERMINOLOGY

If you've even glanced at a pinball machine, you've noticed that these "tables" are littered with lights, bumpers, channels, flippers, and doodads that few players know the names of. Here's your chance to get hip. Toss these terms about to really impress the folks down at the family fun center.

- *Bumper.* Mushroom-shaped object that bounces the ball around the table.

- *Hole.* Either a saucer-shaped depression which temporarily holds the ball or the dreaded out hole—the final abyss into which all pinballs must eventually fall.

- *Plunger.* The spring-loaded thingamajig you pull and release to put the ball into play.

- *Flippers.* The rubber-coated devices you use to trap, deflect, and flip the ball.

- *Indicators.* We know them as lights.

- *Lane.* A channel through which the ball passes. When you first plunge the ball, it passes through a plunge lane. When the ball flashes down the right or left side of the table and into the out hole, it has passed, however regrettably, into an out lane. The return lanes found next to the out lanes channel the ball to the flippers.

- *Drop target.* Gravestone-shaped pieces of plastic that retract when hit by the ball.

- *Spot target.* Electronic switches, generally arranged in banks, that are activated when hit by the ball. Hitting a bank of spot targets usually triggers a special scoring event.

- *Kickback.* A small plunger or flipper that when activated by a special event propels the ball up an out lane and back into play.

- *Slingshot.* The wedge-shaped islands found just above the bottom flippers that when hit cause the ball to bound around like a poodle with a hotfoot.

- *Rollover Button.* The term says it all—a button that is activated when the ball rolls over it.

- *Ramp.* These elevated sections of track are typical of modern-day pinball machines.

- *Tilt.* The unfortunate situation that arises after you've put a little too much oomph into your technique.

- *Playfield.* The surface of the table where the action takes place.

- *Back glass.* The area above the table where the scoring indicators reside.

Somehow these clanging contraptions lined up against the south wall of the O represented to me all that was forbidden in this world. Naturally, I was fascinated. Although I wasn't allowed to actually touch one of the machines, there was nothing to prevent me from standing on a wooden bench and gazing at the garish flashing lights, the representations of improbable women on the back glasses, and the real men locked in haunted combat with the silver balls.

As the years passed and Asteroids, PacMan, and Defender became the rage, the pinball machines were shunted farther down the wall until finally a single machine stood unplayed next to the men's room. The O started serving salads and sweeping the floor. My youth was over and so, it seemed, were the days of pinball.

Fly On, LittleWing

Or they were until programmer Yoshikatsu Fujita and his artist partner and wife, Reiko Nojima, formed LittleWing—a Japanese concern dedicated to the creation of outstanding pinball simulations for the Macintosh—and released their first pingame, Tristan.

Tristan

Amtex Software Corporation

CD

We're a little surprised to hear that Amtex still has Tristan on the market. Although we still drag our copies out every once in a while and are charmed by the game's simplicity and elegance, it looks like a child's toy compared to Little-Wing's current work. The playfield is tiny, the graphics lack the richness of Ms. Nojima's later designs, and there's precious little to bang your ball against. In fact, the only thing that hints at greater things to come is the game's physical modeling. But despite its shortcomings, Tristan plays like a real pinball machine. For this reason, we think Tristan is worth having if you can find it for the right price. It's still a great time-waster and just as addicting as any simple pinball machine can be.

Eight Ball Deluxe

Amtex Software Corporation

Released in 1992, Eight Ball Deluxe is LittleWing's second creation. Unlike Tristan—a game that exists only as bits and bytes—Eight Ball Deluxe is a digital re-creation of a real pinball machine. The game features five-ball play, three flippers, and sound sampled directly from the original Bally machine.

Ancient History

The real-life wood-and-glue Eight Ball Deluxe was a sequel to another Bally creation, Eight Ball. The theme of the earlier table game was a loose interpretation of the 1970s sitcom *Happy Days*. It featured the oh-so-smooth visage of the Fonz draped over a pool table with a hotpants-clad babe—definitely *not* Joanie Cunningham—admiring his form from afar. Wildly popular, Eight Ball was one

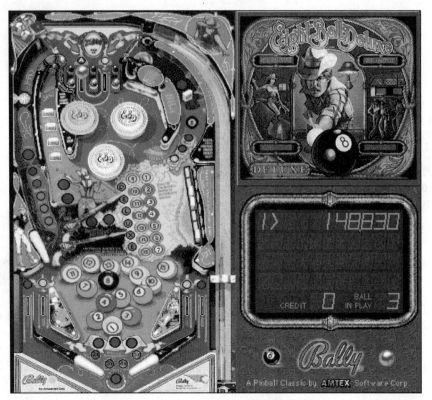

Quit talkin' and start chalkin'!

of the first solid-state pinball games. The inclusion of solid-state technology meant that, unlike its predecessors, Eight Ball actually remembered the positions of the various targets and reset itself accordingly for each player's turn.

Eight Ball Deluxe appeared in 1981 during the height of video arcade madness. As the name implies, it featured a pool hall setting in which players were invited to "Chalk Up!" and knock down drop targets representing striped or solid pool balls. Game play was fast and offered enough variety to entice the kids who didn't care to stand in long lines for Ms. PacMan to give pinball a try. The game won numerous awards during the early 1980s and has since become a classic.

Rack 'Em Up!

Installation is fairly straightforward and requires only the additional step of entering a serial number the first time the game boots up. In a tribute to realism, you must add "coins" to the game by selecting Insert Coin from the File menu or typing the against-all-standards-set-by-Apple keyboard combination,

Command-C. To add players to the game, you again invoke this command to plop more change into the machine and then select Add New Player.

The four control keys—left and right flipper, plunger, and nudge—are preset and cannot be changed. Although the keys are laid out logically, we like to operate our flippers with the same hand and are thankful that later LittleWing games allowed for customization of the keyboard.

Game play is remarkably similar to that of the original machine, although this realism may not tickle every player's fancy. The real Eight Ball Deluxe was a fairly fast machine that featured treacherous out lanes and a nearly magnetic out hole. True to the original, the re-creation is more than a little challenging and, some players may attest, borders on frustrating.

The playfield is laid out beside an image of the back glass. Although static scoring indicators appear on the back glass, they are strictly decorative. But an enlarged and operational indicator is featured below the glass.

In addition to imitating the game play of the original machine, pains were taken to copy the look and sound of Eight Ball Deluxe. Ms. Nojima's graphics are as vibrant and compelling as the original, and the lo-fi sounds emanating from the Mac's speaker are so realistic you may begin searching your keyboard for cigarette burns and beer rings.

GREAT FEATURE

What's to Like

Eight Ball Deluxe is a beautiful game that truly re-creates the feel of a real pinball machine. The sounds, the look, and the realistic movement of the ball combine to create a worthwhile tribute to a classic pinball game. And to prove that the game has at least one foot in the digital domain, the designers also included a special help screen and Magic Eight Ball function. To view the help screen, click on the small silver ball located at the lower right of the score window. A click on the small eight ball in the same window will deliver advice from the great beyond.

Unfortunately, the game does not adjust for larger monitors. Regardless of the size of the monitor you use, the entire playfield is never completely onscreen. Even with screen space to spare, when you pull the plunger, the screen scrolls down and, upon release, quickly scrolls back to its original position.

LOUSY FEATURE

It would be difficult to re-create the busy artwork of the original table. Eight Ball's graphics tend to be jagged, and it's hard to discern detail on the playfield. This in no way interferes with playing the game, but 16-bit color might have made the graphics absolutely inspirational.

High Score

If you're a fan of classic pinball but can't seem to find the floor space for your own machine, Eight Ball Deluxe is for you. Pinball newbies who haven't had a chance to take on such classic machines will find it a challenging, entertaining, and yes, at times maddening experience.

Pros: Faithful re-creation of a classic pinball machine. Authentic sounds, graphics, and game play make this a winner.

Cons: Difficult and frustrating at times. Game does not adjust for larger monitors.

System Requirements: 8-bit color or grayscale monitor, 4MB RAM, 3MB hard disk space, System 6.07 or higher.

EIGHT BALL DELUXE	
Fun factor	4.0
Look and feel	4.5
Value	4.0
Replayability	4.5
Overall	4.0

Crystal Caliburn
StarPlay Productions

With the advent of video games in the late '70s and early '80s, pinball needed to be reinvented. The raw challenge of knocking down a handful of targets and finessing the ball through a particular gate simply couldn't compete with the digital thrill of blasting the bits out of a pixelated cootie. New, faster, and flashier pinball machines that featured ramps, multi-ball play, and a wealth of digitized sounds appeared. LittleWing's third pinball simulation, Crystal Caliburn, is such a machine.

The Sword From the Stone

Crystal Caliburn is an original three-ball machine based on the Arthurian legend. Your job is to offer accolades to the knights of the Round Table by knocking over banks of spot targets, completing the top lane (meaning that you run your ball through each of the three lanes at the top of the machine), and shooting the ramps and return lanes. Once you've accoladed the 12 knights, you must shoot the Glass Island ramp to gain the Holy Grail (worth 500,000 points). If you attain the grail, you have exactly five seconds to shoot the Camelot Castle ramp to deliver the grail to the castle (worth untold riches and, at the very least, a high score).

Holding No Quarter

For Crystal Caliburn, LittleWing significantly reorganized the command interface, the unintuitive Command-C is gone, and Command-I now inserts the coin. Adding up to four additional players is as simple as pulling down the Option menu. The Option menu also contains the Assign Extra Keys command, which allows you to assign alternate keys for the plunger, the flippers, and the nudge function. The game includes background music as well as effect sounds that can be individually switched on and off.

Compared to Eight Ball Deluxe, Crystal Caliburn is slower and more controlled. Rather than careening wildly about the playfield, the ball often seems to float after hitting a stationary target. Nudging is very tolerant, and the surface of the flippers is "soft." We were easily able to trap a ball in an upturned flipper that would have bounced the ball off the glass and into the out hole of a real pinball machine.

The ball angles about the table realistically, and when balls collide during Multi Battle, they seem to act according to the laws of physics. The game exhibits some devilishly difficult regions—the slingshots have a propensity for hurling the ball into the out lanes—but generally, the table is well balanced.

The Lavish Look

The table sports an attractively colorful playfield featuring two pseudo-plexiglass ramps, three bumpers, and a covered Dragon Cave. The back glass features a lovely stained glass window that, were it not for the inclusion of the LittleWing logo, would be a beautiful addition to any church. On 14-inch monitors, the game exhibits the same scrolling effect found in Eight Ball Deluxe, but a full-screen view is now possible on larger monitors.

The jaggedness evident in Eight Ball Deluxe is less apparent in Crystal Caliburn, and the sound is quite clean and bright. The background music is compelling but tends to be noticeably repetitive over time.

Advances

Crystal Caliburn is a modern pinball creation. In addition to getting only three balls for your quarter, new features have been added to entice players seeking the kind of frantic action found in video games. The most amazing of these to players accustomed to old-style machines is Multi Battle.

**GREAT
FEATURE**

There are a couple of ways to trigger a Multi Battle, but suffice to say that with the initiation of this event, three balls start pinging their way around the playfield. With a Multi Battle under way, you can forget about lifting your flippers and carefully planning your next shot. The best you'll be able to do is keep your eyes glued to the bottom of the machine and frantically flap your fingers on the keyboard in an attempt to keep all your balls in the air.

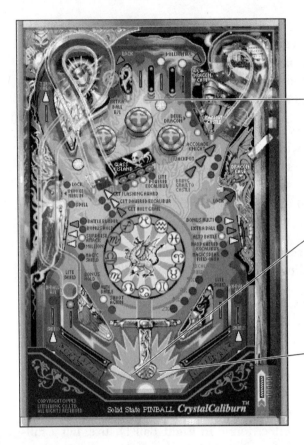

Use the Space Bar to nudge the "table" when the ball is in this area to rack up big bumper points.

Practice flipping the ball up the Camelot Ramp when the ball is moving. In order to bring home the Grail—and a huge score—you must hit this ramp on the fly.

To make the Glass Island Ramp, trap the ball with the right flipper, release the ball, and flip when the ball is in the middle of this orange line.

GREAT FEATURE

Another nice feature is the shields (kickbacks) that are placed in the right and left out lanes. Unlike old-style kickbacks that were activated only by hitting certain targets, these Kickbacks are active at the beginning of the game. Once a shield has been used, you can reactivate it only by shooting either of the two ramps and then running the ball through one of the two return lanes.

Crystal Caliburn features a high score contest. If you are 13 and over and have one of the ten top scores submitted to the game's publisher, StarPlay, each month (you record high scores in a special TeachText file), you win a Crystal Caliburn T-shirt. There are also free T-shirts available to the top three scorers in the 12 and under category. Less-than-top-scorers are welcome to purchase high score shirts for $12.50.

A Pinball Wizard

Crystal Caliburn is our favorite of the LittleWing offerings. It's nicely laid out, features play that is well-balanced between offense and defense, and offers rewards—both personal and of the preshrunk 100% cotton variety—that will keep players coming back again and again.

Pros: Beautifully designed original pinball machine featuring challenging scoring options. The next best thing to the real McCoy.

Cons: Flippers are a trifle forgiving. No beer and peanuts included in the box.

System Requirements: 13-inch, 8-bit color or grayscale monitor, 4MB RAM, 3MB hard disk space, System 6.07 or higher.

CRYSTAL CALIBURN	
Fun factor	4.5
Look and feel	4.5
Value	4.5
Replayability	4.5
Overall	4.5

Loony Labyrinth
StarPlay Productions

CD

Loony Labyrinth is LittleWing's fourth and most beautiful release. Like Crystal Caliburn, the game features a gloriously colorful playfield, LittleWing's remarkable realistic feel, multi-ball play, ramps, and a high score contest.

If a pinball game can be said to have a plot, this is the first that features two story lines. The table's overall theme is Greek mythology, but there is also a time travel element built in. Your first set of tasks is to collect five ancient stones by hitting two Spot Targets and running the Stone Ramp for each stone you collect. Concurrent with this, you must also hit Loony's three bumpers enough times to charge the game's time machine. Once all the stones are collected and the time machine is charged, you have to finesse the ball into the Install Stone Hole. With this accomplished, you access the second stage of the game and are transported back to ancient Crete where you engage in another set of chores to free the nine sacrifices from the grip of the horrific Minotaur. Kill the Minotaur and rack up points to return to the present.

Admittedly, this isn't Book Club material, but the two-tier concept does lend more depth and excitement to the game.

And the Playing Is Easy

Based on criticisms that Crystal Caliburn and Eight Ball Deluxe were too tough for beginning pinball players, Loony Labyrinth was intentionally designed to be a higher-scoring and easier game. This is reflected in the table's design by a wider and somewhat squatter playfield and narrower out lanes. Additionally,

Minotaur Chamber

Loony Ramp

Bumper access

Labyrinth Ramp

To propel the ball to the above locations, flip where indicated.

voice cues have been added to the effects sounds to inform players of the rewards they are collecting and the status of events in the game. If, for example, making one more ramp shot will activate multi-ball play, the game show-like announcer lustily advises, "Shoot for the Labyrinth Ramp!"

As it turns out, the initial release of the game was deemed too easy for skilled players, and a more difficult update was issued two months later. This update limits the number of extra balls one can earn and increases the table's slope. The update feels as though someone had jammed a couple of matchbooks under the back legs of version 1.0.

Loony's New Look

**GREAT
FEATURE**

Reiko Nojima has really hit her stride with Loony Labyrinth. The jaggies found in her early games are gone, and the sandy pastels used to render the playfield are stunning. Improvements have also been made in sound. During the first stage of the game, Loony plays a pumping Tower of Poweresque riff that's funky enough to have you pounding the flipper keys on the upbeats. Stage two features a more traditional Middle Eastern score complete with finger cymbals and wooden flute.

To concentrate more completely on the game, you can turn off the background music. Regrettably, you can't also shut off the announcer without losing the all-important effects sounds.

It's a Ball!

Although we prefer the challenges offered by Crystal Caliburn to Loony Labyrinth's high-scoring play, Loony is also a heck of a fine pinball simulation. LittleWing has pulled out all the stops to create an exciting and accessible game for pinball players of all skill levels.

Pros: The perfect pinball simulation for first-time players. Beautiful graphics and great music. Just about anyone should be able to win one of the T-shirts.

Cons: Slope of the table is a little harsh. No way to shut up the announcer.

System Requirements: 13-inch 8-bit color or grayscale monitor, 4MB RAM, 3MB hard disk space, System 6.07 or higher.

LOONY LABYRINTH	
Fun factor	4.5
Look and feel	4.5
Value	4.5
Replayability	4.5
Overall	4.5

Tips

• The Minotaur Multi is probably the easiest multi-ball feature to activate, but don't be too hasty. One of the toughest tasks on the first level of play is to collect the five stones; this should be your priority. Activate the Stone lights by hitting the Stone Spot Targets, then hit the Minotaur Spot Targets, and finally, lock your ball. Once the ball is locked, your new ball will run the Stone Ramp and collect the stone.

TIP

• As a follow-up to the preceding tip, keep an eye on those flashing Stone indicators during multi-ball play. If you're within the Safety Catch limit—either because multi-ball play has just started or you've activated one of the other multis—let one of the balls drain so that your new ball collects the stone.

• As in Crystal Caliburn, one of the flippers seems to be more precise than the other. Shots taken with the right flipper in Loony Labyrinth are almost always spot-on. The left flipper tends to be less predictable, mainly because the most important shots (the Minotaur Chamber and the Loony Ramp) must be made from the upper part of the flipper. Study the diagram on the previous page for sweet spots.

~~~~~~

Macintosh Reissues

Of course the Macintosh has always been capable of playing more than classic arcade games. A number of tremendously entertaining games that never saw the inside of an arcade were released in the Mac's early days. Regrettably, most of these games are gone forever.

Fortunately, whether due to nostalgia or a paucity of new ideas, a few of the great old games have been brought back to life, some in new and colorful forms. Call us old fogies, but we applaud this trend and hope that one day we'll be able to play such classics as The Colony and Lunar Rescue in full color on our Power Macs. Until that day arrives, we'll content ourselves with once again toppling the Black Knight and, while standing to the west of Zork's legendary white house, typing those three magic words: "Open the mailbox."

The Zork Anthology
Activision

As you may recall from our discussion of interactive fiction, Infocom's Zork games were some of the most popular diversions of their time—yes, even without flashy graphics or sound. Although the command line interface seems antiquated by today's standards, the games are just as rich and challenging as they were over a decade ago.

The White House

The Anthology is contained on a single CD-ROM that carries both the Macintosh and IBM versions of the five original Zork games. As a special bonus, Planetfall, one of the most popular Infocom titles is also included on the disk. The games follow the standard text adventure interface where you must type directions and commands to move your character through the game. The two latter games carry a couple of extra features: Beyond Zork contains an auto-mapping feature along with an endurance meter that measures the amount of abuse you've absorbed. Zork Zero sports crude color graphics, on-line hints, and an undocumented mapping feature.

The Infocom games represent some of the finest examples of text adventures from the golden days of the form. Although, due in part to our rather odd senses of humor, Leather Goddesses of Phobos (LGOP) still holds the number one spot on our text adventure greatest hits list, the Zork series is also outstanding.

INFOCOM NOT DEAD YET

Activision once sold nearly all of the Infocom text adventures in two collections called The Lost Treasures of Infocom (but no Leather Goddesses of Phobos—grrr). By the time you read this book, these collections will be extremely hard to find. If you can find them, snatch 'em up—they're a real bargain.

In their place, Activision has released a five-volume set of many of these classic games. Each $20 CD-ROM volume is based on a theme—Comedy, Sci-Fi, Adventure, Mystery, and Fantasy—and contains four to six games plus two bonus games. Players interested in collecting the series may be a little disappointed to discover that on every single volume, one of the bonus games is Planetfall (Don't get us wrong, we love Planetfall but why not include Shogun, Arthur, or Journey—games included on the CD version of Lost Treasures but omitted here?). Each of the volumes also includes one of the five Zork games.

Like nearly all of the Infocom games the stories are intriguing, the humor refreshing, and the puzzles well-thought-out.

Activision could have expended a little more energy on the total package. The manuals that come with the Zork collection are just plain shoddy—full of typos and misprints and even missing important pages found in the original manuals. Yes, Activision, we do give you credit for including some of the original maps and InvisiClues that were once sold individually, but criminy folks, could hiring a copy editor for the afternoon really cost that much?

Get 'Em While You Can

Interactive fiction isn't for everyone. These games take time, patience, and a reasonable amount of smarts. But the rewards they offer are rich indeed. If you've never played the Zork games before and have even the slightest interest in doing so—now or in the future—buy these jewels before they're lost and gone forever. You won't regret it.

Pros: Some of the best examples of a classic game form. Challenging puzzling accompanied by a rich sense of humor.

Cons: Shoddy manuals.

System requirements: Mac Plus or better, CD-ROM drive, 512K RAM, 2MB hard disk space, System 6.07 and higher.

THE ZORK ANTHOLOGY

Fun factor	4.0
Look and feel	1.0*
Value	4.0
Replayability	2.0
Overall	4.0

*(Hey, they're text adventures!)

TIP

Tip:
• The manual that comes with the Anthology neglects to inform you of Zork Zero's mapping capabilities. To access them, simply type MAP at any prompt.

Lode Runner: The Legend Returns
Sierra On-Line

Way back in 1983, a year before the Mac was born, Douglas Smith created an engaging little game that involved racing a tiny man over a multi-leveled terrain, up and down ladders, and across dangling wires in search of sacks of money. Hot on his trail were at least a couple of nondescript bad guys who, with one touch, caused our hero to wither, fade, and be replaced by one of the remaining runners. Because this was a game of speed and elusion, the protagonist had no weapons other than the ability to temporarily vaporize areas directly to the right or left. What good could this possibly do, you ask? This power served two purposes: Oftentimes treasures were tucked neatly away in underground repositories that could be accessed only by light excavation. And although the nasty boys scored full points in the persistence department, their jumping skills were well below par. Confronted with a temporary pot hole, the goons simply fell in and were trapped while the players gathered their dropped cash and skedaddled.

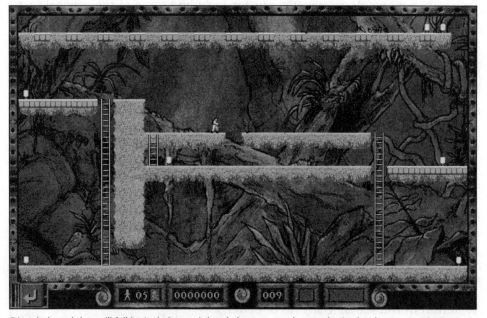

Dig a hole and they will fall in. Lode Runner's hooded creeps are short on brains but long on persistence.

Gorge Sequel

Well, darned if Lode Runner isn't back again in all its enhanced glory. The same little man is there, but he now runs in a lifelike manner and sports dandy white overalls, a black backpack, and some kind of fire-breathing ground digger. The baddies, who haven't improved their leaping one iota, look ominously chic in their new blood-red robes. The background patterns are just as colorful and include such varied environments as a lush rain forest, dank cave, and barren tundra. Other additions include musical accompaniment; nifty new sound effects; color-coded keys that must be obtained in order to open like-hued doors; bombs for clearing paths through solid rock (or for generally creating havoc); jackhammers for digging through steel girders; gloppy stuff that slows everyone to a crawl; and a two-player mode that enables you and a buddy to team up against the evil ones or race competitively for the gold. As with the original game, you can also add extra runners, terminate the runner you're playing with, and start the game at any level of your choosing.

GREAT FEATURE

Even with all these gimmicks, Lode Runner plays pretty much the same as it always did—fast and fun for a while and then fast and not so much fun. The game comes with 150 levels, and frankly, after 40 or 50 of them, we're ready to call it a day. Unfortunately, despite the great new graphics and enhancements, we found that running hither and yon, digging holes, and gathering up golden rewards loses its charm the 704th time around.

To be honest, once we tired of running through the stock Lode Runner levels, we thought it much more fun to create levels of our own with the Game Generator tools and toss our creations onto our favorite online services. These tools provide you with all the goodies you need to devise some absolutely dastardly puzzles that virtually guarantee you months of angry e-mail.

Paying the Price

All this sound and fury isn't free. Using the standard install, you should expect to lose about 11 megabytes of hard disk space. Even PowerBook users won't get off cheaply: their install will eat up a little over four megabytes. We're also not terribly thrilled with the game's initial control screen. Thanks in part to Microsoft Word 6, we realize we're supposed to be living in a one-interface world in which Mac and PC programs look exactly the same. But just for once, pretty please, couldn't we use the interface that's more intuitive rather than the one that sells more copies? Are we really supposed to divine that a hand inside an octagon means quit or that a spiral sometimes means undo and other times means return to the default setting? Sheesh.

RANT

The Mother of all Lodes

Sierra On-Line has certainly done its best to jazz up this old standard, and in most respects, it's done an admirable job. Lode Runner looks great, and the enhancements add new levels of complexity to the game's brain-bending elements. You just need to be careful to play it in small doses. Much as it is with a magnum of fine champagne, the secret to enjoying this game is knowing when to say when.

Pros: Nice graphics. Cool enhancements to a classic.

Cons: Repetitive. Uses a lot of hard disk space.

System Requirements: 13-inch color or grayscale monitor, 4MB RAM, up to 11MB hard disk space, System 6.07 or higher.

LODE RUNNER: THE LEGEND RETURNS	
Fun factor	3.0
Look and feel	4.0
Value	3.5
Replayability	3.0
Overall	3.0

Tip

• When designing your own levels, keep in mind that you can step on the heads of falling bad guys in order to cross a gap. With any luck, players who try your levels won't realize this and will tear their hair out for days.

Dark Castle

Delta Tao

A while back, we heard a rumor that Dark Castle was returning from the dead. "Swell," we thought, "some Hollywood know-nothing has decided to turn this wonderful old game into a CD-ROM-based multimedia extravaganza and will probably cast Robert Urich as Prince Duncan. There's another fond memory down the drain." But then we heard that Dark Castle was going to be released by none other than Delta Tao, one of the coolest companies in the biz. "Well," we thought, "those guys are much too hip to turn this into a CD-ROM game and, heck, considering how much they charge for their software, they couldn't put together the cash to hire Robert Urich's dog. Maybe our memories will be spared."

As it turns out, not only were our memories spared, but thanks to the addition of colorful graphics and a few interface tweaks, our old friend Dark Castle is better than ever.

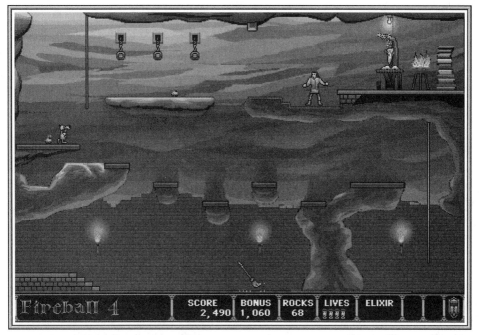

Great balls of fire! *Dark Castle's Prince Duncan is about to receive his fiery reward.*

Maybe You Missed It

Dark Castle was one of the first Macintosh run-and-jump games. The idea was simple: You, in the guise of Prince Duncan, tear around a castle searching for the tools needed to defeat the evil Black Knight. Along the way, you stumble upon bags of stones and bottles of elixir. The stones are meant to be used as weapons against such nasty creatures as venomous rats and bats, mechanized guards, and annoying little guys who prance about squealing, "Nee, Nee, Nee, Nee." The elixirs are used as brief protection against poisonous bites.

The game is divided into four levels, each of which, depending on the level of difficulty you've chosen, contains a varying number of sublevels. So, for example, if you want to want to obtain the shield necessary to protect yourself from the Knight's flung beer steins, you must first dash through a hall of bouncing boulders, past a fire-breathing dragon, in and out of a rat-infested chamber, and finally to a dangerous tower where lightning always strikes the same place twice.

The controls are very simple, but they require you to employ both the mouse and keyboard. The mouse is used to move Duncan's arm up and down and to fling rocks. The keyboard is for jumping, moving the Prince in the four compass directions, and activating special switches and levers. Learning to coordinate the

JOE WILLIAMS REISSUE INTERVIEW

Joe Williams is the 29-year-old president of Delta Tao. He dropped out of Caltech in 1986 to "bum around and write computer games." In 1989, he started Delta Tao, a software company dedicated to changing the philosophical path of computing.

Give us a little background on yourself—name, rank, serial number, greatest hits, why you get to run such a cool software company.

Before we started Delta Tao, the Amazing Timmer (Tim Cotter, our chief engineer) and I did contract programming for Apple. Whenever we wanted a picture in our applications, we found opportunity to moan and complain about the quality (and price!) of paint programs—PixelPaint 1.0 was $599. On a whim, I asked Timmer how long it would take him to whip out "a cheesy little paint program." True to his word, two weeks later he had a fine prototype up and running. It was so great that we quit contracting, moved to Alaska for the summer (of 1989), and wrote Color MacCheese. Besides being cheap, fast, and easy, it was the first paint program to do 32-bit color and antialiasing. We introduced it at Macworld Expo in 1990, where we sold $50,000 worth in our first week—in hand-painted boxes. We started Delta Tao with that money and have kept it chugging happily along ever since. Despite our best efforts, we just keep growing.

As president of Delta Tao, I get all the jobs nobody else wants—marketing, finances, hiring, and so on. Deep down, I just want

to design software, without actually having to write it. Everything we've ever made has had to suffer intense meddling from me. I'm most proud of Spaceward Ho!, Eric's Ultimate Solitaire, and Color MacCheese.

Why reissue Dark Castle?

The original Dark Castle was incredible. Legend has it that Charlie Jackson of Silicon Beach wanted to do a game that was so good other developers would just "give up." They ended up with a winner, too.

Unfortunately, the years have been hard on Dark Castle. Aldus had no interest in games, so they didn't update the code to support new Macintoshes or system software. It eventually came to be that if you weren't running an old Mac Plus, you couldn't play Dark Castle. It was too good a game to let die, so we wangled it for ourselves.

How did you get the rights to it?

Well, it sure wasn't cash. Dark Castle is worth far more than tiny little Delta Tao could possibly pay. We arranged a code swap. We had some technology in our paint programs that Aldus wanted really badly, so we traded it for Dark Castle. That was just the beginning, though—rewriting it took our best guy the better part of a year.

How did you redo it?

Dark Castle was written in hand-tweaked 68000 assembly. That's great—it led to awesome performance on 1987 Macs. Unfortunately, it didn't lend itself to modernization. We didn't want to just reissue an old game, so we had to start over from scratch. We couldn't keep anything—the art and sounds had to be updated, of course, so the code to support them had to be written from the beginning.

Do you have plans for future reissues?

We'll probably do Beyond Dark Castle, but even that isn't certain.

We're not in the business of patching up old games that people remember fondly. We did Dark Castle because it's still a great game by today's standards. Many old games are just old. Just because I spent a lot of time in junior high playing Hammurabi and Lemonade Stand doesn't mean I want to remake them.

two input devices takes some time, but thankfully Delta Tao has provided help via a practice level.

New for Old

Along with the cool new graphics, Dark Castle sports some welcome enhancements. First and foremost is the game's novice, or practice, level. It allows you to try an abbreviated form of the game that, while still presenting all the essential challenges, provides you enough breathing room to master the controls. Other new levels have been added, and although we haven't actually found the thing ourselves, rumor has it that there's a secret level. Also, you can now save a game in progress. You're allowed only one save though; each save overwrites the previous one.

GREAT FEATURE

Of course, Dark Castle wouldn't be Dark Castle without a certain amount of frustration. Just as in the old game, Duncan's arm shoots back to his side after being suspended for a few seconds. This is as much of a drag now as it ever was. And even though we're smack dab in the '90s, the game still presents us with a nine-inch screen. And worst thing of all, the Black Knight's disposition hasn't improved a smidgen since we first met him in 1986.

LOUSY FEATURE

We Like It

But you may not. Compared to modern run-and-jump games like Prince of Persia, Dark Castle seems a little stiff. And some players may find that engaging in the same battles, ducking under the same boulders, and clubbing the same Whip Henchman over and over is a little monotonous. Not us, though. We love the new colors mixed with the old sounds. We're tickled that Delta Tao was able to enhance the game without sacrificing its original character. But mostly we're happy that our old enemy the Dark Knight is back to torment us again.

Pros: New color graphics. New levels. Funny manual.

Cons: Doesn't take advantage of large screens. Can be repetitive.

System Requirements: 256-color Mac, 2.1MB hard disk space, System 6.07 or higher.

DARK CASTLE	
Fun factor	4.0
Look and feel	4.0
Value	4.0
Replayability	3.5
Overall	4.0

Tips

• Those poor wretches hanging in the dungeon know which key will open the door. Watch their faces as you approach each key.

• When you knock out the guards from a distance, hit them from behind. When they come to, they'll be facing away from you and you'll have a better chance to knock them out again.

• Bats first.

• The gargoyles always scream four times before they appear on screen. Don't waste your ammunition by throwing too early.

• Christmas isn't the only holiday that brings special treats.

• Using a copy of the program, check out some of the code resources with ResEdit. Can *you* name the three guys hanging in the dungeon?

Stellar 7
Dynamix

The workaday drudgery of saving the world has taken its toll. With a frosty mug of root beer glistening in the sunshine, you lay back in your lawn chair secure in the knowledge that the aliens have been beaten into submission and are still licking their wounds and pondering why they ever considered grappling with a tough hombre like yourself. Alas, just as the icy chalice of amber sweetness is about to touch your lips, a shadow crosses your reclining form. It's the commander of Earth's defense branch, and he says you're the only one who can stop the contemptuous Gir Draxon, a powerful tyrant bent on complete domination of the known universe.

A Decade Past

Stellar 7 appeared in the early '80s on the old Apple II system and was one of the most popular games of its day. It featured a 3D inside-the-tank style of game

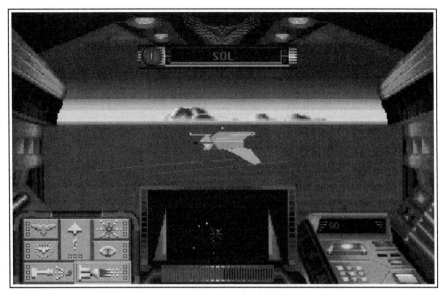

Stellar 7 utilizes the familiar 3D tank view. Check out the Skidder as it slides in front of the Raven.

play and sweeping, smoothly scrolling landscapes. Stellar 7 puts you in a 3D environment in which you are strapped in a craft with your finger on the trigger ready to blow any alien ship to pieces. The original Stellar 7's 3D environment was so far ahead of its time Dynamix saw fit to release it for today's computer systems. While doing so, the company went beyond the game's boundaries and created a new story line complete with animated story panels and a set of new gadgets to enhance the craft's abilities. You are piloting Earth's finest defense vessel, and it comes with Eel Shields, Inviso-Cloak, Super Cannons, and various other additions to help in the battle against Gir Draxon.

A Level Playing Field

The battle is fought on various levels, with at least 12 kinds of enemy weaponry that can come between you and victory, including magnetic mines and laser turrets. Completing a level causes the mother ship to appear. It hovers above the ground and squirts out a Guardian that must be destroyed before you can progress to the next level. Special weapons and accessories can be used to give you the needed edge against tougher competitors, and these can be regenerated by destroying certain enemy units. If, for example, you destroy three enemy Assault Tanks, you are blessed with another Super Cannon module, which of course, must be used with discretion. The craft can be controlled with a joystick or mouse. However, we preferred to use keyboard input for superior speed and flexibility. The graphics in the story panels are purely DOS and have a "blocky" nature that betrays the game's origins. The playing field and the enemies are polygon-based, and the detail can be adjusted to suit your Mac's horsepower, making the game playable on nearly the complete range of Macs still in use today.

Spitting, Not Sleeping

Stellar 7 is an accurate adaptation of the original Apple II product. Its new story line and weapons and the fierce action make it a decent addition to any gamer's library. Those who will appreciate this game are the ones who played it to death on their old Apple IIs while less important activities, such as eating and sleeping, were put on hold.

Pros: Accurate re-creation. New modules add to fun. Adjustable screen detail for slower Macs.

Cons: Blocky graphics in story panels. No digitized voices (which DOS version has). DOS manual with Mac insert.

System Requirements: 1.7MB RAM for System 6.0.7, 4MB of RAM for System 7.0 or later.

STELLAR 7	
Fun factor	3.5
Look and feel	3.0
Value	3.5
Replayability	3.0
Overall	3.5

CD

Sub Battle Simulator
Alliance

Ah, the early days. Reagan was in the White House, Boy George was becoming a bad dream, and the Macintosh entertainment market was dominated by such companies as Epyx, Mindscape, and Silicon Beach Software. This was a time when most Mac owners had few good games to play on their beloved machines. It was 1987, and the bright star of GATO (the first Mac submarine simulator) was fading fast amidst the usual rumors of Apple's demise. Enter Epyx with a black-and-white World War II submarine sim whose box announced that any naval hack wanting to make log entries on this puppy would need at least a 512K Mac. Sub Battle Simulator quickly satisfied the yearning for new missions that the diehards developed after having played GATO for the thousandth time. Although the Mac has never been a major port of call for submarine games, the few that have managed to swim in the marketplace have carved a notch in the Mac's entertainment continuum. Perhaps it's for this reason that Alliance software has seen fit to dredge up the old war horse while giving it color, a smattering of new features, and that mystical beast known as System 7 savvy.

Embellished Memory

Our memory of Sub Battle Simulator is that of a great game which surged past previous offerings to become the best of its genre. Indeed, when the first pixels of the current game's splash screen hit the monitor, one is flooded with fond memories of countless hours spent hunting convoys under cover of night while carefully conserving torpedoes. Playing rereleased classics is like being reunited with a long-absent friend. But when this old comrade comes face to face, it's plain he hasn't aged as gracefully as some of his contemporaries.

DIVE! DIVE! DIVE!

The new Sub Battle Simulator is nearly a copy of the 1987 version. The obvious difference is the color that's been incorporated throughout the game. Sadly however, this is little more than visual candy of the dime store variety; it looks like a badly colorized Ted Turner movie. The graphics are equally antiquated, and although they were impressive in their time, they offer little to today's sophisticated gamer. Sub Battle Simulator gives the option of mouse or keyboard control, both of which are suitably responsive. The game enables you to climb into either a German or American submarine between the years 1939 and 1945. You

RANT

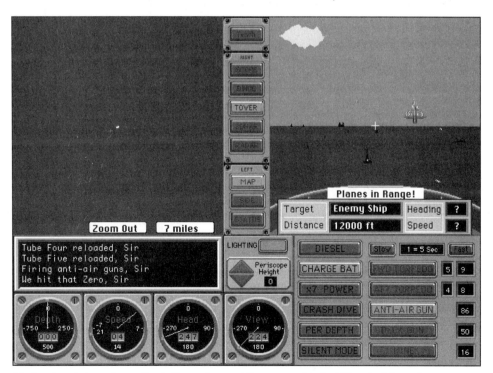

The burning airplane plummeting to the sea is one of the new graphical additions to this re-release.

can take orders for any one of 60 separate missions or challenge yourself to the campaign mode, in which you must survive the entire war. You can adjust the difficulty of game play to a broad spectrum of skill levels.

Periscope Down

Sub Battle Simulator contains few changes to inspire the new user. It has little to entice those already swayed by the infinitely more sophisticated games U-Boat and WolfPack. But it will appeal to—and please—the crowd that made many a captain's log entry all those years ago.

Pros: Accurate re-creation. Wide range of missions. Good value.

Cons: Limited use of color. Crew voices excruciating. Primitive graphics. Average AI.

System Requirements: Mac Plus or better, 2MB RAM for black and white, 4MB RAM for color, 2.3MB hard disk space, System 7 or later.

SUB BATTLE SIMULATOR	
Fun factor	2.5
Look and feel	2.5
Value	4.5
Replayability	3.0
Overall	3.0

3 Traditional Games

It's hard to imagine, but once upon a time people actually played games without the benefit of electricity and cathode ray tubes. Yes, rather than magnetic drives, floppy disks, and random access memory chips, these poor souls had to use playing cards, chess pieces, and other human beings for their entertainment. Fortunately, we live in a digital age in which we can experience pleasures of gaming without fear of being tainted by needless human contact.

Seriously, most traditional games were meant to be played with other people, and the lively conversations and arguments that accompany these games are half the fun. But it's not always possible to find willing flesh-and-blood opponents. When these lean times arise, your Mac is ready to roll up its virtual sleeves and deal a hand of blackjack, take a stroll on the Boardwalk, or whip up an original crossword puzzle.

Electronic gaming is more than just zapping aliens, flying fighter jets, and exploring dungeons. If you're hungry for a hand of gin or simply tired of playing Lazy Susan chess, read on as we explore some new twists on our old favorites.

Word Games—Crossword Puzzles

Picture this: You're in bed on a drizzly Sunday morning. There's a roaring fire in the fireplace and scattered around the room are sections of the Sunday *New York Times*. In one hand you have a cup of freshly brewed coffee, in the other, a pencil and the Sunday crossword. A romantic image, yes?

Okay, now try this: It's this same drizzly Sunday. You've got a color PowerBook balanced on your lap. You've already downloaded and read the day's news, and you're now squinting at the screen trying to come up with a seven-letter word for "heart and lungs of a deer". After cogitating for exactly 12 seconds, you give

Puzzle Master offers little more than a paperback book full of crosswords, but if you have a PowerBook, it may be just the thing for a long flight.

up and select "Reveal one word" from the Solve menu. "Numbles" appears at 34 across.

Yes, electronic crosswords do lose something in the translation, but think of all the digital conveniences you're missing when you scribble on newsprint: timed play, the ability to create original puzzles, on-line hints, and freedom from a bed full of little bits of pink eraser. Until newspapers can match such features, we think these programs bear scrutiny.

Puzzle Master
Centron Software

Take•A•Break! Crosswords
Dynamix

Crossword Wizard
Cogix

All three of these crossword packages contain ready-made puzzles, allow you to print blank puzzles and accompanying clues, and will fill in correct answers on request. Take•A•Break! Crosswords and Crossword Wizard's included puzzles come in a variety of difficulty levels, while Puzzle Master's name tells it all— these are 250 tough puzzles taken from the daily and Sunday editions of the *New York Times*.

Puzzle Master

Although Puzzle Master is consistently more challenging than the other packages, it's the most bare-bones product of the bunch. Unlike the other two products, maneuvering around a Puzzle Master puzzle can be accomplished only with the mouse: you must first click on the number of the answer you'd like to fill in and then specify whether you intend to type a single letter, the down answer, or the across answer. Hints are confined to single letters and entire words. The other two programs are more flexible in this regard and also allow you to reveal only consonants or vowels. And although Puzzle Master has a puzzle creation component, it is extremely basic. While it's possible to build a decent puzzle with its elementary tools, you might more easily accomplish the task with a pencil and a piece of graph paper.

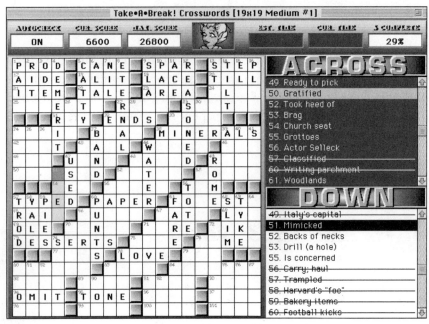

Wanda the Pixie keeps a close eye on you in Take•A•Break! Crosswords.

Take•A•Break! Crosswords

GREAT FEATURE

Take•A•Break! Crosswords does not allow you to create your own puzzles, but in other ways it is a much more complete package. The program carries 750 crosswords from Dell that are divided into three skill levels: Apprentice, Puzzler, and Fanatic. Rather than mousing all over tarnation to enter a word, as you must with Puzzle Master, Take•A•Break! Crosswords allows you to simply click on a clue to move to the appropriate location in the puzzle. Even more convenient is Space Bar toggling of word entry between down and across answers.

LOUSY FEATURE

Take•A•Break! Crosswords sports a couple of features that some people will find adorable; we didn't. The first is an auto-check function that notifies you with an annoying "Unh uh" that you've entered the incorrect word. The other is a Tinkerbell-like pixie named Wanda whose visage sits atop the program's main window and follows the movement of your mouse. It's anyone's guess what purpose Wanda serves. Fortunately, the sound and Wanda can each be sent packing by invoking a couple of simple menu commands.

Crossword Wizard

Crossword Wizard's strength lies not in its included crosswords—there are only five on the CD-ROM—but rather in the nearly magical way it creates original puzzles. Here's how it works:

When the application opens, a window pops up that provides you with four options: open a ready-made puzzle; make a computer-generated original puzzle; build a puzzle from user-supplied words and clues; and create a puzzle from scratch. Asking the program to create an original puzzle for you leads to a window in which you determine how large the puzzle will be—from 7 by 7 to 21 by 21 squares—and whether the clues will be easy, middling, or hard.

Cogix claims that Crossword Wizard can generate more than a million original puzzles. We didn't have the opportunity to try them all out, but the ones we did take a crack at would prove challenging to even the most seasoned puzzler.

Fortunately, you don't need to be an expert player to get something out of this product. For dimwits like us who weren't aware that "canoodle" is a synonym for "caress," Crossword Wizard provides the Idea Wizard, a utility that explains the logic behind the answers and also happens to be a fine thesaurus. And if you can't

GREAT FEATURE

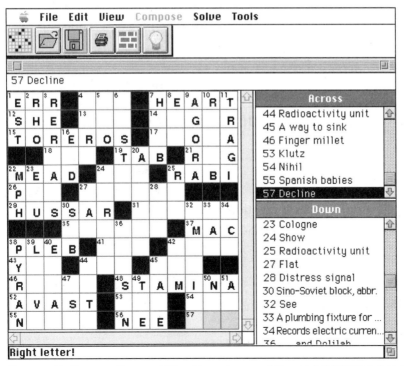

If ever a whiz there was, Crossword Wizard is one because of the wonderful things it does.

think of a four-letter word that begins with e and ends with s that means "sea eagles," check out the Word Builder feature for a list of possible answers.

Proper Word Choice

We're keen on Crossword Wizard, and we recommend it for most people without hesitation. But if you intend to use your PowerBook for a little portable puzzling, we think that either of the other products—both of which use little memory and take up less than 3MB of hard disk space—is a better choice.

PUZZLE MASTER	
Fun factor:	3.5
Look and feel:	2.0
Value:	3.0
Replayability:	3.0
Overall:	3.0

Pros: Challenging puzzles. Puzzle creation component. Good for PowerBooks.

Cons: Mouse-based navigation. Only two hint modes.

System Requirements: Mac Plus or better, 750K RAM, 2.9MB hard disk space, System 6.07 or higher.

TAKE·A·BREAK! CROSSWORDS	
Fun factor:	3.5
Look and feel:	3.5
Value:	3.5
Replayability:	2.5
Overall:	3.5

Pros: Lots of puzzles. Three skill levels. Complete hint modes. Good for PowerBooks.

Cons: No puzzle creation component.

System Requirements: Mac Plus or better, 2MB RAM for System 6, 4MB RAM for System 7, 2.5MB hard disk space, System 6.07 or higher.

Pros: Extremely flexible puzzle creation component. Wonderful hint and help utilities.

Cons: A little large to pack around on a PowerBook.

System Requirements: 4MB RAM, 5.8MB hard disk space, CD-ROM drive, System 7 or later.

CROSSWORD WIZARD	
Fun factor:	4.0
Look and feel:	4.5
Value:	4.0
Replayability:	4.5
Overall:	4.5

Word Games—Scrabble Games

If you've ever wanted to know just how poor your grasp of the English language is, you can do one of two things:

Locate a copy of the *Oxford English Dictionary*, crack it open, and without looking, place your finger anywhere on the page. Odds are you won't be able to pronounce the word you're pointing to—much less know its meaning.

Or play either of these Scrabble simulations.

We don't know about you, but we'd be hard pressed to recall the last time we used the word "uraei" in a sentence. But darned if our computer pals can't pull linguistic nuggets like this one from the included dictionary files of these games. Face facts: Computers are extremely adept at sorting and comparing information. Unless you have a mind like a steel trap and think that memorizing the dictionary is a thrilling way to spend your time, both Scrabble and Maven will beat the pants off you without fail.

But of course the fun is in trying to keep your pants on for as long as possible.

Scrabble
MacPlay

Maven
The Sheppard Company

MacPlay's Scrabble is the officially licensed Milton Bradley version of the game, and this certainly shows in its interface. Behold the traditional curved wooden tray, the salmon-pink double-word-score squares, and the big black star planted smack-dab in the middle of the board. Indeed the main differences between the look of this game and the real thing are the digital timer displayed to the left of the board and the automatic score counter just to the right of each player's name. Oh, and the tiny board, of course. Unfortunately, the game's window won't grow any larger than the nine inches required to display it on the smallest Mac screen, and since the layout must also accommodate each player's set of tiles as well as the timer and a message window, the board had to be scaled down substantially. To get a feel for how this looks, place a real Scrabble board on the ground and play the game while perched atop a 12-foot ladder.

LOUSY FEATURE

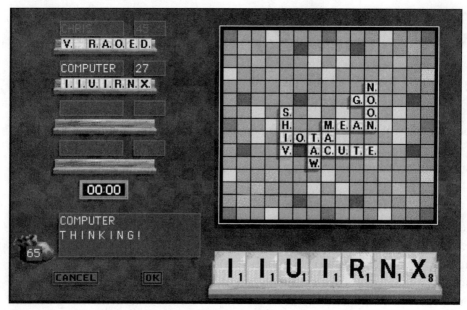

An eight-letter word for little tiny board? How about, "Scrabble?"

Apart from the Lilliputian board, this version of Scrabble is a pretty fair game. It contains such goodies as online hints, an anagram generator, nine computer skill levels, and the Juggle command. Juggle command? No, pressing Command-J doesn't cause the computer to bark out, "Two balls! Now three balls!! Okay, get ready for the flaming torches!!!" Rather, the tried and true juggling technique randomly rearranges your tiles so that it's easier for you to discern new word possibilities.

GREAT FEATURE

We'd recommend MacPlay's Scrabble without hesitation if it weren't for one tiny sticking point: We like Maven better.

Cravin' for Maven

If you've never heard of this game, you needn't be too surprised. It's produced by a small company in Massachusetts and, at the time of this writing, it can be obtained only by calling the Sheppard Company directly. (However, we did hear that a distribution deal might be in the works.)

So why bother with it? After all, Maven doesn't have a juggle command or Scrabble's slick interface. And the game presents the board and tiles in a simple, no-nonsense form that some might consider downright primitive. Ah, but behind this simple exterior beats the heart of a lion. Maven is so smart and so fast that it will cause even the most accomplished Scrabble player to sit back and gawk in appreciative wonder.

The screen size of Maven's board is much larger than Scrabble's, and the tiles, though plain, contain legible letters and numbers. You have the option to display the values of tiles placed on the board and—for those who can never remember whether the light blue squares indicate double- or triple-letter scores—labels for the premium squares. You can also customize the board by adding premium squares to your heart's content.

Maven's Kibitz command is superior to Scrabble's Hint counterpart in two important ways: Not only is it blazingly fast compared to Scrabble, but the hints are also displayed in a single list and are rated from best choice to worst. Scrabble dribbles out a single hint at a time and doesn't seem to factor in the quality of the hint.

But intelligence is what really separates the two games. Maven is capable of playing at 18 skill levels—double that of Scrabble—ranging from Plays Legal Moves to Give Up Hope. But unlike Scrabble, the first few skill levels are not so moronic as to be unplayable (our cats nearly beat Scrabble's first level). Beginning as well as intermediate players will find that Maven's first levels present plenty of challenges, and advanced players will scream in joyous agony at the higher levels. If you're unsure of where to set your skill level, you are free to select Vary Level By Result, which causes Maven to lighten up or bear down depending on your demonstrated prowess.

CHRIS 411		MAVEN 492	
New Game			
1	ague 10	outrated 68	
2	biota 20	poleyn 31	
3	spitz 52	ten 16	
4	jowls 62	brie 14	
5	futz 48	forbye 42	
6	enemy 23	mend 30	
7	sicked 42	rax 38	
8	avail 16	faithing 107	
9	opulence 86	boogies 65	
10	viol 16	wo 23	

Sure, it's not pretty, but Maven is the best Scrabble simulation going on the Mac.

Word to the Wise

People who only dabble at Scrabble will be perfectly satisfied with MacPlay's version of the game—especially if they buy it as part of MacPlay's specially priced Classic Collection bundle, which also includes Monopoly and Risk. Scrabble mavens, however, would be better served by picking up the phone and placing a call to Brian Sheppard in Massachusetts (508-287-0055). Tell him we sent you.

Pros: Traditional board and tiles. Juggle command.

Cons: Tiny board and small game window. Slow hints.

System Requirements: Black and white or 256-color Macintosh, 1.5MB RAM, 4.5MB hard disk space, System 6.07 or higher.

SCRABBLE	
Fun factor:	3.0
Look and feel:	3.0
Value:	4.0
Replayability:	4.0
Overall:	3.5

MAVEN	
Fun factor:	4.5
Look and feel:	3.5
Value:	4.5
Replayability:	4.5
Overall:	4.5

Pros: Very intelligent game. Great Kibitz function. Can place new premium squares on the board.

Cons: Basic graphics.

System Requirements: Mac Plus or better, 1.5MB RAM, 1MB hard disk space, System 6.07 or higher.

Gambling

People are entranced by gambling because, however lopsided the odds, there's a certain thrill in putting your cold hard cash on the line. If Lady Luck is on your side, you could be rolling in cabbage. If not, there goes junior's college fund.

Money is a great motivator. But strip gambling of its main components—the fear of failure and the anticipation of victory—and what have you got? Some fairly uninteresting guessing games or, in the case of slot machines, an overdeveloped right arm.

So why bother with computer gambling simulations? Well, aside from getting a small inkling of just how quickly you can lose great sums of money, the best gambling sims are those that allow you to practice the games and offer help in developing winning strategies.

So stroll with us into the casino, where we'll take in the green felt tables, the clanking chips, and the busloads of pensioners tossing away their Social Security checks. You can't get much more traditional than games of chance, and the Mac has them in spades.

Caesar's Palace
MacPlay

Trump Castle II
Capstone

As indicated by the titles, these two games are all-in-one casino simulations that feature a multitude of gambling diversions. Both programs are situated in gambling meccas, allow four humans to play, and provide players with lines of credit—Trump Castle parts with a paltry $1,000 while the beneficent Caesar allows each player to grab as much as $9,999,999.

Caesar is also more generous than Mr. Trump in the number and variety of the included games. Contained within the walls of the emperor's digs are 15 different games of chance. These include baccarat, roulette, blackjack, pai gow and three varieties of American poker, three kinds of slot machines, craps, and four different video games. Many of the games are divided into tables that offer a range of minimum bets. These range from the poker tables' $1, $2, and $5 minimums to the more extravagant $5, $25, and $100 minimums found at the baccarat table.

Reflecting the fallen fortunes of the ex-real-estate-tycoon-turned-pizza-pitchman, Trump's establishment offers only baccarat, blackjack, roulette, craps, video poker, and a single slot machine.

Hail Caesar

Caesar's Palace is superior to Trump Castle in a number of other ways. Although neither game is drop-dead gorgeous, Trump Castle II is, quite simply, an eyesore. When you enter Trump's casino, you are greeted by a sepia-toned lobby that is pixelated in the worst sort of way. Once you actually get to the games, things don't improve much. The figures on the cards are blocky, the tables are

LOUSY
FEATURE

an unearthly bright green, and the slot machine is cartoonish. This game smells distinctly of a cheap port.

Caesar's little diversion makes better use of graphics and sound. The characters on the cards are easy to discern, the coins make a nice clink when they're deposited in the slot machines, and the cards flip realistically when dealt.

No Training Wheels

GREAT FEATURE

Although neither of the games offers any training to prospective gamblers, Caesar's Palace does give you some control over how the games are conducted. You card counters will be pleased to know that you can determine the number of decks used—from one to eight—in blackjack and baccarat. You can also choose whether the roulette wheel includes 00, the number of drawable cards in poker, and if the high hand must beat the low hand in pai gow. Trump Castle lets you change only the minimum bet at each table.

LOUSY FEATURE

Just because Caesar's Palace looks good in comparison to Trump Castle II, don't get the idea that it's God's gift to gambling. There are some obvious problems with the program. For example, if you fold during one of the poker games, there's no way to speed up the hand or bail out entirely. Instead you must sit and wait while the computer plays to the conclusion of the hand. This can take considerable time when you've chosen to include six total rounds of betting.

This castle is in disrepair. Trump Castle II is our least favorite gambling sim.

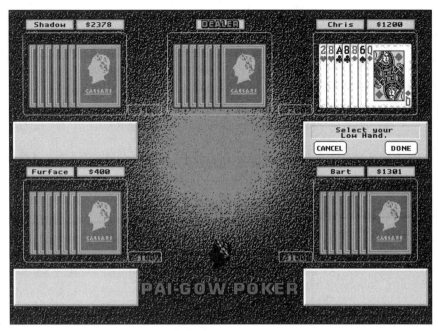

Pai-gow poker is just one of 15 gambling diversions served up at Caesar's Palace.

Also, some of the computer poker players pull some incredibly boneheaded stunts. We stumbled upon an artificial player who, with no chance for a straight or a flush, drew a single card and continued to raise like there was no tomorrow. Considering that bluffing doesn't really come into play, you have to wonder if this faux opponent had taken advantage of some hidden free drink function.

Read 'Em and Weep

While Caesar's Palace is hardly perfect, it does expose you to a variety of games. Pai gow and the electronic gambling machines are very popular in modern casinos, and Caesar's Palace provides a good introduction to these games. Players spending a few hours with Caesar's Palace and the accompanying manual should feel right at home in Atlantic City or Las Vegas. Players basing their gambling plans on Trump Castle may choose to head for the nearest dog track.

Tips

• No matter how hard you try, you can not go over $9,999,999 in Caesar's Palace.

• Forget the slots, it's a sucker's game.

TIP

• Don't bother trying to play poker on the computer against a human opponent. When you do, both hands are dealt face up.

Pros: Decent graphics and sound. Good variety of games. Flexible options.

Cons: Poor artificial intelligence of computer opponents in the poker module.

System Requirements: Black and white or 256-color Macintosh, 2MB RAM, 4.7MB hard disk space, System 6.07 or higher.

CAESAR'S PALACE	
Fun factor:	3.5
Look and feel:	4.0
Value:	4.0
Replayability:	4.0
Overall:	4.0

TRUMP CASTLE II	
Fun factor:	2.0
Look and feel:	1.0
Value:	2.0
Replayability:	2.5
Overall:	2.0

Pros: At least you're not losing real money.

Cons: Ugly graphics. Limited number of games. Few options.

System Requirements: Any Macintosh with 1MB RAM, 1.8MB hard disk space, System 6.07 or higher.

Casino Buddy
Varcon Systems

Casino Master Gold
Centron Software Technologies

Although these two gambling sims contain a variety of games, they are not all-in-one casinos. In other words, don't expect your bankroll to follow you around within them from game to game. The modest Casino Buddy contains keno, roulette, slots, and video poker. Casino Master Gold dispenses with the slot machine but adds blackjack, craps, and red dog to the games in Casino Buddy.

Low-Rent Gambling Houses
Neither of these products is likely to win a prize for graphic design, and they both fall short in the variety of games they offer. Casino Master Gold has a sparse interface, but it contains some helpful elements. For example, the black-

The profit graph is a nice touch, but let's face it Casino Buddy, why do you need it? Video poker is a losing proposition.

jack module allows you to select the number of decks you wish to play with, offers an advice option, and can display four different card counting systems. And each of Casino Master Gold's games keeps track of your win/loss statistics and provides different wagering options. These features hardly amount to stiff competition for such dedicated blackjack applications as Blackjack Trainer and Varcon's Blackjack for Macintosh, but they do offer a reasonable starting ground for players new to card counting. Casino Master Gold also has an extensive manual that explains the rules of the games as well as some betting strategies. Casino Buddy's manual is tiny, but the game provides online assistance that includes betting strategies in roulette and the rules of keno. Casino Buddy also keeps track of win/loss statistics for video poker and the slot machine.

Put Your Money Down

For an all-around gambling sim, we'd still put our shirts on Caesar's Palace. But if we had to choose between these two collections, we'd opt for Casino Master Gold. Yes, the roulette component is a little cheesy (but find one that isn't), and it's a shame that you can't transfer your bank from one game to the other. But the blackjack module is more helpful than the one found in Caesar's Palace, and the variety and usefulness of the included games is superior to those in Casino Buddy.

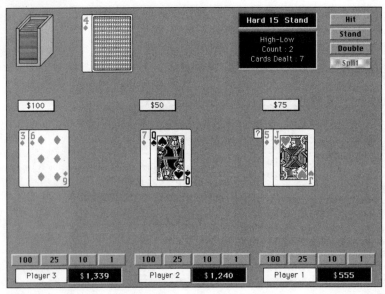

If you have any doubts about whether to hit or stand, Casino Master will set you straight.

Pros: Online help for some games.

Cons: How much fun is an electronic slot machine really?

System Requirements: 256-color Macintosh, 1MB RAM, 2.8MB hard disk space, System 6.07 or higher.

CASINO BUDDY	
Fun factor:	2.5
Look and feel:	2.5
Value:	3.0
Replayability:	2.5
Overall:	2.5

CASINO MASTER GOLD	
Fun factor:	3.5
Look and feel:	3.5
Value:	3.5
Replayability:	3.5
Overall:	3.5

Pros: Advice and card counting components in blackjack. Decent variety of games. Good manual.

Cons: Not an integrated package.

System Requirements: 1MB RAM, 1.5MB hard disk space, System 6 or higher.

Blackjack for Macintosh
Varcon Systems

Blackjack Trainer
ConJelCo

Here's where we get down to brass tacks. These games are designed for those players who want to sharpen their gambling skills in anticipation of making the big score at the casinos. Both games provide you with information regarding counting strategies and allow you to extensively customize the way the game is played.

Because the focus of these games is on teaching rather than entertainment, the interfaces and graphics tend to be less than glorious. Blackjack for Macintosh displays an expansive table that seats seven, and tiny cards with even tinier numbers (fortunately, there is an option to display the card totals for all hands). Blackjack Trainer's interface, though just as barren, is more intimate—it's just you against the dealer.

Taking Instruction
The two games take different approaches to giving out advice. Blackjack for Macintosh sports a small button labeled Hint at the bottom right of the screen. When you're not sure which course to take, a simple click on this button displays the correct answer. Blackjack Trainer assumes that you know what's what until you make a goofy decision. When this occurs, up pops a dialog box that indicates the play you should have made. If you don't care to be admonished further, you can turn this feature off.

Count Us In
In many respects the games are similar, but when it comes to actual counting and strategy drills, the programs part company. In short: Blackjack Trainer has 'em and Blackjack for Macintosh doesn't. Blackjack Trainer's counting drill tosses one to five cards on the table in succession until the entire deck—save one card—has been exhausted. Your job is to guess, based on your card count, the value of that last card.

GREAT FEATURE

The strategy drills place a card on the dealer's side of the table. You are then dealt pair after pair of cards and must determine what the right response is—hit, stand, double, or split—based on your pairs and the dealer's card. This drill can be changed so that you are dealt two-card "soft hands" in which one of the cards is an ace.

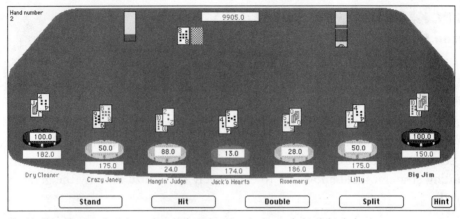

Blackjack for Macintosh ain't much to look at, but there're brains behind this baby.

Cashing Out

If it weren't for Blackjack Trainer's drill modes, we'd have a tough time deciding which program to recommend. ConJelCo's inclusion of these functions in the program make our verdict a no brainer. If you're interested in computer-based blackjack instruction, Blackjack Trainer is the odds-on favorite.

Tip

Although these games are quite helpful, they are not the be-all and end-all of blackjack. We recommend that if you're serious about winning at this game, you pick up one of the many blackjack guides available at your local bookstore.

BLACKJACK FOR MACINTOSH	
Fun factor:	3.5
Look and feel:	2.5
Value:	4.0
Replayability:	4.0
Overall:	3.5

Pros: Multiple-player situations. Card counting features.

Cons: No drills. Tiny cards.

System Requirements: 1.3MB RAM for color, 726K hard disk space, System 6.05 or higher.

Pros: Drills, drills, and more drills.

Cons: A little pricey.

System Requirements: 1MB RAM, 800K hard disk space, System 6 or higher.

```
BLACKJACK
TRAINER

Fun factor:        3.5
Look and feel:     2.5
Value:             4.5
Replayability:     4.0
Overall:           4.0
```

Virtual Vegas Volume 1: Blackjack
Virtual Vegas, Inc.

Virtual Vegas is so flawed in so many ways that it's hard to know where to begin. Let's start with this: Women will loathe this game.

For Those Who Remain

To give them credit, the folks down at Virtual Vegas realized that a blackjack simulation that doesn't offer a training component is likely to be a little dull. So what did they do? Painted the scenery with gorgeous colors, designed some beautiful playing cards, flung in three QuickTime bimbos to deal the cards and provide a little provocative banter, and put the whole thing onto a CD-ROM, where it runs as slow as a tortoise with a foot cramp. Here's the deal:

You are given a $500 stake and can play at any of three stations, each containing a different dealer. Station number one carries a $5 minimum bet and features a blond woman who is supposed to be a bit demure and on the sweet side. Station two has a $25 minimum and a domineering female who reminded Chris enough of an old girlfriend to cause him to lock the door and hide the pointed cutlery. Station three costs you 150 big ones to play and displays the overwhelming charms of a busty brunette.

Cheap Talk

As you play, the bimbettes shimmer onto the video screen to comment on your success or failure, the size of your bet, or your irresistible manliness. These remarks range from almost innocent to overtly sexual. Here are a few examples:

Dealer 3: "I get so upset when people call me a sexpot." (Adjusts her dog collar in a sly manner.) "I mean what gives them that impression?"

Dealer 2: "Keep playing like that and I might just crawl through the screen."

Dealer 3: when you've increased your bet: "I could learn to like you if you keep sticking me with big ones like that."

And finally, Dealer 3 in a moment of innocent conversation:"I should have my breasts enlarged. What do you think?"

At this juncture you are allowed to choose one of three replies:"Well gee, I hardly think it's my place to say." "With a face like yours, I hardly noticed your breasts." "What a coincidence! I just had a similar operation."

RANT

Although we laughed heartily at the third answer, the following response might be more appropriate: "Criminy, lady! Your breasts are bigger than your head! Do you think reading this kind of dreck to 15-year-old boys is going to win you that spot next to Hef when they finally revive Playboy After Dark? Did you rush home clutching this CD and say, 'Look at this, Mom! You'll be so proud! I'm a star!?'"

Slow Action

DANGER

If you've played more than one or two CD-ROM games, you're aware that the folks who cook up these things generally try to devise a way to speed up play by allowing you to copy parts of the game to a hard drive. Not so here. If you copy the application to your drive, the game crashes. Even those with massive hard drives will find it difficult to copy the entire program and accompanying files, many of which are invisible and can be accessed only with a utility such as DiskTop. This lack of forethought makes gameplay unbearably slow. You could easily knock back two or three free virtual cocktails while waiting for the next card to turn.

Got the Idea?

So the game is not only dumb but also slow. The one thing it has going for it, other than making a dandy drink coaster, is that it's really cheap—you can pick up a copy for less than $25. If you *really* like blackjack and you *really* have a lot of time on your hands, you might find some redeeming qualities in Virtual Vegas. If you do, drop us a line. We'd love to know what they are.

Pros: The most attractive blackjack simulation on the market.

Cons: Also the slowest and dumbest.

System Requirements: 13-inch color monitor, 68030 or better Macintosh, 4MB RAM, CD-ROM player.

VIRTUAL VEGAS VOLUME 1: BLACKJACK	
Fun factor:	1.0
Look and feel:	3.0
Value:	3.0
Replayability:	1.5
Overall:	1.5

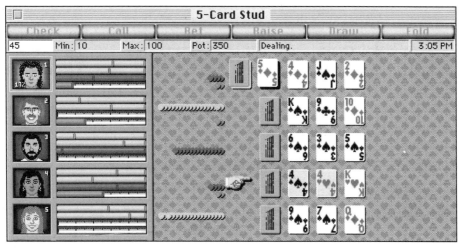

Although the screen size is a tad small, Power Poker is one of the best card game programs available.

Power Poker

Electronic Arts

Card games of all sorts have dwelled and prospered mainly in the shareware world. Few of them have ventured forth into the commercial realm, where most card games have received only moderate success. Why, after all, would anyone pay 40 or 50 bucks for a game if a comparable shareware product was available for $15? More fundamentally, why would anyone forego the complexity that competition with actual humans offers? But Todd Ouzts at Scenario Software has changed the situation with the commercial release of Power Poker, the ultimate in poker simulators. Now we can truly experience the nail-biting pressure of a high stakes poker match with blood-sucking computer opponents and even networked humans.

Know When to Hold 'Em

Booting Power Poker whisks you on a table layout that displays the hands left to right and caricatures of the participants on the far left. These can either be QuickTime players or cartoonlike images. The unsizable game window is a tad small and looks as though it was made with the old 12-inch monitors and Power-Books in mind. Clicking on the deck deals the cards in a snappy fashion. Power Poker contains no less than 109 built-in games. A slew of others can be obtained from online services. And if your online charges are too hefty, Power Poker has a built-in editor that allows you to create your own games. This is great for poker junkies who enjoy such bizarre variations as high/low Anaconda seven-card stud with one-eyed jacks and suicide kings wild.

The interface is mouse-driven, with keyboard equivalents, and is nicely intuitive, leaving your neural networks free to engage in the nuances of building royal flushes (yeah, right). Graphics are not fantastic, but they are crisp and clean, and the on-screen action is adjustable. The QuickTime players are impressive. Each has several clips that come complete with shrugs, smiles, and statements like, "Too rich for me" and "I'll pass." Really dedicated gamers will no doubt opt out of the QuickTime mode to speed game play and avoid hearing the same sound bites 20 thousand times. The dealer's speech is fully digitized—the only gripe we could muster is the absence of an option for a female voice.

Know When to Fold 'Em

**GREAT
FEATURE**

Without question, the artificial intelligence Power Poker possesses is exceptional, and the computer opponents behave much like the masses of organs and connective tissue we call humans. They will run up the pot and are intelligent with hand management. Our only complaint is with the computer's bluffing. Generally if the computer lays down big bets, it's holding a formidable hand. However a large bet can scare off a computer player who's lacking a decent set of cards. Not to worry, though; the silicon adversaries provide plenty of stiff competition, as witnessed by Bart's $2,500 debt! Statistics can be displayed in a graph on an unused portion of the screen.

Know When to Walk Away

As many as ten human opponents can play Power Poker on a network, or even a modem/network combination with AppleTalk Remote Access. As with any game, the ability to face off against your buddies in a four-suit bonanza with the computer taking care of the chips and calculations is a blast. Power Poker lacks a little of the ambiance of a smoke-filled room, but it's the next best thing to being there.

Know When to Stop Quoting Kenny Rogers

The small playing window and tiresome nature of the QuickTime opponents are small detractions from what is the best gambling/card game title on the market. The flexibility, playability, and thoroughness of the game make it an excellent addition to any software library. This is a must have for poker junkies and network gamers.

Pros: Easy to use interface. Good manual. Excellent online instructions. Fantastic flexibility and configurability. Network play.

Cons: QuickTime video opponents can get tiresome. Small game window.

System Requirements: 1MB RAM for System 6.07, 4MB RAM for System 7, 4.6MB hard disk space.

POWER POKER	
Fun factor:	4.5
Look and feel:	3.5
Value:	4.5
Replayability:	4.0
Overall:	4.5

Traditional Card Games

Beyond the sordid world of gambling, there are tamer varieties of card games—you know, the kind you play alone in your spare hours or that mom, dad, junior, and sis play around the kitchen table on a Saturday night. But since mom and dad sold the house to start up the llama ranch and sis won that congressional seat, it's been hard to find enough people to make up a pinochle party.

Fortunately, we have our little computer pals to do—and put up with—our ridiculous bidding. If you like your card games wholesome and homespun, shuffle up to your Mac and check out these games.

Anyone for Cards?
Capstone

Hoyle Classic Card Games
Sierra On-Line

We usually try to keep you in suspense when we're comparing two products that address the same market, but we thought we'd give you a break here and get right to the point. If you'd like to play such traditional card games as cribbage, gin rummy, hearts, pinochle, euchre, and crazy eights on your computer, buy a copy of Anyone for Cards? and avoid Hoyle Classic Card Games like the plague.

How Come?
Simple. Hoyle Classic Card Games is a DOS port so awful that Sierra On-Line should include a written apology in every box. Oh sure, it's packed full of such little goodies as digital sound, background music, animation, and a cast of eccentric

LOUSY FEATURE

Wouldn't you know that the tough woman lawyer who happens to be a whiz at hearts would be named Hillary?

opponents (half of which are characters from other Sierra On-Line games). But the price you pay is steep: 11MB of hard disk space and performance that's slow as tree sap. Add to this Sierra's typically chunky graphics—so chunky, in fact, that it's difficult to tell the difference between a spade and a club—and you've got a real stinker.

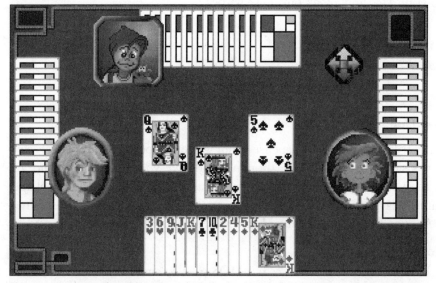

Those are spades on the table and we think that's a King below, but Hoyle Classic Card Games doesn't make it easy to tell with its horrendously chunky graphics.

On the other hand, despite its pedestrian packaging, Anyone for Cards? is a well-implemented and entertaining collection. It contains 12 different card games and includes such eclectic choices as spades, 31, 99, whist, George, and oh hell. Anyone for Cards? also takes up 11MB of hard disk space for the full installation, and it includes digital sound, background music, animation, and a cast of corny opponents, but performance is zippy compared to the Sierra On-Line product, and care was taken to produce legible cards that can be easily arranged by suit or rank.

**GREAT
FEATURE**

Hearts on Fire

Playing sample hands of gin rummy and hearts, we tested the skills of our computer opponents in both games and found them wanting. In gin, opponents routinely threw low cards when a higher discard would have been the smarter play, and these characters don't seem to take into account the kinds of cards you are collecting from the discard pile. In hearts, some of the decisions about card passing were highly questionable. This can be partially accounted for by the skill levels of the opponents, but even artificial players who were ranked as hearts experts set themselves up for huge hits by playing the wrong cards.

We mentioned that Hoyle's Classic Card Games was slow. If Anyone for Cards? has a speed problem, it's that things sometimes move too quickly. Playing gin rummy, for instance, you hardly have a chance to see whether your opponent has picked from the discard pile or the deck before you are presented with his or her discard. Admittedly this speedy play is preferable to Hoyle's dull pace, but it would be nice if Anyone for Cards? included an option to relax the action.

What to Buy?

We've pretty well covered this one. Anyone for Cards? isn't perfect, but it's a darned sight closer than Hoyle Classic Card Games. If you like these sorts of games and are willing to put up with opponents whose play is sometimes less than superhuman, answer "How about me?" to Anyone for Cards?

Pros: Nice variety of games. Flexible options.

Cons: Play is sometimes too fast. Opponents don't always pay attention.

System Requirements: 256-color Macintosh, 4MB RAM, 11MB hard disk space for full installation, System 6.05 or higher.

ANYONE FOR CARDS?	
Fun factor:	4.0
Look and feel:	4.0
Value:	4.0
Replayability:	4.0
Overall:	4.0

Pros: Amusing animation. Contains the greatest hits of traditional card games.

Cons: Awful blocky graphics. Dead slow.

System Requirements: 256-color Macintosh, 4MB RAM, 11MB hard disk space, System 7 or later.

HOYLE CLASSIC CARD GAMES	
Fun factor:	2.0
Look and feel:	2.0
Value:	2.0
Replayability:	2.0
Overall:	2.0

Eric's Ultimate Solitaire
Delta Tao Software

One may ask, "Why buy a commercial solitaire game when there are at least ten good shareware or freeware games out there?" The answer of course is that Eric's Ultimate Solitaire is the best of them all and is worth every penny. This is the cream of the crop in solitaire games and it features 17 of the most popular solitaire games of all time. The folks at Delta Tao have done a typically great job of producing a slick, enjoyable product while sticking to their practical environmental approach by eliminating the wasteful cardboard box and packaging the game in the manual. Those wacky Taoists continue to impress people in the computer game industry with their stands on copy protection and paper wastage.

Eric's Ultimate is the "King" of solitaire games, offering 17 variations.

Deal!

Eric's Ultimate features great color, clear graphics, and a drag-and-drop interface augmented by the necessary shortcuts that make placing a card a mere double-click away. Another handy feature is a tracking device that keeps a log of the overall win/loss percentages and the total time sucked into the computer game void. There are 16 different background colors available, and each of the 17 games has its own unique deck of cards. Animation in Eric's Ultimate is very smooth and can be adjusted to individual tastes. Heck, even the little hand cursor can be set to either right or left-handedness. The written manual describes the rules of every solitaire variation. As might be expected from Delta Tao, these descriptions can be very humorous. If you find yourself without your manual while on a Power-Book outing, the online instructions cover the basics. Amazingly, this game will run on any Macintosh with a floppy drive. It will even run off a floppy-based system (just like in the old days). How many games can say that?

GREAT FEATURE

Fun to Be Alone

This is the best solitaire package on the market, and despite the fact that it is a commercial venture and carries a higher price tag than the shareware fare, it's worth a tad more cashola. Delta Tao has excellent customer support and even includes a *stamped* envelope for you to return with suggestions, no doubt to keep the folks there frosty with ideas for great new games. If you're a solitaire junkie, this is one game you can't be without.

Tip

• Try playing Eric's Ultimate on various holidays. Log in as Weasel.

TIP

Pros: Great color and graphics. Simple, easy interface. Seventeen different games. Runs from disk!

Cons: None.

System Requirements: 256-color Macintosh, 2MB RAM, 671K hard disk space, System 6.05 or greater.

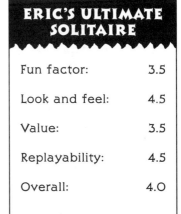

ERIC'S ULTIMATE SOLITAIRE	
Fun factor:	3.5
Look and feel:	4.5
Value:	3.5
Replayability:	4.5
Overall:	4.0

Bridge Games

Every group of amusements, from board games to card games, has one member that is thought to be the most challenging of its kind. Chess is universally considered to be the most complex board game. It takes great dedication and perseverance to be recognized as a Grand Master, or even to become simply an accomplished player. Likewise, bridge is the granddaddy of all card games, and its mastery can take years. In fact, most bridge players say that the education process never stops. As with chess, which has been refined on the computer to an incredible level of ability, the computer would seem a natural nonhuman opponent. However, bridge involves intricate combinations of scoring and bidding that in the past have been difficult to properly emulate. We will look at three contemporary Macintosh bridge games and explore their differences to see if the computer's artificial intelligence has risen to the challenge.

Deluxe Bridge With Omar Sharif
MacPlay

MacPlay's entry in this field is probably the most visible and well known of the Mac bridge games. After all, Omar Sharif is becoming more familiar as a bridge player than an actor, and with his voice in the game and his face on the box the

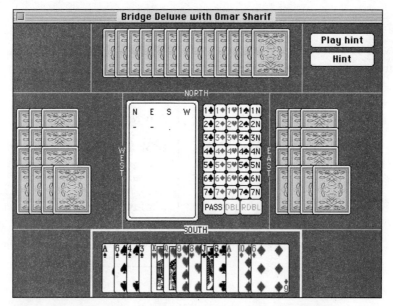

Omar Sharif verbally guides the game in Bridge Deluxe with Omar Sharif.

glitz is certainly not lacking. We found the play in Deluxe Bridge fairly sophisticated, so much so that a novice player might initially find this an obstacle. There are tutorials for different types of hands such as "slam" and "no trump" as well as for regular play. The take-back function allows you to back up in bidding in one step. We had some concerns about the cumulative scoring, which has points going above the line once the game is made, that may be confusing to some as this is not always the method used to score rubber bridge. We also found that the bidding does not always follow logic or common conventions.

At first glance, Deluxe Bridge's graphics appear to be the best of the three reviewed here, but close examination reveals an odd fuzziness that greatly decreases clarity and increases eyestrain. This becomes painfully apparent when trying to see how many tricks each side has garnered because the number of tricks is superimposed on the back of the cards and is sometimes not readable. It should be noted that the card graphics can be changed at any time to help decrease these effects. However, this is not particularly effective. All in all, Deluxe Bridge falls smack in the middle of the other contenders, and offers decent gameplay and value and a big-name star to guide you on the path to bridge excellence.

LOUSY FEATURE

Pros: Fairly sophisticated play. Good value.

Cons: Graphics can cause eyestrain for some.

System Requirements: 256-color Macintosh, 2MB RAM, 1.7MB hard disk space, System 6.07 or higher.

DELUXE BRIDGE WITH OMAR SHARIF	
Fun factor:	3.0
Look and feel:	3.5
Value:	3.5
Replayability:	3.0
Overall:	3.5

BridgeMaster
Capstone

Capstone's entry into the bridge sweepstakes offers the best full-screen playing area of these three games. It can incorporate various conventions as well as rubber, duplicate, and pairs playing styles. BridgeMaster offers four skill levels, but it can sometimes be difficult to tell the difference in gameplay between amateur and pro. Players are given the usual opportunities to configure various game parameters, such as table and card design, game speed, and even gender and playing personality. Hands can be rebid as many times as you like, but there is no feature to allow for replay of a match with the same hands that were played in a previous game.

We generally found the interface to be both better and a tad trickier to manage than its contemporaries. The rewind feature, for example, is a little quirky, but we found the bidding system to be superior, with large bidding squares laid out conveniently for two-click bids. Unfortunately, the play was not particularly sophisticated, and the computer players rarely finesse or ruff and sometimes engage in inappropriate bidding practices. BridgeMaster provides adequate play and reasonable value.

Pros: Three styles of play. Visually pleasing. Can set gender of players.

Cons: Not very sophisticated play. Some parts of interface quirky.

System Requirements: 256-color Macintosh, 4MB RAM, 1.2MB hard disk space, System 6.05 or greater.

BRIDGEMASTER	
Fun factor:	3.0
Look and feel:	4.0
Value:	3.0
Replayability:	3.0
Overall:	3.0

Micro•Bridge Companion
Great Game Products

**GREAT
FEATURE**

Great Game Products supplies us with the unlikely winner of the bridge sweepstakes. You might expect one of the titles from the large publishing houses to be at the pinnacle of bridge gaming, but MBC comes out on top by a full point in every category. It's laid out with the suits separated so that the hands are easy to count, and the cards are small but crisp and easy to read when the large setting is engaged. It allows you to review bidding at any time as well as to replay or rotate hands. An excellent scorecard explains the scores clearly.

MBC offers the choice of rubber bridge, duplicate or "special" hands, for example, avoiding an overruff and picking the right suit. The help system is also exemplary, supplying info on such matters as bidding, play, and scoring, as well as flow charts to help beginners make decisions. Another excellent feature is the statistics card, which keeps track of bidding and tricks. The game seemed to include a greater number of unevenly distributed hands, which makes for more sophisticated bidding and playing. The bottom line is that MBC offers the best

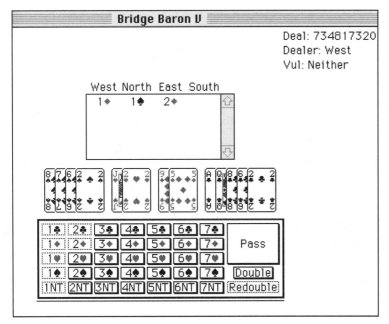

Despite its spartan interface, Micro•Bridge Companion is the smartest of the bridge games.

artificial intelligence of the three contenders, and it has an acceptable interface. These make for a superior and more enjoyable bridge experience.

Pros: Very configurable. Great scorecard. Best AI.

Cons: Visually dull interface.

System Requirements: Color or black and white monitor, 2MB RAM, 544K hard disk space, System 6.07 or greater.

MICRO·BRIDGE COMPANION	
Fun factor:	4.0
Look and feel:	3.5
Value:	4.0
Replayability:	4.0
Overall:	4.0

Board Games

Although board games would seem to be natural candidates for digital translation, attempts to bring them to the Mac have met with mixed success, and while some games, such as chess, are perfectly suited to the computer, others may best be left on the kitchen table.

Risk Deluxe

MacPlay

Of all the available board games, few have caused as many hard feelings and heated arguments as the deceptively simple conquering game of Risk. Its complex web of alliances can literally bring friends to fisticuffs over shattered treaties or unlucky rolls of the dice. Although not complicated in nature, Risk lends itself well to the computer's expertise. Whether the computer version can help to prevent a split lip or terminally damaged friendship is of little concern here. The only important issue involves dealing the final blow to a battle-weary adversary who has been circling the drain for several turns.

What Are Friends For?

Risk involves two to six players spread out over 42 territories on a map of the world. The territories are not geographically accurate. Armies are earned at the beginning of every turn based on the number of territories held by the players. Bonuses are awarded for holding continents over the course of full turns. If a foreign territory is toasted during your turn, a card is placed in front of you and can be exchanged (in sets) for more armies. Ultimately, these diversions regarding continents and cards are unimportant because the real issue is how you are going to manipulate the other players so that you can turn their friendship into a horrible weapon of destruction and take their territories while crushing their morale. Whew! Obviously this game inspires emotion.

Port This!

When Virgin Games first released Risk Deluxe, it was a terrible port from the DOS realm with absolutely no Mac interface or command set. MacPlay should be commended for cleaning it up and dressing it in nicer clothing before rereleasing it to the consuming public. This was of vital importance because there are several freeware Risks in cyberspace that are fun and easy to play. Risk Deluxe uses a point-and-click approach to army placement and territory selection. It contains the necessary options to speed gameplay to acceptable levels for

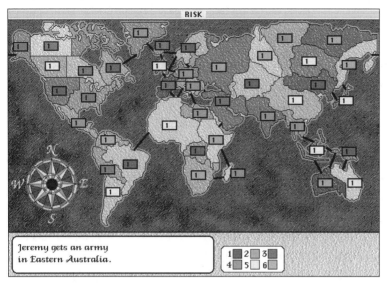

The Risk game board borrows heavily from its cardboard counterpart.

the accomplished player. It also offers variations that the freeware titles have not included: the choice of U.K. or U.S. rule sets; the choice of mission or head-quarters-type games; and a two-player neutral territory version.

The manual notes that some of the delays in action are related to the original port programming that could not be changed without recoding the entire game. However, we understand that such recoding is being considered.

Low-Risk Buy

Risk Deluxe faithfully re-creates the original box version of the game, and although it's clearly stunted by its DOS roots, Risk fans should include it in their libraries along with the freeware versions. Certainly the price is right; Risk Deluxe comes packaged with Monopoly and Scrabble for one low price.

Pros: Offers game variations. Good instructions. Great value.

Cons: Suffers from DOS roots. Interface still somewhat DOSesque.

System Requirements: 13-inch monitor re-quired for color, 2MB RAM, 3.1MB hard disk space, System 6.07 or higher.

RISK DELUXE

Fun factor:	3.0
Look and feel:	2.5
Value:	4.0
Replayability:	3.5
Overall:	3.0

Monopoly
MacPlay

A piece of cardboard, some well-known streets, and an addictive theme were designed and refined into a classic game in 1934 by Charles B. Darrow of Germantown, Pennsylvania. This is without doubt the biggest selling board game of all time. It has caused many a grudge match and made Parker Brothers a small fortune. In North America, most households contain one form or another of this classic capitalist diversion. And there are editions in 23 languages in 33 countries. In the Canadian version, the streets have been given Canadian names and the police officer is a Mounty. The fun of Monopoly lies in the interaction and competition that is created when four or five people sit around a table to make their millions (or thousands as the case may be). It remains to be seen if this classic game can be viable in a computer environment.

Community Chest

There are many variations on the Monopoly rule set, and most folks don't follow the actual rules to a tee. Some say that when landing on Go you receive double salary. Others say that when landing on Free Parking a pile of cash stacked in the center of the board becomes yours. Of course, these are not real rules but variations dreamed up by generations of Monopolists. They are so ingrained in Monopoly folklore that bitter arguments have started over whether collected income taxes should go into the Free Parking fund. In MacPlay's Monopoly,

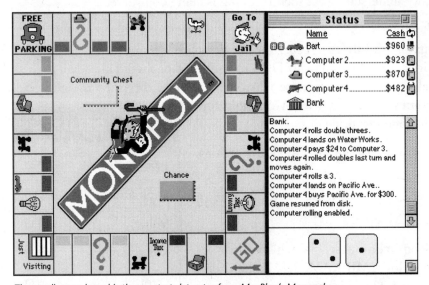

The small game board is the greatest detractor from MacPlay's Monopoly.

most of the common rule misconceptions are available options that can be selected as desired. In fact, all of the necessary extras in game play have been included, from an optional time clock, to a mode that allows for exploration of any "what if."

Go Directly to Jail

The major drawbacks to playing a classic board game like this on your computer involve the lack of human opponents to gripe at when you have rolled doubles three times in a row and are heading to the slammer. Without this, Monopoly seems kind of lifeless, and although all of your computer game opponents can be human, why would you want to sit around a single computer if you can play the board version? Perhaps a network feature would help alleviate this problem, as it did for Power Poker. If you could play against a distant friend via modem, Monopoly would instantly become worth its price (just prior to publication, we learned that Parker Brothers will be releasing an online version of the game that can be played over the Internet). The dice rolling and property management is handled quickly and efficiently, but this is not enough to make playing on the computer better than the real thing. The last complaint we have is about the tiny size of the playing area. It occupies the upper left area of the screen and causes considerable eyestrain over any period of time.

Luxury Tax

Although this is an accurate re-creation of the classic board game, it lacks what good multiplayer board games need: human opponents. The feature list, instructions, and interface are very nice but are hindered by the strangely small board design. For true Monopoly aficionados, this would be a great addition to a collection of related paraphernalia. But if you want to play Monopoly with friends, you'd be better off buying the cardboard version.

Pros: Incorporates unofficial rules. Easy interface. Good instructions.

Cons: Game board is very small. Suffers from a problem inherent in this type of game—if several people want to play, why not use the original version?

System Requirements: 1MB RAM, 1.5MB hard disk space, System 6.07 or higher.

MONOPOLY	
Fun factor:	3.0
Look and feel:	2.5
Value:	3.0
Replayability:	3.5
Overall:	3.0

Mario's Game Gallery
MacPlay

"Hey, goomba! Howsa bouta you and I playa littlea game togeder, eh?"

Would all Italian-Americans offended by that last sentence please raise your hands?

For those of you who count yourself among the offended, this review may be over. You may very well not want your kids playing Mario's Game Gallery, because the above is the kind of stereotyped "Uncle Luigi" dialog you'll hear pouring from your Mac every time your child fires up the game.

Nintendo Tie-In

If you've been in a coma during the past decade, you're probably unfamiliar with Mario. He's a happy little Italian character who is featured in a variety of Nintendo games and on television, cereal boxes, lunch pails, sheets, towels, and pajamas. Mario is much like Barney but is a degree or two less obnoxious.

Mario's Game Gallery is a collection of five traditional games for kids: checkers, go fish, dominoes, backgammon, and yacht (read: yahtzee). In each game, your

Atsa nice! Sit down with Mario and try a little Yacht (zee).

child is matched against the ever-smiling Mario, who chirps such little bits of happy talk as, "That'sa gooda movea!" at the conclusion of each turn. It is possible, of course, to turn off the sound in which case your child can get the messages in print, without dialect.

Cute, Though

Okay, we're too old and politically correct to embrace this game wholeheartedly, but your kids probably aren't. We may be old fogies, but we can appreciate the care that went into designing the individual games and the sound effects and graphics that accompany them. We expect children to be entranced when they march Yoshi and Koopa across the backgammon table or checkerboard. Kids will also enjoy watching a tuna leap out of the deck whenever they must "go fish." What we're not so sure about is how seven-year-old children will feel when Mario demands, "Hey, whatsa takinga so longa?" when they've hesitated for a few seconds before making the next move. Generally the game is extremely encouraging and nonthreatening, but we feel Mario is a little quick to hector, especially in games such as backgammon, which can be tough for young children. We hope that the next iteration of the game includes either a Nag Time Adjuster or an on-screen button that reads, "Hey Mario, get off my back!"

LOUSY FEATURE

Darned Close

Aside from the cultural stereotyping and Mario's impatience, Mario's Game Gallery is a swell little collection of games that should keep your kids entertained for hours on end. The animation and sounds are endearing, and Mario, unlike parents who have put in ten hours at the office, is always ready for another game.

Pros: Great graphics and sound. Fun games.

Cons: Cultural stereotype. Mario's in a hurry.

System Requirements: 256-color Macintosh, 1.7MB RAM, 7MB hard disk space, System 7 or later.

MARIO'S GAME GALLERY	
Fun factor:	4.0
Look and feel:	4.0
Value:	4.0
Replayability:	4.0
Overall:	4.0

Jeopardy
GameTek

Game shows are a staple of the television diet that have maintained their popularity surprisingly well over the years. One of the most popular has finally made its way to the Mac. Yes, it's *Jeopardy!* Alex Trebek and the gang from TV's number one question and answer show have arrived on our beloved machines for some answers in the form of questions.

Daily Double

It's all here, from buzzers to the multitudes of categories and even the voice of good old Alex himself smoothly pronouncing "nnnnno" and "that is correct" at appropriate moments. GameTek has done a superior job of giving this program the look and feel of the actual show. In fact, this is the best interpretation of a game show that we've seen on a Mac. The opening screen is so accurate that a quick glance could make you mistake your computer for a television set tuned in to *Jeopardy*.

Mac Jeopardy has a library of 3,500 questions. It can be played with any combination of human or computer players totaling three. The caricatures are digitized photos of real people, and the four choices from each gender are alright, but all of the choices are stereotypically beautiful people. This may appeal to some, but hey, in real life not everyone looks like Barbie or Ken. The three buzzers are set on the keyboard and can be reconfigured between the Tab key, Space Bar, and Return key. The mouse handles the rest of the category and question choices, and there is a lock-out feature that prevents anyone from ringing a buzzer before everyone has had time to read the question. The game is structured exactly like the TV show, and it includes Jeopardy, Double Jeopardy, and Final Jeopardy.

I'll Take Annoying Features for 500, Alex

There is an occasional sluggishness in some of the buzzer buttons when three people are engaged in play; a person could press his or her button first and still not get first crack at the question. This problem is so incredibly annoying that it alone makes the game unenjoyable when playing against other people. So if you can't play against other people properly, you still have the computer opponents to play against, right? Absolutely one hundred percent wrong. We have never seen computer opponents that were bigger doormats than these. Rarely can they even attempt an answer let alone hit the buzzer button. The other very

RANT

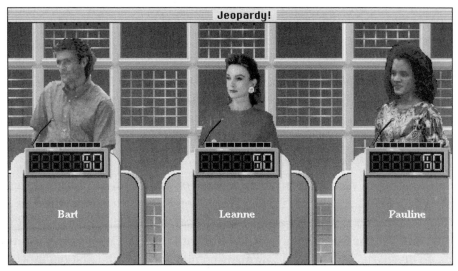

The contestants in Jeopardy are unusually beautiful people, but they answer like doormats.

irritating problem lies in the answer recognition AI. Occasionally you will type in the correct answer only to get a "sorry, that is incorrect" from Alex, and then have him give you the exact answer you just typed in! Give us a break.

Final Jeopardy

GameTek has succeeded in re-creating the look and feel of television's *Jeopardy*. All early indications point toward an enjoyable multiplayer game. However, the problems with computer opponents, buzzers, and answer recognition destroy what could have been an excellent game.

Pros: Great color and graphics. Looks like the real show. Good sound right from the show. Good question base.

Cons: Poor answer recognition. Not compatible with small PowerBook screens. Computer opponents are doormats. Buzzer response sometimes sluggish.

System Requirements: 68030 or better Mac, 1MB RAM, 2MB for color, 2.3MB hard disk space, System 7 or later.

JEOPARDY	
Fun factor:	2.0
Look and feel:	4.5
Value:	2.5
Replayability:	3.0
Overall:	2.5

∿∿∿∿∿∿∿∿∿∿∿∿∿∿∿∿∿∿∿∿∿∿

Chess Games

The popularity of chess, which has been described as one of the most intellectual of human endeavors, has survived such improbable diversions as the hula hoop and Trivial Pursuit. As far as historians can tell, the game originated in India around the sixth century A.D. Without a doubt, anything this long in the tooth must have compelling properties.

The small matter of devising a machine capable of challenging a human at this game was first approached in 1770 when Baron Von Kempelen devised the Turk, a clever chess machine that concealed a chess master who operated the machine's controls. In 1770 this was the only way to deal with the game's staggering complexity. To illustrate, we ask you, How many combinations of the first ten moves in a chess game do you think are possible? Several hundred thousand? Nice try. How about 169,518,829,100,544,000,000,000,000,000? One might expect this number to be called something like "169 mega-giga-gigantoric humongazoids to the tenth power." Actually it's 169.5 octillion. Obviously the awesome level of potential moves in chess could be handled only by a machine of mystical intelligence. Well, ta da! Enter Steve Wozniak and Steve Jobs sitting in a dusty garage assembling an electronic machine that would be used in every home. The computer revolution has brought the game of chess, complete with formidable opponents, into the homes of every person who enjoys the game. Actually, computers can be quite a bit better at the game than most of us. At present, however, there is still no computer (including Deep Thought) that can defeat the world champions of chess.

Battle Chess
MacPlay

One of the many breathtaking scenes in the first Star Wars movie occurred on the *Millennium Falcon* when Cee3PO and Chewbakka were playing a futuristic chesslike game with tiny monsters that actually fought for the squares they occupied. This idea was transferred to the now legendary Battle Chess CD-ROM from MacPlay, which provides the most entertaining title in this group. The sound in Battle Chess is the best of all the games we have played in any genre. It was accomplished with a novel approach to sound delivery. The dialogue, music, and combat scenes all come directly off the CD-ROM into separate speakers connected via the headphone or RCA jacks in the drive. This

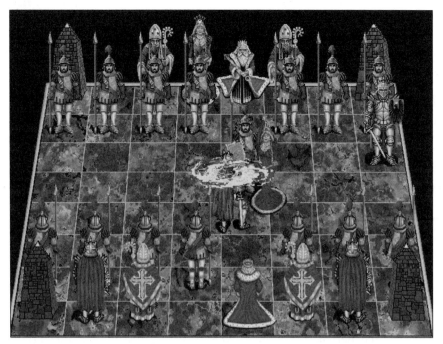

The queen engulfs an unfortunate piece in a swirling vortex of fire. Guess she got the last word.

allows for simultaneous sound from the computer speaker and the separate speakers, making for an incredible auditory experience. When a piece captures another, there are fireworks aplenty, with fully animated and very humorous combat scenes. For example, the action when two knights face off hearkens back to the old Monty Python and the Holy Grail flick in which the Black Knight gets his limbs cut off while insisting his wounds are superficial.

GREAT
FEATURE

The online tutorial in Battle Chess is far and away superior to that of its competitors and includes detailed "personal" explanations of rules for each type of piece. When being tutored on the bishop for example, he will walk onto the screen with a musical fanfare, introduce himself, and proceed to chat for five minutes on the origins of the piece and how it's used in the game. This is all done with a heady but humorous tone that is very captivating. Whether you're a beginning player or a chessaholic, you will probably want to take the time to see the entire tutorial. Gameplay is achieved through mouse work and is smooth and Mac-like, with pull-down menus for choosing from the many available options. There is also a modem play feature that allows two players to face off via either a Mac-to-Mac or a Mac-to-PC link. (Don't forget that you are, after all, playing chess, and a good game is not usually completed in the time it takes to say "exorbitant phone bill.") We think this game is the weakest of the four for complex play but more than adequate for weekend gaming. The only other drawback to Battle Chess is the need for a CD-ROM drive and external speakers to enjoy the fantastic show. MacPlay should get a pat on the back for providing the most entertaining chess game ever to grace the Mac screen.

Pros: Modem play. Fantastic humorous combat. Great tutorial for raw beginners. Awesome sound from CD-ROM.

Cons: Not a high-level chess player. Battle scenes can become tiresome.

System Requirements: Any color Mac, 4MB RAM, System 6.07 or higher, CD ROM drive, external speakers.

BATTLE CHESS	
Fun factor:	5.0
Look and feel:	4.0
Value:	3.5
Replayability:	3.5
Overall:	4.0

Sargon V
Activision

Sargon, the original personal computer chess game, dates back to the moldy days of 1978. Since the program's creators, Dan and Kathe Spracklen, first released it, Sargon has been ported to nearly every computer platform in existence. The earliest version can still be played on an old Commodore Vic 20,

Clunky DOS graphics are the only downfall to Sargon V, the most intelligent Mac chess program.

although you might have to wait a thousand years for the Vic 20 to take its turn. Five generations later, the highest-rated computer chess game (with a rating just below that of a grand master) comes to the Mac with more features then ever before. Everything from tutorials to the Mate Finder is accessible through pull-down menus. The latter feature allows for learning attack strategies and solving chess problems by having the computer find the quickest route to checkmate in any given number of moves. Sargon also includes a beginner mode that high-lights various possible moves for selected pieces.

Sargon V is a very detailed computer chess game, and it incorporates features for the novice and grand master alike. Although it's said that home computer chess programs cannot defeat grand masters, Sargon V will be a formidable enough adversary for the majority of us. For the most features and solid playing styles across all levels of ability, Sargon V is an excellent choice, especially for more experienced players.

Pros: High-level chess play. Many features. Great Mate Finder Feature.

Cons: DOS style graphics. No modem play.

System Requirements: Mac Plus or better, 2.5MB RAM for black and white, 4MB RAM for color, 2MB hard drive space, System 6.07 or higher.

SARGON V	
Fun factor:	3.5
Look and feel:	3.0
Value:	3.5
Replayability:	4.0
Overall:	3.5

CheckMate
MacPlay

CheckMate can be played on a 2D or 3D game board. It provides a level of gameplay above Battle Chess but below Chessmaster 3000 and Sargon. Its excellent manual is complete and explains in detail everything from how to play to the rating system by which chess players are categorized. The strength of Check-Mate lies in its simplicity, bright readable game board, and excellent descriptions of individual pieces, strategy, and chess notation. Test situations, complete with solutions, are included to assist in the learning process, as are notations from various classic chess games. The computer has two difficulty sections. The first can be set to any of 10 levels. These allow beginners to hone their skills before moving on to the strong opponents, which number four. There is also a button that makes opponents use more aggressive strategies in their play. We liked the

GREAT
FEATURE

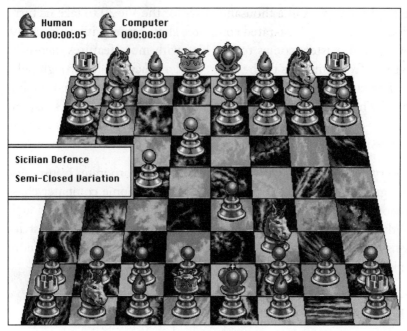

Ease of use and nice graphics make CheckMate a suitable entry level chess program.

small boxes that pop onto the screen to let you know if your game is following the course of any famous historical matches. CheckMate is more than sufficient for armchair chess players, and it offers easy play, healthy opposition, great documentation, and solid value.

Pros: Modem play. Easy interface. Good manual.

Cons: Not for expert chess players. Not as many features as competitors' games.

System Requirements: Any color Mac, 4MB RAM, System 6.07 or higher, CD-ROM drive.

CHECKMATE	
Fun factor:	3.5
Look and feel:	4.0
Value:	4.0
Replayability:	3.5
Overall:	3.5

Chessmaster 3000
The Software Toolworks

The Software Toolworks has gone to great lengths to provide the most configurable chess game on the market. Rather than merely limiting the amount of time the computer thinks, Chessmaster 3000 gives you the ability to alter the computer's playing style so that you can create opponents that are truly different. The feature list in Chessmaster 3000 is the largest in the four games reviewed here; it includes everything from aquatic chess pieces to rules adjustments. Numerous small windows can be toggled to supply information on pieces captured and the computer's thought processes. Hard-core chess players may be less inclined to get excited about such features as the ability to "bend" the 3D board to suit your visual needs. But we should remember that the majority of people in the chess world are not grand masters and that they would be very pleased with Chessmaster 3000's AI and glitzy features. Chessmaster 3000 offers awesome value, many extra features, and, with the exception of BattleChess, the most visually refined graphics of any of the Mac chess programs.

Pros: Large number of features. Great graphics. "Micro" (mini-chessboard) feature allows for background games.

Cons: Custom-made opponents can be pushovers. No modem play.

System Requirements: Any color Mac, 4MB RAM, 3.9MB hard drive space, System 6.07 or higher.

CHESSMASTER 3000

Fun factor:	4.0
Look and feel:	4.0
Value:	3.5
Replayability:	3.5
Overall:	4.0

Chessmaster 3000 offers the most features of any chess program, including this aquatic board variation.

PIZZA OF THE PROGRAMMERS

So what toppings do game programmers prefer on their pizza? you ask. Leaving no question unanswered, here's what we found:

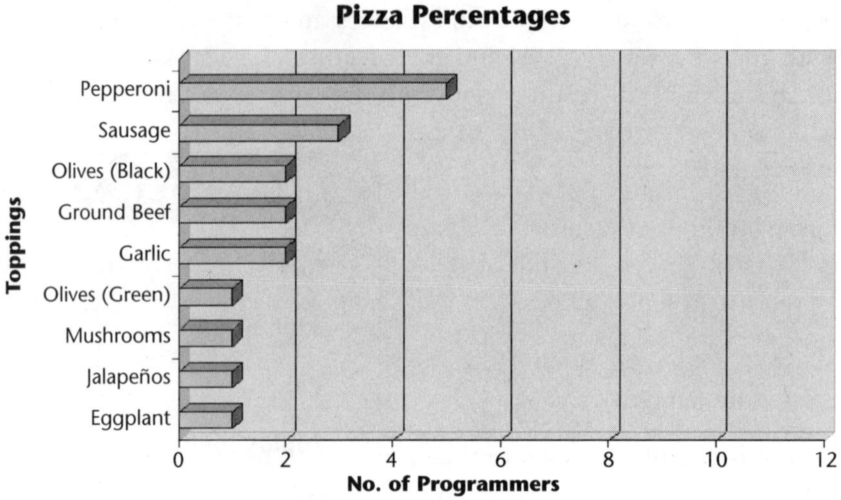

Pizza Percentages

A horizontal bar chart titled "Pizza Percentages" with y-axis "Toppings" and x-axis "No. of Programmers" ranging 0 to 12:
- Pepperoni: 5
- Sausage: 3
- Olives (Black): 2
- Ground Beef: 2
- Garlic: 2
- Olives (Green): 1
- Mushrooms: 1
- Jalapeños: 1
- Eggplant: 1

Chris Crawford (Patton vs. Rommel, Balance of Power): Sorry, I don't eat pizza. It's just a lot of fat smeared on bread. If you're looking for bad habits, I must confess to one: cookies.

Rand Miller (Myst): Ground beef, black olives, onions, lots of cheese, and as little sauce as possible.

Robyn Miller (Myst): Pepperoni, green olives, and anything else with lots of fat and sodium.

Eric Parker (Hellcats Over the Pacific, A-10 Attack!): Pepperoni.

Mark Payne (Co-founder of OMNI Games/SimNet): Pepperoni, sausage, and mushrooms.

Andrew Welch (Ambrosia Software. Maelstrom, Apeiron.): I like plain pizza with a little garlic or perhaps some pepperoni. Actually my preferred programming food is chinese take out.

Joe Williams (President of Delta Tao. Spaceward Ho!): Meat. No plants.

Will Wright (Maxis. SimCity, SimCity 2000): Black olives.

Keith Zabalaoui (President of Atomic Games. V for Victory): Garlic, onion, breaded eggplant, and italian sausage. Lots of cheese and when I'm feeling *really* feisty, you can add some jalapenos.

Modern Mac Gaming

With the introduction of the colorful Mac II, the era of modern Macintosh gaming begins. Whether your taste runs to sports, arcade action, adventure, avionics, mystery, science fiction, or simple mayhem, you'll find it all here.

CHAPTER 4: Sports

CHAPTER 5: Arcade Games

CHAPTER 6: Brain Games

CHAPTER 7: Maxis

CHAPTER 8: Adventure Games

CHAPTER 9: Science Fiction

CHAPTER 10: First-Person-Perspective Shoot-'Em-Ups

CHAPTER 11: Conquest Games

CHAPTER 12: War Games

CHAPTER 13: Flight Simulations

CHAPTER 14: Hardware

4 | Sports

Judging by the number of people willing to sit through godawful Super Bowl half time shows and by the frequency of bar brawls generated by differences of opinion about baseball statistics, competitive sport holds an element of attraction for most humans. Considering this, isn't it odd that sports games are so underrepresented on the Macintosh?

Yes, there are a couple of good football simulations that will bring out the Vince Lombardi in those even mildly interested in the game, and sure, golf is nicely covered by Links Pro and PGA Tour Golf III, and okay, Slam Dunk! is a mighty fine basketball coaching sim. But where are the great baseball, tennis, soccer, rugby, and Aussie Rules football games? Surely the Sega and Nintendo crowd aren't the only people interested in laying on a squeeze play or going for the three-pointer at the buzzer.

It's time to send this message to Mac programmers: We have enough space shoot-'em-ups to hold our interest for a while. We hope your future efforts will cause this chapter to grow significantly in a second edition. Until they do, our readers will have to be content with the following small but worthy collection of Mac sports games.

Golf

PGA Tour Golf III
Electronic Arts

Links Pro
Access

Digital golf presents a puzzle. In real golf, the trick is to get a small ball into a not-much-larger hole by whacking the ball with a stick that has a knob on the end of it. Golf's challenge arises from the way in which it hobbles the player with inefficient equipment. After all, if you could use a lacrosse stick to launch the ball or, better yet, some kind of laser-guided bazooka, the game would be a piece of cake. Once you move the game into the digital domain, thereby removing much of the difficulty caused by the equipment, where's the challenge?

According to both PGA Tour Golf III and Links Pro, the answer is timing.

Digital golf reduces all the trials of the perfect golf swing to these two elements: where you stop your back swing and at what angle the face of the club hits the ball. Here's how it's implemented in these games:

Your main view is peering down the course from above and behind the player. Both games present you with a stroke meter that represents the arcing progress of your stroke. Links Pro places this meter at the bottom of the screen, and PGA Tour superimposes it over the player's swing. To begin your swing in Links Pro, click and hold on the mouse. Up go the player's arms. When you reach the apex of your back swing, release the mouse. Down go the player's arms. To determine where the club hits the ball (the contact area), click once again. *Whack!* the player follows through. PGA Tour uses similar controls, the only differences being that you can use the Space Bar instead of the mouse and there's no need to hold the button down once the stroke is initiated.

Easy enough? Well, no. Although both games' meters have marks indicating where you should click in order to produce a precise stroke, this is easier said than done. The meters move very quickly, and timing the click correctly is difficult. If you click beyond the optimum point on your backswing, you will hit the ball with more force but are more likely to hit wildly to the left or right. Clicking below this point, the ball's flight will be more controlled but will travel a shorter distance. Missing the bottom mark causes the ball to veer off in one direction or the other. The situation is further complicated by the fact that the downstroke is much faster than the backstroke. PGA Tour allows you to select player levels on which the contact area is more forgiving; you can be a little sloppier with your final click and still produce a shot that's straight and true. Links Pro players are not afforded this luxury.

TIP

"Make me wear brightly colored polyester, will you? … " our intrepid author screams from PGA Tour Golf III's first tee.

Tee Up

Each game offers the following: the option to draw or fade (push or pull) your shot to either side; a mulligan feature that allows you to play your last shot over; instant replays (Links Pro lets you save these shots for later replay); and a "caddie" that automatically chooses clubs for your next shot.

A savvy golfer may sometimes wonder if Links Pro's caddie is in the employ of his or her opponent. Apparently the caddie's choices are determined by mathematics alone. For example, a nine iron is capable of propelling a ball 135 yards, and by gosh, if you're 130 yards out, that's the club you're given. But, try using that nine iron when you're standing under a low overhanging tree. You should consider the caddie's choices as suggestions only and feel free to pick other clubs. You can also choose to turn the caddie off.

PGA Tour allows you to set three different caddie levels: Novice, Amateur, and Pro. These ratings reflect your abilities, not the caddie's. Novice club choices take into account not only distance but also the lie of the ball (whether you're on the fairway, in a sand trap, or knee-deep in the rough). Moving up through Amateur and Pro, PGA Tour's caddie no longer factors in lie and its decisions become a little more questionable. This caddie cannot be turned off.

The two games also provide you with the option to play different courses. PGA Tour includes three courses but makes no provision for adding more. Links Pro comes with only the Harbour Town Golf Links but allows you to add additional courses for a cost of around $30 per course. At the time of this writing, Access offers six add-on courses, including Pebble Beach, Firestone Country Club, Prairie Dunes, and a fantasy course named Devil's Island. According to Access representatives, a new course should be released every two to three months.

Duffers Like Us

The two games provide you with a variety of computer competitors. As the name implies, PGA Tour contains a platoon of such professional golfers as Tom Kite, Craig Stadler, and Fuzzy Zoeller. You can compete against these athletes in any of the six included tournaments or play a skins game, in which each hole is played for a cash prize. Using Links Pro, you can go up against a "recorded" player whose game is exactly the same each time through the course.

We found the level of competition to be frustrating in both games. We understand that these guys are supposed to be good, but superhuman? During a Links Pro game, an opponent dropped a 116-yard chip shot right in the hole. In a PGA Tour matchup, Tom Kite holed out from a distance of 48 feet while in a sand trap.

HARBOUR TOWN
Bart Palmer   -1
Hole: 4 Par: 3 Shots: 0
Ball to Pin: 196 YD.

Skip
Grid
Profile

Setup Top Scores Drop

SWING 31

● Address
● Draw
● Straight
● Fade
● Chip ● User1
● Putt ● User2

0   31

Gimmie Rotate CLUB

Lie

ON THE TEE WIND

Chris Gonzales : Swing at it!
Bart Palmer : Where's my niblick?

Send

Networked player Bart Palmer prepares to give the ball a ride in Links Pro.

We've been lulled to sleep by enough televised golf matches to know that shots like this happen in real life once about every blue moon. In these virtual games, they're routine. For the next revision of each game, we would suggest the addition of a few computerized schleps so duffers like us don't feel so intimidated.

We would be remiss if we didn't mention that Links Pro lets you create your own schleps using the Record Game option. Just select Record Game from the New Game dialog box to keep an accurate record of every shot you make in the proceeding game. You can then play against yourself or swap these games with your friends. If, for example, Chris wanted to find out if Bart's supposed digital golfing prowess is just so much hot air, we could each record a game, swap files online, and play against the other's recorded games. To keep you honest, mulligans are also recorded and gimmies are disabled.

**GREAT
FEATURE**

Looking Good

We'll let you in on a little secret: One day prior to turning in this chapter, we discovered that PGA Tour Golf III had been released—this after we'd written a less-than-glowing review of the cartoonish PGA Tour Golf II. With a sense of relief, we're pleased to say that the latest version greatly improves upon the last.

GREAT
FEATURE

To begin with, Electronic Arts has made huge strides in the game's graphics and sound. The players are more lifelike than those in II, and the graphics are every bit as good as those in Links Pro. Links Pro's sound still has an edge on PGA Tour's, though. With Links Pro, you can control your player's choice of clubs with voice commands (if you have Apple's Speech Recognition software running), and the game tosses in such comments from the player as: "Go in the hole!" "Get legs!" "Be the club!" and the mysterious, "Purry!" PGA Tour dispenses with such remarks and instead substitutes a suitably subdued announcer who analyzes your situation once you've hit the green.

Of course, these goodies take their toll on performance. Both games can take a long time to create each scene if you're using anything but a speedy 040 or Power Mac. Links Pro offers the option to create lower-resolution graphics to speed up the game.

GREAT
FEATURE

PGA Tour fails to compete with Links Pro in network play. Actually, PGA Tour offers no networking whatsoever. Links Pro lets you play live against up to seven other players over a network or against a single player via ARA. This adds a wonderful dimension to the game and is one of the main reasons we continue to recommend Links Pro over PGA Tour.

LOUSY
FEATURE

PGA Tour is now a much better game than it was, but we do have a couple of complaints: You can not copy parts of the game from the CD-ROM to your hard drive in order to speed up performance. Also, there's no speed governor on the stroke meter. If you're running a slower Mac, the stroke meter moves slowly and you have loads of time to place your clicks accurately. If you have a fast Mac, such as a Power Mac, the stroke meter zips along, leaving you frantically pounding on the Space Bar in a vain attempt to execute a precise shot. We find it odd that you're punished for having a faster machine and pray this will be fixed in an update.

The 19th Hole

Although we're tickled that PGA Tour is now a darned fine golf sim, we still have to give the nod to Links Pro because of its networking features, recordable replays and games, add-on courses, and predictable stroke meter. We hope that Electronic Arts will continue to improve upon PGA Tour and anxiously look forward to version IV.

Tips

PGA Tour Golf III

• If you have a fast Mac and want to gain more control over the stroke meter, do exactly the opposite of what the manual suggests: Turn on a *lot* of extensions and control panels. This will slow the entire game down, which may be just as frustrating as not being able to hit the ball accurately, but at least you won't find yourself wallowing about in a sand trap after every other stroke.

Links Pro

• Use the multiple windows mode to keep the Green View open. This gives you a better idea of where doglegs are and where to place your shots.

• For chipping to the green, use the pitching wedge rather than the default eight iron. It's easier to control.

• (This applies to both games.) Practice putting. It does you no good to get on the green in two if you three-putt the hole.

PGA TOUR GOLF III	
Fun factor:	4.0
Look and feel:	3.5
Value:	4.0
Replayability:	4.0
Overall	4.0

Pros: Fast golf sim that plays well. Works in black and white.

Cons: Look-in-the-manual copy protection. No network play.

System Requirements: 256-color monitor, 33MHz-68040 processor or better, double player-speed CD-ROM, 8MB RAM plus 5MB of virtual memory, 10MB hard disk space, System 7.1 or later.

LINKS PRO	
Fun factor:	4.5
Look and feel:	4.5
Value:	4.5
Replayability:	4.5
Overall:	4.5

Pros: Great golf sim. Wonderful graphics and sound. Network play.

Cons: Requires fast Mac.

System Requirements: 13-inch, 256-color monitor, 4MB RAM (8MB recommended), 4MB hard disk space, System 6.07 or higher.

Basketball

CD

Slam Dunk!
Patrick Halvorsen

Slam Dunk! is not the Macintosh equivalent of NBA Jam. There's no trash talking, no tennis shoe endorsements, no retiring of player numbers, no arcade action. Slam Dunk! appoints you coach of the top college teams and of all the American pro teams.

You may recall that in the days before the game was dominated by overly sensitive, high-priced players, coaches used to run the teams. Well, those days have returned—at least to your Mac.

Jump!

Slam Dunk! is loaded with the stats of numerous basketball players and teams from particular years. (The version included on our CD-ROM contains 1994 NBA and a selection of 1994 NCAA teams. Many additional years and teams are available online). As coach all you have to do is pick a couple of teams, determine

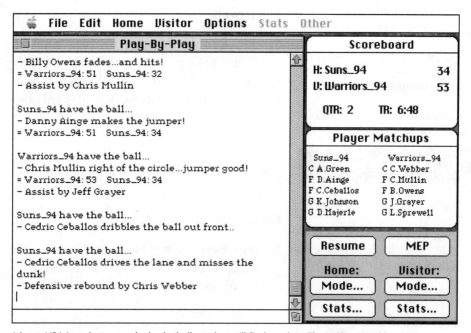

It's not NBA Jam, but wannabe basketball coaches will find much to like in Slam Dunk!

who will play which positions, make substitutions, choose the style of play, and decide whether a little double-teaming is in order to keep a player like Charles Barkley in line.

The action takes place in text form in the Play-By-Play window. Once you hit the Jump button, the game begins with a line such as "Warriors_94 win the jump." From there, the plays tick by at a rate of up to five seconds between each play. When this Delay option is set to the higher end of the scale it allows you to stop the game and make substitutions. Setting the rate to zero facilitates playing a "what if" game in which the computer controls both teams. The delay can be changed throughout the game.

The computer stops the game at user-defined intervals throughout the game so that you can view the various players' stats and make changes. The stats are quite complete and include everything from number of fouls to points scored and minutes played. You can also select how often the computer will check its teams for substitutions (from once a minute to once every quarter of a game).

More Than a Game

Slam Dunk! is not only a fine coaching sim, it's also a great source of information. Using the Stats menu, you can display an amazing number of statistics on individual players as well as teams. And if you have your own stats, you're welcome to create teams from scratch or to edit existing teams.

GREAT FEATURE

For all this, author Patrick Halvorsen asks a measly $25. When you send in your shareware fee, you'll be given the latest version of the game, a guide to entering statistics to create your own teams (you'll need it!), and as many teams as he can smush onto a couple of floppies.

If you've ever had dreams of coaching the finest basketball teams in the world, this is your chance. Slam Dunk! is a must have for every Macintosh-equipped basketball fanatic.

Pros: Wonderful basketball coaching sim. Tons of stats. Bargain.

Cons: A somewhat longer delay for slow readers would be nice.

System Requirements: Mac Classic or better, 800K RAM, 1.5MB hard disk space, System 6.05 or higher.

SLAM DUNK!	
Fun factor:	4.0
Look and feel:	3.0
Value:	5.0
Replayability:	4.0
Overall:	4.0

Boxing

4D Boxing
Electronic Arts/DSI

Other than one early endeavor to bring the sport of Mohammed Ali and George Foreman to a 68000 processor, there were essentially no decent attempts to capture boxing on the Mac before 1991. Fortunately for fans of this brutal sport, Electronic Arts and DSI have provided a modern boxing simulation by the name of 4D Boxing, a 3D multiangle extravaganza complete with cutting edge Tru-Motion technology. If you have anything faster than an LC and can still find 4D Boxing in the stores, this game will give you hours of fun and fast-paced action.

Fight!

4D Boxing attempts to capture the combative nature of the sport by letting you create and train your own boxers to your exacting specifications. Each fighter you make can be trained or adjusted in eight different categories ranging from height and weight to shorts color. There are even a couple of female characters in the "head bank."

Three routes are available to budding fighters. First there's the Practice mode, which basically does what it says by allowing you to hone your skills for future events. Next there's the Main Event, which enables you to fight your way up a list of 50 opponents of increasing ferocity and skill. Finally the Exhibition area lets you face off against your favorite opponents in a slug fest to the death (well, not quite).

True-To-Life, Tru-Motion

The soul of the 4D Boxing game engine is Tru-Motion animation, which closely mimics human movement. Countless hours of boxers performing all sorts of maneuvers were videotaped and incorporated into a wire-frame animation model that behaves as subtly as a real boxer would. The results are very impressive indeed, and although the fighters are polygon-based, they're the most realistic sports figures we've ever seen. It's surprising that this technology wasn't a bigger hit when it first came out. The ring can be viewed from nine camera angles, any of which can be alternated between stationary and flying-camera. This adds amazing realism to 4D Boxing, but the icing on the cake is the game's ability to show any of the camera angles in instant-replay or video-playback modes.

4D Boxing's Tru-Motion animations are fast, fierce, and lifelike.

Knocked Out By Copy Protection

4D Boxing just about has it all: functional keyboard controls; great animation and sound; challenging action whether you're playing the computer or sparring with a friend; even a decent price. Unfortunately, it also has manual-based copy protection. Every time you boot 4D Boxing, you must look up the picture of a boxer in the manual, which is particularly annoying due to the difference in color between the character you are asked to find (in black and white) and the example you are given. All we can say is that 4D Boxing was released in 1991, when this form of buyer punishment was still in vogue; perhaps today it wouldn't bear such a burden. Regardless of this felony, 4D Boxing is still the best (and admittedly the only) boxing game available for the Mac. Those who love the sport won't be disappointed.

LOUSY FEATURE

Pros: Fantastic realistic fighting motion and animation. Lots of challenge.

Cons: Manual-based copy protection scheme.

System Requirements: Mac Plus or better, 1MB RAM for black and white, 2MB RAM for color, 1.9MB hard disk space, System 6.07 or higher.

4D BOXING	
Fun factor:	3.5
Look and feel:	4.0
Value:	3.0
Replayability:	3.0
Overall:	3.5

Racquetball

Club Racquetball

Virgin Games

In the years since 1984, there have been two attempts at bringing racquetball to the Mac's screen, neither of which succeeded in providing a great gaming experience. Smash Hit Racquetball was the first (and probably the best) of the pair, and like so many older games, is no longer compatible with contemporary Mac systems. Enter Virgin Games with an attempt to fill the gap with Club Racquetball, a simulation designed to capture the realism and fun of competing in tournament racquetball.

A Slew of Options

LOUSY FEATURE

Club Racquetball lets you choose from tournament or practice play, but it limits the number of tournament opponents to four, which is apparently intended to supply countless hours of competitive fun. We quickly tired of the four opponents and feel that selective amnesia would be a boon to those wanting variety. Game play follows standard rules, and a display box comments on the outcome of the last shot, be it a serve that fell short or a volley that bounced twice. The background graphics give a reasonable 3D atmosphere to the court, and the players are smoothly animated but have a slightly clunky appearance. There are the usual court sounds and voices announcing fouls on serves and other events. You have access to a slew of options, from ball shadowing to changing animation speed and defining scoring parameters.

Out of Control

LOUSY FEATURE

We found the controls awkward, and although we tried, we never became fully proficient at managing our players. Player movement is controlled through the keyboard, while the aiming of the shot is accomplished with the mouse. Power adjustment (in the swing) is also controlled by the keyboard, and this makes it very difficult to change the power of your shot while still trying to maneuver your player. If you're not very dexterous, you can probably forget about becoming truly accomplished at maneuvering and shooting, but fortunately there are some options—such as automatic hit—which can make things easier for the beginner.

Club Racquetball is graphically impressive but falls short in supplying adequate controls for smooth play.

Double Fault

Club Racquetball won't run on many PowerBooks despite the box's ambiguous claims of color and black and white compatibility. There is a message deep in the bowels of the manual saying that the game wasn't tested on any of the Power-Books and therefore might not work on them. But you shouldn't have to fork over cash just to find out you can't use a game. This is sorta like getting a cup of Ovaltine when you're expecting Colombian fresh roasted coffee.

RANT

The other annoying aspect of Club Racquetball is its tendency to crash in the middle of games or when moving between programs in the Finder. In fact, when Club crashes, it takes the whole system with it, so instead of sipping a cold brew after the game, you may have to settle for a cold reboot instead.

DANGER

Falls Short

Club Racquetball is a good idea, but it needs to be exorcised of its resident bugs and have its interface and control set overhauled to become a great game. As it is now, it looks good at first glance, but once you get to know it, you'll be looking for an excuse to end the relationship.

Pros: Decent graphics. Good sound.

Cons: Full of bugs. Does not work on PowerBooks. Only four opponents. Awkward controls.

System Requirements: Any desktop Mac, 2MB RAM, 1.3MB hard disk space, System 6.0.5 or higher.

CLUB RACQUETBALL	
Fun factor:	2.0
Look and feel:	2.0
Value:	2.0
Replayability:	2.0
Overall:	2.0

Football

CD

PlayMaker Football
PlayMaker Inc.

Brøderbund Software's 1989 debut of PlayMaker Football marked the beginning of a phenomenon so singular in the Mac community that it deserves special recognition. We are referring to the cult following that has grown up around this game. Die-hard fans are known to organize leagues with distant opponents and work toward playoff and championship games. Of course, we know that the only serious football league in the world is the one that's also the oldest existing league. Yep, you guessed it: the Canadian Football League (CFL) is Bart's idea of three-down heaven. Despite PlayMaker's propensity for the four-down variety of ball, it is the best coaching-level football game on the market.

Down, Set, Hut!

GREAT
FEATURE

PlayMaker Football puts you in command of a football team that you can either inherit from the team folder or draft yourself. Each team is made up of 30 players who can be substituted to your liking as new offensive and defensive situations arise. When constructing a team, you can assign points according to speed, ability, strength, and intelligence. You even have the option of adjusting individual players' levels of discipline. Another aspect of setup involves devising a play book from which to run the team's on-field activities. This means assigning types

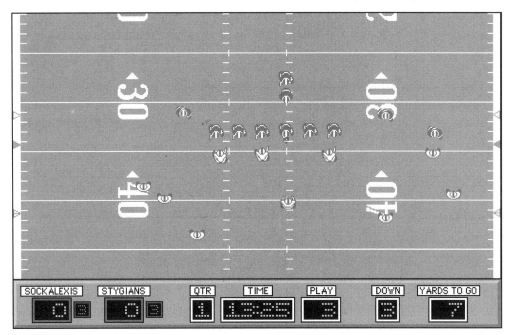

Leagues scattered throughout cyberspace play PlayMaker Football through online services and the Internet.

of blocking, movement, running, catching, and so forth for each individual play, as well as giving any extraneous instructions to particular players who are important to the outcome of the plays. You also get to set up the artificial intelligence that will be used when your team is facing the enemy on its home turf (another computer, which you will not be at). This involves setting parameters for what kind of plays to call in certain situations, what priority to give plays, and what sort of risks you're willing to take in any given circumstance. Game play itself involves making coaching decisions in real time while the computer decides the outcome of each play.

The graphics are very plain, but for those who are really into coaching in Play-Maker leagues, the lack of eye candy doesn't seem to matter. However, Play-Maker Inc. has promised better graphics and modem/network play in the future.

Touchdown!
PlayMaker Football continues to be the premiere coaching-level football game on the Mac and is sure to remain in the online realm for years to come due to the strong support from its legion of fans. Although, considering current Mac technology, we would have appreciated better graphics and sound, PlayMaker

Football is available from online services as a demo and can also be run straight off the CD-ROM included with this book.

Pros: Good coaching game. Cult following. Infinitely replayable in various PlayMaker Leagues.

Cons: Poor graphics. No network or modem play.

System Requirements: Mac Plus or better, 512K RAM, 7MB hard disk space, System 6.07 or higher.

PLAYMAKER FOOTBALL	
Fun factor:	3.0
Look and feel:	2.5
Value:	3.5
Replayability:	4.5
Overall:	3.5

Tom Landry Strategy Football
Merit Studios

Tom Landry Strategy Football is another in the line of coaching-based football games relying on quick, real-time decision making. Unfortunately, the only thing that's assured in this game is the greatness of the coach whose name adorns the title. TLSF is another example of what can happen when a company assumes that a lousy port from an even lousier computer can be unleashed on Mac users.

Crash, Bang, Boom
TLSF allows you to control the coaching reigns of an existing professional or college football team and guide it through a simulated season or through exhibition games with unique situations. For instance, a game could be started with a foot of snow on the turf and with the score tied at the two-minute warning. Coaching decisions are resolved by setting percentages for certain formations and categories of play and by calling plays as situations arise on the field. You always have the option of calling a special play to take advantage of the clock or to blitz the heck out of the enemy QB. And if you're in a tight spot, Tom can even suggest a play for you. TLSF keeps track of individual player's statistics, of team standings, and of leaders in different categories.

Long Bomb

Unfortunately, TLSF spends more time crashing your system and rearranging the color palette than providing enjoyable game play. The manual is atrocious; it was designed for Amiga and DOS machines and contains only an insert for Mac enthusiasts. The interface lacks such basic features as a menu bar or a standard control set. No effort was made to make this game work under any version of the

RANT

Mac's MultiFinder system, which means that once you're in TLSF, you're in it, and you'll probably have to do a cold reboot to get out of the program after it's crashed on you. Suffice it to say that Merit software should have looked more closely at what Mac gamers are used to in terms of software functionality and quality. Topping it all off is the added bonus of manual-based copy protection, which is sure to punish you for buying this game every single time you boot it up.

If Only

If a small amount of effort were made to clean up the bugs and interface of this game, Mac users would likely embrace it as a quality product. Sadly however, Tom Landry Strategy Football is nowhere near being ready to be the premiere Mac football simulation. We hope it can live up to its potential in future versions.

Pros: Very customizable. Decent animation.

Cons: Buggy. Poor Mac interface. No Mac manual.

System Requirements: 13-inch 256-color monitor, 4MB RAM, 4.5MB hard disk space, System 6.07 or higher.

TOM LANDRY STRATEGY FOOTBALL	
Fun factor:	2.0
Look and feel:	1.5
Value:	1.5
Replayability:	2.0
Overall:	1.5

5 Arcade Games

At the mention of arcade games, many people's thoughts drift back to those heady days when the country's youth gathered at local convenience stores to stuff their faces with Pop Rocks and Slurpees and to try their luck with such coin-op games as PacMan, Galaxian, and Donkey Kong. But, of course, the roots of arcade games run much deeper than that.

~~~~~~

The Fable

From what we hear, these games began a few millennia ago in a small pastoral district of the Peloponnesus. There a young shepherd named Spiro, bored with tending sheep and tripping over his garments, decided to give up the shepherding trade and journey across Greece to seek his fortune.

After many days' travel, the erstwhile shepherd found himself in a beautiful resort community on the Aegean shore. Making his way along the promenade, young Spiro gaped in wonder as he beheld the shining sea, the T-shirt and pottery vendors in their multicolored robes, and the finely dressed citizens who strolled leisurely on the marbled causeway.

"Oh, man," the lad is alleged to have uttered, "check out the chicks!"

Alas, poor Spiro, sporting both the clothing and aroma of his former profession, knew he was unlikely to attract the attention of these high-born ladies, although he did try. He walked up and down the promenade for hours, smiling and trying desperately to catch the attention of the young women. But they saw only a filthy shepherd-in-transition and quickly averted their eyes.

"Surely," Spiro thought, "there must be something I can do to make them notice me." And then he had an idea.

As you can imagine, shepherding is not a terribly demanding job. After a few years, the excitement of standing on a rocky hill and watching dozens of sheep champing at rough grass begins to lose its luster. Because comic books had not yet been invented, Spiro had taken up rock throwing as a way to pass the long hours. Each day he would throw chunks of marble a little farther and a little more accurately until he could knock an olive from a tree branch at 200 paces. This skill would now serve him well.

Spiro rushed over to one of the pottery vendors beside the promenade and, with his last few coins, purchased six terra-cotta urns. Gathering the urns in his arms, he took them to the edge of the sea and placed five pebbles in the base of each one. Working carefully, he set the urns on the water and gave each one a gentle push.

When he returned to the promenade, the pottery vendor said to him, "Are you mad, boy? You just bought those and now you're giving them to the sea?"

"Watch this," Spiro said confidently.

The boy reached down and gathered up several stones. As a crowd began to gather, he turned toward the sea and heaved one of the stones.

CRASH! One of the urns exploded in shards.

"Ahh!" the crowd said.

Spiro tossed another stone.

SMASH! Another urn sank to the bottom.

"Ooohh!" the crowd oohed.

"Here now," a burly man said as he pushed through the crowd, "that's not so hard. Let me have a try!"

"Certainly," said Spiro. "I'd be happy for you to try your luck. But sir, I paid for those urns, and I'd like to be the one to break them. I am, however, willing to sell you the chance to try. Tell you what I'm gonna do: If you break an urn on your first throw, there will be no charge. If you miss, you must pay me for the urn."

"Well, I don't know … " the blowhard began.

"Oh come on," chimed in an attractive young woman at his side. "Don't you want to prove to me how big and strong you are?"

"Gimme that rock, kid."

Well, the fellow missed, of course—as did hundreds of other people over the course of the next days, weeks, and months. Spiro eventually hired his own potting concern, and from time to time he'd smash the occasional jug to demonstrate just how easy it really was.

The Moral

We can thank Spiro not only for supplying the museums of the world with hundred of pounds of shattered Greek pottery but also for providing us with the very first arcade game. From ancient Greece to modern suburbia, from smashing urns with a rock to zapping encroaching space critters with a 34th-century death ray, Spiro's tale demonstrates that the requirements of the arcade remain constant: a steady hand, an unwavering eye, the desire to impress others, and most importantly, the knowledge that timing is everything.

~~~~~~

Running and Jumping

Since the early days of Macintosh gaming, otherwise steady and faithful folk have developed an odd inclination to propel tiny digital alter egos across wide chasms, hang electronic Everymen from cliffs by their pixelated fingernails, and square off their champions against enemies whose dispositions can be described as anything but sunny. Let's face it, opportunities for the kind of swashing and buckling enjoyed by the likes of Errol Flynn are fairly limited in this workaday world. And in the computer age, why take the risk when you can live vicariously through the likes of the Prince of Persia or a magnificent Stormlord?

Prince of Persia I
Prince of Persia II, The Shadow
& The Flame

CD

Brøderbund

If it's swashbuckling you're after, the Prince of Persia has it by the bucketful. The plot is similar to that of the animated Disney feature *Aladdin* but without that awful song that's crept into so many weddings lately. In both games, you play the poor prince who wants nothing more than to be in the arms of the fair princess. Unfortunately, Grand Vizier Jaffar also has his eye on the sultan's daughter and, through her, the royal throne. The evil Vizier has magic, and you've got two strong legs, a pure heart, and a certain skill with long pointed cutlery.

Prince of Persia I begins with your little turbaned self thrust into the bowels of the castle's dungeon. From there you must run, jump, clamber, and generally make a nuisance of yourself with the local security forces through 12 labyrinthine levels of the castle before engaging in the big showdown with Jaffar.

Volume II takes you back to the castle just 11 days after your marriage to the princess. Jaffar has inexplicably returned from the grave—of course he *is* magical, and some serious mojo can be invoked when a sequel is involved—to take the guise of the prince and place you, the real McCoy, under arrest. Fortunately, you escape your guard's clutches and once again have the opportunity to commit severe mayhem on those who embody all that is wicked.

You Move Me

The most remarkable thing about the two Prince of Persias is the characters' lifelike movements. Creator Jordan Mechner spent a good deal of time filming

The Flying Heads are just one of the horrors encountered by the Prince of Persia.

live actors leaping about and engaging in sword play. He then digitized the action and used it to model the characters. Thanks to his efforts, when you send your prince scampering across a pit of death-dealing spikes, a real person seems to be doing the scampering.

GREAT FEATURE

The games are similar in terms of your control over the prince. Using a combination of keys, you cause him to tiptoe, run, jump up, crouch down, perform a standing or running leap, hang from a ledge, and, of course, whip out a sword and hack his opponents to bits. The games differ in their graphics and variety of enemies.

Prince of Persia I takes place within the corridors and dungeons of the castle. Although this scenery was pretty impressive when the game first came out in 1992, it now looks drab compared to that of Prince of Persia II. Many of the scenes in the sequel are spectacularly rendered.

GREAT FEATURE

And although Prince of Persia I contains enough baddies to keep your prince hopping, they're strictly amateur hour compared to the creeps you'll find in PoP II. In addition to the usual guards and skeletons, there are screaming disembodied heads, snakes, and guys with weird bird heads. As if this weren't enough, Mr. Mechner has also included quicksand, lava pools, and floor traps that spit poison darts.

But Be Warned

Although these games hold a special place in our hearts, we should mention a couple of minor objections:

To begin with, if you have an aversion to graphic violence—or perhaps more importantly, if you have a child you'd like to see develop an aversion to violence—the PoPs may not be for you. When the prince is pincushioned by an array of nasty spikes, he bleeds early and often and the event is accompanied by a fairly gruesome sound. Likewise when the prince fails to clear the chomping jaws of death in PoP I.

CD

Secondly, the games are copy protected with a look-in-the-manual protection scheme. PoP I's scheme is not a one-time affair and is particularly annoying. Fortunately, you can patch the program with a copy of PoP Patcher, a clever little utility we've included on our CD-ROM that removes the copy protection.

LOUSY
FEATURE

Lastly, the games are timed. If you don't manage to work your way out of the mess before the timer runs out, you've got to return to the beginning and try, try again. Although the timer element adds urgency to the games, we feel it's an unnecessary gimmick.

Aside from these gripes, we really love these games. If you have a robust constitution, you will too.

Pros: Tremendous movement of the characters. Good graphics in Prince of Persia I. Outstanding graphics in Prince of Persia II.

Cons: Look-in-the-manual copy protection. Timed games. Violence may be too graphic for young children and the faint of heart.

System Requirements:
Prince of Persia I: Mac Plus or better, 2MB RAM for black and white (2.5MB for System 7), 2MB for color (4MB for System 7), 1MB hard disk space, System 6.02 or higher.

Prince of Persia II: 8-bit color monitor, 4MB RAM, 15MB hard disk space, System 6.07 or higher.

PRINCE OF PERSIA I	
Fun factor	4.5
Look and feel	4.0
Value	4.5
Replayability	2.0
Overall	4.5

PRINCE OF PERSIA II	
Fun factor	4.5
Look and feel	4.5
Value	4.5
Replayability	2.0
Overall	4.5

Tips
Prince of Persia I
• Save, save, save! You're working under a time limit, and you must hoard every second. As soon as you enter a new level, save the game. Then explore the level until you know it inside and out. Restart the level and run through it as quickly as possible.

• To discover loose tiles that may lead to secret rooms, jump up as soon as you enter a room. Loose tiles will clatter.

• In both games, keep an eye on the color of the potions. Not all of them are good for you.

Prince of Persia II
• After a battle, watch the bottom right section of the screen to see if any blue bottles indicating the near presence of an enemy appear. If so, don't put your sword away—there's more action to come.

• Just before the flying heads attack, they will hesitate. This is your moment to strike.

• In Prince of Persia I, the prince automatically draws his sword. Not so in the sequel, in which, before hazarding beyond the current screen, it's not a bad idea to draw you sword, just in case a baddie stands nearby.

Deliverance
Inline Design
(Bundled with eight other titles on CD-ROM)

Youngsters have always gravitated to arcades to dump seemingly endless supplies of their parents' quarters into various pinball and video game machines. In contemporary game parlors, the machines that consistently horde the lion's share of the coinage are those that glorify the kick-and-punch, hack-and-slash, rip-the-heart-out-and-hold-it-high mentality. These types of games have been bypassed repeatedly by Mac game developers, most likely because competition with video monstrosities like Sega or Nintendo resemble Ross Perot going ten rounds with Mike Tyson. No doubt many parents were relieved to find that their computer purchases needn't encourage video game violence nor the expenditure of the hundreds of hours needed to master those games.

Deliverance brings solid action without tasteless violence while letting one live vicariously through the exploits of a Stormlord warrior who roams castles,

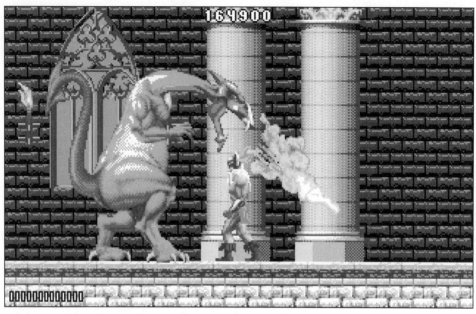

After you complete the first level you have the joy of facing off against this nasty fire-breathing dragon.

forests, and skies swinging a silver battle axe as his graying locks dance around his helmet. Your quest is to travel the landscape of Llyn Cerrig in search of Tnarom, the evil one who has imprisoned the Fairies. Who makes this stuff up, anyway? But of course, what would this breed of game be without suitably absurd story lines?

Conan, Here We Come

Basically the game has you maneuvering your warrior through a series of four levels that are displayed in a side-scrolling manner that keeps your character in the center of the screen at all times. These games demand aggressive ordnance. You therefore wield a silver battle axe that automatically regenerates after you heave it at the enemy. Those players who prefer the Conan carve-and-mangle method of damage delivery can make the most of intimate situations by swinging their axes front to back in a suitably barbaric manner.

Getting your intentions across to the Stormlord is accomplished by a keyboard or joystick, and both sets of controls are very responsive, reliable, and easy to learn. The Powers That Be supply three lives, and completing a level brings up a 12-character code that allows you to start from that point in your next game. From floor sections that bite at your feet to aliens that look like they come from

H. R. Geiger (creator of the aliens in the *Aliens* movie), the creatures in Deliverance provide a suitable range of challenges.

Deliverance need not be played on a warp-speed computer; it'll smoke on any contemporary Mac. Only those with machines slower than an LC II will be tinkering with the performance-enhancing options. Animation is fluid and includes some nice nuances, such as the movement of the Stormlord's hair and the stream of fire spewed by the first guardian (we like to call him "Smoky"). Sound is digitized and acceptably complete, with the grunts, groans, and splats you'd expect. The violence quotient is low; the killing is of cartoon-type characters who exude green blood and explode in puffs of smoke. Deliverance lacks some of the in-your-face butchery that drives many games of this species.

GREAT FEATURE

Final Analysis

Deliverance is an excellent representation of this type of Mac arcade game. It will challenge—albeit briefly—the Sega and Nintendo machines' tenures as the arcade champions in the households of the video generation. Smooth graphics, nifty animation, easy to master game play, and a not-too-violent disposition make this game a must addition to the gamer's library.

Pros: Easy controls. Nice animation. Speed-optimizing options. Doesn't exploit violence. Comes in incredibly priced nine-on-one CD-ROM.

Cons: In full-screen mode, the graphics are a little blocky. Low replayability; cannot save at any spot.

System Requirements: 16 or 256-color Mac, 4 MB RAM, 3.4MB hard disk space, System 6.07 or higher.

DELIVERANCE	
Fun factor	3.5
Look and feel	3.5
Value	4.5
Replayability	2.0
Overall	3.5

Tips

• Throwing an axe in midair will make you jump slightly farther.

• Use battle mode often (swinging your axe closely). It limits your mobility but protects your back and front and generally does more damage per swing.

• To defeat the poisonous gas machine, throw axes until you hit something solid and then go to work on it.

TIP

CD

Out of this World
MacPlay

Those who are familiar with Out of this World may think we've lost our marbles by including this game in the chapter on arcade games. We can hear them now: "Out of this World is an adventure game. These guys are bogus."

To those individuals, we place our lips firmly together and, expelling air rapidly, produce a rude noise. If these critical readers will just venture back a few pages to the introduction of this chapter, they will see words to this effect: in arcade games, timing is everything.

Ppbbbbttttt

Out of this World does indeed have many characteristics of an adventure game. To begin with, the plot goes something like this: You are a young nuclear scientist named Lester Knight Chaykin. Late one night, you are conducting a particle acceleration experiment at the lab during a violent electrical storm. Just as you engage the experiment, a bolt of lightning strikes the building, travels down the accelerator shaft, hits your computer terminal, and—BLOOEY!—a large hole appears where your keister was previously planted.

TIP

Next thing you know, you and your desk are taking the deep six in a tentacle-infested pool in a place that is definitely not Kansas. If you know what's good for you, you swim to the surface and your adventure ... er, *arcade* adventure begins.

Arcadian Action

We'll admit this is a mean mess of plot for a typical arcade game. But Out of this World is anything but typical. To begin with, the look of the game is fairly remarkable. The characters are composed of polygons that shift and reform as the character moves. Although this animation technique doesn't allow for fine details, the motion achieved is surprisingly lifelike. The color palette is also quite nice—muted blues, purples, and grays that create just the right other-worldly atmosphere.

GREAT
FEATURE

But while Out of this World explores the I-can't-stand-this-place-and-I-want-to-go-home adventure theme thoroughly, success in the game depends not so much on solving puzzles or collecting items as it does on how quickly you can squeeze off a laser blast and duck before that big goon down the hall reduces you to your chemical elements. This isn't one of those games in which events change from session to session. Next time you play, this particular creep will be standing in this particular hallway, and if you can't work out a way to run, crouch, and

This beautiful scene belies the danger that lurks throughout Out of This World.

fire before he wastes you, you're going to start seeing the screen that reads "PRESS SHIFT TO CONTINUE" in your sleep.

It Seems So Easy

The game has very basic controls. Simply tap the left or right arrow keys to move in the obvious directions. The down arrow causes Lester to crouch; the up arrow is used for jumping; pressing Shift fires your weapon. To run, press the Shift key in combination with the left or right arrow keys. The menus are just as straightforward as this.

To make the game playable on a variety of Macs, you can select from four screen sizes. Those with less-powerful machines will definitely want to run Out of this World at the smallest window size; anything larger tends to make the animation jerky. Power Mac and AV Macsters will find that the game screams along at the letterbox size of 640 x 400 resolution.

GREAT FEATURE

There's not much to dislike about Out of this World. Sure, getting killed over and over isn't all it's cracked up to be, and it would be nice if the game supported larger screen resolutions for players with big monitors, but these gripes are small potatoes. For the most part, Out of this World is quite simply out of this world.

Pros: Lifelike movement of the characters. Good plot. Cool action. Comes on one floppy.

Cons: Screen resolution no bigger than 640 x 400. You'll need a reasonably fast Mac to get the most benefit from the game.

System Requirements: 256-color Mac, 2MB RAM, 2MB hard disk space, System 6.07 or higher.

OUT OF THIS WORLD	
Fun factor	4.0
Look and feel	4.0
Value	4.0
Replayability	1.5
Overall	4.0

TIP

Tips

• Use the 5 key on the keypad to kneel when firing. You'll be a smaller target if you do.

• Follow the locals; they know the territory better than you do.

• Why bother with keys when you can use your weapon's powerblast option?

• Unless you absolutely need to make a run for it, dodge in and out of the next screen to ascertain the lay of the land. This may give you time to devise a plan of attack.

CD

Flashback
MacPlay

Flashback is another fine running-and-jumping adventure from the French game designers at Delphine, the same folks responsible for Out of this World. In this production, you play graduate student and part-time secret agent Conrad Hart. In a plot all too similar to an Arnold Schwarzenegger vehicle, you have escaped the clutches of the bad guys and, due to a fall from an exploding hover bike, lost your memory in a hostile world. Your mission is to totally recall your lost memories and stop the interlopers from destroying humanity.

The Grand View

Unlike Out of this World, whose letterbox movie styling lends a cinematic feel to the action, Flashback's look is akin to that found in the Prince of Persia games. Similar to the PoPs, each screen contains up to three discreet elevations. Conrad may enter the screen at ground level. On a tree branch above sits a gun-toting mutant, and from a suspension bridge dangling above the mutant sits a key card that just might help him open that intractable gate located three screens to the

Flashback's trees are impossible to kill. Not that you aren't welcome to try …

left. The artwork is quite lush, but because Delphine used bitmapped graphics rather than the polygon modeling techniques found in Out of this World, Flashback is considerably more detailed.

The game's controls are as simple as those found in Out of this World: four movement keys assigned to up, down, left, and right, and a couple of modifier keys for drawing your weapon, firing, and operating switches. Flashback maintains the same outstanding motion modeling found in Out of this World, but in this newer game, your character not only performs simple jumps and crouches but also more complex rolls. And unlike any of the other running-and-jumping games we've played, in this game, you can actually carry your weapon at the ready when you perform a complex motion. You can draw your gun, roll under a low tree branch, and blow that nasty Cyborg away without fear of bumping your head. Very nice.

GREAT FEATURE

You'll Be Back

LOUSY FEATURE

Although in most respects Flashback is a great arcade game, we do have one complaint: timing. We understand that hand-eye coordination is the bread and butter of arcade games, but if these demands are too exacting, the game becomes a chore rather than a challenge. We think Flashback is just a little too picky about when you press the modifier key that causes Conrad to leap from point A to point B. Look, we're pros. We're quite accustomed to being gnawed by the screaming heads when we can't whip out our swords quickly enough in Prince of Persia II. But having to repeatedly run and leap, run and leap, just to climb up a level is pointless. We wish the game was more forgiving in situations that are not life threatening.

Aside from these moments of frustration, Flashback, with its colorful landscapes, fierce action, and outstanding motion modeling, is a worthy addition to the running-and-jumping genre.

Pros: Wonderful motion modeling. Brisk action.

Cons: Hand-eye coordination demands are too exacting.

System Requirements: 256-color Mac, 1.5MB RAM, 7MB hard disk space, System 6.07 or higher.

FLASHBACK	
Fun factor	4.0
Look and feel	4.0
Value	4.0
Replayability	1.5
Overall	4.0

TIP

Tips

• When you first begin playing, set skill level to easy. The first level contains many flat areas where you can practice rolling, crouching, running, jumping, and firing without fear of some nastiness occurring.

• It is sometimes difficult to find objects dropped by other characters. Make sure you check around downed baddies for items they no longer have use for.

~~~~~~

CD-ROM Arcade Games

We know what you're saying. What are CD-ROM games doing in the arcade section of this book? Conventional wisdom suggests that the speed restrictions in CD-ROM drives would make the placement of such software in this area a goof of epic proportions. However, CyberFlix has overcome the arcade exile endured by CD-ROM games by creating a sort of "arcatainment" hybrid that incorporates elements of space melodrama and arcade action. A couple of years ago, pundits suggested we were about to experience the dawn of a new era in CD-ROM games. Players salivated as they foresaw a future in which high-quality warp-speed games were coming off CDs as though they were being sucked straight off RAM disks. Alas, Scotty has not been able to get the warp engines past impulse power, and the lone examples of this technology are the CyberFlix titles. However, both Lunicus and Jump Raven have very impressive technology, and despite their shortcomings, they are still capable of enslaving you in a cybersuit complete with a photon matrix plasma weapon. Full credit goes to Bill Appleton, Cyber-Flix founder and creator of the great Supercard application, for stretching the technological boundaries of CD-ROM entertainment.

Lunicus

CyberFlix

In the year 2023, a few crusty paleontologists dug up a discarded alien artifact. When given to the proper authorities, the artifact's components and technology were used to help humans better their condition and create a world of peace, love, and happiness. The U.N. then went on to develop the moon base Lunicus, where you are now stationed. Unfortunately, the aliens are a tad miffed that their belongings were used to help creatures who could otherwise have been used as slaves in their own back yard. So with a chip on their shoulders (if they have shoulders), the aliens decide to invade Earth and show the humans just how peeved they really are.

From Russia with Love

After the 3D-rendered opening sequence, you find yourself standing by your bed on the Lunicus station. Your goal on Day One is to peruse the base and rap with the crew about moon base stuff as well as banter about this alien threat that seems to have come up. The crew is a multinational collection of moon dwellers who are there solely for the development of the melodrama. Vladamir Molotov

How's my favorite Medical Officer?

What's the briefing about?

Are you busy tonight?

Bye for now, Sasha.

Have a chat with Cyber Puppet "Sasha" before you head into the heated action.

routinely refers to you as Slug, but deep down he's a great guy. The love interest is supplied by Dr. Sasha Serenskaya, born and raised in Kiev, but unfortunately she is not presently interested in any romantic notions.

When you see a character in the hallway, you click on it and up pops a Cyber Puppet. A Cyber Puppet is a talking head that raises its eyebrows, blinks, and moves its mouth semi-appropriately with the dialog. Cyber Puppets remind one of an old Saturday Night Live skit in which Bill Murray spoofs a dubbed Hercules movie. Interaction with the Puppets is achieved through clicking on a selection of predetermined questions. Once you have a foothold in the story, Lunicus takes a tumultuous turn toward the violent as you travel to Earth to meet the alien menace.

Smooth Moves

The incorporation of graphics and animation into game play is what really makes Lunicus tick. After the opening-day sequences, which are reminiscent of Spaceship Warlock, the technological advances really shine. Movement through the corridors and streets is silky smooth, although you must move in "blocks," and once committed to moving forward a space, you must do so. According to Bill Appleton (Lunicus's creator), all the animation is "hard coded" without the use of a secondary program such as MacroMind Director. The result is very impressive fluid animations in the battle zone that bring the nasties to life. However, because the processing and memory overhead required to move smoothly around the maze is so high, certain compromises had to be made in the action. For example, if you are standing in one spot, a Drone Bomb will come after you and explode on contact. If, on the other hand, you are moving through the corridors of the maze, the Bombs will pass right through you, inflicting no damage whatsoever.

GREAT FEATURE

There are only occasional delays during play. These occur when moving from Lunicus to Earth, or from a building to the street. At this time, Lunicus loads information necessary for the next round of play to your hard drive for quicker access. Although this feels like a stopgap measure, these short delays do not detract from the game, but instead they let you have another sip of your hard-earned soft drink before returning to battle. Because the battle scenes in Lunicus seem to be arranged in loops, the action can tend to be repetitive. We also found that the loops enable you to cheat your way to success. You cannot leave a level until you have killed all the enemies; the elevator is jammed unless you have done this. However, if you enter the elevator but then get out on the same floor, the lockers that contain ammo will have been restocked.

TIP

The Bottom Line
Lunicus is an excellent example of the impressive technology developed by the folks at CyberFlix. The game combines adventure allure with action punch, and although the battles can become a tad tedious, it certainly will hold many hours of entertainment for those who enjoy in-your-face combat.

Pros: Fast game play. Combined allures of action and adventure. Smooth graphics and animation. Attractive interface.

Cons: Processing overhead makes it easy to avoid the bad guys and stock up on supplies. Predictable plot line allows only for male protagonist. Battles can become repetitive.

System Requirements: Mac II, 4MB RAM, hard disk, CD-ROM drive, System 6.07 or higher.

LUNICUS	
Fun factor	3.0
Look and feel	4.0
Value	3.0
Replayability	2.0
Overall	3.0

Jump Raven
CyberFlix

It's the future, and pollution and global warming have killed millions. Most animals still alive are kept in fortified reserves as genetic samples. Conditions in the world's cities have deteriorated so dramatically that the law lies in the hands of whomever has the biggest guns, which in this case means renegade bands of Skinheads. The world has really gone to hell in a hand basket, but at least the population has not nuked itself into the Stone Age. The Skinheads have hijacked many of the pods containing the only remaining genetic material of much of Earth's life. Your mission is to ride your Jump Raven ship into the heart of New York to battle the Cyberpunks and Genetic Warlords. Only with complete success can the fate of Earth's animals (including humans) be secure.

Cybermucous

As with Lunicus, Jump Raven does not begin with blazing gunfire. In fact, you are treated to a long journey through the streets of a futuristic New York, past colorful animated billboards (advertising Mucus Off and Bazooka Hut), on your way to a meeting with your boss, Lou Battaglia. The opening sequence is

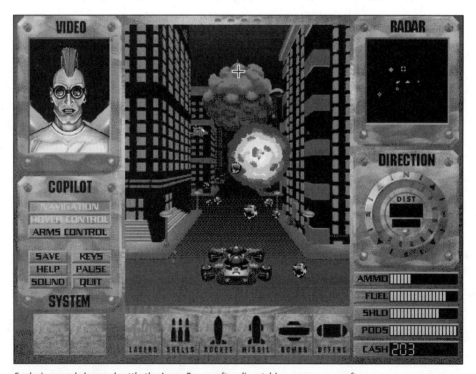

Explosions and shrapnel rattle the Jump Raven after dispatching an enemy craft.

beautifully drawn, and it has smooth scrolling and a fun sound track that even includes noises rising up from the street. "Control those annoying Fungi with Mucus Off!" is just one of the slogans spouted within the engulfing ambiance of the score.

Choose Your Weapons

After you've absorbed the fantastic opening sequence, you are forwarded to the instructional area to bone up on modern Jump Raven technique. From there, you can go to the briefing room to get the details on the foes you must knock heads with on the streets of New York. The Skinheads are a nasty bunch who use four different kinds of craft to prowl the avenues and side streets. You are then supplied with some nice clanky bits of cash and are shipped off to the Weapons Lady to equip your craft with the latest in futuristic weaponry. These include lasers, rockets, bombs, missiles, and defensive weapons, all with four levels of sophistication and cost. The Weapons Lady is more than willing to supply you with detailed information on all the items for sale, but her responses to your choices become somewhat monotonous.

Probably the most important decision you make before you are thrown to the wolves (so to speak) is which copilot you will share your craft with. There are six to choose from, each with a particular attitude and set of skills. The only other decision you must ponder is that of which music will accompany you on your mission. You have four choices, which are impressive but thankfully can be turned off when they become repetitive.

GREAT FEATURE

A Hair-Raising Experience

Once you're on the streets of New York, the battle begins in earnest. You assign your copilot to navigate or manage the hover controls, and before you know it you have several Skinheads in your face shouting insults and lobbing grenades. The action is fast and furious, and the animation provides some downright outrageous effects. Game play is fast, and as with Lunicus, Jump Raven utilizes available hard drive space to store the levels and leave game play to move along in an impressively seamless manner.

The controls are configurable. Placing gunfire is accomplished through mouse work; movement and hovering is keyboard-oriented.

Cyber Puppets Live!

CyberFlix has carried over the Cyber Puppet technology developed in Lunicus. The same mouth, eye, and brow movements occur in the Jump Raven characters to make for a more realistic interaction. Unfortunately, we noticed that

DANGER

some of the language used in Jump Raven is not suitable for the age group that this game would appeal to most. The nature of some of the comments, while adding to the flavor of the game, are not politically correct, nor are they particularly tasteful.

A Step (or Two) Beyond Lunicus

Jump Raven truly goes a step beyond Lunicus with its superb animation, environmental story line, and hair-raising action. There is definitely something disconcerting about seeing taunting video images of foes you are trying to eliminate. Raven has aspects of adventure, drama, and in-your-face combat combined in a package with lush sound, spectacular graphics, animation, and movielike cinematic sequences. So latch your canopy, activate the honing device, and power up your lasers! You're in for a heck of a fight!

Pros: Fast game play. Timely environmental story line. Incredible animation. Attractive interface. Tasks can be delegated to copilot. Built-in instructions.

Cons: Hardware requirements will exclude some users. Language too strong for youngsters. Battles can become repetitive. Enemies are not particularly intelligent.

System Requirements: Mac II, 4MB RAM, hard disk, System 6.07 or higher.

JUMP RAVEN	
Fun factor	3.5
Look and feel	4.5
Value	3.5
Replayability	3.5
Overall	4.0

TIP

Tip

• Take over arms control when going after a number of tanks or a pod base. Save your missiles for the base.

More Arcade Action

Astro Chase 3D

MacPlay

Astro Chase 3D is a first-person-perspective arcade game that takes place in our galaxy's distant future. Thanks to the development of the FTL (Faster Than Light) drive, earthlings have been able to pack up their troubles in their old kit bags and shuffle off to the four corners of the Milky Way for the purposes of colonization. Real estate and resources are plentiful and cheap, and wars and conflict are but memories of a barbaric past.

Regrettably, the good times are not destined to last. From the far reaches of the cosmos have come a testy alien force that has quickly thrown up an impenetrable force field around the solar system and, in a particularly unfriendly display of its might, vaporized a sizable chunk of a neighboring star system.

Your job is to pilot a secret weapon, the Ultraship, and blast the baddies and their nefarious Mega Mines out of the cosmos. If one of the Mega Mines touches Earth—resulting in a stupendous explosion and massive loss of life—the game is over and you've got egg on your face.

This Ultraship is a fairly nifty craft. It can fire in many directions, turn and flip into reverse on a dime, and comes standard with Warp Drive for those times when you're *really* in a hurry. This performance comes at a cost, though: You must constantly be on the lookout for Energy Generators that can fulfill your ship's nagging fuel requirements.

The View From the Deck

Astro Chase 3D opens with an introductory scene that highlights the game's proprietary technology, the Software Accelerated Graphics Engine (S.A.G.E.).

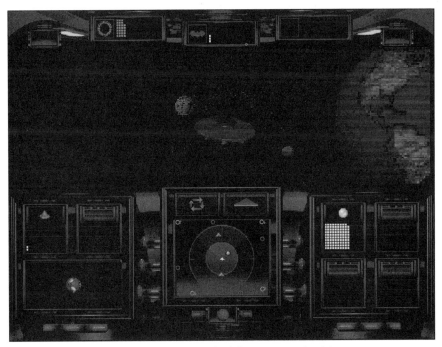

One of the deadly Mega Mines is to your left. That's home over on the right.

According to the manual, "S.A.G.E. manipulates bit-mapped graphics so quickly and with such memory efficiency that it can render highly detailed and realistic environments in real time." Translation: the graphics are a touch grainy because only every other line is drawn on-screen and movement is incredibly smooth.

GREAT
FEATURE

This every-other-line scheme has since been used in other games to speed the action on less-than-beefy Macs. Generally it's a poor compromise because it tends to wash out the color graphics, but in this case it works extremely well. The view from the deck of the Ultraship is dark to begin with—there are no street lights in outer space—and the graininess inherent in the process actually enhances the look of the gray asteroids and dim planets.

We Want Control

The Ultraship can be controlled in a number of ways: via the mouse, keyboard commands, the Gravis MouseStick II, or the Gravis GamePad. The manual suggests that the proper way to pilot the ship and gun down threatening objects is to use the mouse as a dual-function controller. This is one of those rare occasions when it's best to ignore the manual. Precise mouse control is difficult at best, and you're better off using the keyboard. But when you do so, take care. Here's why:

LOUSY
FEATURE

When flying and fighting by keyboard, the manual suggests that you use the keypad, and a couple of letter keys, and the Shift and Command and Option and Control keys, and, and, and … phooey!

TIP

Ultimately you need to use only the four cursor keys for navigation and the left-hand controls to fire the weapons, flip from forward to reverse, blast into Warp Drive, and toggle between the different weapons. True, this does change the strategy a bit and means that you can fire only in the forward direction. Still, you can beat this game without *ever* shooting from the sides or behind, deploying one of the exotic weapons, or picking up a shield at a Shield Depot.

Tripping Digits

Maybe our flying fingers give us an advantage, but we doubt it. We gave the manual a cursory glance before firing up the game and progressed to Level 34 before even considering the use of the powerful Cosmic Energy Weapon or bothering to investigate one of the Shield Depots. With just six levels remaining, it dawned on us that piloting the Ultraship in this way makes Astro Chase 3D a little too easy.

That's not to say that the last ten levels are exactly a stroll in the park—the cramp in our firing finger will attest to that. At Level 30, for example, the Mega Mines sport a satellite known as a Mega Mine Guardian, which orbits rapidly around the mine. One touch from this guardian and you're shrapnel. If you manage to slink past the guardian, you face an additional challenge: the mines now drain power from your ship if you come in contact with them. But, after one or two encounters with the newly enhanced mines, we found that the back-and-forth maneuver we had perfected to obtain power from the Energy Generators held us in good stead here. Moving to and fro—remember, the Ultraship never stops moving in one direction or another—it was relatively easy to stay out of range of the guardian and knock out the mine.

End of the Chase

Once you settle on a comfortable playing style, Astro Chase 3D is a fast-paced and not overly taxing diversion. The game features great graphics and fluid motion but ultimately suffers by making things too easy for seasoned arcade players capable of independent hand and finger motion. A skill-level option would ameliorate this problem, but until the day it's added, we'll look elsewhere for greater challenges.

Pros: Responsive space ship that turns on a dime. Good atmospheric graphics.

Cons: Poor implementation of mouse and keyboard controls. Too easy.

System Requirements: Color Mac, 1.8MB RAM, 6MB hard disk space, System 6.07 or higher.

ASTRO CHASE 3D	
Fun factor	3.0
Look and feel	4.0
Value	3.0
Replayability	2.0
Overall	3.0

Tip

• Learn to quickly throw your ship from forward into reverse and back again. This do-si-do maneuver will help you get a full charge at the power stations in the least amount of time and will also keep you just out of range of the deadly satellites.

TIP

Eat My Photons
Eccentric Software

RANT

With more exciting releases penetrating the Mac games market, we are seeing an increasing slew of great games that will suck tens of thousands of work-hours out of the U.S. economy. What does this prospect lead to? High expectations, that's what. And Eat My Photons doesn't even whet the old whistle. The best thing about this game is that my cat played with the box for about five minutes.

Been Done Before

Eat my Photons could be described as Stellar 7 and Zone of Avoidance combined. The goal is to protect your base from approaching drones (and later fighters) that want nothing more than to blow you, or your base, to kingdom come. You initially have a choice of fighting a space-based challenge or to blast on good old terra firma. The ground-based game closely resembles the venerable Stellar 7 and involves cruising around blowing up drones that are honing in on your base. This quickly becomes monotonous due to a built-in tracking system that leads you directly to the next foe. Follow the arrow, shoot, follow the arrow, shoot. You get the idea. Navigation with your radar is next to useless because the obstacles littered over the landscape do little but add to the considerable clutter on your radar screen. Why bother having a radar screen when the blips on it are so close together they're indistinguishable from each other? The space portion of the game is similar and only adds the dimension of 3D flight and increases your dependence on the targeting computer. Following a targeting cursor may be a blast for some, but. ...

Out of Control

Keyboard control is the input method of choice and keeps your fingers close to the weapons-selection control and targeting keys while you maneuver. Speed control is achieved with keys 1 to 10 representing 10 to 100 percent throttle. You also have control over weaponry selection and mouse sensitivity. Unfortunately, Eat My Photons doesn't feel right. Lining up bad guys to wax them is extremely difficult because the motion of your craft traps you in an endless cycle of over-compensating. The "lead" on the controls makes small adjustments difficult, to say the least.

LOUSY FEATURE

Eat This!

Graphically, Eat My Photons falls into the middle of the pack, and although the sound is adequate, its repetitive nature can become annoying. Adding some network play, better graphics (especially 256 colors), and improving on the radar/targeting system would have greatly improved this game. If you are thinking about Eat My Photons, stay home and order pizza. However, if you've already laid out the cash for this game, you'll find the Eat My Photons cheat on our CD-ROM.

Pros: Online help. Two types of battle (space and ground).

Cons: No network play. Repetitive. Sometimes cluttered graphics. Movement controls cumbersome and difficult.

System Requirements: 68030 Mac or better, 2.5MB RAM, hard disk, System 7 or later.

EAT MY PHOTONS	
Fun factor	2.0
Look and feel	2.5
Value	2.5
Replayability	2.0
Overall	2.5

Crystal Quest with Critter Editor
Crystal Crazy

Casady & Greene

If you own a Macintosh and have never played either of the Crystal Quests then:

A. You've been held prisoner in a dank grotto by an evil gnome for the past ten years.

B. You belong to an obscure religious cult that disallows pleasure in any form.

C. You bought your Mac this very day and fully intend to find out what all the hubbub is about.

The Hubbub

Crystal Quest has been out for a long time, and for good reason. It is one of the most mindless yet entertaining arcade games ever made for the Macintosh. The basic idea is simple: You control a flying bedpan, and using your mouse, zip around the computer screen picking up crystals and bonus points. Once you've collected the crystals, you make a beeline for the now open gate at the bottom of the screen. End of round.

Unfortunately, it's not as easy as it sounds. Complicating matters are the goofy creatures whose *raison d'être* is to cause you grievous harm. You must avoid these deadly critters plus tiptoe—if a bedpan can be said to tiptoe—around the mines that are scattered about like so much deadly confetti.

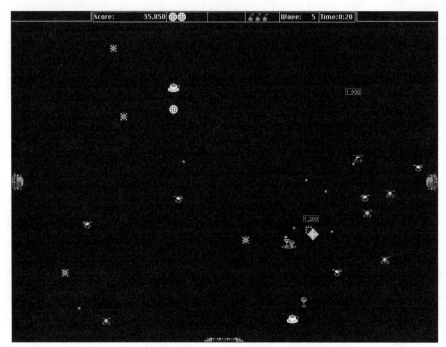

Just like a bull in a china shop, Crystal Crazy gives you the opportunity to bust the joint up.

Of course, you're not completely defenseless. You're equipped with a gun that shoots only in the direction you're moving. You can also pick up and activate small bombs that destroy any aliens lingering about on the screen. These bombs are mighty effective, but they are in limited supply and must be used judiciously.

New and Improved

Crystal Crazy plays off the same basic theme as the original game. The difference lies in the objectives of each round. Round one begins in familiar territory—grab the crystals and get out. In round two, however, Crystal Crazy demands that you use your bedpan to smash a collection of highly breakable objects against the walls—all the while avoiding the spring-loaded boxing gloves. Other tasks include sinking pool balls in the correct order and covering and uncovering paintings by scrubbing your ship over floating canvases.

Considering the difficulty of these new tasks, it's only fair that the game should also provide you with an opportunity to upgrade your weapons and shields. So be it. You can now arm your pan with such projectiles as guided missiles and capti-vators (bullets that ensnare the aliens) and such defensive coverings as the Rubber Hat and the prickly Mace Head.

Critter Editor

Unfortunately, Crystal Crazy does not come with the Critter Editor that's bundled with Crystal Quest. Even though the sequel contains a nice assortment of wacky creatures and tremendously funny sounds, it would be nice if you could create your own custom critters in this game as well.

Our guess is that Casady & Greene excluded the Critter Editor in the sequel simply to keep Crystal Quest alive. The variety of its missions does make Crystal Crazy a more engaging game than Crystal Quest. The one advantage the earlier game has over the sequel is this ability to plaster your brother-in-law's mug onto one of the game's more hideous creatures.

For some of us, that's reason enough to buy.

Crystal Quest with Critter Editor

Pros: A classic Mac arcade game that runs on older machines. Highly addictive. Critter Editor included.

Cons: Can get repetitive.

System Requirements: Mac Plus or better, 600K RAM, less than 1MB hard disk space, System 6.02 or higher.

Crystal Crazy

Pros: An upgraded classic Mac arcade game that runs on older machines. Highly addictive.

Cons: No Critter Editor.

System Requirements: Mac Plus or better, 3MB RAM, 3.4MB hard disk space, System 6.02 or higher.

CRYSTAL QUEST WITH CRITTER EDITOR	
Fun factor	3.5
Look and feel	3.0
Value	3.5
Replayability	4.0
Overall	3.5

CRYSTAL CRAZY	
Fun factor	4.0
Look and feel	4.0
Value	4.0
Replayability	4.0
Overall	4.0

Tips

• This is a game of survival. In the bonus rounds, don't bother picking up extra points until you've grabbed every smart bomb you can lay your hands on.

• Memorize the colors of the balls used in pool so that you don't need to waste time looking for the tiny numbers. (1: yellow, 2: blue, 3: red, etc.)

• Fire your nastier weapons through the black holes.

Spaceway 2000
Casady & Greene

Casady & Greene games tend to be colorful and fast-paced and to feature the oddest storylines. Spaceway 2000 is no exception.

In an apparent reaction to the freeway shootings that were all the rage in Los Angeles a few years back, programmers Jeffrey Robbin and john calhoun devised a game in which the player's mission is to shuttle cargo across the galaxies' freeways while being harassed and pummeled by an inconceivably nasty lot of armed and dangerous aliens. Think of it as drag racing with an Uzi—definitely not your typical shoot-'em-up fare.

Step On the Gas

Each of the 100 levels of play begins with you parked at the entrance of a cosmic causeway. Your ship is a two-speed job that is initially equipped with a laser cannon and automatic shields. As you careen down the highway, you have the opportunity to pick up small crates containing such items as more-powerful weapons, stronger shields, heartier engines, and blue crystals that provide you with extra lives. Your goal is to reach the end of the road in one piece.

This seemingly simple task is made difficult by your fellow travelers, who would like nothing better than to see your license—and you—permanently suspended. You are also hampered by your ship's engines, which whisk you by the galactic goodies when in high gear and leave you open to attack from your much speedier rivals when downshifted. And regrettably, your high school physics teacher was wrong: there are indeed boundaries in space, and they're patrolled by mechanized weapons known as Wall Creeps. No matter how good your engines, off-roading is not an option.

Turn the Wheel

Spaceway 2000 is deceptively simple to run. You have exactly five controls to concern yourself with: left turn, right turn, gear shift, and fore and aft weapons. And although the default keys are well chosen, you have the opportunity to change them to your liking.

The difficulty of the game is embodied by this one little word: inertia. Take a look at those controls one more time. See any listing for retro-rockets? Right, there are none. Your ship never stops moving in a given direction unless there's something in the way to stop it—such as a wall or asteroid—or you whip your ship around and apply thrust in a different direction.

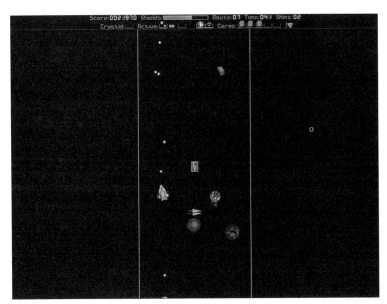

You think commuting on Earth is tough? Try it on Spaceway 2000.

Given these conditions, the ship is a bear to operate, and herein lies the real challenges. Granted it's tough being zapped from all sides by cranky commuters, but imagine being heaped with this same abuse while bashing about willy nilly with nary a hope of getting your vehicle under control.

It's a Blast

Spaceway 2000 is a kick to play if you like your action fast and frustrating. Although you may find that some of the action tends toward the repetitive, enough new elements are introduced throughout the game that you won't be bored for long. By no means is this an easy game, and we could hardly blame you if, while playing at the higher levels, you muttered the kind of expletives you normally reserve for that real-life tailgating jerk in the BMW.

Pros: Fast and furious action. Delightful graphics and sound.

Cons: Can be frustratingly difficult. The action can get repetitive over time.

System Requirements: 68020 Mac or better, System 6.05 and higher. Memory and hard disk requirements depend on the size and bit depth of the monitor used.

SPACEWAY 2000	
Fun factor	4.0
Look and feel	4.0
Value	4.0
Replayability	4.0
Overall	4.0

CD

Tubular Worlds
Dongleware

If you've done much traveling, you know what it's like to find yourself standing in the midst of the local Firetoad Festival thinking to yourself, "Things sure are different around here." It's likely this feeling will creep over you as you play the side-scrolling space shoot-'em-up Tubular Worlds.

Vaguely Familiar

You know the drill. You pilot a fighter taking on the toughest aliens the planet Titanos can toss at you. In order to prove you're the best, you must dodge in and out of rocky canyons, around floating space cooties, and amongst some nasty looking viscera while annihilating anything that moves. You pick up weapon-enhancing power-ups, shields, and bonus tokens that provide you with extra ships. Rather than viewing the action from the side, as in most side-scrolling arcade games, your perspective is from above your craft.

Been There, Sorta

We realize this sounds like standard arcade fare and in many ways it is.

You pilot ship.

You shoot things and they blow up.

If they shoot you, you blow up.

Repeat.

It's only when you reach the fourth round of each level of this game that you begin to realize that something for which you have no cultural reference is going on here. While the first three rounds present the usual cannons, tanks, and alien fighters, the fourth round suddenly takes a turn to the bizarre. For instance:

After making your way through the frantic first rounds of level one, you find yourself dropped into a seemingly empty desert. Just as you become accustomed to the serenity of your surroundings, in waddles a newtlike creature who emits a green death ray from his eyes. You keep firing and dodging the rays until the creature dies. A few seconds pass and then a much larger horned lizard approaches. It too wishes you an unpleasant day and attempts to drip a caustic substance onto your craft. Again you dodge until you are forced to make your way back to the creature's tail section. Here a birthing which can only be described as "icky" takes place. You kill the potato-bug youths as they appear until it's time to move back to the creature's head. More nastiness ensues.

This is not your typical arcade fare.

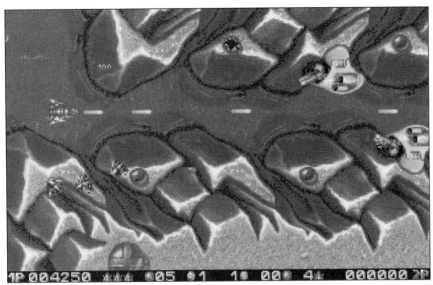

Through the canyons, through the meanies, through the gruesome, icky, stuff ...

Fun, But

We're willing to accept the idea that this disturbing vision has some meaning for someone somewhere and that we just don't have a wide enough view of things. But there are a few things about Tubular Worlds that simply don't work.

To begin with, there's no way to save your game. If you lose one of your ships, you're placed back at the beginning of that round, and that seems logical enough to us. But if you're on your last ship and it gets swallowed by a hideous creature, you're back at square one even if you've made your way through the rigors of the first nine rounds. Unlike with similar games, there's no way to enter codes to directly access the higher levels.

LOUSY FEATURE

And this makes the game incredibly repetitive. If players have demonstrated they can get through the first three rounds, why make them do it over and over?

Also, there is so much on-screen action that it's often difficult to discern what's happening. You're firing tens of green bullets a second, that cannon over there is firing different green bullets, a dozen small alien fighters swing in from the bottom of the screen, gas bubbles erupt small blue capsules ... We understand that this is supposed to be challenging, but jeez, let up on the clutter.

LOUSY FEATURE

Lastly, if you play in full-screen mode, the graphics have a tendency to get a little chunky. Although not as bad as some of the old DOS ports, cleaner lines would have been nice.

Good, Though

If you can live with these flaws, Tubular Worlds isn't a bad arcade game. It's full of action and contains some of the most interesting enemies we've ever had the dubious pleasure to meet. Despite our complaints, we've actually played it quite a bit, if only to see what other sorts of demented creatures lurk on the next screen.

Pros: Lots of action. Fluid animation.

Cons: No way to save a game or begin at higher levels.

System Requirements: 256-color monitor, 68020 Mac or better, 4MB RAM, System 6.04 or higher.

TUBULAR WORLDS	
Fun factor	3.5
Look and feel	3.0
Value	3.0
Replayability	2.5
Overall	3.0

Tips

• From the left side of the screen, position yourself about a third of the way in. This keeps you away from the dangerous edge of the screen but gives you enough room to see upcoming goodies and baddies.

• When dealing with the horned lizard at the end of the first level, stay to the bottom left of the screen. Her piercing gaze never travels that far. Wait until she switches into one-eyeball mode to take a better shot.

Zone Warrior

Casady & Greene

Afer firing up this game, experienced gamers might think that this game is simply a sequel to the somewhat flawed 3D space flight simulation game, ZOA (The Zone of Avoidance). They would be wrong. Zone Warrior is actually the same game as ZOA except for vastly improved performance, graphics, and sound. Zone Warrior is the game that ZOA should have been.

Back On the Ship

Once again you're back on the Seen-It-In-2001 spinning-wheel space station. Alien nasties, up to their old hijinx, have lobbed a passel of isocahedral projectiles at your home sweet home and you must fly out into the great void to gun them down. If one of these projectiles hits the station, a section breaks off and becomes so much space debris. When enough sections break off, the station disappears and you are truly hosed and homeless. If you manage to destroy all of

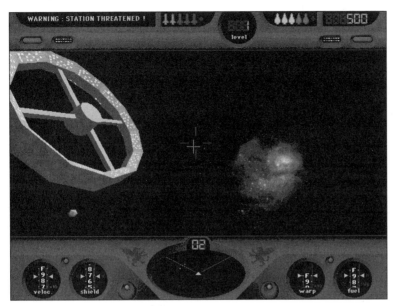

The Wheel of Misfortune: Zone Warrior's space station.

the projectiles and keep the station in pristine condition, a helpful tractor beam emerges from the docking bay to bring your ship effortlessly home. Of course, if the station is nicked, you must return your ship to the station *sans* tractor beam and herein lies the crux of Zone Warrior—parking the ship.

Although our personal experience is a bit limited in this regard, we understand that jetting around in a weightless vacuum is trickier than flying a prop plane. When flying a plane, you almost always know where the ground is, but in space there's no up or down and no horizon with which to orient yourself. Plus, when you land a plane, you rarely need to worry that the runway will be slowly rotating.

Zone Warrior's controls are quite simple. Similar to a flight simulator, you manage movement along the x and y axes with the mouse, keyboard or joystick. To roll the ship from side to side—an absolutely vital skill to master if you have hopes of docking your ship—use the arrow keys. Precise control of the ship takes much practice and is the biggest challenge of the game.

More Power

Zone Warrior is for Power Macs only and will not run on a 680-anything. Even though this may irk users with 680x0 Macs, we applaud this decision. All too often, we see "fat" games—meaning that they contain both native Power Mac and 680x0 code—that run beautifully with the PowerPC processor, but are just wretched on even the speediest 68040 machines.

GREAT FEATURE

If you're lucky enough to have equipment that allows you to play the game, you will immediately see why Zone Warrior requires this kind of processing muscle. The detail and performance of the station, projectiles, and enemy ships is quite remarkable. And the movement of your vehicle is so smooth and convincing that you might experience a degree of motion sickness.

Back and Beautiful

We're tickled that Casady & Greene gave ZOA another try. The interface is cleaner, the graphics are stupendous, and the game takes full advantage of the wonders of PowerPC technology. We're sorry that 680x0 players are left in the lurch but perhaps while waiting to trade up, they can pick up ZOA I and try to imagine what they're missing.

Pros: Fantastic graphics and smooth movement. Works on Power Macs only.

Cons: Can induce motion sickness. Works on Power Macs only.

System requirements: Power Mac, 4MB RAM, 2MB hard disk space, System 7.1.2 and later.

ZONE WARRIOR	
Fun factor	4.O
Look and feel	4.5
Value	4.O
Replayability	4.O
Overall	4.O

CD

Glider Pro
Casady & Greene

Whether it was to slam a paper airplane into the side of Billy Rassmusan's head in sixth-grade English class or just to see whose paper creation could float the farthest on a warm summer breeze, paper airplanes have held a place in the hearts of folks everywhere. Unfortunately, evergreen deforestation and depletion of the rain forest make wasting paper on such frivolity a risky proposition for someone with a good conscience. Okay, perhaps we haven't quite reached the point of banning parchment from uses other than literary endeavors, but we can still conserve paper by flying our paper airplanes vicariously through john calhoun's fabulous Glider Pro. Who knows, perhaps we can even find a way to save a few whales in the process.

Fly the Not-So-Friendly Skies

It doesn't get much simpler than this. You are in command of a hand-crafted papyrus glider that must be maneuvered through an endless parade of rooms in a rather drafty house that is heated by a temperamental forced air furnace. You should remember that hot air rises, water kills, and gravity is the ultimate

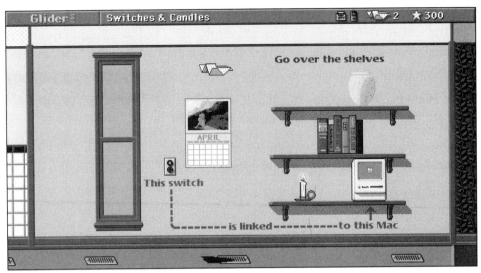

The Demo House has detailed explanations to help you learn the ins and outs of Glider Pro.

destroyer of your flight. You have but five controls at your disposal: left, right, thrust, fire, and change orientation. To keep from becoming another casualty statistic, you must ride the air currents and avoid obstacles such as bookshelves, tables, the floor, and leaking pipes. The glider can quickly become kindling for the fireplace if you fly too close to an open flame. That same flame, however, can be just the ticket to supply you with enough lift to move you into the kitchen for a snack or lift you through a window to the outside world. While navigating the various obstacles, you can pad your score by nabbing the occasional bonus clocks or free gliders that sit perilously close to the edge of a coffee table or wall cabinet. Glider Pro comes complete with the four-hundred-and-some room Slumberland house, a demo house for the novice, and an empty house for those anxious to design their own castles complete with paper shredders and jumping fish. If you are really feeling adventurous you can ask a friend to join you in the Two Player Mode which allows simultaneous flight through the house. This changes the complexion of the game considerably and forces you to consider the extra real estate occupied by the other player so that the two of you can work together to make it through each room.

GREAT FEATURE

Riding the Updraft

john calhoun has produced an outstanding, simple, addictive, fluid game that holds the potential to send quite a few couples to marriage counseling. Many players will look up from their "short" games to find the sun rising from its slumber and but a few short hours remaining until they are due at work. Of course, it does not help matters that Glider Pro comes with a complete house

DANGER

editor that lets you create your own masterpiece of frustration. This, combined with the endless flow of new houses constantly being uploaded onto online services and every BBS from here to Baghdad, is sure to decrease the GNP in most first world countries.

Pros: High-quality graphics and sound. Easy to learn. Room editor. Two-player option. Great value.

Cons: No practice mode for individual rooms.

System Requirements: 16 or 256-color Mac, hard disk, System 7 or later (Power Mac-native).

GLIDER PRO	
Fun factor	4.0
Look and feel	4.0
Value	4.0
Replayability	3.5
Overall	4.0

TIP

Note: Rumor has it that Slumberland contains dozens of secret rooms accessible through hidden transporter pads. The pads can be discovered only by passing over them. Good luck!

Power Pete

CD

MacPlay

A level of violence is inherent in nearly every electronic arcade game. Whether it's vaporizing space cooties with advanced laser weapons, piercing a lackey with a saber, or dueling it out with a sneering cowpoke, if it's an arcade game, something's going to die. Given the horrid violence found in some of these games, is it any wonder parents are reluctant to have their kids play them? But what about the children? Denied the pleasures of the arcade, where are the poor little ones to go for fun?

RANT

Oh sure, they could go *outside*. Yes, they could run for the pure joy of it; breathe in sweet, fresh air; see something of this grand world; but jeez, why would you want them to do *that* when they could be planted in front of a computer screen wasting their precious youths on mindless shoot-'em-ups? Why, if we were running this nation we'd ...

Oh, sorry. We've got to stop turning into Rush Limbaugh when we're writing this stuff.

The fact is there's very little in the arcade realm that's appropriate for children whose ages fall in the single digits.

Such creatures as fuzzy bunnies and scary cavemen abound in Power Pete.

Until Now, That Is

This situation has been admirably remedied by the release of Power Pete, a Pangea/MacPlay arcade game that is the cutest darned shoot-'em-up you or your child are likely to encounter. Here's the setup:

It's after midnight at the local Toy Mart and all the toys have come out to play, but not all of them play nicely. Throughout the various departments, small communities have formed. Evil gingerbread men stalk Candy Cane Lane. Killer clowns, evil rabbits, and jack-in-the-boxes join together in the Magic Funhouse.

Meanwhile, one of the cages in the Stuffed Animal Zoo breaks open, and the store is flooded with Fuzzy Bunnies. Silly rabbits! Don't they know that Toy Mart can be a dangerous place for bunnies? Who will save these cuddly creatures from the uncaring clutches of the other toys? None other than Power Pete, the most powerful and popular action figure in the entire universe!

Ah, but there is danger for Pete as well. Since his sales figures have skyrocketed, the other toys have become quite jealous and resentful. Many of them would like

THE PAIN OF PLAYING

Strange Sensations

The Vorglins are set to escape the gravity field. A bead of sweat forms on your brow as you tighten your grip on the joystick and prepare for the inevitable flurry of photon blasts the Vorglin fleet will unleash on your tiny craft. With teeth clenched and blood pressure soaring, you begin to hammer relentlessly on button A, thus releasing the awesome power of your Zyphton lasers. Ahhh victory! But wait, what's that strange sensation? Why do your wrists and fingers feel as though they've suffered through a Jane Fonda workout video after being run over by a Mack truck? You'd better stop right there, because you might be suffering from what medical experts refer to as RSI, or repetitive strain injury, and it's no laughing matter.

Get a Grip

Repetitive strain injury is a catchall phrase many doctors use to describe the debilitating pain caused by repetitive activities, usually in the arms and hands. Experts say the pain and swelling that can impinge on nerve function is largely due to the repeated stress placed on muscle tendons and ligament structures. Tendons are the bits of tissue that anchor muscles to bones or other body parts. The places where they do this are called "insertion sites," and they are where chronic inflammation can often occur. In fact, this is the genesis of "tennis elbow," a condition that has haunted many a weekend Boris Becker. The RSI injury that consistently captures the most press attention is carpal tunnel syndrome. This is particularly nasty because it involves the compression of the median nerve, which runs through a narrow tunnel (the carpal tunnel) in the wrist and is responsible for the functioning of the first two fingers and the thumb. If this condition progresses, in extreme cases it can result in permanent

nothing better than to see Pete—in a somewhat battered condition—wind up in the bargain bin.

They're Playing with You

Pete begins his journey in the Prehistoric Plaza. To collect the bunnies, he must avoid the deadly tar pits, scoot between the rows of palm trees and modeling-clay plateaus, and seek out the stone hammers that open the intractable granite doors. This wouldn't be so difficult were it not for the bone-throwing cavemen and thick-skinned dinosaurs who are in constant pursuit.

Fortunately, Pete comes equipped with a rifle that shoots little suction-cup darts. As malevolent toys approach, you must turn Pete toward his aggressors and fire. If you hit the enemy and the weapon you're employing is powerful enough, the enemy vanishes in a shower of confetti and jawbreakers. To earn an extra life, pick up 500 jawbreakers.

damage to the median nerve. Just try playing Power Pete without the use of your first two fingers, and you'll see why it is important that we all are aware of this potential problem.

Is Beating RSI Pie in the Sky?

Admittedly, some people will be able to perform very repetitive data entry tasks, piano playing, and game playing without ever developing a repetitive strain injury. However, most people are susceptible to some degree, and any compelling game with the need for action controls has the potential to lead to an RSI. As with all medical problems, prevention is by far the best weapon in combating these injuries. Good posture and ergonomics are the number-one factors to be aware of, and there are special keyboards with wrist supports and angled keys to prevent wrist strain. There are also special gloves made of a spandex material that support and keep the wrists warm when engaging in keyboard tasks, and special braces that prevent the over-flexion of the wrist joint.

Perhaps the best early warning mechanism is your own good sense. Remember that keyboards and joysticks require only light pressure on the buttons, not intense pounding. Many people find that joysticks and game pads tend to be less traumatic than keyboard controls, and this is especially true when keyboard movement comes into play. A joystick requires only gripping the stick and rotating it, whereas keyboard movement often will result in frenzied pounding on the keys to maneuver. The most underrated prevention activity is simply taking a break. Lifting your hands off the keyboard and doing some light finger stretching every 20 minutes will go a long way in maintaining the health of the metacarpals and phalanges you love so much. If you are having this kind of pain, you should consult your doctor.

TIP

These enemies might also carry deadlier weapons and the kind of special power-ups that destroy any nearby toys or give Pete perky feet. Of course, the only way to find out what they may be packing is to blow the other toys to bits. But heck, that's the fun of the game! And just check out this list of weapons: Double-Barreled Gumball Blaster, Toothpaste Gun, and the strictly tongue-in-cheek Summer Fun Backyard Flamethrower. Come on Mom, is this fun or what!?

It's Toyriffic!

Power Pete is the cutest thing going in the arcade market. It's simple to operate, the animation is delightful, and the sounds are absolutely endearing. Despite the packaging and content, adults will have as much fun with this game as kids. Yes, at a certain level, Power Pete reeks of violence, but its violence is packaged in such an innocuous form that even the most peace-loving among us will be drawn in by the game's many charms.

If you have children, save Power Pete for one of those rainy days when it's too blustery to go outside and the kids need something to keep them occupied. When the sun comes out and the kids have gone out to play, try Pete yourself. You'll have a wonderful time.

Pros: Cute as a button and tons of fun.

Cons: For best performance, a speedy Mac is necessary.

System Requirements: 25MHz-68030 or faster Mac, 4.9MB RAM, 1MB hard disk space, System 7 or later, CD-ROM drive.

POWER PETE	
Fun factor	5.0
Look and feel	5.0
Value	5.0
Replayability	4.0
Overall	5.0

Tip

• Although it may seem like so much heartless slaughter, stand at the opening of the cavemen's lair and start firing. These stupid creatures will file out in waves to be destroyed. Once the wave has passed, dash in and out of the cave to pick up the many power-ups.

6 | Brain Games

As much as we enjoy a laser-locked face-off with Galactic Slime-weasels and winging our way across hostile desert lands, there are times when it's a relief to stow away the joystick and fire up something a little more cerebral. Whether it's a motion puzzler like Tetris that demands nimble fingers and a keen eye, or a sit-motionless-and-ponder mind twister like 3 in Three, the Mac has a lot to offer electronic puzzlers.

If your mind is your most prized organ—or if you just like to take it for a run around the block every once in a while—these Mac games are for you.

Blobbo
Glenn Andreas Software

This $20 shareware jewel from Glenn Andreas is cute as a tiny yellow button. You control a small creature named Blobbo, who looks a bit like a dollop of egg custard. Little Blobbo, who's been a bad blob, has been sent to his rooms, and you must help him pick up all his toy chests. Unfortunately for you, Blobbo's not about to tell you how to avoid the series of booby traps he's set. These traps may be as transparent as precariously balanced bowling balls or as devious as little smiley faces that stick to Blobbo like glue and make it impossible for you maneuver.

Custardy Conundrum

The trick to Blobbo is to figure out the operating rules of the objects in the game. For example, there are a number of bodies of water that Blobbo must cross. He doesn't swim, so you must depend on the canoes that you hew out of palm trees to transport him across these waterways. The hard part is to determine which direction the current flows and when the best time is to leave the canoe. Through a great deal of trial and error—thank goodness for the Restart Screen command—you may discover that you should shove Blobbo out of the canoe as it passes the second island, pick up a toy chest, and then reboard the boat as it passes the back side of the island.

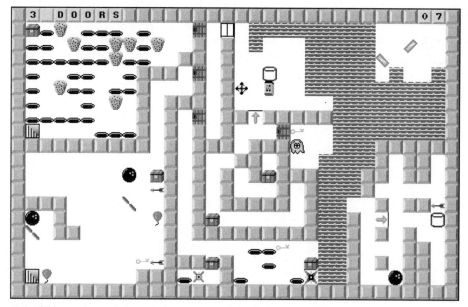

Little Blobbo needs your help to navigate a maze of deadly booby traps.

Blobbo is an untimed turn-based game. When you move Blobbo one space, every other mobile object moves one space as well. It requires no dexterity and provides lots of time for you to ruminate on the delightfully devilish puzzles. The graphics are hardly spectacular but are quite endearing in their own way. The sounds are also charming.

The Price You Pay

All 25 levels are accessible in the unregistered version of the game, and we include it on our CD-ROM as Blobbo Lite. In addition to gaining the satisfaction of doing the right thing, registering Blobbo allows you to create your own levels. If your conscience and a new creative outlet aren't enough to compel you to register, the best reason of all may be that you'll also receive the solutions to the 25 included levels. Give Blobbo a try and tell us if this isn't strong incentive indeed.

Pros: Simple controls. Tough puzzles. Cute game.

Cons: Only 25 included levels.

System Requirements: Mac Plus or better, 800K RAM, 1.2MB hard disk space, System 6.08 or higher.

BLOBBO	
Fun factor	4.5
Look and feel	3.5
Value	5.0
Replayability	2.0
Overall	4.0

Ishido

MacPlay

Chris bought Ishido back in 1990 and regrets to this very day that he didn't buy the limited-edition wooden box version when he had the chance. This is one of our all-time favorite brain games and we're just tickled that MacPlay not only brought it back from the dead but also resisted—except for a few minor tweaks—the temptation to mess with a good thing.

Meditate on This

You are presented with a 12- by 8-square board and 72 tiles. The tiles come in six different colors and are marked with one of six symbols—a slate-gray stone stamped with the yin/yang symbol, for example. The object of the game is to place each stone so that it matches the color or symbol of adjacent stones. In the case of a two-way match, the placed stone must match one adjacent stone's color and the other's symbol. A three-way match must match the color or symbol of

It would be tough to find a more beautiful or challenging brain game than MacPlay's classic, Ishido.

two of the stones, and the other characteristic of the third stone. The all-important four-way match must split this color/symbol match both ways. Your ultimate goal is to use all 72 tiles and make as many four-way matches as possible.

GREAT FEATURE

These four-way matches not only bring you big points, they engage one of the more charming aspects of the game: the online oracle. It works this way:

At the beginning of each game, you type in the kind of question that you might ask your local voodoo doctor, such as, "What future is there in playing computer games all day?" When you complete a four-way match, up pops the oracle with a groovy answer that's wide-ranging enough to apply to your question.

In addition to the oracle, Ishido contains other nice extras. You can custom design your own tiles and boards. Additionally, you can play competitively or cooperatively with another human or with the computer.

Your Fortune

Puzzlers and solitaire players will name their children and pets after this game—it's that good. Everything from the sound to the graphics to the gameplay is brilliant. Buy it, buy it, buy it!

Pros: Lush graphics. Great sound. Tremendous solitaire game.

Cons: No limited-edition wooden box version.

System Requirements: Mac Plus or better, 1MB RAM for black and white, 2MB for color, 3MB hard disk space, System 6.07 or higher.

ISHIDO	
Fun factor	5.0
Look and feel	5.0
Value	5.0
Replayability	4.5
Overall	5.0

Inline Greatest Hits Game Pak
Distributed by Focus Enhancements

We discuss a few of the games found on this CD-ROM compilation in other parts of the book: you'll find Firefall Arcade and Deliverance in the Arcade Games chapter. Although these games are tempting enough on their own, the real reason to buy the Game Pak is to obtain Inline's brain games. Few publishers produced such a quality collection of mind benders, and now you can have them all for an unbelievable price. If puzzling is your passion, this collection is worth more than a cursory look.

3 in Three

Cliff Johnson, creator of one of the great early Mac games, The Fool's Errand, took his brilliant game design to a new level with 1991's 3 in Three. This classic brainer begins when a freak power surge jolts a lonely number 3 from a spreadsheet and sends it into the confounding bowels of a computer, where only firm dedication to conquering quandaries can lead to the 3 being returned to its rightful place in the computer's RAM.

When Numbers Get Serious

Taking on 3 in Three thrusts you into an arduous journey complete with animated introductory and end-game sequences as well as over 80 perplexing mind stumpers to unravel along the way. Five or six puzzles are initially available, and the rest become active as the others are solved. It's the carrot dangling in front of the old schnoz—nice tidbits of reward for the brain that solves the earlier challenges. The puzzles range from various word games to numeric problems, and although they generally continue on this slant, there's a heap of variety to keep the proceedings fresh. Most of the transitions between puzzles are filled with animated sequences to ensure that the user remain involved with the plot and doesn't wander off to play Myst or other such drivel.

Number 9, Number 9, Number 9

**GREAT
FEATURE**

Its intuitive puzzle interfaces and Mac pull-down menus make navigating through the realm of 3 in Three a breeze. Fortunately, if you get stuck on one puzzle, there are always four or five others you can switch to in a jiffy to keep your noggin fresh and eyes wide. Don't expect to be solving 3 in Three in three hours, three days, three weeks, or even three months. Well, maybe three months. Some puzzles are fairly easy to get a grip on, but there are two or three that require very deep thought indeed. It's a good idea to keep an anagram maker, like Chuck Girssom's Karma Manager, on hand to help with some of the multiple-lettered word puzzles you'll be sure to encounter.

In This Case, Three Is Not a Crowd

3 in Three is a prime example of that rare breed of computer game with true staying power. Originally released in 1991, it still commands respect from publishers and gamers alike; it is an excellent value for anyone who enjoys a great brain game. No doubt it will sit on hard drives for months or years while users occasionally chip away at a puzzle or two. Despite its age, 3 in Three is still one of the better puzzle compilations available, and its humorous story line will be a boon to youngsters and adults alike.

Cogito

Imagine a particularly diabolical version of Rubik's Cube with cool graphics and a soundtrack reminiscent of bad German synthesizer music from the mid-70s. Now consider that when you try to turn the top row of the cube one notch to the left, the bottom row moves two notches to the right. That's the idea behind Cogito.

Each of the 120 levels begins with a pattern of markers—nine markers arranged in a square, for example—that are placed on a 9 by 9 grid. This pattern is then scrambled, and your job is to put it back together again by pushing arrows that move the corresponding rows and columns. In the first couple of levels, this is a simple task. But once you progress past these initial levels, the arrow buttons no longer move the rows and columns the way you would expect. For example, instead of moving a row one space to the left, pushing an arrow key may cause a row that is six spaces away to shift two spaces to the right. As you move through the levels, the relationship between the arrows, rows, and columns becomes even more convoluted.

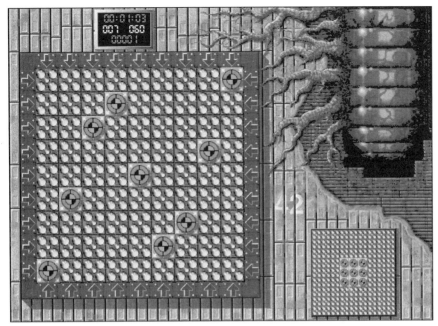

So you push this arrow and then it moves left. ... No. Hmm. Okay, you push this arrow, and that one moves up. ... Drat! Cogito is one tough brain game.

Is Timing Everything?

You can time your progress through each level as well as track the number of moves it takes to restore the markers to their original shapes. It's anyone's guess why you'd want to do this—there's no high score sheet or head-to-head mode—but the information is there if you want it.

This is one of the tougher brain games around. If you liked the Cube, you'll love this game. If, like us, you laughed gleefully after whacking Rubik's hellish device with the business end of a ball peen hammer, you may want to do you and your blood pressure a favor and opt to play another of the Inline classics.

DANGER

Darwin's Dilemma

In a world of harsh labeling laws, a better title for Darwin's Dilemma might have been A Rather Loose Interpretation of Evolution as Applied to a Computer Game in Which You, in the Guise of a Funny Bearded Fellow Who Looks More Like R. Crumb's Mr. Natural Than Charles Darwin, Are Asked to Collide and Merge Icons Representing Life Forms—Ranging From Squishy Amoebas to Toucans—on a 13 by 7 Grid With the Goal of Merging Enough of These Darned Icons to Finally Arrive at the Ultimate Icon, Homo Sapiens.

Of course, the adjusted title doesn't have the alliterative pizzazz of Darwin's Dilemma, but then the truth rarely does.

Icon Do It Myself!

The game opens with a mix of 16 icons representing five primitive species scattered randomly about on a 13 by 7 grid. You are called upon to merge the like icons so that they evolve into an icon representing the next highest form of life. For example, four starfish shoved together become a single jellyfish. Merge four jellyfish and you get a crab. Since the icons rarely line up, you need to maneuver your icons to advantageous positions by clanking them up against unlike icons. Your vehicle for all this clanking and merging is Darwin, a little bearded guy whom you place in various positions on the grid and instruct to kick icons in particular directions.

The rub is that unlike icons may get jammed together in such a way that Darwin can't get a purchase on them because they're blocked by other icons. In these situations, he gives a couple of impotent kicks, turns to you, and lifts his hands in despair.

Hoisted on this particular petard, it's time to do a swap. Swapping involves changing Darwin's position with that of an icon. To begin the swap, simply place Darwin where you'd like that paramecium, say, to be, center the arrow on the microbe in question, double-click, and—huzzah!—they've switched places. You are given eight swaps at the beginning of the game and earn an additional two for each of the 24 levels you can complete. If you burn through your swaps and don't complete the game, you lose.

Extra! Extra!

GREAT FEATURE

If this whole animals-and-plants thing leaves you cold, you can create and determine the distribution of your own icons with the Icon Editor. Rather than flora and fauna, you can insert an image of your good-for-nothing brother-in-law, who can evolve into a cow pie. The heinous possibilities are limited only by a 32- by 32-pixel grid, 256 colors, and your imagination.

TIP

Darwin's Dilemma can be a real forehead crinkler. The slatted brow becomes even more pronounced if you assume that every game is winnable. Save yourself the frustration. At times you'll simply be dealt a bad hand and you'll be better off starting over rather than banging your head against the screen.

Of course you can still place a few dents in your monitor's case even while playing games you can win. Darwin's Dilemma is often frustrating, but for the true puzzler, it's a magnificent challenge.

The Tinies

If you have tendencies that predispose you to rearranging and manipulating of fuzzy ping-pong balls in confined spaces, The Tinies might be just what you're looking for. Let's set this up: There's this planet called Sklumph, and its inhabitants are small-brained fuzz balls who are into griping and annoying practical jokes. Although they need to be guided to their beds at night, they are smart enough to have developed a space ship which has been commandeered by some especially nasty Tinies. These furry giblets are planning to land on Earth and annoy the inhabitants into submission. Your job is to go through the hundred levels of the space craft and put all the Tinies safely into their respective berths for a safe, uneventful trip home.

Fuzzy Golf Balls From Hell

The Tinies are manipulated by grabbing them with a device that enables movement in any available direction. However, Tinies are not equipped with four-wheel disk brakes, so they'll keep on truckin in whichever direction they're started until they ram into something. This forces you to consider using obstacles as well as other Tinies to create paths to appropriate resting places. This is by far the most challenging aspect of game play. The Tinies' constant taunting and monotonous music will eventually take their toll on most players. Fortunately, the music can be toggled off, and the faces the Tinies make at you becomes an acceptable annoyance. Of course, when first running the game, these little creatures displaying their tonsils, teeth, and gums can be mildly amusing, but after 15 levels, what the Tinies do is minimally important because the ol' clock is the main enemy here. Each level has a specific time limit, and failure to succeed on any given level ensures a repeat performance.

LOUSY
FEATURE

Tiny Appeal

While putting taunting fuzzy annoyances to sleep may be the highlight of a child's day, we didn't find that The Tinies could rise above average in the crowded world of great brain games. The controls are a tad funky and cause unnecessary collisions with walls and obstacles, and the level of challenge isn't enough for tried and true brain game aficionados. Add those factors to the rather displeasing key word needed to start at a selected level, and The Tinies alone isn't really worth it, though a good value in the nine-game package.

LOUSY
FEATURE

Tip

• If you need to have your Tiny pass over a teleporter of the same color, place another Tiny of a different color on top of the teleporter exit. The color-coded dynamite will only explode the Tiny of the same color. All others can pass over it safely.

TIP

S.C.Out

This attractive motion puzzler has an incredibly complex plot line that, as far as we can tell, adds nothing to the game. We'll save a tree or two and summarize as follows: You control a small tank on a moonbase. Your mission is to drive around each of 100 levels of the base, locate an immobile yet heavily armored alien, place a nuclear grenade next to its face, set it off from a distance, and blow said alien to the great beyond.

This would be easy enough were it not for all the odd devices, traps, and tank-eating worms scattered about the tiled floors. Although the online documentation reveals the purpose of some of these objects, most of the really nasty ones are left for you to discover on your own. Thankfully, the new items are introduced gradually throughout the game.

Another hitch is that your little tank can only carry one object at a time. If, for example, you've just picked up a missile with the intention of cremating a troublesome worm but discover that the worm is behind a locked door, you must find a key, swap the missile for the key, unlock the door, swap the key for the missile, and finally end the worm's tedious life. Sure, scooting back and forth discarding and retrieving objects is a little tiresome, but it forces you to prioritize your actions and, in some cases, is the linchpin to certain levels' puzzles.

Time Is on Your Side

Even though this is a motion puzzler, it includes a few occasions on which you'll have to race through a level. Hand-eye coordination and timing do play a part in the proceedings, but for the most part, you can park your tank on a safe spot and think things over for as long as you like. Unfortunately, you won't be able to plan the campaign for the entire level because you can only see 14 tiles across and 10 tiles down at any one time; there is no map overview.

RANT

As with such other Inline puzzlers as The Tinies and Cogito, you earn the password to the next level at the completion of the last. As much as we like these games, we think this password-access stuff is for the birds. If you've only made it to level 13 and feel like taking a peek at level 99, what's the harm? Sure you'll have to live with the guilt of being a big, fat, cheater, but who are software designers to take on the role of conscience cops? Because we find this so annoying, we're including all the passwords to S.C.Out on our CD-ROM. We'll assume you can deal with your self-image on your own.

Aside from the password issue, S.C.Out is another quality Inline puzzler. It's a great looking game that can be enjoyed by players of all ages.

Tip

• Type NOWALL in the password box to allow your tank to drive over any and all nonthreatening obstacles. (This takes all the fun out of the game, of course, but go ahead, give it a try!)

Tesseræ

Tesseræ is defined as "small squares of colored stone or glass inlaid to form a mosaic." As the author reminds us, Tesseræ is also a tantalizing puzzle game for the Macintosh. Some of the best brain games in history have drunk from the well of simplicity, and Tesseræ is no different. The built-in "hide" feature that quickly engages a mock screen saver will no doubt protect many from the wrath of anal retentive middle managers intent on catching employees goofing off. Unfortunately, Tesseræ is so terribly addictive that middle managers everywhere should fear the productivity loss this game could bring about. Even those players who normally demand action in their games will find themselves mesmerized by the calm simplicity and primary colors of this diversion.

GREAT
FEATURE

Click Clack, I Was Taken Aback

The goal of the game is to eliminate all but one of the tiles from a grid (called a mosaic) that can vary in size and shape. The easiest grid is a basic rectangular 6 by 8 mosaic that looks easy enough but will probably leave most first-time users

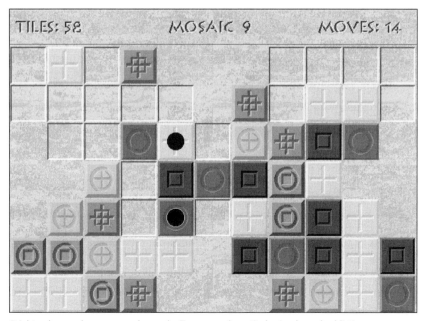

Bright colors and easy gameplay make Tesseræ a deceptively simple and addicting game.

piecing together the remnants of their shattered pride after the initial round. The tiles are brightly colored and come in seven varieties: three primary tiles and four that are combinations of the first three. The tiles are removed from the board by jumping them over other tiles. This process involves a nice smooth animation of the tiles flipping over each other with a solid "click clack" sound that gives a satisfaction reminiscent of pushing the "popamatic" die roller on an old Milton-Bradley game. The online instructions are complete and include animations of flipping tiles to illustrate the various combinations needed to master the game. Although Tesseræ excels on a color Mac, the black-and-white version is decent and works on anything from a Mac Plus on up (including a PowerBook 100).

Tesseræ Anonymous

This is an excellent example of software that is challenging, addictive, visually pleasing, and highly intuitive without being complex or confusing. Everyone in the family will have many hours of fun clickity-clacking along, trying to reduce the mosaic to only one remaining tile so as to enjoy the nifty animation of that last tile disintegrating and blowing away in an electronic wind. Anyone who has this game at work would be wise to remember that Command-H takes one to the boss screen.

System Requirements: CD-ROM player, 256-color Mac for some games (most run in black and white), 3MB RAM for System 6, 4MB RAM for System 7, 20MB hard disk space, System 6.07 or higher.

INLINE GREATEST HITS GAME PAK	
Fun factor	4.5
Look and feel	4.0
Value	5.0
Replayability	varies*
Overall	4.5

* Depends on game

CD

Oxyd
Oxyd Magnum!
Dongleware Publishing

These two games from Germany's Dongleware may be the coolest motion puzzlers on the planet. The games' underlying concept is deceptively simple: Using the mouse, scoot a black marble around a tiled landscape and uncover pairs of matching colored tokens by touching the marble to each token's outer casing. Easy, eh? Hardly.

To begin with, there are any number of obstacles in your marble's path that must be avoided or moved. Some require a gentle shove, others a whack with a

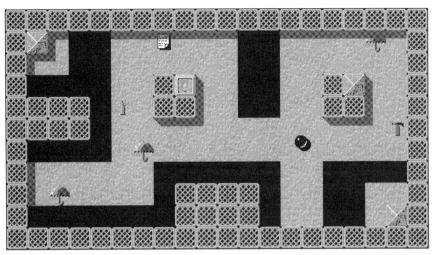

Maybe one of those umbrellas will help you float Oxyd Magnum!'s black marble across the dark maw of death.

hammer, and still others must be blown up with a small bomb. There are also large holes scattered about and unless you can skirt them or find an umbrella token to help you float over these pits, you'll board the deadly express elevator to Loserville. Oh, and did we mention the reverse tiles that cause your marble to journey in the direction opposite the one in which you move your mouse? Levels that feature this reverse action are invariably dotted with pits or death stones that shatter your marble with a single touch.

These are just a few of the delightfully devilish objects that you'll find in the games. Although the manuals do not explain the purpose of everything you're likely to encounter, small scraps of paper that provide some helpful hints are scattered about the levels.

The Hand and the Eye

The realistic physical modeling of the games compounds your difficulties. When you bang your marble against a large chunk of masonry, the marble bounces back with a good deal of force. If there happens to be a pit behind you and you're not careful, the marble falls over the edge and you're again on your way to Hades. The Oxyds require a great deal of concentration, and we strongly suggest that you avoid caffeinated beverages before you take them on—a steady hand as well as a sharp mind is key to conquering these games.

Both games contain 100 single-player levels and an additional 100 levels intended to be played cooperatively/competitively over a network. You'll find a copy of the first game on our CD-ROM. The first ten levels are yours to play for ever and a day. To play beyond these levels, you must purchase the Oxyd book that contains codes that allow you to move through the other 90 levels. Oxyd Magnum! is sold commercially and is completely code-free.

So fire up your CD-ROM player and give Oxyd a try. We think you'll be absolutely charmed and perplexed by this fine European puzzler.

TIP

Tips

• In Oxyd, the level 10 Meditation level resets all the password numbers from level 11 onward. Therefore, if you've already gone past level 10, do not repeat it (or allow anyone else to repeat it). If you do, your old passwords will not work and you'll have to start again.

• To protect yourself from this happening, make a copy of the Oxyd Preferences file (located in the System Folder's Preferences folder), and store it in a safe place. This file contains the password settings. If the passwords should be reset, copy the saved Preferences file back to the Preferences folder.

Pros: Wonderful graphics and sound. Very challenging brain games. Shareware version allows you to try before you buy.

Cons: Password entry to levels. Copy protection code book for Oxyd is inconvenient to use.

System Requirements: Mac Plus or better, 1MB RAM, 1MB hard disk space, System 6.01 or higher.

OXYD & OXYD MAGNUM!	
Fun factor	4.5
Look and feel	4.5
Value	4.5
Replayability	2.0
Overall	4.5

CD

Troubled Souls
MacSoft

GREAT FEATURE

There have been many incarnations of the pipe-fitting style of games that require various sections of piping to be connected properly in order for them to be counted as points on a tally. Troubled Souls is the newest and by far the most sophisticated of the lot. It marries supercool 3D graphics to stunning music and game play that cruises along at a compelling pace. With only three lives (represented by hands with beating hearts in them) you must strive to attain the highest possible score in order to be recognized on the coveted Fool's List.

If you can hold it together long enough to get a high score, you can hang your head proudly in the Fool's List.

Sadistic Souls

Troubled Souls begins when pieces of macabre tubing start dropping down a tube at regular intervals. The tubing comes in the form of curves, straight pieces, intersections, and even bizarre eyeball-laden pipes that are used to create self-contained systems. When a complete connection is made, the system disappears from the screen and you are rewarded with a number of points based on the complexity of your morbid creation. As the game progresses, the various pieces of piping start coming labeled with body parts. This makes it more difficult to proceed because loops can only be made with pipe from the same groups. For example, pipes with eyes cannot be mixed with hand pipes or brain pipes or ventral gluteus pipes. The level rises every time you complete 13 loops. As would be expected, this means a faster drop rate and a smaller working area. If you can complete the 13 levels, you are treated to an animated finale. Sadistic souls can continue to play with ever-increasing levels of difficulty.

Have a Heart

This was the first commercial programming effort for the prodigal 17-year-old Randy Reddig, a feat for which he should be highly commended. The graphics and background animation are absolutely top notch, and the game plays smoothly. Although it's not incredibly original, it is very addictive. We're dying to see what will spring forth next from this wonderful lad; if it's anything like Troubled Souls, it'll be great.

Pros: Easy to play. Fun graphics and animation. Cool music.

Cons: Can become repetitive after a few hours of play.

System Requirements: System 6.07 or higher, 4MB RAM, 2.7MB hard disk space.

TROUBLED SOULS	
Fun factor	3.5
Look and feel	5.0
Value	4.0
Replayability	3.0
Overall	4.0

Diamonds
Varcon Systems

This little gem has been praised from here to eternity by such journals as *MacUser* and *Macworld* for good reason. It is one of the most addicting motion puzzlers on the market. Diamonds is a faster game than Oxyd, and it requires deft hand-eye coordination. It can be learned in seconds but takes days to defeat.

Another Marble Game!?

You start each of the 30 levels with a pale blue marble. In order to complete the round, you must remove bricks on a landscape by banging a constantly ping-ponging marble against like-colored bricks and then against the diamond bricks—all the while avoiding the death-head bricks that spell your marble's destruction. This would be child's play were all the bricks of the same color. Of course, they're not.

To change the color of the marble, guide it to one of the paintbrush bricks distributed throughout each level. The twist is that there are no pale blue paintbrush bricks. Therefore, you must remove all of these bricks before you change the marble's color.

To add another touch of exquisite misery, the later levels contain reverse bricks that cause the marble to go in the direction opposite the one you indicate. So now not only do you have to avoid the colored paintbrushes and the death-head bricks, but you also have to remember to press the left arrow key when you want the marble to go to the right. Oh, and one more thing: You'll also find some bricks that contain locks and others that contain the keys to those locks. To open certain passageways, you'll have to navigate back through the death-head maze to first change your marble to the appropriate brick color, then trot over to pick up the key, and finally, bounce back again to open the lock.

New Levels

The problem with many puzzle games is that once you've solved the puzzles, the games serve only as useless collections of bytes on your hard drive. Not so with Diamonds. Tucked away in the game is an editor that allows you to create your own levels and swap them with your Diamonds-bearing friends. If you have no friends to swap with or are too darned lazy to come up with your own levels, you can purchase More Diamonds, which contains another 40 levels.

GREAT FEATURE

The game runs in black and white as well as color and comes with a musical soundtrack that, although pretty decent as these thing go, can get awfully repetitive (though you can switch it off). The graphics are quite good, and the game provides an option to paste your own custom PICT file in the background.

Diamonds is a customizable motion puzzle game that provides days of entertainment and can be run on a PowerBook. What more could you possibly ask for? If you like fast action with your puzzles, you've got to have this game.

Tips

• If you've changed the color of the marble before you've nailed all the pale blue bricks, don't just dive for the closest death-head in order to continue the game. Clear any bricks you can with the tools at hand. Then, and only then, commit suicide.

TIP

• You'll have to slap some bricks from the side, and oftentimes there will be a death-head or unwanted paintbrush brick on the other side. When hitting bricks from the side, try to do so while the marble is traveling in the opposite direction of the dangerous brick. (For example, if a death-head is one brick above the one you want to hit, try to slap it when the marble is headed down.) This is necessary because there is a slight delay after the key is pressed and before the marble moves.

Pros: Arcadelike action in a puzzle game. Built-in level editor. Customizable backgrounds. Good PowerBook game.

Cons: Music gets annoying after a while.

System Requirements: Mac Plus or better, 1.3MB RAM, 800K hard disk space, System 6.05 or higher.

DIAMONDS	
Fun factor	4.5
Look and feel	4.5
Value	4.5
Replayability	4.0
Overall	4.5

The Even More Incredible Machine
Dynamix

Once in a while, a great game comes along that challenges our noggins in ways previously not imagined. In the case of the Incredible Machine, it came along for the wrong platform, but we can forgive this oversight because the sequel is now available for the Mac, and although it's late, it's graphically superior to its DOS counterpart. Although this may sound like just another puzzle game, the revolutionary nature of this program makes it one of the top cranium crankers in this family of games.

Ever Play Mousetrap?

Once upon a time there was a board game called Mousetrap that involved setting up a series of physical chain reactions that would eventually capture a mouse. That's the premise of The Even More Incredible Machine (hereafter known as TIM)—a set of sequential events something like this: ball falls onto seesaw; seesaw pulls string; string opens door; you get the idea. TIM sets forth 160 different puzzles to solve with the help of 55 separate aparatii. These devices include everything from dynamite (which usually requires a candle or a magnifying glass to light) to a cat (who runs when its tail is squashed). Of course some of the items can be used in several ways. For instance, you can tempt a mouse with a morsel of cheese or spook it with a cat. The 160 levels can be tackled one by one. There is also the free-form mode, with which you can create whatever spectacular machines you can imagine. The puzzles progress in difficulty. The first 15 or so are there to help the user get a grip on the interface and various mechanisms.

**GREAT
FEATURE**

PhundaMental Physics

The animation in TIM is reminiscent of some of computer pinball games, and it strives for realism in every physical aspect. Of course, not everything is dyed in the wool "real life," and in fact, some of the animations, such as those of a gun shooting or a kettle boiling, are hilariously comical. Despite the fantastic sound and animation that would seem to need heavy horsepower, the faster machines are pretty much too quick, and some of the humorous and critical aspects of the animations can be lost when trying to solve a real mind bender. If the game becomes tiresome, there is always the game box to play with. It's an assembler's nightmare that includes a built-in cats tail that when pulled causes the middle portion of the packaging to flip over. While this is kinda cute, it's a glitzy frill that's ultimately a waste of paper and resources that a great game like this does not need in order to sell well.

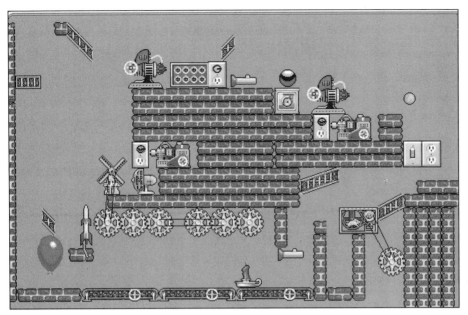

Over 50 comical contraptions help make The Even More Incredible Machine a ground-breaking brain game.

ACK! Copy Protection

Copy protection is the bane of any real gamer. Of course, tasteful and well-done copy protection is acceptable, but having to refer to the manual every time you boot the game (even if the game was just running and you haven't shut down) is downright annoying. Features like this ensure that a game is just licking the envelope rather then pushing it. Despite the obnoxious copy protection, The Incredible Machine is an excellent game and will provide countless hours of enjoyable problem solving. It's good to see such innovative thinking going into the brain game genre.

RANT

Pros: Great fun. Innovative game play. Smooth animation. Fun graphics.

Cons: Annoying key word feature for saved games. Password copy protection.

System Requirements: Mac Plus or better, 2MB RAM with System 6, 4MB RAM with System 7, 2.8MB hard disk space, System 6.05 or higher.

THE EVEN MORE INCREDIBLE MACHINE	
Fun factor	4.5
Look and feel	4.5
Value	4.0
Replayability	4.0
Overall	4.0

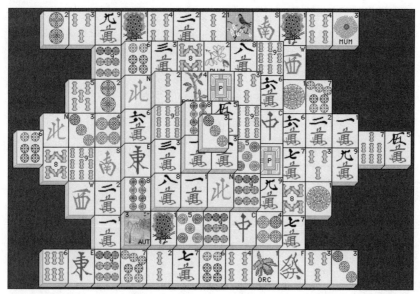

A variation of the ancient and addictive game of mah-jongg has been brought to the Mac in Shanghai II, The Dragon's Eye.

Shanghai II, The Dragon's Eye
Activision

As we have previously mentioned, the early days of 1986 did not offer Mac enthusiasts very much in the way of good gaming. Probably the best early brain game was Shanghai, a simple mah-jongg-based tile game that was conceived and developed by Brodie Lockard. Mr. Lockard was also involved (to a lesser degree) in the creation of Shanghai II. For those who aren't familiar with mah-jongg, it's a 3,000-year-old Chinese game that is so addictive it was banned in Philadelphia in the 1920s. Shanghai isn't mah-jongg, but it borrows some of its content to create an irresistible gaming experience.

Beautiful Tiles

Figuring this one out without reading the paragraph of basic instructions might prove a bit difficult. The concept, however, is simple enough. There are 144 randomized tiles of seven different suits laid out in the shape (initially) of a dragon. Don't worry if you don't see the dragon, these figures share anatomical accuracy with astrological figures in the stars. The tiles can be removed from the board only in matching pairs, and only tiles that are "free" can be removed. Any tile unable to freely slide to the left or right or with another tile on top of it is considered locked, and it cannot be removed. This makes the order in which the tiles are removed of critical importance. If you're faced with two identical tiles whose removal isn't essential, it might be prudent to save them for a tight spot later in the game. Shanghai II is endowed with 16 preset layouts as well as a layout editor for an unlimited number of board variations. The tiles are beautifully drawn, and there are ten built-in tile sets ranging from fantasy figures to animals of the world. When the tiles are removed, there is a short animation and a corresponding sound (such as the roar of a lion) for whatever tiles are removed. We found ourselves rushing through the tile sets just to see the various animations the figures offer. For those hopelessly addicted to Shanghai II, there are custom tile sets available from the author for a small fee.

GREAT FEATURE

The Dragon Doesn't Drag On

A complete game of Shanghai can often be played in under 30 minutes. Beside the solitaire mode there is a challenge setting which allows for nail-biting head-to-head action that's played against the relentless timer. Shanghai II and its predecessor are classic entertainment. One or both of them must have been on our hard drives for almost a decade.

Pros: Great color and sound. Fun animations. Unlimited variety of layouts. Easy to play.

Cons: Addictive.

System Requirements: Mac Plus or better, 4MB RAM, 5MB hard disk space, System 6.05 or higher.

SHANGHAI II, THE DRAGON'S EYE	
Fun factor	3.5
Look and feel	4.5
Value	4.0
Replayability	4.0
Overall	4.0

Minefield
BugByte, Inc.

MacMines
Cary Torkelson

Super Mines
Callisto

These are three different versions of the classic mines game—one freeware, one shareware, and the last a (currently) commercial product. Mines is another one of those simple brain games that turns out to be anything but simple once you start playing. To begin the game, click on one of the squares in the playfield and hope a hidden mine doesn't blow you to bits. If you survive the click, a numeral or group of empty spaces replaces the square. Empty spaces represent safe areas, and numerals indicate how many hidden mines are adjacent to that square. For example, if you uncover a 1, a single mine is hidden beneath one of the eight squares surrounding the numbered square. Through the process of elimination—and a little luck—you should be able to navigate your way safely through the minefield.

Minefield

Kendall Redburn's freeware Minefield features three skill levels. The Beginner level contains a 10 by 10 minefield; Intermediate boosts this number to 20 by 10; and Expert tops out at 20 by 15. Like other mines games, it sports two counters; one indicates elapsed time and the other the number of remaining hidden mines.

Even though this is freeware, you must register the game in order to unlock the Master and Guru levels. When you register, BugByte offers you discounts on its shareware software. In the Master level, the vast empty spaces that contain neither mines nor numbers are not automatically revealed and you must uncover each space individually. In Guru mode, none of the squares are revealed when you click on them. Instead, a number is revealed for only as long as you click and hold on the square. This level is only for those with photographic memories.

BugByte also offers Minefield Deluxe, a shareware version of the game that allows you to create your own minefields and take hints from a cute little teddy bear named Earl Gray.

MacMines

Cary Torkelson's $15 version of the basic mines game also comes with three skill levels. With it, you can also create custom levels that go as high as a 60 by 60 minefield containing as many as 999 mines. In addition to being the only shareware version of mines we looked at that doesn't hobble the game in order to solicit shareware fees, MacMines contains a couple of options not found in these other games.

GREAT
FEATURE

The Moving Mines option causes a single mine to periodically pack up and move from one location to another. With this option switched on, squares that you've marked as explosive may no longer be so and previously benign areas may now be deadly. The Randomizer option places a single randomizer square on the minefield. When you uncover it, all of the mines move to new locations. We also like the Stupidity Avoidance option—not that *we'd* ever need it—that ensures a mine you've marked as active won't explode if you click it again.

Super Mines

Callisto's take on the game is more flexible than Kendall's and Cary's. The minefield is still there, but it now comes in four layouts: Square Grid, Hex Grid, Parquet, and Large & Small. These different layouts are not just for aesthetic purposes. The pieces of the minefield are no longer square-shaped and therefore do not have eight pieces touching them. Large & Small, for example, has nine points of contact for some of its pieces.

Unlike the other two games, Super Mines provides you with five lives and chucks in one extra life for each minefield you clear, although you can also play the traditional one-exploded-mine-and-you're-dead version of the game by selecting the Mini Mines option. And as with Minefield, you can ask for hints if you get stuck.

Tiptoe Through the Minefields with Me

You'll find copies of Minefield and MacMines on our CD-ROM. These games both offer worthwhile enhancements to the basic mines game, and we think they're just swell. Super Mines is in a state of transition as we write this. According to the inside dope, Apple will be bundling some of Callisto's games at a future date. Super Mines may not be included in that bundle but could be available free online. If you have access to an online service, run a search to see if Super Mines is there. It's definitely worth the download time.

Tip for All Mines Games

• You can quickly find mines when a 1 is placed in an inside corner. Since the 1 is only exposed on that single corner, the mine has to be in the one open spot.

TIP

Pros: Fine representative of the traditional mines game. Guru level will challenge the most hardened mines junkie.

Cons: Have to register the freeware version to unlock the entire game.

System Requirements: Mac Plus or better, 400K RAM, 180K hard disk space, System 6.07 or higher.

MINEFIELD	
Fun factor	4.0
Look and feel	4.0
Value	5.0
Replayability	4.0
Overall	4.0

Pros: Another fine representative of the traditional mines game. Moving Mines and Randomizer options add extra difficulty.

Cons: No option for creating minefields from scratch.

System Requirements: Mac Plus or better, 400K RAM, 190K hard disk space, System 6.07 or higher.

MACMINES	
Fun factor	4.O
Look and feel	4.O
Value	4.5
Replayability	4.O
Overall	4.O

Pros: Yet another fine representative of the traditional mines game. Varied shapes of minefield pieces add more complexity to the game. Multiple lives.

Cons: No option for creating minefields from scratch.

System Requirements: Mac Plus or better, 1MB RAM, 800K hard disk space, System 6.07 or higher.

SUPER MINES	
Fun factor	4.O
Look and feel	4.O
Value	4.O
Replayability	4.O
Overall	4.O

CD

Chiral
Ambrosia Software

Ambrosia keeps churning out fantastic shareware that's often superior in quality to many of its commercial counterparts. In the case of Chiral, even though it deals with covalent bonding and multiple molecules, it's pretty much the same game as Troubled Souls. Now we're not suggesting that there's any borrowing of material by either party, but there's enough similarity to make a comparison. Much as in the manner of Hornet and Falcon, these two games have the same basic premise. Chiral, which is defined as "symmetry between molecules," has the great music and comical sound bites we've come to expect from the fine minds at Ambrosia, and of course the graphics are like 3D-rendered eye candy.

Constantly Falling

Although the underlying theme of Chiral lies in the field of chemistry, you won't need a Ph.D. to become a successful Chiralist. The basic goal is to build molecules by matching up atoms with the correct number of bonds. If a molecule is to be removed from the playing area, there can be no unmatched bonds in it. As with Troubled Souls, the pieces are constantly falling into a receptacle from which you get the individual atoms to build chemical bonds previously only dreamed of by chemists. You must always build a certain number of molecules with minimum numbers of atoms in them. So although a three- or four-atom molecule looks good and will disappear from the screen, it doesn't count toward getting you out of the present level of play. Fortunately, there is the Schzapp. The Schzapp is an electrical charge that will zap the test tube of its atomic contents when it becomes full; if no Schzapp existed, the game would effectively be over at that point. The Schzapp can be earned in the bonus rounds, and for all intents and purposes, it amounts to an extra life.

GREAT
FEATURE

Mr. Wizard Never Had It This Good

Chiral is simply the latest brain teaser in Ambrosia's ever-growing line of entertainment software. Anything Ambrosia puts out turns to gold, and Chiral is no different. For fast-paced, colorful, funky action, this is as good as any, and as usual the shareware price is ridiculously low for such high quality. You can have a look at Chiral on the CD-ROM in this book.

Pros: Great graphics and sound. Great price. Multiple challenge levels.

Cons: Online documentation adequate but not up to Ambrosia's usual standards.

System Requirements: Mac Plus or better, 800K RAM, 704K hard disk space, System 6.05 or higher.

CHIRAL	
Fun factor	4.0
Look and feel	4.5
Value	5.0
Replayability	3.5
Overall	4.0

Tetris Gold

Spectrum HoloByte

Talk to any Reagan-era State Department bigwig and he'll tell you that the Soviet Union collapsed due to the economic pressures inherent in a massive arms build-up.

Nonsense, we say.

The truth is that the Soviet people got a taste for capitalism when they realized that Amerikanskis were willing to throw away millions upon millions of dollars on a silly little brain game called Tetris.

"Boris," we can imagine one former Party member saying to another, "you can keep the collective. I'm trading in my cabbage shares for a black market Commodore-64."

Spectrum HoloByte has been cranking out Tetris and its sequels for nearly a decade. Because these games are no longer huge sellers on their own, the company has collected them all on a single CD-ROM called Tetris Gold. Here's what you'll find on this bargain-priced silver disc:

Tetris

We think we can safely assert that the number of people who haven't played this game and those who have never seen a toaster-oven are about equal. If you are one of these few folks, this is how to play the game:

Geometric shapes made out of four squares drop from the top of the Tetris window. Your job is to shift and swivel these shapes so that they fit neatly together and form complete lines at the bottom of the screen. As lines are completed, they vanish from the screen. If you fail to complete lines, the shapes pile atop each other until they reach the top of the window and the game ends. As you progress through the ten rounds of the game, the pieces fall more rapidly.

A Classic

Tetris is just about the perfect motion brain game. It's very simple to play and extremely addicting. It also runs on PowerBooks and such vintage Macs as the Plus and SE. If you've had a Mac for more than a few weeks, you probably own this game. If you're new to the Macintosh and would like to try out a little Tetris action, read the section called Tetris Clones.

Welltris

Welltris was the first Tetris spin-off and is still one of the more challenging versions of the game. The dropping pieces remain, but they now fall in three dimensions. That's right, the straight-ahead 2D view is out and the well is in.

As the game opens, you peer down the shaft of a deep well. Suddenly, a multi-segmented shape slithers down one of the well's walls. To maneuver the shape into position, you must rotate the object as well as slip it around the four sides of the well. This would be a simple enough process if the four walls were all you had to deal with. But like all good wells, this one has a bottom, and you must also account for the fact that these shapes will fit where they can in the bottom of the well and then bend up the sides. As with Tetris, the ultimate object of the

TETRIS CLONES

If you really only want to play Tetris, there's no need to buy the Tetris Gold CD-ROM—or even the original Tetris for that matter. Steve Chamberlin's $10 shareware Tetris Max 2.4 is a better version of Tetris than Tetris.

CD

Not only do you get all the usual features of Tetris, but unlike the original, you can customize the keyboard controls, rotate pieces either clockwise or counter-clockwise, and choose different backgrounds, piece shapes, and music. Registered users can even set Tetris Max to Autoplay—a mode in which the computer demonstrates what a truly weak player you are by effortlessly slamming pieces into place in rapid succession. Registered owners can also purchase a four-disk set of additional music, backgrounds, and piece shapes for $10.

Rodney and Brenda Jacks's $10 shareware gem, Jewelbox, is related to Tetris but doesn't present the game in the way Tetris Max does. In this game, you control a string of three different dropping jewels. Rather than forming lines, your mission is to line up three jewels of the same variety horizontally, vertically, or diagonally. As with Tetris Max, Jewelbox contains a very good background music score that, unlike the music found in the Spectrum HoloByte 'Tris games, doesn't get on your nerves during the first three minutes of play.

You'll find both games on the CD-ROM. We expect you'll like them as much as we do and will, like all good electronic citizens, dutifully pay your shareware fees.

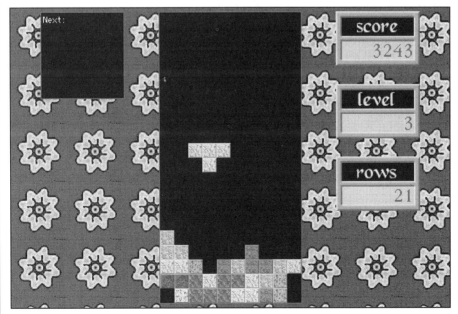

Steve Chamberlin's Tetris Max 2.4 is all the Tetris you'll ever need.

of the well and then bend up the sides. As with Tetris, the ultimate object of the game is to form complete lines in the bottom of the well.

Not Quite a Classic

Welltris suffers from the same problem as some of the other Tetris spin-offs—it lacks Tetris's elegant simplicity. We have nothing against tough brain busters, but if we have to think too hard for too long, we're likely to take our puzzling elsewhere.

Tetris is one of those rare games that is perfectly balanced between thought and reaction, and any good Tetris player will testify to the existence of that intuitive trance state you enter after playing the game for a while. Although Welltris is fine in short spurts, it requires too much cogitating to allow you to become one with the game.

Faces

When this game first hit the scene, a few of us wondered if perhaps the Tetris well was starting to run dry. Once again we were called upon to move dropping objects around a painted window. This time the objects were face slices: chins, mouths, noses, eyes, and foreheads. The point of the game was to assemble faces by ganging together these parts in sequence. If you could assemble a "perfect face"—one made out of a single individual's face—so much the better.

Frankly, we thought Faces was a yawner then, and it doesn't look any better in retrospect. It's mainly noteworthy because it's the first Tris game that offered head-to-head play over modem and AppleTalk.

Wordtris

Wordtris is a far more worthy effort than its cousin Faces. Stop us if you've heard this before, but you are presented with a group of falling blocks that must be positioned so that they form lines. The kicker is that these blocks have letters printed on them and the only way to remove the stockpiled blocks is to form words horizontally or vertically. The game comes with a 60,000-plus word dictionary that allows you to check on the viability of the formed words. If your vocabulary is more, er, colorful than the dictionary allows, the game includes the option to add your own words.

**GREAT
FEATURE**

Wordtris is something of a cross between Scrabble and juggling. If you're one of those people who can't stop fidgeting while waiting for your Scrabble partner to lay down a word, Wordtris could be just what the lexicologist ordered.

If you think that lion's breath is bad, watch what these bombs do to those puny blocks in Super Tetris.

Super Tetris

We now take you to an imaginary conference room at the offices of a totally imaginary software publisher:

"Alexey, sweetie, we've done the 'Tris thing to death, but we still think there's a little gold left in this mine. What can you give us?"

"Perhaps the public is ready for our latest game, Cowtris. You steer the falling cattle to the ..."

"Too bovine, babe. It'll never fly in the 'burbs."

"Well then, there's Calcutris. You start with the cosine of ..."

"We dig your mathematical roots, A.P., but it won't sell outside of Cal Tech and M.I.T. Look, is there any way that you could just do Tetris again? Ya know, toss in some networking stuff, some explosions ..."

"Explosions?"

"The kids eat up bombs, sugar. Yeah, that's it. Explosions and special detonator blocks! Bonus blocks! The works!"

"*Da,* if you insist, I can do the works."

All kidding aside, Super Tetris is a fine effort. Once again, the little block shapes fall and, as before, you are expected to form complete lines. But this time around the bottom of the game window contains rubble—a hodgepodge of game pieces and bonus tokens. The key to clearing the rubble are the bombs that drop from above when you successfully complete lines.

Bombs serve two purposes: They destroy any blocks they come in contact with, and they activate the bonus pieces that are lodged in the rubble. These bonuses include such things as detonator blocks that remove pieces in a 3 by 3 area and tokens that cause the next dropped piece to become the ever-welcome, blue, straight-sided square piece. Along with the bombs, Super Tetris offers a networking option as well as the opportunity for cooperative and competitive play on the same computer.

Super Duper?

After the original Tetris, Super Tetris is the most compelling reason to buy the Tetris Gold CD-ROM. We're still not convinced that the original game needed much improvement, but if it had to be done, Super Tetris is as good a sequel as we're likely to see.

Pros: All the Tetris games in one bargain package.

Cons: Not all games are as good as Tetris.

System Requirements: CD-ROM player, Mac Plus or later for black and white, Mac II or later for color, 4MB RAM, hard disk, System 7.0 or later.

TETRIS GOLD	
Fun factor	4.O
Look and feel	4.O
Value	4.5
Replayability	4.O
Overall	4.O

BreakThru

Spectrum HoloByte

You could hardly blame a savvy Mac gamer for picking up the BreakThru box and swiveling it around a bit in search of the word "Tetris." After all, the box sports the bright red and yellow design of all the other 'Tris games, there are colored blocks featured on the face of the box, and isn't that Tetris designer Alexey Pajitnov's smiling visage up in the left-hand corner?

Sometimes you *can* tell a book by its cover. Although the 'Tris name is missing and Alexey apparently did little more than lend his picture and name to the game, BreakThru is as much a Tetris spin-off as any of the games found on the Tetris Gold CD-ROM.

sirteT

BreakThru is kind of a retrograde inversion of Tetris. Instead of filling in the missing bricks from a wall, with the ultimate goal of tearing it down, you tear down the wall by removing like-colored bricks.

At the beginning of each round, a complete wall made up of different-colored bricks is displayed against a decorative background. Using the mouse or keyboard, select like-colored groups of bricks to make them vanish. As the bricks disappear, the rest of the wall shifts down to fill the void. Meanwhile, single bricks float overhead and occasionally drop down onto the wall. As empty columns appear beside the wall, you can shift the wall from side to side to aid in the placement of these new bricks. The round ends when all the bricks are cleared.

Of course, Alexey wouldn't lend his name to such a product if that was the extent of the game. Unlike Tetris, BreakThru games have player-selectable time limits. And as with Super Tetris, bombs are included in this game. You can explode these bombs only when they are on the bottom row of bricks or when another bomb drops down upon them. In later levels, the game also includes pesky tin cans and spiders that must be removed by bombs, and small rockets that take out any bricks in their paths.

BreakThru offers three two-player modes—Cooperative, Competitive, and Dual Wall—that are, regrettably, not networkable. These modes are fun, but because playing the game with the keyboard is cumbersome, the lucky player with mouse control has a distinct advantage.

LOUSY FEATURE

Been There, Done That

Playing BreakThru is a bit like watching the latest Star Trek spin-off. It's fine entertainment, but after a while you begin to wonder if the fountain of original ideas has run dry. Tetris was a great game, and BreakThru is a pretty good game. But Alexey, it's time to give it a rest.

Pros: More Tetris-like fun.

Cons: More Tetris-like fun.

System Requirements: 256-color or 16-grayscale Mac, 68020 processor or better, 4MB RAM, 8.5MB hard disk space, System 6.07 or higher.

BREAKTHRU	
Fun factor	3.5
Look and feel	4.0
Value	3.0
Replayability	3.0
Overall	3.5

Lemmings
Oh No! More Lemmings
Psygnosis

Lemmings are furry little creatures noted for their mass migratory patterns. They've also touted as foolish animals who willingly fling themselves off cliffs by the thousands. This, of course, is a myth, and it is also the basis for this Psygnosis duo of games for the Mac. The little guys just stroll around by the hundreds waiting for you to show them the way to a better life, or at least the next level.

Fun, Tricky, Taxing, or Mayhem?

Lemmings begins when a group of beasts descend onto the playing area and begin walking aimlessly across the terrain. These critters are so brainless they'll march off a cliff and plummet to their deaths without a second thought. This is where you come in. You direct the little varmints through the many obstacles offered up on each level and guide them to safety. To progress to the next level, you must rescue a certain percentage of Lemmings from whatever Lemming squasher lies in their way. There are pools of acid, high cliffs, lava flows, and even electric devices to be wary of when chaperoning Lemmings across your screen. To aid you in saving the fuzzies, there are limited amounts of equipment that can be attached to individual Lemmings. These juicy extras include diggers, climbers, blockers, bridge builders, and pick-wielding diggers. They can be applied to any lemming in the interests of helping the others. And if you get annoyed, there's even a Doomsday button that explodes each lemming into a cozy ball of flame and debris. There are four levels of difficulty: Fun, Tricky, Taxing, and Mayhem. Each of these contains 30 levels. New players should have a go at the Fun setting before tackling more challenging levels.

Obnoxious Copy Protection

RANT

Copy protection is offensive, and we're considering cooking up a big pot of pasta so we can engage in a wet noodle flogging of Psygnosis. In the case of Lemmings, accessing the game requires that you find a faintly printed picture of a lemming in some asinine pose somewhere in the manual, select the correct number from a list of 29 on each page, then type it in. Although the protection scheme is said to be random, we've found that we're asked for a code every single time we boot Lemmings. Now, of course pirating is a problem in the industry, but we don't want to go before a board of inquisition every time we get a hankering to play a game.

Best of All Platforms

The Mac version of the Lemmings duo has the best graphics and animation of any version. The four-channel music is fantastic, and there are nice touches like exploding lemmings shouting, "Oh, no!" only moments before little lemming bits are splattered all over the screen. The animation is smooth and fun, and both Lemmings games will run on all PowerBooks as well as most Macs.

GREAT FEATURE

Fun Game, Bad Copy Protection

The Lemmings games are challenging, colorful, easy-to-play puzzle/action games. The graphics and animation compel you to play just to see what will happen when the next lemming gets ground up in a trap or falls into a vat of acid. This is a prime example of a great game that's been cruelly marred by a copy protection scheme that punishes the humble user who forked over hard-earned cash for the product. Despite this major annoyance, Lemmings and Oh No! More Lemmings are destined to enjoy longevity in the computer gaming world. And we can hope that Psygnosis will find a different method of copy protection for future releases.

Pros: Great graphics, sound, and animation. Compelling, fun gameplay. Works well on all Macs. Blowing up Lemmings is fun.

Cons: Barbaric copy protection scheme. Codes necessary for saved games.

System Requirements: Mac Plus or better, 800K RAM, 704K hard disk space, System 6.05 or higher.

LEMMINGS OH NO! MORE LEMMINGS	
Fun factor	3.5
Look and feel	3.5
Value	4.0
Replayability	2.0
Overall	3.0

ClockWerx

Spectrum HoloByte

Many people will buy ClockWerx because Alexey Pajitnov has his mug slapped all over the front of the box. But as with BreakThru, if you read the caption next to the picture carefully, you'll notice that it says that Mr. Pajitnov *introduces* Clock-Werx. Heck, Alexey could introduce us to you but it doesn't mean that he had anything to do with our creation (although we'll ask our mothers just to be sure).

ClockWerx was around long before Alexey got into the introduction racket. In its first incarnation, ClockWerx was known as Spin Doctor and was created by Callisto. (Spin Doctor may now be bundled with certain Apple products. Keep

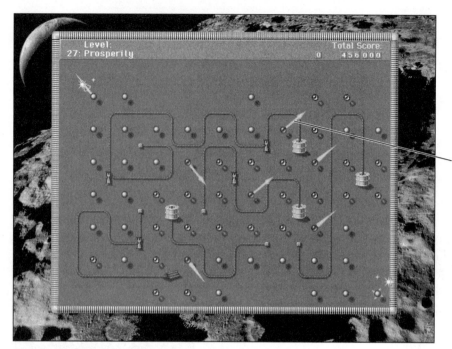

Clock hand

"Time keeps on slippin', slippin', slippin' into the future." Would that it were so easy or inevitable in ClockWerx.

your eyes peeled.) Spectrum HoloByte took Spin Doctor and added a clock theme, some extra bonuses and baddies, and a two-player challenge mode.

Doctoring Spin Doctor

The ClockWerx playfield is made up of a number of dots. You control a spinning clock hand that you must move around the field until you reach the Goal Dot. Along the way, you'll encounter such goodies as bonus dots and hourglass tokens that can add to your score as well as such deadly items as opposing clock hands, exploding spikes, and oil and acid droplets.

You are provided with just four controls: Swing, Bounce, Flip, and Reverse. Swinging and flipping cause your clock hand to attach itself to the dot nearest the hand's rotation. You can only move from dot to dot. When you hit the swing button, the hand continues in the same direction in which it was previously traveling—imagine a gymnast performing a series of handsprings with each contact point representing one of the dots. Flipping sends the hand in the direction opposite the one in which it was traveling—over, under, over, under. Bouncing causes the hand to stay put but to reverse directions once it comes in contact with the next dot. Reverse is like bouncing except that the hand immediately changes direction rather than waiting for the next dot.

You'd think that a game with such rudimentary controls would be a walk-over, but that's not the case. Because you're constantly changing directions and rotation, it's very easy to get confused. Throw in the pressure of a rapidly approaching acid drop, and things can get quite hairy.

Learning to Flip

Most good brain games begin with simple levels that provide safe training grounds and then gradually progress to more challenging situations. Recognizing that mastering the controls is the key to this game, its designers created one of the best online tutorials in the Macintosh gaming world. As you begin the game, the first few levels are annotated to tell you exactly what each object is and how to deal with it. ClockWerx also contains an excellent Help menu. It's so good, in fact, that you should never have to open the manual except to answer the one-time copy protection question.

GREAT FEATURE

Whether or not Alexey Pajitnov did more than glance at this game and sign a model's release during his lunch break is irrelevant. ClockWerx is a tremendous brain game that will provide you with weeks of enjoyment. Joyous huzzahs to Spectrum HoloByte for adding some terrific enhancements and bringing this game to a wider audience.

Pros: Simple controls. Great interface. Very challenging.

Cons: Music won't play with RAM Doubler or virtual memory switched on. Requires a 16-grayscale or 256-color display and so won't run on some PowerBooks.

System Requirements: 256-color or 16-grayscale monitor, 25MHz-68030 processor or better, CD-ROM drive, 4MB RAM without music, 5MB RAM with music, 5MB hard disk space, System 7 or later.

CLOCKWERX	
Fun factor	4.5
Look and feel	4.5
Value	4.5
Replayability	4.0
Overall	4.5

7 } Maxis

Hold on a durned minute, you're probably thinking, why does a single software company merit an entire chapter in this book? Bungie doesn't get a chapter, and they make cool stuff. Graphic Simulations and ParSoft produce great flight sims, yet they're confined to a couple of reviews. And Rand and Robyn Miller get a single lousy interview? What's the deal?

As one-time President and lifelong country music aficionado George Bush might have put it, Maxis has earned this honor because of "the vision thing." Name one other software company that, when you mention its name, users immediately know the kind of product they'll be getting (insert your own derisive Microsoft crack here). Whether it's SimCity, SimAnt, A-Train, SimTown, or El-Fish, Maxis products have a common thread: They are based on construction rather than destruction, and for the most part, they are open-ended—even when you've attained the highest rewards the simulation has to offer, there's always something left to tinker with.

~~~~~~

SIMply Empowering

Underlying each SimWhatever is the power to take a complex active system—whether it's city planning, crop rotation, or the component parts of life itself—and make it your own. That's right. Your town. Your ant colony. Your high-rise. This is pretty empowering stuff, and it goes beyond mere entertainment. If these simulations weren't so engrossing, we might suspect a hidden educational intent.

All Maxis simulations are remarkable to one degree or another. Sure we have our favorites, and there are also those that don't exactly ring our bells (Bart says, "Yeah, like A-Train!" and Chris says, "Oh, shut up"). Regardless, each one offers the rich reward of providing the player with absolute control over a load of electronic creatures who have no power to retaliate. These things are a megalomaniac's dream come true.

So sit down and prepare to play many roles—mayor, farmer, landlord, engineer, ant, God. Maxis provides you with the tools necessary to fill these job descriptions. All you have to do is prove that you're up to the challenge.

History

Back in 1984, a contract programmer for Brøderbund named Will Wright started work on his next game. Intended for the Commodore 64, this project would be a departure for Wright—no blowing up munitions bases with a helicopter as in his earlier Nintendo game, Raid on Bungeling Bay. This game would promote building rather than destroying. Its name was SimCity.

When Wright submitted the completed SimCity to Brøderbund, the company was unable to find a place for it in its lineup and passed on the game. Undaunted, Wright filed SimCity away and began work on another Brøderbund project.

Meanwhile (actually, a little later on), Jeff Braun was thinking seriously about entering the computer game publishing business. A nonprogramming, self-described computer nerd, Braun was interested in producing games for adults that went beyond the typical shoot-'em-up fare that was so popular with teenagers. The main hurdle he saw was finding people to create the games.

Always an innovative thinker, Braun and a colleague who was also looking for technical talent used the old pizza-beer-and-computer-games-party gambit to draw in techies from around the San Francisco Bay Area. During one party,

WILL WRIGHT INTERVIEW

What's your programming background?

My first programming was in college around 1977 using FORTRAN and keypunch cards. I really didn't like it very much. Around 1980, I bought an Apple II Plus (a friend talked me into it) and started playing with it. I was instantly hooked. I taught myself to program it first in AppleSoft Basic, next in Apple Pascal, and later in 6502 assembler. The first game I bought was the first FS3 flight simulator with wireframe graphics. I thought it was so cool.

I bought a Commodore 64 when it first came out and decided I would attempt to write a game for it. My first game was on the C64; it was called Raid on Bungeling Bay. It was about 8,000 lines of assembly code and was published by Brøderbund Software. It did okay in the U.S. In Japan, it was one of the first U.S. games put on the 8-bit Nintendo and sold about 750,000 copies.

How did Maxis start and what was your role in its birth?

Here's the real story: Back around 1985, I was working on the first version of SimCity (on the C64) when I discovered that Brøderbund was actually a front for a secret government organization dedicated to ruling the world. Their plan was to brainwash our children with their games by embedding mimetic tags that would only be activated years later in another product—Carmen San Diego Rules the World

(due 1998). I withheld my discovery of the plot and decided I must thwart their evil plans. So when I met Jeff Braun—who is actually a benevolent alien from Barnard's Star sent to protect humanity from itself—we knew what we had to do. Our first step was to design a mimetic antibody to defeat the evil mimetic tag. Once we had that, we needed to distribute it as widely as possible—ideally to the same education-oriented audience that had experienced Carmen. So I redesigned SimCity with the antibody and we started Maxis to sell it. Fortunately, Brøderbund didn't suspect what we were up to, and we got them to sign us up as an affiliate label for our first few years. Otherwise we probably wouldn't have gotten Maxis off the ground.

What was your role in the other Sim games?

For SimEarth, SimAnt, and SimCity 2000, I was a codesigner and coprogrammer. I wrote about half the code and did about half the design (with Fred Haslam on SimEarth and SimCity 2000, and with Justin McCormick on SimAnt). On the other Sim games, I gave feedback to the designers, but I did no coding myself.

Maxis is famous for the constructive simulations that are largely based on your work. Could Maxis exist without you or Jeff?

Maxis could exist at this point based on inertia, but Jeff and I make it a point to keep pushing it into new directions to keep things fresh. Jeff and I have made a nice team through the years. We share much of the same vision, but our specific interests and talents don't overlap very much. He enjoys business, and I enjoy technology. We both like to play games. He builds the company, and I work on the products. Jeff loves to interact with people—which I find rather tiring at times. I prefer to build and interact with mechanisms.

Are you and Maxis so tied to the SimX idea that it would be impossible for you to produce another kind of game?

We are looking to branch out soon into other areas. We brought on a new group recently (SimLabs) which, despite the name, will be doing some very non-Sim titles for us. The group is headed by Ihor Wolosenko, who was the founder of Synapse Software back in the early '80s. Ihor is a tremendously creative individual, and I really enjoy working with him.

Some years ago, you created a simulation for Chevron. Do you see Maxis creating more simulations for industry?

We tried that for a few years, and it didn't

quite work out for us. The problem is that when you start dealing with industries like that, you end up spending more time negotiating contracts than developing software. And as it turns out, the return for your investment is much lower than you would get in the entertainment industry. It was an interesting learning experience though. We ended up spinning that group off into a new company called Thinking Tools.

Maxis seems to take customer suggestions to heart. Do you consider the customer/user base a primary source of new ideas and inspiration?

Yes. I'm on the networks almost every night reading user comments and suggestions. After SimCity came out, I kept a box in my office of all the letters with SimCity suggestions. I read them all before starting on the design for SimCity 2000. The tricky part is to decide how to distill the thousands of suggestions into a fun game. It's not just a matter of piling in all the features that the players ask for. There's an old Japanese saying: "Your garden is not complete until there is nothing else that you can remove." I think this applies nicely to games also.

Braun met Wright and convinced the reluctant programmer to show him the nearly forgotten SimCity. Braun was more than a little impressed with what he saw. He and Wright formed a partnership and spent the next two years at Maxis headquarters—an apartment in Moraga, California—creating versions of SimCity for the Mac and PC. After it was released, sales were slow until *Time* magazine ran a full-page article on the game. With the publication of that article, sales of SimCity skyrocketed and Maxis took its first giant step toward becoming the SimEmpire we know and love today.

SimCity Classic

This is it—Will Wright's first system simulation, released by Maxis in 1989. Surely you're familiar with it. No? Okay, here's the short story: You take on the role of a mayor and city planner who designs, builds, and maintains an ever-expanding metropolis. In order to succeed, you must provide jobs, housing, transportation, electricity, and a degree of stability in regards to crime, fire protection, pollution, and traffic. When you have a moment, you'll also need to take on taxation and budgeting chores. And just to keep you on your toes, a number of random disasters occur to test how solid your design really is.

I'm Looking Over a Tan Bulldozer

Compared to the whizzy 3D interfaces of later Maxis products such as A-Train and SimCity 2000, SimCity Classic looks positively remedial. Rather than the rich colors used in these later sims, all objects in SimCity are represented via a more basic palette, and your view is from a 2D vantage directly over the city.

The main edit window, where the serious work takes place, contains a menu bar that sports all the tools you'll need to lay down industrial, commercial, and residential zones as well as police and fire stations, power plants, parks, roads, rail lines, electrical lines, seaports, and airports. The Map window shows an overview of the entire area and carries a set of tools that provide a graphic glimpse of where such things as wealth, pollution, and crime are concentrated. Using these tools, you can readily determine where your money and resources are most needed. For further evidence of your success or failure, bring up the Evaluation window, which indicates just how tickled or terrorized your citizens are by your ministrations.

Sim-ple Beginnings

The game begins with a barren landscape. You can choose to take the first landscape offered or generate one that's more to your liking. Once the landscape is firmly in place, select from a beginning budget of $20,000, $10,000, or $5,000—the lower the amount, the greater the game's difficulty.

The first thing your citizens need is power, and they don't much care that it's generated by a smelly coal-burning plant (though they'll certainly have opinions later). Next they'll need jobs and little homes to call their own; in the early

SIMCITY CD-ROM

SimCity Classic, SimCity 2000, SimCity Enhanced CD-ROM. … Anyone cruising the aisles of their local software dealer is likely to be confused about exactly which version of SimCity is which. Let the confusion end here.

SimCity 2000 is the new and improved version of the original game. The SimCity CD-ROM is SimCity Classic with better color graphics, voice-annotated tools, and a passel of QuickTime movies showing clips of such things as complaining city workers, news footage of the game's various disasters, and occasional peeks into the lives of the citizenry.

We love SimCity Classic and SimCity 2000 but are less enthusiastic about the SimCity Enhanced CD-ROM. Don't get us wrong; at first the movies and sound are tons o' fun—the opening sequence in particular is marvelous—but after a very short time we questioned whether all the glitzy add-ons really enhanced the game in a significant way. After all, our eyesight is still pretty keen and we really don't need someone telling us for the umpteenth time that we've selected the Road tool. And although the movies are cute the first couple of times around, we grew weary of the reruns.

We recommend that before buying the CD-ROM version of the game, you pick up copies of SimCity Classic and SimCity 2000. If after playing these two wonderful simulations you still hunger for more SimCity, toddle on down to your local dealer and demo a copy of the SimCity Enhanced CD-ROM.

stages of the simulation, this means industrial and residential zones. Of course, the Sims have to get to work, and they'll expect you to lay down a road or two as well.

As time passes and your city grows, the Sims will also demand such things as police protection, a seaport, an airport, and a stadium. It seems the greedy little things never stop their whining. Eventually they also get fed up with the polluting factories and congested roads they screamed for earlier and expect you to balance commercial and environmental considerations and add public transportation. Of course, you've got to pay for all the goodies. But be careful; the Sims hate being taxed and will move out of town if they think you're being too greedy.

For the Goal-Oriented

Recognizing that there are some people who expect games to have an ending, Maxis includes a scenarios file with SimCity. These scenarios include such disasters as the 1906 San Francisco earthquake, a nuclear meltdown in a Boston of the future, and the infamous 1956 Godzilla attack on Tokyo. Your job is to handle the disasters as they take place and then rebuild the city within the allotted time.

But Who Needs Classic When You Can Have 2000?

Given that SimCity 2000 improves greatly on the original simulation, why purchase the classic? We'll give you three reasons: 1. If you have an older Macintosh (we mean Mac Plus through IIcx), SimCity 2000 will either not run on your machine or will run so slowly that it's hardly worth playing. 2. SimCity Classic runs in black and white and doesn't take up much hard disk space or memory and is therefore ideal for PowerBooks. 3. Most importantly, SimCity Classic has an elegant simplicity. As much as we like SimCity 2000, we sometimes long for less complicated pleasures. With SimCity Classic, you can implement a couple of changes, sit back, and directly observe the effect your actions have had on the simulation. We're not sure this beats a cool 3D interface or fusion reactors, but in its own way, it's quite a treat.

KEYS TO THE CITY

Behind the scenes, SimCity uses a model based on something called cellular automata. Here's the general idea of how it applies to the game: SimCity is broken up into tiles. The tiles are programmed to contain a set of rules and conditions under which they operate. A police station, for example, requires funding and electricity to work properly, and when these conditions are met, it emanates a web of protection to nearby tiles.

Tiles respond not only according to current conditions but also to the tiles around them. If a police station is placed next to a residential property that has deteriorated due to high crime (which may be due to low property values based on pollution and traffic congestion), the residential tile reacts to the police station's influence, and the residential property is upgraded. This change ripples through the entire city and can alter the community's concerns about the overall effect of crime. At the same time, the Police Station reacts to the crime rate of the neighborhood, and its influence changes depending on the pull of those conditions.

This is the simulation at its most basic level. We have been assured that there are all kinds of other processes taking place among nonadjacent tiles. But because we're just a couple of jamokes who set out to write a book about computer games, we'll take this on faith and move on. This stuff is way over our heads.

TIP

Tip

• Type FUND to receive an extra $10,000.

Pros: Urban planning can be fun! Great for low-powered Macs and PowerBooks.

Cons: Get back to us; we're thinking about it.

System Requirements: Mac Plus or better, 1MB RAM for black and white, 2MB RAM for color, 1.5MB hard disk space, System 6.02 or higher.

SIMCITY CLASSIC	
Fun factor:	4.5
Look and feel:	4.0
Value:	4.0
Replayability:	4.0
Overall:	4.0

CD

SimCity 2000

It's amazing what a difference four years can make. Oh sure, it doesn't seem that long, but think of the effect four years has on a high school student: in as a quivering freshman and out as a self-actualized senior. But nowhere did four years bring about such a dramatic change as it did in SimCity. What began as a simple little city simulation with a 16-color, 2D interface blossomed into a not-quite-so simple big city simulation with a stunning, 3D, 256-color interface.

Ch-ch-ch-changes

In SimCity 2000, along with visual enhancements, you'll discover a Terrain Editor (including controls for adjusting altitude); a new set of scenarios; subway and water systems; libraries, zoos, and prisons; huge human beehives called arcologies; alternative power systems; the ability to issue city bonds; on-screen advisors; and a number of savory little rewards for the successful mayor. Whew! The folks at Maxis were busy in the interim.

GREAT FEATURE

In addition, you now have more flexibility when placing zones. In the original version, zones were quite large and a little unwieldy. SimCity 2000 has wisely dropped these large blocks and instead allows you to place much smaller zones (one-ninth the size of the originals, if you must know). You can now, for instance, place residential zones along an uneven coastline.

Another cool feature is the ability to encourage or discourage certain industries in your metropolis by raising and lowering tax rates. For the sake of argument, let's say that you've been carrying a grudge against a particular oil company for an oil spill in a state well north and west of Canada. If you'd like to get that tiger out of your city's tank, simply open the City Industry window and jerk the tax rate on the petrochemical industry up to a whopping 20%. Just watch those plants shut down and those unemployment numbers rise!

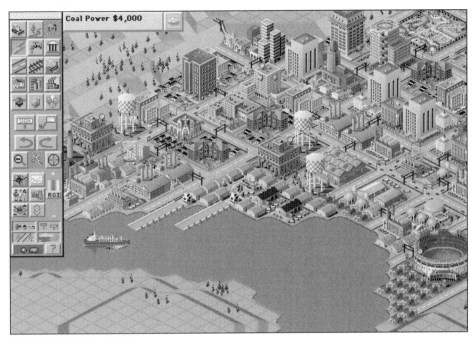

Looks like your ship is just about to come in. Maxis's SimCity 2000 is beautiful to behold.

Tough Urban Decisions

These additional features add complexity to the situations you will find yourself trying to resolve. For example, the road-versus-public transportation decision now includes the thorny issue of location. If rail and subway stations aren't conveniently placed, the citizens boycott the system. Or consider libraries: Without enough public libraries, your Sims dumb down once released from school. The result is that the intellectual pool of your city is not sufficiently deep to attract high-tech industries.

You also face the military base dilemma. Once your population reaches 60,000, you are offered a military base. The military brings cash to your community and helps protect you in case of alien attack—yes, there's a monster that sometimes rains fire, trees, or windmills down on your town—but bases also increase traffic problems and cause the crime rate to climb. It's a dilemma, to be sure.

A Demanding Process

We've barely scratched the surface of the wonderful new treats contained in the latest incarnation of SimCity. Suffice it to say that this is a complex simulation that should keep you fiddling and tinkering for months on end. But be warned: Those of you with slower Macs may find yourselves mucking with the simulation just to make it playable. SimCity 2000 demands a lot of oomph from your

DANGER

processor and if you're running something less peppy than a 68040, you may experience sluggish performance. If this is the case, we suggest you turn off the music (which we're not wild about anyway) and sound effects, and make the edit window as small as is manageable. After making these changes, you should notice a modest boost in speed.

One other little nit we'd like to pick is the lack of an Undo command. Although the interface is beautiful, the grid's angle makes it difficult to determine exactly where you're clicking. When using the bulldozer, for example, it's not uncommon to miss the square you're after and instead pulverize that expensive college you just laid down. We'd really like to be able to correct these little mouse miscalculations with quick taps of the Command and Z keys, but alas, it is impossible. We hope that SimCity 3000—should there be such a product—addresses this problem.

Our Demands Are Met

But enough griping. SimCity 2000 is a beautiful, challenging, and entertaining update to a program that was a winner to begin with. If you've got the processing power to push this sim around—or own a slower Mac and are a patient sort—we unhesitatingly suggest that you pick up a copy. It's Sim-ply marvelous.

TIP

Tips

• In version 1.0 of the game, type PORNTIPSGUZZARDO to get an extra cash reward.

• To earn the same reward in version 1.1, bring the Map window to the front, type PIRN, click on the floating Status window, and then type TOPSGUZZARDO.

• At the beginning of a new city, type FUND. A window will appear asking if you'd like to take out a bond at 25% interest. Answer yes. Repeat this step, again answering yes. Now click on the $ icon in the menu bar, click the Open Book icon next to Bond Payments and click Issue Bond. A window will appear stating the decimal percentage of the current rate. Click the Yes button. You will now receive 1.5 million dollars a year for free for the rest of the game.

• If you use this last cheat, give the Sims a break and drop the tax rate down to zero. Watch your city take off!

• As with most Maxis sims, type JOKE for just that.

• Keep an eye out for Captain Hero and Nessie.

Pros: Urban planning can still be fun! Wonderfully rich graphics. New disasters.

Cons: Can run slowly on older Macs. No bulldoze undo.

System Requirements: 256-color monitor, LC or better, 4MB RAM, 5MB hard disk space, System 7.0 or later.

SIMCITY 2000	
Fun factor:	4.5
Look and feel:	4.5
Value:	4.5
Replayability:	4.5
Overall	4.5

SimTown

SimCity and SimCity 2000 are a couple of the best computer games ever magnetically encoded on floppy disks. Unfortunately, for a youngster whose chronometer hasn't yet reached double digits, they aren't exactly simple (no pun intended) games to play. In fact, between the two SimCity games, you could start a small library with the various books and FAQs available in bookstores and in cyberspace. Enter Maxis with the latest incarnation: SimTown, a graphically plush and intellectually scaled-down version of the games that spearheaded the sim genre. SimTown is aimed at kids aged 8 to 12 and is appropriately paced for this group both in complexity and intellectual challenge.

You almost need a Power Mac to make SimTown's very high-quality graphics flow.

Environmentali-sim

The goal of SimTown is to design and build a small town with cozy homes, fast food eateries, libraries, movie theaters, parks, and even haunted houses. Money is a nonissue, however, and the only restrictions to building with reckless abandon lie in the natural resources you have at your disposal. Cut down your forests to build a couple more office buildings and BANG! before you know it you're living on a veritable Easter Island with no timber resources and a bevy of giant stone heads lining the shore. The growth of the small municipality must always be balanced against the available resources of timber, crops, and water or you'll be faced with something of an eco-crisis. Trees can be replanted, however, and garbage recycled with the use of natural resource credits that you earn on a month-by-month basis. Like its parent program, SimTown has its share of disasters that can wreak mayhem on your suburb. These are called Eco-Villains and five come in such forms as Food Pigs and Litter Bugs, but they can be augmented by the triggering of a drought, earthquake, or fire. To keep on top of any problems, the Sims can be asked for their input, but the newspaper is the most reliable and concise source of information.

Happy, Happy Fun Day

GREAT FEATURE

The overall tone of SimTown is very upbeat and, well, happy. Even when the chips are down, there is an air of optimism about everything. Although this may be somewhat nauseating for adults, it certainly can't hurt the kids to hear constant positives in this age of media-induced negativism. The strength of Sim-Town lies in the rich graphics that can be zoomed up to show the fantastic detail each building has been endowed with: a Chinese restaurant shaped like a take-out box; haunted houses worthy of a place in *Psycho*; a television station complete with satellite dishes and call letters. Even the pedestrians are beautifully rendered and will make comments to you when clicked on. Users can have their very own Sims that they can dress in the ways they see fit and can list their likes and dislikes and even keep diaries for them. All of the controls in SimTown are accessed simply by clicking on the desired icons.

Molasses

LOUSY FEATURE

Although almost everything about this game works very well for children of this age group, the speed of gameplay does not. In fact, a Kasparov versus Deep Thought chess game seems like a roller coaster ride compared to SimTown on a 030 Mac. By the time you read this, however, version 1.1 should be out and will solve some of the speed problems. But we advise that you have at least a 040 Mac or a Power Mac before you venture into SimTown.

Pros: Easy to learn. Great graphics. Appropriate for age group.

Cons: Slow. Hardware intensive.

System Requirements: 256-color monitor, 25MHz-68030 processor or better, 4MB RAM, CD-ROM player and/or 21MB hard disk space, System 6.07 or higher.

SIMTOWN	
Fun factor:	3.0
Look and feel:	3.5
Value:	3.5
Replayability:	3.0
Overall:	3.0

SimEarth

In the beginning, Will Wright created the Sims and placed them in the City. The marketplace saw all that Maxis had made and proclaimed that it was good. And although Will had finished the work he had been doing, he did not rest. "Bigger and better," he mused. "SimCounty? SimCongressionalDistrict? Sim-TimeZone?" Small thinking. "SimUniverse?" Too big to fit on a disk. "Hallelu-jah!" he shouted. "SimEarth!"

How on SimEarth?

Maxis's second simulation takes the player from the birth of an Earth-like plan-et, complete with the creation of an atmosphere and oceans, through the processes of evolution and civilization to the point of exodus, where intelligent life has developed the technology to spread its seed throughout the universe. You have only 10 billion years to accomplish this task before your sun becomes a red giant and gives all life a terminal tan.

Once your world is formed, you have the power to alter many developments. You control such forces as continental drift, solar input, and reproduction and mutation rates. As supreme being, you can also trigger natural disasters, includ-ing earthquakes and meteor strikes. Once life has begun with the humble prokaryote (a single-celled microbe), you may place any of 14 life forms ranging from these microscopic cooties to mammals on your planet. It's possible that humans will not emerge as the dominant species and that your orb will be ruled by amphibians or cockroaches.

Learning Through Play

As with many of the other Maxis simulations, the small changes you implement have larger repercussions. Based on James Lovelock's Gaia hypothesis, SimEarth views the earth's varied systems as a self-regulating whole. So, for example, if you throw enough carbon dioxide into the atmosphere through the burning of fossil fuels, you're likely to see a change in air temperature and quality that will adversely affect your life forms.

Like SimCity, SimEarth also comes with an assortment of preset scenarios. The challenges you face include creating a land-based civilization in a completely water-covered world, bringing your planet out of its stone age, and helping it survive such modern-day problems as famine, global warming, and nuclear proliferation. If you prefer to work off-planet, you can also attempt to terraform the hostile environs of Mars and Venus.

Down to Earth

The program's creators have thrown in a number of gimmicks and graphics to spice up what could otherwise be a dry enterprise. Do you secretly fear insects? Fine, wield the extinction tool and wipe 'em out! While we appreciate these extra touches, we still found SimEarth to be less rollicking fun than its predecessor, SimCity. If you're looking for a little light entertainment, SimEarth may not be your cup of decaf latté. But if you're seeking a greater understanding and deeper appreciation of your home sweet home, SimEarth may be just the ticket.

MAXIS MANUALS

They say the true test of great Macintosh software is whether or not you never need to open the manual. While we generally agree with this statement, there are those rare occasions when the manual is so informative and so cleverly written that it shouldn't be missed. Maxis manuals fall into this category.

You don't need to be a writer to appreciate the brilliance that Michael Bremer and Tom Bentley bring to the Maxis documentation. Some of these simulations are extremely complex, yet Michael and Tom's prose is always clear and chock-full of fascinating facts and humor. If we may be so bold, we think the manuals are nearly as entertaining as the software.

If you purchase a Maxis product, we command you to RTFM (read the friggin' manual), if not for the valuable information it contains, then for your own enjoyment.

Pros: Great earth science tool. Rare opportunity to play God.

Cons: Not a lot of laughs.

System Requirements: Mac Plus or better, 1MB RAM for black and white, 2MB RAM for color, 1.5MB hard disk space, System 6.02 or higher.

SIMEARTH	
Fun factor:	4.0
Look and feel:	4.0
Value:	4.0
Replayability:	4.0
Overall:	4.0

SimLife

SimLife is the flip side of the SimEarth coin. Both simulations deal with species survival and domination. But rather than working from the outside in—exploring the effects of environment on your life forms—as you do in SimEarth, you work from the inside out—playing with the genetic and behavioral functions of your resident plant and animal life in order for them to survive in a given environment.

In the Beginning

Because this is a Maxis toy, you get to play God. Your first act is to create a new world, complete with mountains, seas, and temperature and moisture zones. Your next likely steps are to strew a few life forms over the landscape, watch them struggle and die off in short order, and wonder what all the fuss was about. Even gods have their off days, and sometimes it takes a little forethought to create a functional ecosystem.

SimLife provides a number of tools for altering the geography of your world as well as the genetic makeup of its inhabitants. As deity, you have the power to manipulate such things as an animal's gender, life span, social patterns, diet, and size. Likewise, you decide the sex of your creature, whether it will grow on land or in water, and what conditions are optimal for its growth. Impatient deities willing to upset the delicate balance of the ecosystem can change their organisms' genetic structures on the fly. If you find, for instance, that your vegetarian stegavarks are having trouble making it in an arid climate with nothing to eat save cockaroos, you can turn them into desert-dwelling carnivores with a couple of clicks.

At the End

SimLife suffers from the same wonderful complexity as SimEarth. Don't expect fireworks. Your reward for putting together a self-sustaining world is the satisfaction of doing it. Although Maxis has attempted to inject some humor into the proceedings by supplying whimsical animals and a pun-filled manual, SimLife is a serious study. Users looking for sparkly lights and specific goals might find SimLife a bit dull. Were SimLife still being sold at its original list price of around $60, we doubt we'd send one and all rushing down to the software store to pick up a copy, but since it is now available for less than $25 and is included with the original SimCity and SimAnt in the SimClassics bundle, we think it's worth a look for anyone who has even a marginal interest in controlling the destiny of all life on Earth.

SIMLIFE	
Fun factor:	3.5
Look and feel:	4.0
Value:	4.5
Replayability:	4.0
Overall:	4.0

Pros: Very powerful and scholarly simulation. Another chance to play God.

Cons: Can be quite complicated. A little dry.

System Requirements: Mac SE or better, 2MB RAM for black and white, 2.5MB RAM for color, 2MB hard disk space, System 6.02 or higher.

A-Train

No, this is not a Duke Ellington Orchestra simulation or a toy train construction set. At first glance, A-Train might be mistaken for SimCity II. After all, both simulations focus on the successful development of a large city featuring residential, commercial, industrial, and recreational properties. But while SimCity places you in the position of a benevolent urban planner nurturing an uncongested, smogless utopia, A-Train asks you to become a financial mogul bent on the profitable and unregulated development of the surrounding countryside.

If A-Train has a spiritual cousin, it's Maxis's other Japanese import, SimTower. For both these simulations, transportation and scheduling are the unifying elements; elevators for SimTower, and, of course, trains for A-Train. Both games demand that your transportation systems be logically laid out so that the greatest amount of material (this also includes passengers) are moved with efficiency. Pull off these scheduling miracles and the world is your oyster. Fail and you're out of business.

Peering Down the Track

You open A-Train to a bird's-eye view of an Art Deco landscape featuring chugging trains hauling in building materials from an off-screen metropolis. Depending on the scenario you've chosen—A-Train contains six, ranging from

The A-Train chugs slowly around your metropolis.

the pastoral and easy New Town to the under-funded and difficult Multi-City Connection—your trains wend their ways through meadows, mountain ranges, and towering skyscrapers.

To earn enough lucre to win the simulation, you must first slap on your engineer's cap and design a viable railway system that delivers building materials to undeveloped locations and later brings passengers to live and work in your burg. After you've plunked down a few tracks and trains, you will become more involved in financial matters as you learn to route and schedule rail traffic, take on bank loans, flutter a few dollars on the stock market, and buy and sell properties.

From Across the Pacific

A-Train was created in Japan, and it has a different character than the home-grown Maxis simulations. It does not have the ecological bent other Maxis toys tend to have. And because wheeling and dealing properties is considered a crass way to make money in Japanese culture, you're taxed up the wazoo on capital gains profits (Monopoly must not be a big seller in Japan). Finally, bankruptcy is not the respectable institution that it is in American culture, and the game ends when you run out of cash.

Of course A-Train has the usual Maxis treats, and you won't feel out to sea with the simulation. Tables and graphs detail the success or failure of your railroad, properties, and investments. Players with color systems can watch their towns change from day to night and season to season. (Santa Claus even appears on December 24th!) And the latest version of the game includes the A-Train Construction Set, a set of tools for creating your own custom layouts.

LOUSY FEATURE

Unfortunately, the price you pay for these goodies is a slowdown in performance that suggests you're riding on a Zzzz train. We've heard that A-Train runs much more quickly under System 6.07. If you'd prefer not to buy a faster Mac just to play with this sim, you might want to give the ancient system software route a try. Once A-Train gets up steam, though, you should encounter enough challenges to keep you busy all the livelong day.

TIP

Tips

• If you have an older version of A-Train that doesn't contain the Construction Set, here's a way to hack scenario files with ResEdit to give you the big bux:

1. Open a saved game file with ResEdit (always work on a copy).
2. Open the SAms resource.
3. Open the ID 0 resource (it's the only resource in there).
4. Change the first eight digits in the first line to 02EBAE40 (those are zeros).
5. Save the file and quit ResEdit.

When you next open the scenario, you should have 49 million dollars.

• Stock dividends are paid out on July 1st. To sneak your way into the market, purchase stocks before midnight on June 30th, collect the dividends on the following day, and then sell the stocks.

Pros: Cool train/financial simulation. Who thought scheduling trains could be so fascinating?

Cons: S-L-O-W on older machines.

System Requirements: Mac Plus or better, 1MB RAM for black and white, 2MB RAM for color, 1.5MB hard disk space, System 6.05 or higher.

A-TRAIN	
Fun factor:	4.0
Look and feel:	4.0
Value:	4.0
Replayability:	4.0
Overall:	4.0

TAKING OR LEAVING THE A-TRAIN

Bart: Were you half asleep when you reviewed A-Train? You like this game?

Chris: Completely awake, and yeah, I like A-Train. What's your beef?

B: To begin with, you need to make a $10,000 investment just to get the darned thing to move faster than frozen molasses.

C: You're completely off the mark. I first played A-Train on a IIcx (okay, it was an accelerated cx), but it moved along fast enough. Plus it's not as if there isn't plenty to keep you occupied while your trains are chugging around the track.

B: I first ran A-Train on an LC III, running System 7. What a joke! I was able to read the entire manual during the first turn. And what's with System 7 performance anyway? It runs twice as fast under System 6! You shouldn't have to change your operating system for a game, for crying out loud!

C: Easy on the exclamation marks. Okay, so it's slow on older machines. But I don't think it's fair to ask game companies to dumb down their games just for slower machines. What about the folks who bought the high-priced stuff? Aren't they entitled to play games that are more complex and that take advantage of that power?

B: I contend that A-Train is unusually slow for what the game is. A properly coded game should run faster.

C: Properly coded!? So then SimCity 2000 isn't properly coded? Myst isn't properly coded? Marathon isn't properly coded? Code's got nothing to do with it. Richer graphics and complex processes demand more horse power.

B: Also, I found A-Train harder to learn than it should have been. Picking it up and tinkering didn't work. I read the manual and I still didn't get it. Any game that takes this much effort to learn is destined for a small dedicated audience.

C: Which would explain why the game only sold a trillion and six copies in Japan. Look, there's nothing wrong with a game being demanding. Sure, A-Train is complex, and not everyone is going to think that running trains efficiently is as much fun as gunning down Venutian Xkclaxarzoids, but don't discount a game simply because it's hard. Some people enjoy thinking while they play. I say that A-Train is extremely stimulating when run on a fast Mac.

B: And I think A-Train is one slow and overly complicated mode of transportation.

SimTower

Here's SimTower in a nutshell: Build a very tall building full of offices, eateries, hotel rooms, shops, and condos, and make the elevators operate well enough so the tenants don't get fed up with you and your building and take their pixelated lives (and cash) elsewhere. Simple enough, yes?

Simple enough, no. Things aren't too bad in the early stages of the simulation. You're given two million bucks to start building your little paradise in the sky. Just grab the lobby tool and lay down floor one. Now add a couple of fast food joints on the next floor, a level of offices above that, and stairs to connect the whole mess. Sure enough, little white-collar drones flock to the building, put down their tiny briefcases, and rent your brand-spanking-new offices. A few days pass and money starts flowing in from office rents and food receipts. Naturally you'll want to use this money to make your tower bigger and better.

As you add more floors and exceed 300 tenants, your tower moves from a measly one-star rating to a grand and exalted two stars. To continue on through all five stars to the coveted Tower rating, your building must rise to a height of 100 floors and operate at something near peak performance. If you haven't guessed, the peak performance aspect of the simulation is the rub.

Once you get past a handful of floors, you've got to start including elevators—your tenants have a limited interest in developing their calf muscles. At first, a couple of elevator shafts and cars are plenty to keep the natives happy. But as you add floors and thus attract more people to your building, you'll notice your once-happy tenants starting to turn first a shade of gray, then pink, and finally corpuscle red as they queue up for the now inadequate elevators. Red tenants are unhappy tenants, and unless you end these long lines, they will move out and take their little wallets stuffed with the evergreen with them. And you know what that means: no cash, no construction.

So it's time to face the elevator music of this simulation: scheduling.

Be still my beating heart.

Boom Shacka-Laka-Laka

In addition to scheduling elevators and adding to your vertical empire, you also control such things as office rents, condo prices, the placement of security and cleaning personnel, and how often the movie theaters change films. For the most part, these are simple tasks and rarely detract from your main job of moving bodies efficiently around the building.

Cool three-story lobby and spiral staircase, eh? For your SimTower to have them, you have to know the trick.

To find out how you're doing, pull up the Map window, which details which tenants in the building are happy, complacent, or completely ticked off with your little operation. Tenant complaints appear in an information box and include noisy neighbors, high rents, poor location, and unclean hotel rooms. Some tenants are generally unhappy with conditions but refuse to explain their discontent. You can identify these folk by their high stress levels. To check these levels, simply click the magnifying glass tool on one of the figures in a room. If the meter reads blue, everything is hunky-dory. If yellow, then they are fair to middlin'. Red and they're ready to move right out. You can track these malcontents and any other tenants by double-clicking on them and assigning names to them.

Tower of Power

SimTower contains some of the most intriguing parts of two other Maxis products: the scheduling component of A-Train and the please-us-or-we-split attitude of SimCity. And as a hybrid it works fairly well. The graphics are great, and the background sounds take at least ten minutes before they really get on your nerves (yes, you can turn them off). SimTower is more goal-oriented than either of the other sims and a little less complicated—and for people who find other Maxis toys too open-ended and convoluted, this may make SimTower more attractive.

LOUSY FEATURE

But there are also some glaring problems. To begin with, the simulation runs very slowly once you exceed a handful of floors. The only way around this is to turn off all animation and sound and make your edit window as small as possible. This hardly makes for an optimal playing environment.

For another thing, except for lobbies, you have to lay down each unit individually. This is fine in the early floors, where you're just placing an office or two. But when you want to smear in five floors of hotel rooms, you can't do it in a single stroke. We also don't care for the way condominiums are handled. Once in place, tenants move in so quickly that oftentimes you can't adjust sale prices. And when these same tenants become righteously indignant about their neighbors, it's impossible to appease them by lowering the costs of their units. Instead you have to wait until they're so fed up that they move out before you can adjust pricing for the next tenants—provided that you notice when the units are empty and get to them in time. Finally, because the game is so goal-oriented, we think that SimTower is less replayable than the other Maxis products—when you've successfully built one tower, we can't imagine that you'd rush to do it all over again.

These problems, particularly the sim's lack of get-up-and-go, may be annoying enough to keep SimTower from making a Maxis fanatic's top five list—it surely won't make ours before a Power Mac native version is released. And that's a darned shame, because without the interminable waits, SimTower is more fun than a game about elevator scheduling has a right to be.

TIP

Tips

• To generate some quick cash at the very beginning of the game, choose the Lobby tool, scroll to the very bottom left corner of the edit window—that's right, down in the dirt—and click. You'll be rewarded with an extra two million smackers.

• To add a three-story lobby at the beginning of the game, hold down Option-Shift while placing the first floor. Add a staircase to get a completely awesome spiral staircase. But don't go too wild at first—these larger lobbies are expensive.

• In version 1.1 of SimTower, you cannot invoke the extra cash cheat as well as the three-story lobby cheat. It's one or the other.

• If you want to quickly replace one unit with another, skip the Bulldozer tool and instead hold down the Shift key when laying in the new unit. The old unit will be destroyed and the new one put in its place.

• If you want to add soundproofing to such noisy units as ballrooms and movie theaters, don't place adjoining units right next to them. Instead, allow a little extra space. That gray material absorbs some of the noise.

Pros: Great graphics and animation. Option to track as many as 65,000 tenants. Less open-ended than other Maxis sims.

Cons: Unit placement could be more flexible. Less open-ended than other Maxis sims. Glacially slow once things get going.

System Requirements: 256-color monitor, 68030 or better, 4MB RAM, 4MB hard disk space, System 6.02 or higher.

SIMTOWER	
Fun factor:	3.5
Look and feel:	3.0
Value:	3.5
Replayability:	2.5
Overall:	3.0

SimAnt

"I got ants in my pants and I wanna dance!"

These famous words from James Brown, other than having the word "ants" in them, have absolutely nothing to do with this review of SimAnt. But in order for us to put James Brown's name in the index (we're after extreme hiptitude here), we had to slip a reference in somewhere. Now that we've finished with that little piece of business, let's get on with the review.

Not About James Brown

Billed as the Electric Ant Colony, SimAnt is all that and more. You are born as a working class member of a small colony of black ants. You have such responsibilities as foraging for food; expanding the nest for the ever-growing supply of eggs; defending your home from invaders; overrunning the nests of the evil red ants; and avoiding the champing jaws of spiders and ant lions, as well as the mincing blades of a rotary lawnmower. Oh, and you should try to have a little fun along the way.

SimAnt takes place in an innocent looking suburban backyard. Ostensibly, your goal is to gather your six-legged buddies around you and kill the red ants' queen. If you perform this task successfully for the 50 different quadrants that make up the yard and house, you drive the human residents from their home and win the

DECISIONS, DECISIONS

Okay, you caught us. We like most everything that Maxis makes, but how does this help you, the confused software shopper who's surreptitiously reading this in the book aisle of the local Electronics Emporium in the hope that we'll direct you to the very best Maxis sim? We really shouldn't be doing this—we're saving our buying advice for paying readers—but we'll give you a break this one time. (This selfless gesture alone should convince you to buy the book.) Here now is Chris and Bart's Maxis Top Five Games list:

Chris	Bart
1. SimCity 2000	**1.** SimCity 2000
2. SimCity Classic	**2.** SimCity Classic
3. SimEarth	**3.** RoboSport
4. A-Train	**4.** SimAnt
5. Widget Workshop	**5.** SimEarth

Of course, our choices are purely subjective and are not based on the same criteria for each product. For example, we agree that although SimCity 2000 is a great city planning tool, it's mostly a lot of fun to play with. SimEarth, on the other hand, isn't exactly a laugh riot, but it does contain a marvelous educational component. We'd like SimTower a lot more if it ran more quickly. As our networking expert, Bart loves RoboSport's head-to-head capabilities and thinks SimAnt is just a kick in the pants. You know where we each stand on A-Train.

game. It's likely that you'll lose sight of this goal as you spend more and more time learning about the particular foibles of ants and less and less time devising offensive and defensive strategies.

Your Ant Comes to Visit

SimAnt's interface is typical of a Maxis simulation. The Map window displays the big picture and details the location of the red nest, food, spiders, and the odd caterpillar. And the edit window gives you a closer view of the action where tasks such as foraging for food, building defenses, digging tunnels, and recruiting troops are performed. To move your ant around this window, simply place your cursor on the ultimate destination and click.

The simulation can be played in four modes: Tutorial, Quick Game, Full Game, and Experimental. Tutorial is a fine run through of the basic components of the simulation. Quick Game and Full Game are the goal-oriented modes—you're out to get the red guys at any cost. And Experimental is where you really get your antennae wet: You can try any stupid ant trick you like—including laying down alarm scents or dousing the area with insecticide—without incurring the guilt of killing real living creatures.

This isn't Your Father's Ant Farm

Myrmecology (the study of ants) is never far from the surface of this simulation. Even with its obvious game elements, SimAnt is one of Maxis's most science-oriented products. The manual is a veritable encyclopedia of ant-cillary information, and in order to do well in your battles with the red hordes, you really have to get your entomological chops down.

SimAnt is frighteningly well done, so much so that if you have an aversion to insects—and we weren't aware that we did until we started spending time with this thing—it could creep you out over time. The ants are that real. Our only other problem with the sim is that there's no included auto-feed option. We'd like to be able to switch into Experimental mode, run our ant farm over the long term in the background, and check on it from time to time. Unfortunately, the ants have to be fed so often that you can't leave them to their own devices for long before they starve to death.

If you don't mind the convincing illusion that your Macintosh is full of crawly critters and you think having the ultimate ant farm is just about the coolest thing anyone could aspire to, you'll love SimAnt. If you're not convinced but know a bargain when you see one, take a look at SimClassics, which includes SimAnt, SimCity Classic, and SimLife. Over time you may find that you're just buggy about this sim.

Tips

• Press the Mystery button. All kinds of cool things happen.

• The spider isn't terribly bright. If it's nearby, hide behind a rock.

TIP

Pros: Buggy software that doesn't crash. Realistic animation.

Cons: Have to keep the little buggers fed.

System Requirements: Mac Plus or better, 1MB RAM for black and white, 2MB RAM for color, 1.5MB hard disk space, System 6.02 or higher.

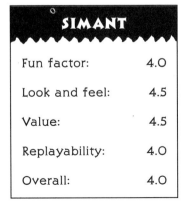

SIMANT	
Fun factor:	4.0
Look and feel:	4.5
Value:	4.5
Replayability:	4.0
Overall:	4.0

SimFarm

At one time or another, every suburban gardener leans on a hoe, wipes the sweat from his or her brow, and while gazing over tiny plots of tomatoes and green beans, thinks, "Ah, to be a farmer. Living off God's green earth. Now that would be the life!" If ever there was an argument that this kind of thinking is completely fatheaded, that argument is SimFarm. If we were to paraphrase this simulation in song, it might go something like this:

Old McMaxis had a farm,
E-I-E-I-O
And on this farm there were some weeds and bugs and fungus and infertile soil,
E-I-E-I-O
With a spray, spray here,
And a spray, spray there,
And a spray, spray over there too,
And while we're at it, a spray, spray, spray next to that fence,
And, oh what the hay, let's douse the whole darned farm with spray,
E-I-E-I-O.

Yes, according to SimFarm's almanac, the successful farmer will spend most of the time applying one form of chemical or another to the soil when not busy selling off diseased pigs or rusty farm machinery. "Keep Manhattan, just give me that countryside" indeed.

A Tough Row to Hoe

You begin your SimFarm with $40,000, a farmhouse, and a plot of land studded with rocks and trees. Your first chore is to grab the Bulldozer tool and remove any objects that might interfere with your crops. Once the field is clear, it's time to take your little nest egg and tool down to the John Deere dealership where you'll purchase a tractor, planter, sprayer, harvester, trailer, and truck (you could lease 'em, but in the long run it's a losing strategy). Toss these items in a bag and head over to the True Value Shack and Tobacc' outlet for your small silo and large and small sheds. Chuck these babies into the back of the truck and skedaddle on home so you can park all your new toys in the sheds before the rain starts falling and rusts them three ways to Sunday.

Now you'll need to select a crop and put it in the ground. Just pick a crop from the pull-down menu and plop it somewhere on your property. Good. But wait a gol-darned minute! What's that Wave icon next to your Crop icon? Well shoot, it looks like your field is flooded. Guess it's time to put in an irrigation ditch to drain off that excess water. There, that's better. But hold on, Nelly! Now there's

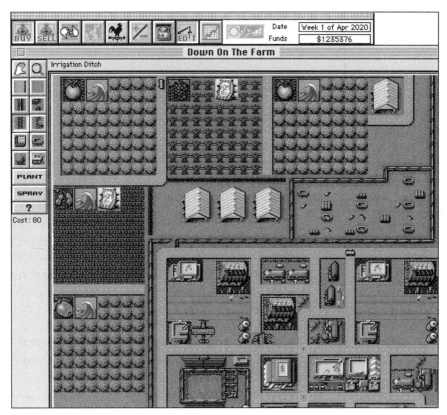

Down on the SimFarm, it appears that your grapes and goobers need another spraying. So what else is new?

a Wiggly Worm icon! Whoops, you've got some kind of bug infestation and it's time to start working that sprayer.

The crop seems to have finally stabilized, so what say you purchase an extra plot of land and toss some pigs onto it. Oh, and don't forget to feed and water those little oinkers or, sure as shootin', they'll break down that fence and eat up all your crops. You say they're looking a might peaked? Better take the loss and sell 'em off, you're working on some mighty lean bacon.

Ah, the crop is finally ready for harvest. Here's your chance to make back some of that money. Out come the harvester and trailer to pick the fruits of your labor and—Land o' Goshen!—these dag-nabbed spuds are fulla worms and worth squat in the market! You're nearly out of cash, and how are you supposed to make it with a silo full of rotten tubers?

Well, you could always visit the bank for a loan; try again with a different crop; install a complete irrigation system; look into the futures market; or pray for rain.

No Garden of Eden

As should be abundantly clear, SimFarming is more involved than sitting on the front porch and watching the virtual wheat wave lazily in the breeze. There's always some chore to be taken on, and if you're not quick on the draw, you could see your farming dreams go up in a cloud of locusts. Yes, locusts are just one of the additional disasters that can befall you, although, as with other Maxis sims, you can turn these disasters off.

SimFarm may be the most fiddleacious of the Maxis sims. For those who just can't get enough tinkering, it could be the greatest invention since the cotton gin. But unlike the SimCities and SimTower, fiddling is not so much an option as a necessity. The minute you turn your back, another problem (literally) crops up and it's time to haul out the sprayer. This coupled with the fact that spraying is such a major part of the simulation may drive some users to distraction. We're willing to accept that squirting plants with noxious chemicals is an important part of farming, but if we wanted to experience the tedium of reality, we wouldn't be playing a computer game in the first place.

LOUSY FEATURE

Apart from the spraying annoyance, SimFarm is a lot more fun than it sounds. The interface is up to Maxis's exemplary standards, and of course the manual is both enlightening and a hoot to boot. If your farm does particularly well, you'll be visited by Carmen Mooranda, who performs an exotic dance not often seen in these parts. You'll also be rewarded with a keyboard-controlled crop duster ride. It's not an F/18 Hornet, but for an add-on treat, it's not bad.

With a couple of tweaks, this could be one of our favorite Maxis toys. There are countless decisions to be made and nearly as many gewgaws to futz with as in SimLife. But honestly, Maxis, until you implement an auto-spray function, how you gonna keep 'em down on the farm?

Pros: You'll learn more about farm life than you ever wanted to know. Typically swell Maxis graphics and interface.

Cons: Can't we please hire someone to do the spraying for us?

System Requirements: LC or better, 1MB RAM, 5MB hard disk space, System 7.0 or later.

SIMFARM	
Fun factor:	3.5
Look and feel:	4.0
Value:	3.5
Replayability:	3.5
Overall:	3.5

El-Fish

Aquariums have a certain appeal for many people. Unfortunately, though, not everyone has the patience or financial wherewithal that a colorful collection of tropical sea creatures requires. Back in the autumn days of the Apple II series of computers, there was a little program called Fishies that emulated an aquarium on the monochrome monitors that were then the display standard. At the time, it seemed like a novel idea to have your computer sitting in the background gurgling happily while sea horses bobbed across the screen instead of compiling spreadsheets or noisily hammering out a resume on an ImageWriter printer. Since then, we have been doused with several fish tank programs, most notably the Fish screen saver module from the After Dark collection. The limitations of these diversions lie in the two-dimensional and mechanical nature of the water-bound vertebrates. Enter El-Fish, a new take on an old theme that truly puts a tub of fish-filled water on your desk, complete with ultrarealistic fishy movements.

Go Fish

El-Fish is a stand-alone application that enables your computer to become an aquarium stocked with exotic fish from around the globe. You begin with a few preset varieties of fish to watch glide through the virtual waters inside your monitor, but where the fish come from and how they evolve is up to you. A map enables you to drop an electronic hook anywhere in the world to catch various fish for your aquatic purposes. Pairs of fish can be bred together again and again to accentuate favorable features or traits, and if you're feeling really crazy, the big clock can be fast forwarded a few millennia to see how the little gaffers evolve. When evolving any species, the amount of color and shape variation can be controlled with a scroll bar, while the whole three- or four-thousand-year process only takes about 15 to 20 seconds. It's well worth the wait for those marine biologists just dying to know if any white sharks are going to evolve into Greg Norman.

Gotcha Hook, Line, and Sinker

The real beauty of El-Fish lies in the animation of the fish, and the tanks they swim in. The fish are presented, and swim in, three dimensions using the same fluid movement of real fish. It's an incredible sight to behold; this technology is light years ahead of any other fish-tank kind of program and makes you do a double take to make sure someone hasn't converted their Trinitron into a goldfish bowl. So what's the catch you ask? Horsepower. El-Fish requires a fair bit of guts to make the animation smooth, and each animated fish takes up a megabyte of hard disk space, making it difficult to keep all the sea creatures looking realistic.

GREAT FEATURE

Fortunately, with the entry-level Mac fast becoming the 040, most folks should have no trouble handling the processor demands of this software "toy."

Fishy Fun

El-Fish fits the classification of software toy like a hand fits a glove; it is neither a game nor an educational program. Of course, there really is no beginning or end to it and no particular purpose or obstacle to overcome when "playing" (for lack of a better word) with it. But El-Fish does a great job of creating the most realistic and visually breathtaking artificial aquarium available for the Mac. What use that is to average Mac users is up to them.

Pros: Breathtaking fish animation. Great color. Fish can be bred and evolved for greater variety.

Cons: Slow on 68030 machines. No beginning or end. A memory and hard disk hog.

System Requirements: 256-color monitor, LC or better, 3.5MB RAM, 10MB hard disk space, System 7.0 or later.

EL-FISH	
Fun factor:	4.0
Look and feel:	4.5
Value:	4.0
Replayability:	4.0
Overall:	4.0

Widget Workshop

With dwindling grades, slumping interest, and general fiscal apathy, education in America has begun turning toward flashy multimedia-based learning to provide the wakeup call for today's youth. The level of distracting entertainment youngsters are exposed to has reached a fever pitch, and it's not gonna ease up one iota in the foreseeable future. Some (not all) members of the MTV generation would much rather spend 25 hours exploring every last geographical detail of Donkey Kong Country than learning something as seemingly insignificant as reading or writing. A few pioneering souls have harnessed the power of nifty gadgetry to create educational material designed to covertly seduce unwilling juveniles into learning. Television shows like *Beakman's World* and *Bill Nye the Science Guy* have replaced the relatively mundane science shows of the past with highly polished, trendy, in-your-face erudition. With computers continuing to hold a place in today's schools, it's only logical that a wave of edutainment software woo today's youth into healthy learning, even if it is camouflaged by tree-stealing Eco-Villains. Maxis pioneered the software toy concept and has adapted it successfully into the Widget Workshop, a virtual science lab that's a mad scientist's idea of utopia.

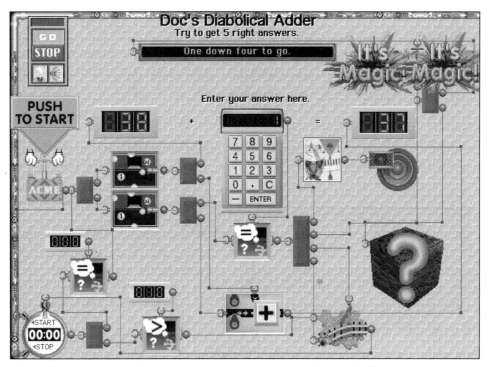

Widget Workshop is so versatile that science games can be created with minimal effort.

Mad Science 101

Widget Workshop allows you to become a card-carrying Mad Scientist in 25 easy steps without ever so much as touching an Erlenmeyer flask. Despite the lack of dangerous chemicals, electricity, and a trusty sidekick with spinal problems, this is a powerful and fun tool that allows for scientific experimentation in everything from gravity to secret code generators. WW includes a puzzle section and the Free Play area. The 25-step introductory tutorial takes place in the latter location and involves wading through 42 pages of manual, which some will no doubt find a tad grueling. Fortunately, there's a set of puzzle widgets that can be accessed at any time, as can the design area, where you can create such items as a shoe-size calculator. This can be used to fit your feet with fuzzy foam slippers while en route to devising a tool best suited to ruling the world.

Super Digit Fidget Widget

The Widget Workshop laboratory houses the control box and tool tray from which all things widget are developed. The tool tray includes literally hundreds of various parts and doohickeys for creating machines of scientific wonder designed specifically to aid in learning about the world while having fun doing it. The parts are laid out in icon format with their function displayed at the top of the tool bar when the pointer is moved over them, thus offering a variation of balloon help that's always on. Placement of switches, stop watches, and even a human heart is achieved with a simple click and drag. Perhaps the greatest limitation of WW is the size of the screen in relation to the bulk of the tools. On a 14-inch monitor, there is a definite limitation for those who want to explore the outer reaches of widgetdom. WW will no doubt have myriad uses in schools and homes around the world. It's easy to picture a teacher asking his or her students to break into groups of four, boot up their Macs, and design widgets for figuring out how long it would take Steve Jobs to fall 1,300 feet on Mars with an 512K Mac tied to each foot.

Where There's a Widget, There's a Way

Widget Workshop is a versatile and entertaining piece of software that truly shows what educational software could be: fun and—hold on to your hats—educational! The lack of extra widget work room on smaller monitors is a minor gripe that occurs only because of the desire to keep creating interesting machines with which to learn about science. This is a great addition to the software libraries of kids of all ages.

Pros: Easy to learn. Very versatile. Fun for all ages. Powerful tool for exploring beginner science.

Cons: Work area slightly limited on smaller monitors.

System Requirements: 256-color monitor, LC or better, 4MB RAM, 7MB hard disk space, System 6.05 or higher.

WIDGET WORKSHOP	
Fun factor:	4.0
Look and feel:	4.5
Value:	4.0
Replayability:	4.0
Overall:	4.0

8 Adventure Games

Ah, the call of adventure—from the confines of dank and musty catacombs to the far reaches of a hostile galaxy to a MYSTerious island world. So don your pith helmet, recharge that laser blaster, and unfurl the magic scroll. Your fantastic journeys begin here.

∧∼∼∼∼∼∼∼∼∼∼∼∼∼∼∼∼∼∼∼∼∼∼∼∼∼∼∧

Puzzling Adventures

Since the early days of interactive fiction, puzzle solving has been a major component of adventure gaming. Although the interfaces have changed over the years with the inclusion of animation, stereo sound, and 3D-rendered landscapes, the basic concept remains the same: You want to get from Point A to Point B but there's no clear path between them.

Myst
Cyan, Inc.
Published by Brøderbund

In mid-1993, CD-ROM gaming was a pretty sad affair. Sure, thanks in part to Apple's deep discounting of external CD-ROM players and the inclusion of internal players on new systems, game publishers could now comfortably produce CD-ROM titles without fearing that the market was too shallow to support them. But regrettably few game publishers knew how to effectively exploit the medium. The games included complex 3D graphics, QuickTime movies, and huge sound files but lacked one thing: fun. Sad to say, many of these things were created by skillful artists who lacked a keen sense of game design.

Those of us rummaging through the then-current CD-ROM games were more than a little dismayed. "Surely," we thought, "someone somewhere will know what to do with these silver discs and create a landmark CD-ROM game."

Someone did: Rand and Robyn Miller, two brothers in Washington State who were known for the delightful children's games The Manhole, Cosmic Osmo, and Spelunx and the Caves of Mr. Seudo.

Getting MYSTy

Myst is a game of discovery, and we won't spoil your fun by revealing too many of its plot points. But here's the premise: Atrus, a rather talented author, has picked up an arcane trick from his father that enables him to write books that literally transport the reader to fantastic lands. So adept at this skill is Atrus that he has stocked three shelves of Myst Island's library with these magical tomes. With horror, Atrus discovers that his books are being destroyed and his fantastic lands ransacked. As the island's population is limited to the writer and his sons Sirrus and Achenar, suspicion for these nefarious deeds rests heavily on his progeny. Somehow the book linking our world to Myst Island finds its way to you, who are left to unravel its mysteries.

Even rendered in grayscale, Myst's graphics are breathtaking.

Your adventure begins with an aerial tour of the hazy, tree-encrusted Myst Island. After this brief QuickTime flight over the stunning landscape, you are plunked down on the island's dock. From there your job is to explore the island, solve puzzles that gain you access to other lands, and gather clues to reveal the identity of the book-destroying perpetrator. As it turns out, this is not a particularly easy task.

Myst is one of those games that gives you virtually no instruction. The information provided in this review is actually a bit more than you're likely to glean from the manual and the back of the box. Although this can be confounding at first, a quick jaunt around the island is enough to provide sufficient information to start you on your way. One of the charms of the game is that you are free to make discoveries at your own pace in a nonthreatening environment. There is no game clock; the puzzles need not be solved in any particular order; and nothing in the game will cause your untimely end. You're welcome to try any boneheaded thing you like without fear that something really bad is going to leap out and cleave you in two.

GREAT FEATURE

Inside the MYSTery

At the time Myst was created, most Mac games available on CD-ROM were put together with Macromedia Director, a program that, among other things, provides developers with a highly sophisticated animation system. The drawback to

Director is that the processing requirements for animation slow down already poky CD-ROM performance. The Miller boys elected to forgo this route and take another, more familiar path. Although they had experimented extensively with Director, Rand and Robyn chose to use their old buddy HyperCard as the engine to drive Myst.

Because Myst is HyperCard-based, it has a different look than games created with Director. Each scene is presented as a 3D-rendered, stationary backdrop. Any animation that may occur is contained within QuickTime windows that are seamlessly integrated into that backdrop. Navigation is controlled by clicking on the screen in the direction you want to move. Likewise, objects are activated by clicking or, in the case of levers, clicking and dragging. As you move from one location to another, each scene cross-fades to the next. If these fades seem too slow, you can opt for fast transitions that fling you directly to the next scene.

Although it may seem as if the Millers were not taking advantage of the latest and greatest whiz-bang technology, working within the limitations of Hyper-Card actually enhanced the game. Myst isn't a shoot-'em-up. There's not a darn thing chasing you, and a good deal of your time is spent staring at the screen and tapping thoughtfully on your noggin. There's really no need for fully animated Director sequences when you have such pleasant scenery, Chris Brandkamp's soothing environmental sounds, and delightfully diverting toys scattered throughout the game.

Don't get us wrong—Myst doesn't ignore the elements that make CD-ROM the delivery system of choice for huge games. Like any worthwhile 462MB game, Myst plays to the strengths of the medium: 2,500 ray-traced images that will, on occasion, cause your jaw to drop in admiration; 66 minutes of QuickTime animation; over 40 minutes of original music; and megabytes of digital-audio sound effects. The difference between Myst and some other CD-ROM games is that the technology is not the star of the show. Yes, you will be absolutely knocked out by the graphics, the live-action QuickTime sequences are stunning, and the musical score—cinematic in its scope—enhances the feel of the game without being intrusive. But Myst is more than just a collection of sparkly graphics and stirring sound. The substance of the game is every bit as good as the package.

**GREAT
FEATURE**

The danger inherent in fantasy/adventure games is that plot lines can become convoluted and farfetched. Not so here. Myst's narrative is straightforward and simple enough to be believable given the surreal nature of your surroundings. In addition, information that drives the plot is released at an even pace. You learn as you go and don't feel as if someone had tacked on a harebrained ending simply to tie up loose ends.

The puzzles, like all good puzzles, are tough but fair and require only that you pay attention to everything going on around you (well, perhaps a little musical training and a compass would help). Observation, both aural and visual, is the key. There's not an unjust trick in the bunch, and once you find an answer you may wonder why you didn't get it hours earlier.

TIP

This Close to Perfect

We hate to knock a product that has set a new standard in computer gaming, but we do have two small complaints. First, when you click your cursor to the left or right side of the screen, you turn either 90 or 180 degrees, depending on whether the designers thought it important for you to see what was to the side of you. We understand that some of these views might seem extraneous, but in some areas the scenery is so similar that you can become disoriented. This results in extra clicks between one scene and another to determine exactly where you are.

Second, when you save a game in progress and then come back to that game later, you are transported to the opening location of the scenario. Although everything you've accomplished up to the point of the save is still intact when you return, you may have to travel a fair piece in order to return to the spot where you saved the game. This occurs more often than you'd expect because much of the information you need to complete a task is contained in books stored on Myst Island and the only other way to retain that information is to scribble it down. For lazy sods like us who are unwilling to transcribe page after page of text, this means restoring a game saved from Myst Island, looking something up, re-restoring to the first location, and then tramping back to where you began. Switching into Zip Mode, an option that allows you to traverse a path in a few leaps rather than several steps, helps considerably in these situations.

LOUSY
FEATURE

A Classic Nonetheless

Along with the CD-ROM (which contains, in addition to the game, a 14-minute QuickTime movie of the making of Myst), the game package includes a notebook for jotting down your observations and three game hints to get you started. If these hints are insufficient and you can't pry the answers from another player, a couple of hint books are available, and we've found complete walk-thrus online. Personally, we can't understand why anyone would want to rush through the game by getting an easy answer. With Myst's beautiful look, lush sound, and compelling plot line and puzzles, it's over all too soon.

INTERVIEW WITH RAND AND ROBYN MILLER

Call it luck, call it kismet, call it anything but late for lunch, Chris was fortunate enough to secure an interview with Cyan's Rand and Robyn Miller just weeks after the release of their legendary adventure game Myst.

Nearly two years later, the brothers were kind enough to take a few moments away from the development of Myst II—you can blame us for any shipping delays—to grant us a second exclusive interview.

We begin by whisking you back to the autumn of 1993:

How did you begin programming and designing games?

Rand: I have been programming for years—since Junior High. When HyperCard was first released, I saw a lot of potential in the program. Linking pictures to other pictures was made simple, simple enough for non-programmers. I thought it would be a great idea to create a sort of children's book, one in which you'd flip through pages clicking on things that would interest you. The only problem was that I wasn't an artist. So I sent HyperCard to Robyn along with an outline of my idea. He took off.

Robyn: I was immediately infatuated with HyperCard and started drawing pictures and linking them together. Much of the inspiration for that original project came from adventure games. I wanted a world where I could wander around yet where I wouldn't die and go back to the beginning. The Manhole was this world.

Rand: After finishing this world, doing Cosmic Osmo seemed like the next natural step. It was a wacky Science Fiction world.

But when we finished the disk version of Cosmic Osmo, we were ready to begin a world with a goal. We began formulating story ideas and even made proposals, but unfortunately, we had already typecast ourselves as children's entertainment creators.

Robyn: We continued on doing additional titles—Cosmic Osmo CD-ROM and Spelunx—but all the while our ideas of what our goal-oriented world would be continued to evolve.

And thus Myst. How were your ideas finally realized?

Robyn: Sunsoft, a Japanese corporation, had licensed and converted a version of The Manhole for a NEC game machine in Japan. They approached us with the vision of doing something on a grand scale. We told them our idea, and they loved it. They provided the resources we needed, and we jumped in. Later, we showed some of the work we had done to Brøderbund. They were equally impressed and were interested in the Mac and MPC platforms, which we had kept the rights to.

Did you have free reign to throw anything you liked into Myst and present it to your sponsors as a fait accompli, or did you have to go through some kind of approval process?

Rand: Obviously on a product this size, there is no carte blanche. But both companies are very easy to work with and had great suggestions. Brøderbund gave us a lot of very valuable input that really improved the gameplay. In a way, it's good having someone look over your shoulder; it forces you to not work in a vacuum. But they kept their distance—looking over our shoulders, but not breathing down our necks.

Who does what? And is there much crossover in your responsibilities? For instance, who's the dreamer and who's the pragmatist?

Robyn: I'm the dreamer.

Rand: Yeah, in your dreams!

Robyn: Ohh! Quick!

Rand: Actually we both come up with the ideas. We created the story together. All that is done regarding design, story, puzzles, and even interface is done together.

Robyn: This may come easy for us because we're brothers. We think a lot alike. In those ways we don't think alike, well, our relationship allows some good healthy arguments. We spent a lot of time designing Myst. After this design process was done, we began the implementation. This is where we separated the work out and everyone began work. But everyone has some hand in the design process, just like actors have a hand in a theatrical story. Everyone tweaks. And we had some really great people working with us on Myst.

Robyn, you were responsible for the music on the project. What kind of background do you have in music, and how did you determine the character of the themes?

Robyn: Background in music? I wish I had more. I play a little guitar and a very little piano. I think of the computer as my instrument; it's what I know how to "play." I

compose sitting at the computer, half plunking things out on the keyboard, half editing notes with the mouse. It seems to work. As far as determining the character of the themes, I just look at the room I'm writing a piece for and try to feel how that room sounds. Sometimes I get this feeling or mood completely wrong. But fortunately I'm surrounded by people who aren't afraid to say so!

Rand: That's right!

Do you guys play the characters of the brothers in Myst, and how reflective are their attributes to your own personalities?

Robyn: Who said we played the characters of the brothers?

Rand: Ridiculous! This is how vicious rumors are started!

Robyn: We're sorry, but the people who played the characters in Myst would like to remain anonymous.

Rand: And any similarities to persons living or dead is purely coincidental.

Okay, but speaking of brothers, how easy is it to work with your sibling? The creative process can be difficult enough without the additional baggage of an entire lifetime together. Did you collaborate even as kids?

Rand: We get along great. Competition doesn't really occur, because Robyn knows I'm smarter than he is. He's learned to live with that.

Robyn: Oh, what a joker! Ha! Actually we didn't do much together as kids, because I was younger. But we did a lot together as a family. Our parents are incredible people. Somehow, with the added grace of God, they raised four boys who are all almost best friends.

Rand: I love you too Robyn. (Sob.)

What do your parents think of your work?

Robyn: They think Myst is the greatest thing in the world. However, Mom would fall asleep if she actually sat down and played it.

Rand, in the Making of Myst you mentioned that Robyn had some stupid ideas. Can you share a couple of them with us?

Robyn: No, he can't. Next question.

Oops. Okay, let's switch from the personal to the technical. Macromedia Director seems to be the program of choice for CD-ROM entertainment designers, yet for Myst you stuck with HyperCard. Why?

Rand: It's true that we're very familiar with HyperCard. It's very easy for us to work with, and that's a very viable reason. But there are others. Director was originally created as an animation program, and it's an excellent animation program, but it's not a great interactive multimedia program. They seemed to have shoved interactive capabilities into the wrong paradigm. The Lingo language is especially screwy. HyperTalk is an elegant language, and the HyperCard paradigm is a perfect paradigm for what we do. We are able to add features to HyperCard where we need them. We are able to subtract features where it will speed

things up. We're certainly not married to HyperCard, and we will switch to the first good alternative that comes along. But surprisingly nothing has come along.

Robyn: And what Rand says holds true for any of the tools we use. We use Strata StudioPro, for example. But we want to be careful not to be married to that tool or any one tool at the expense of the quality of our worlds. We also have to be wary not to leave a tool hastily just because everybody else does it that way. Director is a perfect example of a tool which everyone seems to use because … well, because everyone just seems to use it. But that's not a good enough reason. Director is not the best tool for us.

Myst has a slow and thoughtful, sometimes haunting feel to it. Everything you've included, from the graphics to the ambient sound and music to the pacing of the game reflects a central theme and design philosophy. Tell us about that philosophy.

Robyn: We have many philosophies regarding the creation of goal-oriented worlds.

Rand: Like it should be completely non-linear.

Robyn: Also, the player should not die. It just slows things down for no reason.

Rand: Game design, or what we like to call world design, is of utmost importance. Myst may look nice and sound nice, but it would be just another junky game if it wasn't for captivating puzzles and an interesting story.

Robyn: We spent a lot of time on detail. Detail in every aspect is important. But holes in the plot drive people nuts.

Water images recur throughout Myst. Does this have something to do with the kind of meditative tone you set for the game, or was it simply a device to keep your worlds limited to the confines of an island, and thus allow you to work within a world of manageable size?

Rand: A meditative tone for the game? You're getting deep on us! The worlds are all islands for one very simple reason: water provides a very natural boundary. It tends to be frustrating when you're wandering through an environment and you see somewhere you want to go—like a city street or a forest—but for some inexplicable reason you can't go there! A lot of games tend to suffer from this. One of our philosophies in these interactive worlds is that if you see somewhere you want to go, you should be able to go there. Water is a good way to say, "Sorry, there's nothing here."

So what's next? One of Myst's characters indicates that there is more to come, and I've also heard a buzz online about a prequel.

Robyn: It wasn't far into the design process that we realized there would have to be a prehistory to the entire thing. Where did Atrus come from? Where does this strange Myst world come from? There were these and many other questions to be answered. We felt we needed these answers. So as we were working on Myst, we began to write a story that answered these questions. But this prehistory also presented many new questions. Because of the prehistory, the Myst game was evolving slightly. Out of that evolution emerged the ideas for what Myst II will be. So the Myst prehistory, Myst the CD-ROM, and Myst II began to become inextricably entwined. At this point, we are working on our third or fourth draft of the prehistory. When we're finished, we hope to get this novel into people's hands; it is all part of the Myst experience. The prehistory answers much that may seem unexplained in Myst.

Rand: Like why the heck is there a big crack in a field of stars during the intro?

Robyn: Exactly.

And after Myst II? Have you given up on children's games?

Rand: We're obviously anxious to begin Myst II, and we will as soon as physically possible. We'll be pushing things even more as far as technology and level of detail are concerned. After that, well, new ideas usually aren't a problem for us. We'll just be implementing them to take advantage of hardware and software that we can only dream about today. Have we given up on children's games? We never close any doors. We really love kids and we love our kids. But we also have a special interest in worlds for older audiences. We're just creating these worlds the way that appeals to us, and it just so happens that other people enjoy them as well. Ironically, our one regret in doing Myst is that we can't really have the pleasure of experiencing this game that we designed as something we'd like to play.

———————

My, how things change in a year and a half. Myst has become a bona fide phenomena, selling in the hundreds of thousands on both the Macintosh and PC platform. The brothers Miller have become celebrities, appearing in the pages of every major news and media magazine across the globe, on MTV, and, most recently, in ads for the GAP. Not bad for a couple of guys who like to create fantastic worlds, draw pictures, and mess with computers.

Here's where things stand as of the summer of 1995:

Since we last spoke, you've become the first superstars of multimedia. For a couple of pretty down-to-earth guys, this must be awfully strange. How has this sudden rush of fame changed your lives and work? And what sort of pressure does the huge success of Myst place on you for your future projects?

Robyn: I can't really say that the fame has effected our lives in any negative or positive way. We're still people who are just doing stuff that we really want to do. Oftentimes doors are opened up to us because of what we've done, but our personal lives still stay very personal and secure. I can't say that the fame will never affect our lives; we definitely see it as something to beware of and to guard ourselves against. It must be a very easy trap to fall into.

Rand: Fame is kind of relative. It's not as if people recognize us when we're walking down the street. Not all that much has changed from a personal standpoint. On the business end, the exposure has been great for opening doors.

Last time you also mentioned that a Myst novel was in the works. What's going on with the book and what other Myst-related products are simmering?

Rand: The Myst novel is underway. This has been a bit of an ordeal for us. The story behind Myst has been there from the beginning, but putting it in novel form takes a skill set that neither of us has, and time that neither of us has. So it's been a slow process. Working with authors and editors and publishers has been an interesting experience. We're really excited about finishing the novel and finally revealing the events that lead up to the Myst experience.

There is a calendar with some never-before-scenes from Myst. And we're trying to be a bit more aggressive on the merchandising front—only because there are so many cool Myst items that we'd like to have! The Myst soundtrack should be available soon at a record store near you. We still are waiting until the time is right to start considering movie options again; we have that on hold right now. But when it's all said and done, we really need to focus on what we think we do best: interactive.

Give us a rundown on Myst II. Will the next adventure take up where the last left off?

Rand: The story continues—the questions are answered. What book is Atrus writing into? Where is Catherine? Who is the foe that Atrus is worried about? The sequel will pick up just where Myst left off, in D'ni, which is, by the way, the only part from Myst that you'll see in the sequel.

What technological changes have you made with the new game?

Rand: We have two areas of technology: generating the content and delivering the content. We're concentrating most of our technological advances in the generating content area. Better graphics, better sound, better music, better quality in all areas. The images that we're creating are much more detailed than we did in Myst. We're using SGI workstations, which give us much more control and speed. We're letting other folks concentrate on the content delivery improvements for us: better video compression, faster CD-ROM drives, more colors, better sound, new technologies.

In retrospect, is there anything you would have done differently with Myst I?

Robyn: Absolutely. The day we finished Myst I there were things we knew we would have done differently, which is why we were so anxious to start on the next project. We probably could have worked on Myst indefinitely, perfecting it and perfecting it, but there are obvious problems with that method of operation. We'd never get the project out!

For each of our projects, we do the best we can with the resources we have, get the project out there and get on to the next project. This doesn't mean we publish junk. There is a certain level of quality and inventiveness that we will always demand, but with each new project this bar should raise a bit, or a lot! With each new project we demand more and more from ourselves. We see what we did wrong with the previous project and improve in those areas for the next project. The medium (CD-ROM) is in such an infant stage right now that these improvements are probably going to be much greater jumps forward than those in already matured mediums such as movies. Interactive is in a stage of definition, and there is so much room for improvement.

What happens when you get tired of being the Myst guys? Suppose you get through Myst II and decide it's time for a change yet your public clamors for Myst III. Do you feel free to drop it if something else piques your interest?

Robyn: It would be very difficult for us to imagine a Myst III. We built the Myst universe to be based on two games and a book. When the Myst sequel is finished, the Myst story will be finished, and I don't see how we could continue it. I don't see how we'd even want to continue it. We're working on Myst II right now because all of us here at Cyan are very excited about the project. We know we can do it justice. We know it's a viable and exciting project that has real challenges for us. Yeah, it's true that the public may want more after that, but we have so many other dreams that we'd like to pursue.

Rand: Here's how we look at it. If we decide not to give Myst III to the clamoring public, we plan on giving them something else that makes them forget all about Myst III.

Tips

We love this game so much we don't want to spoil it for you. But there are a couple of hidden goodies you might look for:

TIP

• Open the Channelwood folder found in the Myst Graphics folder. Copy the file Holo-AMouth.MooV to your hard drive. Using a utility such as FileTyper or Snitch, change the file type to **MooV**. Now open the movie with a QuickTime movie player. (For your convenience we put one on our CD-ROM. It's called Peter's Player). Holding down the Shift key, double-click on the movie window to play the movie backward and hear a secret message.

• Poke around in the graphics files with a resource editor such as ResEdit. The Millers didn't use every graphic file they created for the game, and there are a few intriguing extras floating about on the disc.

Pros: One of the greatest computer games ever made. Graphics to die for. Brilliant sound effects and musical score. Great story and logical puzzles.

Cons: The game eventually ends. Puzzles may prove too difficult for younger players.

System Requirements: 8-bit 256-color Macintosh, CD-ROM drive, 4MB RAM, (2.5MB free RAM), 3MB hard disk space, System 7 or higher, QuickTime 1.6 and Sound Manager 3.0 (provided).

MYST	
Fun factor:	5.0
Look and feel:	5.0
Value:	5.0
Replayability:	2.0
Overall:	5.0

Jewels of the Oracle
Discis Entertainment

Many adventure games have certain elements of puzzles embedded within them while others display the riddles without camouflage. One could almost call Jewels of the Oracle a true puzzle game, but its CD-ROM roots and thinly veiled plot line place it in a gray area somewhere between these genres. However one categorizes Jewels of the Oracle, it's an impressive collection of over 30 puzzles with stunning graphics that is sure to baffle and entertain a wide variety of gamers.

Temple of Jewels

The attempt to solve the puzzles takes place in a temple constructed by an ancient civilization bent on cultivating in its young the ways of logic and reason rather than war and combat. Its keeper is a talking upside-down triangle. Yep, an angular butler with a knack for speaking in riddles. Fun, eh? You begin play by watching a brilliant multicolored diamond-shaped jewel spin and explode in a cascade of color. This blast distributes gems around the temple. Each has a puzzle for you to solve to ensure its return to the mother gem. Old Eternal

Triangle Face is there to guide you with sometimes confusing verbal clues. But maybe we're being too hard on this guy. Actually, this character's animation is excellent, and it adds substantially to the game.

The puzzles range from peg-and-tile games to geometric and maze conundrums. But often the real challenge is to figure out what the problem is in the first place. The two hints per puzzle offered by the triangle are often more confusing than helpful, and there are never any direct instructions included with the puzzles. This isn't a drawback though. We think it's actually a feature. It makes you take the time to figure out the purpose of the puzzle as well as the method for solving it. This bi-level complexity adds to the satisfaction one receives when decisively kicking the problem's butt.

Atmosphere

The artwork and the animated transition sequences when moving from location to location are nicely rendered and conjure up the atmosphere of an ancient temple. However, the ancient symbols aren't always very distinct, perhaps because of the coloring, and it's easy to get confused as to where you have and haven't been in your quest. The game offers only 8-bit color, but it mentions that there might be a version for Power Macs that will take advantage of the "thousands of colors" option these Macs enjoy. This alone would help alleviate some eye strain. The movie sequences are fantastic, but if you tire of their effect they can be turned off in exchange for straight screen swaps.

No Need for Insect Spray

Jewels of the Oracle runs smoothly, and we did not detect any bugs when running on either an 040 or a PPC. The interface is point and click and you have access to the menu bar whenever you need it. Although we found the speed of navigation reasonable, it would be nice to have a more direct way to access the individual puzzles. We got tired of moving around the central well.

Oracle Time

Jewels of the Oracle is essentially an excellent puzzle game in a pseudo-adventure wrapper. It is bathed in rich graphic and animated detail. Our best advice is that if you like puzzle games, 3 in Three for example, the Jewels of the Oracle will not disappoint, and the great rendered art and beautiful sound will be icing on the cake. Sit back and take your time with Jewels. There's no maiden in distress to save, or evil warlock to overthrow—just puzzles to be solved without fear of reprisal.

Pros: Great graphics. Puzzles fairly difficult. Non-linear.

Cons: Very little instruction or manual
help. Moving around can get to be a drag
once the game is mastered.

System Requirements: 256-color monitor, 25MHz 040 or better, 4MB RAM,
1MB hard disk space, System 7.1 or later,
double-speed CD-ROM drive.

JEWELS OF THE ORACLE	
Fun factor:	3.0
Look and feel:	3.0
Value:	3.5
Replayability:	4.0
Overall:	3.5

Hunting and Gathering

These games are direct descendants of early text adventures, and they typically
put you in a landscape in which you must grab the proper goodies before winning your way to the end.

King's Quest VII: The Princeless Bride
Sierra On-Line

RANT

Sharp-eyed readers will notice that we don't cover many Sierra On-Line games
in this book. Here's the reason: Most of them aren't worth the floppies they're
printed on. That's not to say that the content isn't worthwhile—many Sierra
games are actually quite good—it's just that the company has steadfastly refused
to provide Mac gamers with anything but unwieldy and ugly ports of their PC
products. Add Sierra's wretched marketing support and you've got little to
endear yourself to a Macintosh game reviewer.

Roberta Williams' latest, King's Quest VII, is an exception. The original PC
game was a marvel to begin with. The graphics are beautiful, the animation is
charming, the storyline engaging, and, for the most part, the characters are nicely realized. Sierra had a good thing from the get go and didn't mess it up when
bringing it to the Mac.

Walt Would Have Loved This (or Maybe Sued)

In what is more than a simple homage to Disney, King's Quest VII is a fully animated adventure in the style of the Buena Vista school. The game begins with a
sweeping opening complete with a theme song that's not good enough to cause

Talking mice, tiny houses, full animation . . . looks as if the latest installment of King's Quest has taken a side road to the Magic Kingdom.

Whitney Houston to lose any sleep but that is impressive for a computer game. After this musical interlude, the story begins.

Princess Rosella, like all good fairy tale princesses, has made up her mind to marry for love rather than political convenience. Her practical mother, Queen Valanice, urges her to consider the dull yet wealthy prince who lives a couple of kingdoms away. As her mother natters on about these matters, Rosella sees a tempting vision in a nearby pool. Spunky lass that she is, Rosella plunges into the pool only to be whirled away to an enchanted land. Mom, no doubt anxious to test her CPR skills, dives in after her daughter and is likewise drawn away.

The two women find themselves in wholly different parts of the enchanted Land of Eldritch. Your job is to solve a series of puzzles and reunite mother and daughter. This will be done over the courses of six chapters that alternate between the trials of Valanice and Rosella.

The Look We Love

Generally, KQ VII offers standard adventure game activity: collect objects, use or trade them to solve a puzzle, and move to the next situation. Although the

GREAT
FEATURE

puzzles vary in their degree of logic and difficulty, few will flummox moderately experienced adventure gamers. What sets King's Quest VII apart from other adventures is the look of the game. The art and animation is remarkable.

KQ VII's characters do not lumber about like Robbie the Robot in front of a gauzy backdrop. Playing KQ VII is like being inside a middle-grade, late-model animated Disney feature. When you click on an area of the screen you'd like Rosella and Valanice to go to, they waltz over as smoothly as you please. The characters they interact with are just as animated. Even inventory items pop up as 3D rotatable images.

Although the main flavor of the graphics is pure Disney, there are other influences as well. The speeding rabbit found in Chapter 1 is a cross between Warner Brothers' Bugs Bunny and the Road Runner. And a later chapter that features a Halloweenish landscape borrows liberally from Tim Burton's *Nightmare Before Christmas*.

Interface Issues

GREAT
FEATURE

KQ VII's interface is a mixed bag. On the positive side, the game is very friendly in that it allows you to begin with any chapter you like. If you're having a tough time with one chapter, progress doesn't have to stop. Just start on another chapter and come back to the problem area later. Also, if your character suffers a serious mishap and dies, you can take back your last move and try a different tactic. Very nice.

LOUSY
FEATURE

Less friendly is the lack of a reasonable save function. To save the game you must quit—not by pressing Command-Q, but by selecting Quit within the game. Pressing Command-Q quickly ends the game without saving, leaving you to begin again from your last "official" save. Very bad.

Crowning the King

But considering the fine design and delightful look of the game we're willing to live with this lumpy save scheme. Visually, Roberta Williams and crew have done a superb job with this latest installment of the King's Quest saga. The content may not be anything special, but for sheer animated delight, you won't find another game like it.

Pros: Revolutionary animation for a computer game. Decent puzzles. Good voice characterizations.

Cons: Awful save scheme.

System Requirements: 8-bit 13-inch color monitor, 68040 Mac or better, 8MB RAM, 20MB hard disk space, System 7.01 or later, double-speed CD-ROM drive.

KING'S QUEST VII	
Fun factor:	4.0
Look and feel:	5.0
Value:	4.0
Replayability:	2.0
Overall:	4.0

Return to Zork
Activision

In the early days of computer game playing, when text adventures ruled the land, gaming was akin to reading a book and playing chess at the same time. With the advent of graphics, the text genre faded from popularity and took with it some of the greatest games of the time, the Zork series. But Activision recently brought forth a CD-ROM adventure that takes advantage of state-of-the-art technology while attempting to make the connection to the venerable Zork games.

Mail Call

The Zorkian delights commence when the mailbox is opened and Lady Luck shines down on you with a vacation sweepstakes victory that sends you, all expenses paid, to the Valley of the Sparrows. Ah, but there have been a couple of minor changes in the itinerary. It seems the valley has been appropriately renamed the Valley of the Vultures and the town of East Shanbar has disappeared. Not to worry though, you can pick yourself up by the bootstraps (hint: also pick up a rock and use some good old-fashioned ingenuity to figure out what the heck is the matter in River City).

Along the way you'll meet cleverly presented video actors who have been incorporated seamlessly into the graphic backgrounds and who can chat up a storm. Interacting with the characters is critical for survival and for enjoying the game. You'll quickly get a taste of the excellent acting that went into Return to Zork when you meet up with the lighthouse keeper who rewrites the definition of a fool's paradise. Getting from place to place usually requires some cerebral fortitude not unlike that required when plowing through the old text games. However, the visual clues certainly give one an advantage that's easy to capitalize on. The game is easy enough for most players to finish, but if you're getting impatient or just want to zip through, we've included a walk-thru on the enclosed CD-ROM.

CD

Half 'n' Half

Graphically, Return to Zork is a mishmash of DOS-level and Mac screen art. The animated sequences are low resolution, but some of the still screens are as good as we've seen. The video integration is exceptionally crisp, and there are no stutters or stammers when conversing with characters, even on Power Macs running in emulation. We did notice, however, that some of the animated transitions were dropped by slower machines, no doubt to reduce the load on the CPUs. We also found that if you're unaware of the existence of the transitions, they aren't really missed. The interface is unique and uses appropriate tools for different situations. For example, when talking to a character, you get a choice of demeanor ranging from threatening to bored and are also offered a choice of topics to query about. Inventory is accessible with a tap on the Space Bar. As with all games of this type, it's a good idea to pick up whatever you find in your travels, no matter how insignificant the objects may seem. Believe us, you'll never know when you might need some item to solve a puzzle.

Hail the Return to Zork!

Despite its obvious DOS roots and non-Mac interface, this game has a lot going for it. It'll require some fairly serious patience and perseverance to beat

Return to Zork marked the comeback of Infocom to the Mac computer scene. It is highlighted by excellent acting and great video incorporation.

the darned thing, but it's worth it in the end, and you can aid your quest by saving at any time. Although it's possible to meet an early demise, it certainly isn't the norm, and the complex story keeps interest high. Return to Zork's real pleasure is delivered by the actors Infocom hired. They definitely make the game. Zork should stand as an example to game designers who think they can act. Hey, get professionals. They really, really make a difference.

DANGER

Pros: Can't be solved in a couple hours. Great acting. Interesting and functional interface.

Cons: DOS graphics in some areas. Cuts out transition scenes on slower Macs.

System Requirements: 256 color monitor, LC III or better, 4MB RAM, 100K, 3MB or 50MB hard disk space (depending on installation selected), System 7 or later, CD-ROM drive.

RETURN TO ZORK	
Fun factor:	4.0
Look and feel:	3.5
Value:	4.0
Replayability:	3.5
Overall:	3.5

Paparazzi! Tales of Tinseltown

Museworthy
published by Activision

In this game, you play a hungry young photographer bent on success in Tinseltown, the world's glamour capitol. To survive and eventually triumph, you must dash about its glittery environs snapping compromising pictures of the local movers and shakers and sell your photographic wares to either the highest bidder or to those agencies or individuals who can do you the most good. You have exactly two weeks to snap shots of the game's 24 celebrities. During this time, you must maintain a positive bank balance and a reputation just seemly enough to keep you from being ridden out of town on a rail.

Your Day Begins

Your photo opportunities arise during two sessions each day—one in the morning and the other in the evening. Clues regarding the location of target celebrities are provided by the day's television programs, recorded videophone messages, and gossip sessions at a local bar and a camera store. A typical session would run thusly:

You wake up to a sassy radio alarm and are faced with the game's interface, the Palminator 2000. In the upper-left corner of the Palminator 2000 is a video window where TV programs and video messages appear. Across the bottom of the

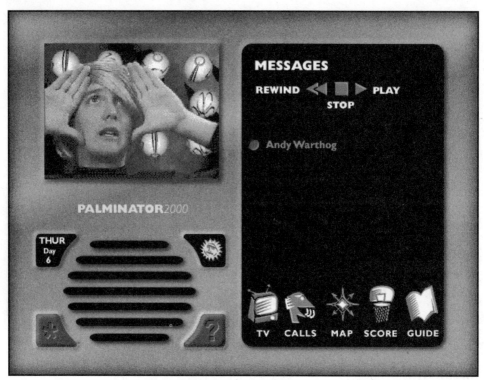

How long does Andy Warhol have to be dead before the people who made Paparazzi decide that he's no longer topical?

Palminator 2000 are five icons: TV, Calls, Map, Score, and Guide. To glean your first set of clues, surf through the six TV channels to catch local news, interview programs, or advertisements. You can then choose to review your video messages. These messages may include assignments from an editor, threatening messages from an unknown hoodlum, or nagging calls from your mother.

With this information under your belt, you click on the Map button to reveal an overhead view of Tinseltown's 13 locations. These include the Soop-R Val-U Leed-R Mar-kit, the Fallen Arches Country Club, the Aroma Motel, and the dangerous Alley. Clicking on the map whisks you to a location.

There the interface changes to a viewfinder that includes a Snap button for taking pictures and a Flee button for getting out while the getting's good. When you arrive at a location, a video sequence plays out in the viewfinder. When something juicy comes along, snap it quickly. You're allowed only two shots, so you have to make them good—the tabloids don't pay for pictures of people innocently standing around. Once you have your pictures, hit the Flee button to view your developed pictures. If they are marketable, up pops a bid window.

The Real Scoop

According to the press release, Paparazzi! Tales of Tinseltown is "a fast-moving satirical comedy." Mmmmaybe. We don't dispute the fact that it's supposed to be comedic; the television sequences are obviously intended to be funny, as are some of the video messages. But the humor tends to be broad and obvious and rarely rises above the level of your typical high school talent show. For example, a number of the game's celebrities are based on real celebs—Cher, Madonna, Rush Limbaugh, Liz Taylor, Michael Jackson—so we must endure jokes about Cher's plastic surgery and endorsement of cheesy beauty products, Rush being whipped into a sexual frenzy by feminazis, and Liz Taylor's radical fluctuations in weight. We heard Leno and Letterman do this stuff years ago, and it wasn't that funny the first time around.

LOUSY FEATURE

But maybe we hit the game on the wrong day. Humor is subjective, and we're willing to admit that everyone else on earth may think this game is a laugh riot. Fine. If we must be critical, let's move on to the more objective area of gameplay.

Point and ... No, Wait a Minute

Paparazzi has some real problems in terms of gameplay. To begin with, the game is extremely difficult to win simply because some vital elements were left out of the interface.

LOUSY FEATURE

You have a limited number of chances to bag each celebrity. Some can be caught only once. During each photo session you may travel to only two locations in the game. If you are unable to divine from the oftentimes obscure clues where a celebrity is due to appear, you may have lost the only opportunity to get your shot. Because there's no way to save and later return to your position in the game, you can't go back and get the shot after returning. You have to start all over again.

If you're fortunate enough to pick the right location, you may still miss the shot because you weren't able to intuit where the game's designers wanted you to snap the shot. For example, it seems to us that snapping a picture of America's teen sweetheart accepting a lit joint from a disreputable rocker would be worth *something* to the tabloids. But no, you have to get a shot of her inhaling. Because you have only the two shots to burn, you could easily snap too quickly and miss your opportunity.

Those Annoying Paparazzi

The folks responsible for this game got some of the elements right: The interface is slick, the TV sequences are well produced, the acting is believable, and the musical score is professional. Unfortunately, they strayed in two crucial areas: writing and game design. We didn't think it was that funny, but you might. We didn't think it was well thought out, and you probably won't either.

Pros: Slick interface. Professional job on video sequences.

Cons: Humor didn't tickle us. Poor game design.

System Requirements: 8-bit 13-inch color monitor, 68040 Mac or better, 4.4MB RAM, 22MB hard disk space, System 7.1.2 or later, double-speed CD-ROM drive.

PAPARAZZI! TALES OF TINSELTOWN!	
Fun factor:	2.5
Look and feel:	3.5
Value:	2.5
Replayability:	2.0
Overall:	2.5

JauntTrooper Mission: THUNDERBOLT
MegaCorp

By last count, this game has gone through four name changes. Originally it was called DoomsDay 2000 and was playable on VAX machines. Author Dave Scheifler then ported it to the Mac and sold it by mail order under the same name. In 1992, the game was picked up and enhanced by Casady & Greene, where it became Mission: THUNDERBOLT. After the game was temporarily dropped from Casady & Greene's catalog, the rights reverted to Dave, who released it as shareware under the original DoomsDay 2000 title. After adding a new opening screen and introduction, Dave renamed the game JauntTrooper Mission: THUNDERBOLT. Meanwhile, Casady & Greene released a CD-ROM called Macworld Game Hall of Fame that contains its version of Mission: THUNDERBOLT plus Crystal Quest, Crystal Crazy, Sky Shadow, and Glider 4.0. We include the last shareware version, JauntTrooper Mission: THUNDERBOLT on our CD-ROM.

Whatever you call the darned game, it ranks as one of Chris's all-time favorites. Here's the gist of it:

Earth is a mess. In a world devastated by nuclear attack, uncouth aliens have crept across what's left of the inhabitable land. Your mission is to travel down through level after level of an underground laboratory and recover an anti-matter device that will spell T-H-E E-N-D for the otherworlders. As you journey through the lab, you find powerful weapons, strange devices, pills of many colors, and loads of nasty aliens.

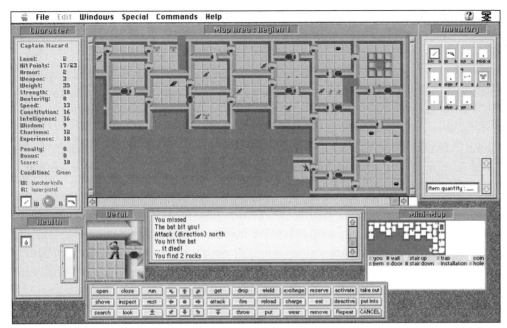

Stop looking at this picture of JauntTrooper Mission: THUNDERBOLT and play the game!

Sounds like typical adventure fare, eh? All part of the Let's-Go-Someplace-and-Kill-the-Bad-Guys-and-Collect-Loads-of-Loot-While-We're-at-It school of adventure gaming. Ah, but there's a difference in this game. The difference is *choice*.

You Choose

In most games of this type, there's only one way to accomplish your goal: Kill all the bad guys, take a healing potion when you're under the weather, and move to the next exit via the proscribed doorway. First-Person-Perspective-Shoot-'Em-Ups still operate under these rules. JauntTrooper doesn't limit you to these few options.

To begin with, Dave tries to model the world more realistically by allowing you to use the particular tools you discover in a number of ways. For example, if you have a crowbar in your possession and the patience to use it, is there any reason on earth why you shouldn't be allowed to knock a hole through a wall rather than search for a less convenient exit? Likewise, if the stairs down to the next level are blocked, why not use your pickax to smash a hole in the floor? And if a bribe or amiable chat helps you make friends and influence others, why not try it?

Because the game is so open, it provides many possibilities for developing individual strategies. For example: There is one beast called the Icky Lump that is particularly frustrating. Lumps travel in packs and don't do a lot of damage when they attack you, but they multiply at a tremendous rate, especially after you've stirred them up by attacking them. The one beneficial aspect of Lumps is that when you kill them they drop the significant amounts of cash they are carrying. Although many players simply start a new game once they hit a lump infestation, wily folks have discovered that if you contain the lumps in a penned-off area, you can harvest them for their gold. And what-do-you-know, there's a device in the game that allows you to create barriers. Chris was absolutely tickled when he figured out this strategy. Dave later told him that it's an accepted technique known as Icky Lump Farming. The game abounds with such possibilities.

TIP

GREAT FEATURE

Another aspect of the game that keeps it from getting stale is the random distribution of weapons, aliens, and pills. For instance, a particular round of game play may be filled with blaster rifles whereas another may not contain any. And with each new game the properties of the many different pills change—a silver pill may heal in one game but cause blindness in the next.

Try It and Buy It

When we set out to write this book, Chris vowed that even if he had to stand outside Dave Scheifler's house and whine piteously into the night he would find a way to place a copy of JauntTrooper on the CD-ROM. Fortunately, Dave's a very nice guy and gave us permission to include the demo version without Chris's having to whine. Dave also mentioned that two additional missions based on Mission: THUNDERBOLT will be available soon. You'll be able to transfer characters and their inventories from Mission: THUNDERBOLT to the next mission, so hang on to those oddly-shaped coins.

We implore you to play this game and register for the full version if you like what you see. You won't get brilliant 3D color graphics or jaw-dropping animation, but you'll have the opportunity to play one of the most inspired games on any platform.

Pros: Open structure that changes with each new game. Inspired design. Can take a long time to play.

Cons: Can take a long time to play (weeks).

System Requirements: Any Mac with 8-bit color monitor, 2.4MB RAM, 9.5MB hard disk space, System 6.03 or higher.

JAUNTTROOPER MISSION: THUNDERBOLT

Fun factor:	5.0
Look and feel:	3.5
Value:	4.5
Replayability:	4.0
Overall:	4.5

~~~~~~

Dark and Scary Places

If, as a child, you loved cheesy monster movies or experienced a secret thrill when your big brother leaped suddenly from behind a doorway shouting "Boo!" these games are for you. Creaking floorboards, pools of blood, and deadly mystery are the stuff of these dark and scary places.

The 7th Guest
Trilobyte/Virgin Games

T7G is set in an old house owned by an eccentric toy maker, Henry Stauf. This grinning cue ball has a mysterious rags-to-riches background that seems drenched in the blood of the children he's sold his handmade toys to. Mr. Stauf has invited seven guests to his house for a weekend of, shall we say, fun? Stauf, Stauf. Hmmm, a quick rearranging of letters and you have Faust, the man who sold his soul to Lucifer himself. Coincidence? After you soak up a ten-minute cinematic introduction, the game begins in earnest. You proceed from the lobby of Mr. Stauf's house, witness apparitions, and stumble across puzzles (22 in all) whose completion provides further access to various areas of the house. Usually completing a puzzle gives you information about why you are in the house and how you got there. If a puzzle becomes too perplexing, you can skip on down to the library to get a clue from Stauf's clue book. If you need to return thrice for a clue, the puzzle is automatically solved, but you're denied the pleasure of the animated treat provided successful sleuths.

GREAT FEATURE

An Idle Keyboard Is the Devil's Playground

Movement around the old house is achieved with mouse clicks. The cursor takes the shape of a skeletal hand that either beckons you forward or waves from side to side denying you access. Whenever the curse is about to trip a supernatural event, it changes to a set of chattering teeth to alert you to a creepy occurrence. While the interface is nicely rendered and filled with cute animations, you never have access to the Mac's menu bar and can only save and quit from a Ouija board screen. Overall though, one would not immediately guess that this is a port from DOS, which it is. This definitely bodes well for Trilobyte, which obviously put considerable effort into making T7G acceptable for Mac users.

Devilish Perspective

The method by which the three-dimensional environment is presented is what really grabs you about T7G. Its use of perspective as you move about the house is absolutely stunning, and although every move is pretty much a preset maneuver, you can't help but feel that this program is a precursor to virtual reality gaming. A cinematic undertone to moving around a room gives gameplay a palpable feel and compels you to peek around the next corner. Solving puzzles, and thus opening doors, becomes extra gratifying when you are privy to supernatural events and ghostly images, the latter of which use video (with real actors) to add to the experience. You'll want to have at least a fast 030 machine, and you can really make T7G cook with gas if you can muster an LC 475 or 575. Performance on slower machines is augmented by an automatic shrinking of the active screen. Most players probably will never have to endure the smaller format unless they are using a Power Mac, on which The 7th Guest in emulation takes a substantial performance hit.

Give the Devil His Due

The Seventh Guest is an excellent game worthy of any Mac's CD-ROM drive spindle. The second CD in the T7G pack is strictly audio. It contains creepy music written especially for listening to whilst wandering the halls of Stauf's mansion. Incidentally, the 11th Hour (the sequel to T7G) is due out sometime this millennium and promises to take the concept to a higher level. If we were pitching The 7th Guest to a movie studio, we'd likely say it's 3 in Three meets MYST in a virtual reality environment. Whatever it's pitched as, it's a great game.

Pros: Fantastic pseudo-virtual reality environment. Impressive incorporation of video. Good mixture of challenge levels.

Cons: Nonstandard interface. Requires 040 to really cook.

System Requirements: 256 color monitor, 20 MHz 030 or better, 4MB RAM, 7MB hard disk space, System 7 or later, CD-ROM drive.

THE 7TH GUEST	
Fun factor:	4.0
Look and feel:	4.5
Value:	4.0
Replayability:	3.0
Overall:	4.0

CD

Alone in the Dark
I•Motion/Infogrames/MacPlay

If you've ever played one of Sierra On-Line's Leisure Suit Larry games but wished you could move around in an environment like the one in 4D Boxing, Alone in the Dark is here to answer your prayers. Originally a DOS game, Alone in the Dark uses a three-dimensional environment and polygon-based characters that move realistically. This game was a huge hit on DOS machines, and nothing has been lost in the translation.

Get ready to face off against demons galore when you take on the challenge of walking through the impressive 3D world of Alone in the Dark.

Creepsville

Amazingly, Alone in the Dark allows the user to choose either a male or female protagonist. This is rare in computer gaming. The game centers around a creepy old mansion that was owned by the recently demised Jeremy Hartwood, an artist who imitated Vincent van Gogh both in life and death. Playing either private eye Edward Carnby or Edward's niece Emily, you venture into the demon-infested halls of Hartwood's mansion to find the reason for his untimely death. As with most adventures, you can pick up objects and employ them to uncover clues to the mystery. You embark on your quest in the attic and work downward through the house, always alert to visual clues that might lead to information or even a secret passage.

GREAT
FEATURE

Looking Over Your Shoulder

Navigating Alone in the Dark's environment is a highly unique experience because your view of the action is constantly changing between nine separate camera angles. Depending on where you're moving or what part of a room you're in, the angle changes automatically to give you a different view. The use of perspective is stunning and adds tremendously to gameplay. The screen art, color, fluid motion, and perspective contribute to a very engrossing experience in which we found ourselves actually getting creeped out when faced with a gargoyle.

GREAT
FEATURE

When moving around a room, you'll occasionally step on hot spots and cause meanies to come looking for you. But not to worry; the background music will start up and warn you of any imminent danger. Remember to search every room thoroughly and read any scraps of paper you come across; you never know how you might piece together the answers to questions.

When doing battle, we noticed that view changes sometimes made it difficult to judge the enemy's distance and that this could cause kicks and punches to miss. This merely requires a little getting used to. Before you know it you'll be kicking demon butt with the best of them.

Keyboard or Nothing

Control in Alone in the Dark is limited to keyboard commands, although game parameters can be adjusted using either menus or key commands. Overall, the controls are easy to learn, with the basic movement coming from the numeric keypad, and the inventory and modes settings from a couple of other keys. We found that we didn't need a reference card to learn the keys and that a few minutes of game play was enough to establish a comfortable rapport with the command set.

Don't Be Afraid of the Dark

Alone in the Dark is a pleasure to play once you've gotten the hang of managing a three-dimensional character from multiple camera angles. The real joy of this game arises from its ability to pull the user into the story. In fact, we got the same feeling of being drawn into the game playing Alone in the Dark that we encountered when we first booted MYST. Don't get us wrong—this game should not be compared directly to MYST, but the atmosphere, great animation, and use of perspective make Alone in the Dark a winner.

Pros: Fantastic use of perspective. Compelling story and atmosphere draws you in. Both male and female protagonist available. Runs well on most Macs.

Cons: No built-in joystick support. Interface takes a while to get used to.

System Requirements: 256-color monitor, 68040 or PowerPC suggested, 3MB RAM, 7MB hard disk space, System 6.0.7 or higher.

ALONE IN THE DARK	
Fun factor:	4.0
Look and feel:	4.5
Value:	4.0
Replayability:	2.5
Overall:	4.0

Quest Adventures

We recall our high school days when cliques of (mainly) boys would hang out in study hall fiercely scribbling in small notebooks and proclaiming that they were going to invoke the Spell of Unsightly Warts and turn their schoolmates into packs of toads. Although this aberrant behavior might have been due to drug abuse, the more likely explanation lies elsewhere, with Dungeons & Dragons. Playing D&D probably hasn't ceased, but there is now an alternative. The practice of assembling and outfitting a group of magical creatures has moved to the digital domain. If you aspire to wizardry, some of the games reviewed below should be in your bag of tricks.

Ultima III
PlayMaker/Origin

In 1983, the third installation in the great Ultima role-playing series was released for Apple II, IBM, and Commodore 64 computers. The game was a huge success, laying the groundwork for literally hundreds of other games. In 1985, Origin released its only Mac title, Exodus: Ultima III. The box included the usual books of Amber Runes and the Liturgy of Truth as well as a cloth map of the mysterious land of Sosaria. But somewhere along the line a system software upgrade made Ultima III unplayable, and Origin decided to bow out of the Mac gaming derby for the next ten years. Ah, but there is light at the end of the tunnel, and PlayMaker recently resurrected this grand old game, colorized it, and made it compatible for new generations to learn the roots of role-playing games.

Secrets of Sosaria

After the demise of the wizards Mondain and Minax, peace flowed through the land of Sosaria. But times are turning dark again with rumors of the rise of the Great Earth Serpent and the resurrection of all that is evil in the land. On that happy note, Exodus: Ultima III begins. (This was the game that first allowed a party of four adventurers to join together in order to explore—and conquer.) It's a substantial thing, really—the inclusion of multiple party members allows for a wizard, a cleric, and a couple of fighters if you wish. The bottom line is that you can customize your party to your liking. The premise is the same as that of many role-playing games: wander the countryside and destroy travelling bands of evil monsters while solving the bigger problem, in this case, the Great Earth Snake.

Color at Last

It took only ten years, but Ultima III has finally come to the Mac in living color and in full-screen format. The game is pretty much what it was a decade ago, with some minor art and color adjustments, and the interface is exactly the same. Moving around can be purely a mouse activity, or the arrow keys can be employed. In fact, there is an extensive keyboard command set that is exquisitely displayed in the online reference section along with the various appropriate charts that are so critical to the Ultima games.

An Old Friend Returns

Although there are plenty of other quality shareware role-playing games available, Exodus: Ultima III is a proven commercial game that was a huge hit and that kind of pulls on our heart strings when we reminisce about childhoods spent trying to destroy that darned snake. The graphics have been substantially updated, and the online help is excellent, so you have no excuse not to play this game and send in your shareware fee. Heck, at least you can try it before you buy. There's a copy of Exodus: Ultima III on the included CD-ROM.

CD

ULTIMA III	
Fun factor:	3.5
Look and feel:	3.0
Value:	3.5
Replayability:	3.0
Overall:	3.5

Pros: Proven game. Updated graphics. Compelling. Low shareware price.

Cons: Totally outdated by today's technology.

System Requirements: 256-color monitor, Mac II or better, 3MB RAM, 3.2MB hard drive space, System 7 or later.

Advanced Dungeons and Dragons Series, Collector's Edition
SSI/MacSoft

Over the last few years SSI has churned out five Advanced Dungeon and Dragons adventures of increasing complexity. With the release of Might and Magic III, it became obvious that the interface utilized in the SSI games had reached the end of its life. This prompted SSI to release the complete Forgotten Realms series on one CD-ROM for the Mac. After the last segment of the Forgotten Realms games (Pools of Darkness), SSI released Unlimited Adventures, a construction set for creating your very own Forgotten Realms adventures. SSI has been rumored to be working on converting Dark Suns to the Mac, which will utilize a 16-bit engine and provide a more realistic gaming environment, but frankly we have no idea if SSI has shelved the Mac project or not.

A Port Is a Port of Course of Course

These games closely follow the Dungeons and Dragons theme. For true role-playing gamers, there can be no better framework to play in. Unfortunately, what are otherwise great games are clobbered by a pure DOS interface and graphics whose resolution is one-quarter that of what Mac users expect. Undoubtedly, hard core D&Ders won't blink an eye at the crummy interface and spectacularly annoying copy protection schemes, but for most gamers we must recommend moving on to another title. Don't get us wrong—the story-lines and D&D realism are great, but they're packaged in a shell that's unplayable by today's standards.

LOUSY FEATURE

Forty Lashes With a Floppy Disk

SSI and MacSoft went to the trouble of repackaging all these games in a nice new box with a shiny CD-ROM and all the appropriate documentation and then left all the manual-based copy protection on. What were they thinking? The CD is protection enough, and hey, these games are so far out of date technological-ly that they're hardly worth the trouble. Come on, get it together next time; nobody's gonna bother copying them. We don't appreciate having to look up a cryptic code every time we want to play one of the games we forked over hard-earned cash for.

RANT

Does Creating Adventures Create Fun?

Unlimited Adventures allows you to play God with every aspect of game play; you are limited only by your imagination. One can only guess how much time could be spent creating an epic AD&D saga the size of Pools of Darkness. You could spend hours adjusting every nuance of battle, monsters, overland areas, and nonplayer characters. In light of this, it is foreseeable that adventures supe-rior to the Forgotten Realms series could be produced by end users. Adjusting the nitty gritty of the game requires either an extensive knowledge of AD&D or a thorough reading of the extensive manual. The question is whether or not there are enough people out there with the desire to create their own AD&D adventure.

DANGER

A Dying Breed

As adventure games, the Forgotten Realms series succeeds in providing inter-esting quests, puzzles, and story lines. You can utilize a wide variety of monsters, weapons and spells in game play, and this series will give ardent AD&D folks plenty of enjoyment. However, the interface, graphics, and copy protection stink. Enough said.

Pros: Follows Advanced Dungeons and Dragons theme.

Cons: Poor graphics for the Mac platform. Copy protection nauseating. Poor interface. Not Power Mac compatible.

System Requirements: Any desktop Mac (except PowerPC), 4MB RAM, System 7 or later, CD-ROM drive.

ADVANCED D&D SERIES	
Fun factor:	2.0
Look and feel:	2.0
Value:	3.5
Replayability:	3.0
Overall:	2.5

Quest For Glory I: So You Want to Be a Hero?

Sierra On-Line

We know you secretly want to live life on the edge as a renegade adventurer. Why else would you bother to enroll in the Famous Adventurer's Correspondence School? This is the crux of Quest for Glory I: So You Want to Be a Hero. If you're crinkling your face and groaning over the prospect of another adventure game in the style of King's Quest, take a deep breath, crack open a cold one, and park your seat back in front of the computer because Quest for Glory is refreshingly different.

Heroics 101

The major difference between Quest for Glory and other Sierra adventure games is the addition of role-playing. Right from the start, you have the choice of beginning the expedition as a thief, magic user, or fighter. Of course as the game progresses, various important attributes of your character can be improved: strength, intelligence, vitality, luck, and magic. And numerous skills, such as climbing and picking locks, can be learned or acquired over time. Probably the best way for a beginner to get a feel for the game is to start as a fighter and hack and slash his or her way to victory. The thief and magic user characters require a little more finesse in order to achieve the rank of truly famous adventurer. There is a slightly different storyline for each character, and this adds somewhat to the game's replayability and is especially nice if you really love hobnobbing with elves and goblins and such.

TIP

Quest for Glory I is a fun little game from Sierra that strays from the Sierra tradition by incorporating role-playing. Let's go troll hunting!

Me and My Mouse

Although a port, Quest for Glory's graphics are certainly acceptable for the kind of game it is. The interface is neither Mac nor DOS; it's its own entity. The command bar is accessed simply by moving the mouse to the upper portion of the screen and clicking on the appropriate box. Each box offers access to a different control strip. All means of interacting with the environment can be accomplished with a minimal learning curve, although this layered approach can sometimes be cumbersome. Movement is achieved by simply clicking the mouse on the area of the screen you wish to be. If the route there is impassable, your character will not move. If you are dying to move around using the keypad, it can be arranged, but this is one game that can be played quite comfortably with just a mouse. We found that the interface generally fits in with the feeling of the game, the low-resolution graphics and the animation quite nicely. Character involvement ranges from the scary to the farcical, but all in all adds to the storyline.

The Price is Right

Quest for Glory I is really an exercise in fun and makes an excellent addition to any gaming library for a number of reasons: The interface is easy to use and is completely mouse driven, there's a good smattering of humor throughout, and the game is very inexpensive. The DOS side of the world is up to Quest for Glory 5, so we have a ways to go to catch up. But when a game is this much fun and this good a value, more versions should follow.

Pros: Great value. Role-playing game. Good sound. Sense of humor.

Cons: Graphics are low resolution. The odd bug appears.

System Requirements: Any 256-color Mac, 4MB RAM, 10MB hard disk space, System 7 or later, supports General MIDI and Roland MT/CM-32.

QUEST FOR GLORY I	
Fun factor:	3.0
Look and feel:	3.5
Value:	4.5
Replayability:	3.0
Overall:	3.5

Might & Magic III Worlds of Xeen
New World Computing

The Mac's decade of existence has yielded precious few role-playing dungeons and dragons games, and as is often the case, many of the games that trickled into the land of point and click were but weak translations sloppily moved from other platforms. However, New World Computing has bucked the trend by successfully porting its long-running Might and Magic series of games to the Mac without offending the traditionally elitist Mac gaming crowd (ourselves included). Might and Magic III hit the scene in early 1993 and delivered a knockout punch by winning several accolades as one of the top games of the year. The long-awaited twin sequels to M&M III, the Clouds of Xeen and the Darkside of Xeen (which were sold separately for the DOS platform as M&M IV and M&M V), were paired on a single CD-ROM for Mac users and interwoven, thus creating a very large single game with multiple quests entitled World of Xeen.

Do You Believe in Magic?
These epic journeys begin in front of a cozy bed-and-breakfast in relatively safe towns (and safe truly is a relative term in these games). Character generation and party building take place at the inns. Although you're always given a party that could see you through the perils of game play, we found it considerably more fun to create our own characters from scratch. This requires a little more time and, heaven forbid, reading the manual a bit, but the joy of controlling a character such as Bartor the Blunderous is unsurpassed. In the case of the Worlds of Xeen,

a party of up to six characters can be assembled from such expected characters as dwarfs, elves, humans, and ogres. Any ardent D&D player will tell you that a good mix of muscle, magic, and thievery is critical to success. Generally speaking, if you can rustle up a fighter, a cleric, a wizard, and a thief, you've covered the basics. The vacancies can be filled by picking from a host of other characters, such as rangers or paladins.

The Adventure Begins

Once your party has been put together, the game just sorta begins as the group wanders into the realm of Xeen (or the Isles of Terra in M&M III). There are many mini-quests to accomplish along the road to ultimate victory, and you come across them simply by chatting with characters in the game or by bumping into hideous monsters bent on sucking your brains out with straws. Might and Magic III comes with no less than 112 monsters to battle, and the Worlds of Xeen certainly doesn't disappoint if you're looking for some carefree carnage. For those more bent on puzzles (on a grand scale), The Worlds of Xeen CD-ROM offers the option of reducing the amount of combat that must be endured during the course of the game. This small allowance makes the game much more appealing to those who want to finish the ordeal within their lifetimes. We found Xeen's lower-combat Adventurer setting to have quite enough hack and slash, thank you very much.

GREAT FEATURE

It will take weeks or months of occasional gameplay to reach the final stages of these games. However, their difficulty level is very reasonable, and unless foolishness is a hallmark of your personality, making progress shouldn't require Herculean effort. But if the sun has gone behind the clouds and you're about ready to take a ball peen hammer to your monitor, there's always the hint books (which have to be purchased separately) or a hint line to guide you through the rough areas. Heck, the hint books will just about smack you in the face with the answers if you really want them to, but we found that frequent head blows with obvious hints tended to change the chemistry of the games more than we wanted.

TIP

Worlds of Color

The result of M&M's use of the Mac's graphical capabilities is a mixed bag. Although the graphics are clear and considerably more impressive when compared directly with those of the DOS game, they have a somewhat cartoony appearance. However, the color is brilliant and we consider the cartoon-like quality of the graphics to be more than acceptable. It remains to be seen if Lords of Midnight and Dungeon Master II will rival this quality when they're released. The animations are nicely done considering the volume of material involved in

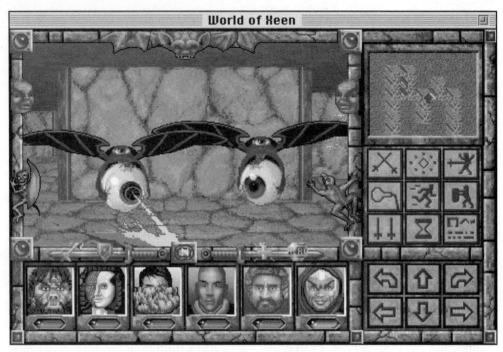

New World Computing's Worlds of Xeen remains the best role-playing game on the market. It can easily suck two months of your life into the computer.

these games, and it's good to see the incorporation of humor in the face-offs against the various nasties.

Might and Magic utilizes a 3D forward window perspective with a decorative border that serves multiple purposes. Various gems and creatures lining the window move in special situations to indicate secret rooms, direction, and even imminent decapitation. The interface is point and click with single-key equivalents for most commands. Cross-controller capability makes the game functional with mouse, keyboard, or both. Invariably most players will enjoy a mouse/keyboard combination. We commend New World Computing for their efforts with the M&M interface; they've added just the right amount of Mac feeling to the existing control set.

What the Worlds of Xeen Can Do for You

The 1995 release of the Worlds of Xeen provided what is essentially M&M 4 and 5 together on one CD. What is impressive however, is that NWC has incorporated a level of play that involves a crossover between the two worlds, something the DOS platform does not have without the separate purchase of both

GREAT FEATURE

games. Also, minor interface adjustments were made, most notably the incorporation of speech when players are interacting with game characters. This adds a bundle to the feel of the game, and we found ourselves enjoying Xeen more than M&M III despite the similarities in game play. The other notable difference between Xeen and M&M III lies in the omission of two characters. The party has a maximum of six bodies, down from eight in M&M III.

Premier Role-Playing

Despite the delay in arriving from the world of DOS, both Might and Magic III and the Worlds of Xeen CD are excellent games that remain at the pinnacle of commercial role-playing games for the Mac. We readily recommend both games. Keep in mind, however, that the Worlds of Xeen requires a CD-ROM drive and a little more horsepower for acceptable game play. The level of challenge, great graphics, and ergonomic interface make either game a pleasure to play for all but those who despise these "elfy" sort of games.

MIGHT & MAGIC III	
Fun factor:	4.O
Look and feel:	4.O
Value:	4.O
Replayability:	3.O
Overall:	3.5

WORLDS OF XEEN	
Fun factor:	4.O
Look and feel:	4.O
Value:	4.5
Replayability:	4.O
Overall:	4.5

Might & Magic III System Requirements: Any desktop Mac, 2MB RAM for black and white, 4MB RAM for color, 15MB hard drive space, System 7 or later.

Pros: Great graphics. Digitized speech (Worlds of Xeen). Challenging yet not too challenging. Everything D&D fans love. WOX really cooks on Power Macs (with the PPC patch that's included on this book's enclosed CD-ROM).

CD

Cons: Worlds of Xeen requires horsepower. Takes up lots of disk space. Not Power-PC native.

Worlds of Xeen System Requirements: Mac IIci or better, 3MB RAM, 3MB hard drive space. System 7 or later.

Digital Environments

How do you classify products such as Madness of Roland, Quantum Gate, and Gadget? As games? Movies? Exploratory environments? Digital picture books?

Although these products have minor gaming elements, they aren't games, and for this reason we've chosen not to rate them. Some are digital movies in which the viewer has little or no effect on the plot or outcome. Others are interactive environments intended only for exploration.

For lack of a better term, we call them digital environments. They're a side road to computer entertainment upon which the viewer is occasionally free to wander through the surroundings, activate an interesting device, and learn something of the local inhabitants.

Alice
L-Zone
Gadget
Synergy, Inc.

These three products are by Japanese artist and director Haruhiko Shono. Each is a visual treat.

Alice

Shono's earliest release, Alice, is billed as an interactive museum, and it is exactly that. Containing elements of Lewis Carroll's *Alice in Wonderland*, Alice is a showcase for the paintings of Kuniyoshi Kaneko and the music of Kazuhiko Kato. The piece contains 13 rooms filled with Kaneko's sometimes graphic artwork and interactive objects created by Shono.

Alice contains one gaming element—collecting 53 playing cards (the regular deck plus the joker) hidden among 12 of the rooms. Each card reveals one of Alice's secrets. The joker divulges the mystery of leaving the museum.

DANGER

Warning: If you are offended by artistic depictions of naked human beings, avoid Alice. We thought the paintings were intriguing (if a little disturbing). You may not.

L-Zone

L-Zone is an exploratory environment set in an abandoned automated city of the future. Working in linear fashion, you travel about the domed city interacting with various machines and devices left there by a mad scientist. If there's a point to the enterprise other than the joy of making beautifully rendered devices come to life and observing their operation, it's to activate all the machinery to reveal the secret of the city and escape to the outside world.

The environment is accompanied by a techno-synthesizer sound track that, although adding to the mechanized feel of the city, may not be to everyone's liking (Chris, an analog synth junkie, thought it was cool).

Gadget

Shono's most linear work, Gadget, is an interactive novel that takes place in a gloomily sterile, machine-laden environment. The artwork and video is Shono at his most impressive and oppressive (image a widget-smitten Edward Hopper working in Eastern Europe circa 1930). Koji Ueno contributes a beautifully realized industrial score that relies on percussion instruments and low strings.

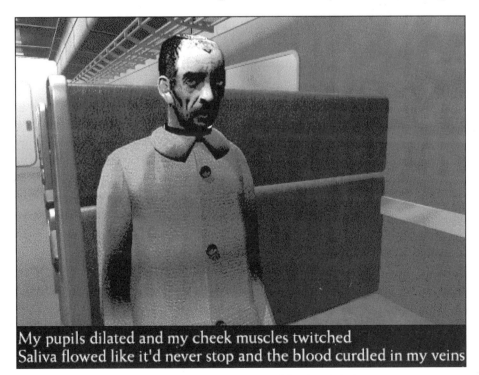

My pupils dilated and my cheek muscles twitched
Saliva flowed like it'd never stop and the blood curdled in my veins

Just one of the disturbing characters you'll encounter in Haruhiko Shono's Gadget.

The sweeping black-and-white QuickTime videos that are sprinkled about the piece are equally impressive.

Gadget's storyline is confounding at times, and users expecting a neat plot and sensible resolution will be disappointed. But the plot is most definitely not the point. Rather, Gadget is a showcase for Shono's substantial design and directorial skills.

Summary

Alice, L-Zone, and Gadget are no more games than a coffee table book full of glossy artwork is a novel. These interactive CD-ROMs are visual and aural delights that can be enjoyed time and again.

The Madness of Roland
HyperBole Studios

The Madness of Roland is by far the closest thing we've seen to a virtual book. It's so unique we are at somewhat of a loss to describe it, but suffice to say that the creator of both the program and the story has done an excellent job of melding books and multimedia. The man responsible for this enthralling creation is Greg Roach, a playwright who holds an M.F.A. in directing and who has dedicated the last four years of his work to HyperBole Studios. The result is thought-provoking multilayered stories embedded within the realm of CD-ROM technology.

Medieval Fantasy Extraordinaire

The place is France, the time, a long-ago era of knights and kings. One man, Roland, stands between a brutal invading army and Paris. The vengeful Mandricardo, humiliated by Roland in battle, seeks to have the enchantress Angelica consume Roland's spirit with madness. It's a heck of a compelling story and the best adaptation of a book for a computer we've ever seen. Roland can be described as an interactive novel of sorts. It's all here: text, speech, video, and a great interface. We should stress that this is not a game but rather a hybrid entertainment package that pulls you into a fantastic story and completely engulfs you with sound clips and well-acted video.

GREAT FEATURE

Although the Madness of Roland is arranged as a book, the story is presented in a very unique way. Every phase of it is told separately by the main characters, who have completely different and often contradictory, perceptions of events. This is an absolutely fabulous aspect of (we want to say gameplay but can't) the book, and it draws the reader/watcher/listener into pondering the authenticity of characters'

The Madness of Roland is a unique multimedia book that incorporates speech, video, and excellent acting into a compelling story.

faculties and taking sides. Over 500MB of QuickTime video, pictures, and sound went into the Madness of Roland, but if you're feeling old fashioned, you can simply print out the 70-odd-page book and take it to bed for a cozy read.

The Beginning of a New Genre

The Madness of Roland demonstrates clearly that the personal computer can be a powerful story telling tool right up there with film and television. As the author Greg Roach tells you in the 25MB QuickTime movie entitled "Author's Notes," he hopes The Madness of Roland inspires people to read some of the great books out there. Roland is a blending of active and passive interaction in which the element of imagination is not sucked into a vortex, as it is when watching television, and it shows that the computer can truly be a medium for critical works. And to add to all these positive comments, our cats liked the story too.

**GREAT
FEATURE**

Quantum Gate
HyperBole Studios
Distributed by WEA

Quantum Gate is Greg Roach's second interactive movie. In this dark science fiction tale, Roach shifts from the medieval setting of The Madness of Roland to an apocalyptic 21st century.

Earth has reached an insurmountable environmental crisis. You view Quantum Gate from the perspective of Drew Griffin, a young military recruit who has signed on to help avert this crisis. Drew's job is to protect a group of miners working on a distant world. These miners are attempting to extract from the planet an ore that may help reverse the damage done to Mother Earth. The local inhabitants, a race of buglike critters, are none too happy about this invasion and strongly resist the interlopers.

If this were the extent of the plot, you'd have the makings of a fair-to-middlin' arcade game. But remember, this isn't a game. And it turns out, things may not be what they seem. Another recruit, Private Michaels has put two and two together and come up with five. Something definitely stinks about this mission. Through interactions with Michaels and the other characters, the awful truth of Quantum Gate is slowly revealed.

Lights, Camera, Action

We should admit that our blood runs cold whenever we see a CD-ROM product boasting live actors. Oftentimes, the performances are godawful. But this is not the case with Quantum Gate. Roach pulls fine performances from the talented cast. Jamie Callahan, who plays Michaels, and James Black, who assumes the role of the malevolent Colonel Saunders, are particularly good.

Another problem with most interactive movies is that the plot and screenwriting tend to be weak. Roach handles both admirably. Quantum Gate's story exceeds the caliber of many Hollywood blockbusters, and the dialog is quite believable. Roach takes the time to relate the main story and small subplots properly, by carefully relating small pieces of information. Throughout Quantum Gate, we are treated to a number of Griffin's memories that flesh out his character and provide motivation for his being in his wretched situation.

Small QuickTime movie windows such as these are part of Quantum Gate's interface.

The Silver Screen

Quantum Gate's interface is typical of interactive adventures: click on the screen to turn left or right and to move forward. One distracting element of the interface is that when you are not moving, the screen is displayed in wide-screen letterbox format. When you click to move, the sides scroll in to produce a square video window in which the traveling sequence plays out. The letterbox reappears when you stop. This constant reminder of the interface interrupts the flow of the movie and makes it difficult for you to remain fully engaged.

GREAT FEATURE

In a nod to the gaming market, Roach includes an arcadelike shoot-'em-up that represents the battle interface during the bug-killing portion of the movie. You can play with this game outside the confines of the movie, but Roach should have left it out altogether. It adds little to the plot, looks cheap, and, because it's CD-ROM-based, responds terribly.

Aside from this poorly implemented game, Quantum Gate provides an example of how good interactive film making can be. We've seen Quantum Gate in the catalogs for around $30. This is a significant improvement over the initial list price of $80 and makes it close to affordable for a product you're likely to put on the shelf after a single viewing.

LOUSY FEATURE

We understand that a sequel to Quantum Gate that features three different endings and more interactivity than the original is on the way. We're convinced of Mr. Roach's skills and talents and anxiously await its arrival.

9 ⟩ Science Fiction

Take two parts spaceship, six parts futuristic weaponry, three-quarters of a cup of alien terror, a dash of time travel, and what do you have? Right, one of the most popular computer gaming genres—science fiction adventures.

Generally contained on CD-ROMs, these games are sonic and visual gems pumped full of QuickTime video, rendered graphics, and huge sound files. Not for those with weak Macs, they are also the most processor-demanding games around.

Spaceship Warlock
Reactor

Reactor, a company founded by former comic book writer Mike Saenz, was one of the first to jump on the CD-ROM band wagon with a ground-breaking game bulging at the seams with over 125MB of data. Hey, stop laughing! We know there are several games on the market around the two-gigabyte range now. But back in 1990, that was really something. In fact, we consider Spaceship Warlock to be one of the first games to push the technology envelope by requiring 3.5MB free RAM and at least a 13-inch monitor. Keep in mind that in 1990, the Mac LC with 2MB RAM and a 12-inch monitor was the norm for many. Warlock upped the ante considerably.

STELLA!!!

Playing Spaceship Warlock is sort of like getting trapped in a campy '50s science fiction movie complete with a supporting cast of characters with names like Hammer, Starbird, and our personal favorite, Stella. The journey begins after wrangling your way onto an interstellar cruise ship called the *Belshazzar* where opulence is redefined and the limits of good taste are stretched like Gumby. Through a series of coincidences, you are thrust into cahoots with a band of rebels in the spaceship *Warlock*. They are bent on ending the evil domination of humankind by the Kroll empire. The story progresses easily, and on today's faster machines the entire game can be completed in a few hours. But the game's brevity shouldn't detract from its appeal. After all, Warlock is more than half a decade old, and it still kicks butt on many modern games for sheer entertainment value.

Macromedia Forever

Warlock was one of the first CD-ROM games to utilize Macromedia Director to manage the on-screen animation. Although this is considered passé in some circles, it still works for many games, and Warlock is a prime example of how it should be done. Navigating the Warlock world is strictly point and click, making the learning curve a horizontal line. Hey, a couple of Airedale terriers could paw their way through this game in a single work day. Picking up objects is equally simple, utilizing the click-and-drag method all Mac users are familiar with. Performance is a non-issue for anyone with a Mac made after 1993, and

Spaceship Warlock was the first CD-ROM game billed as an interactive movie game. It's still fun to horse around with.

Warlock occupies only 125MB on the CD, so you may want to just copy it over to your hard drive to make the screen transitions more zippy.

Still Fresh

Spaceship Warlock sold a pile of copies and was one of the hottest games of 1991. It's still available, and the great color, sound, animation, and obtuse sense of humor still make it a fun game to run through on a rainy Sunday.

It'd be nice if Reactor came out with some more titles. After tempting us with demos for Screaming Metal and Necromancer, the folks down at Reactor are rewriting the books on vaporware.

Pros: Nice graphics and animation. Fun sense of humor. Easy to play. Fast on today's machines.

Cons: Can be finished in a couple hours. Not particularly challenging.

System Requirements: 13-inch color monitor, 3.5MB RAM, CD-ROM drive.

SPACESHIP WARLOCK	
Fun factor:	4.0
Look and feel:	3.5
Value:	3.0
Replayability:	2.5
Overall:	3.5

The Journeyman Project
Presto Studios

The Journeyman Project was the next step in the evolution of the science fiction adventure after Spaceship Warlock. It was also the largest game on a CD-ROM to that date, taking up over 400MB of space. And it was the first title with truly rendered graphics throughout the entire game and a digitized soundtrack that showed the level of ambiance that could be achieved with music. The first versions of the game were painfully slow at times, but version 1.2 is up to 400% faster in some places and certainly runs acceptably on all contemporary Macs.

It's About Time

It's 2318 and you're reveling in the fact that humanity has enjoyed a peaceful coexistence since the inception of a unified world government 200 years ago. No war or suffering, lots of clean air, and everybody's happy. Anyway, an alien race made contact ten years ago asking if we wanted to join their ranks. The aliens imposed a ten-year time limit on giving an answer, and now the time has come. The twist lies in the fact that time travel has become possible and, what do you know, you work for the very organization that makes possible these futuristic forays in time. This is a secret association called the Temporal Protectorate that keeps a special record of history stored in prehistoric Earth as a reference when distortions are suspected.

It seems that the decision whether or not to join the aliens is being altered by the past. Someone has gone back in time to change Earth's thinking on alien influences. Unfortunately, it's happened on your shift, so you're gonna have to put down that jelly-filled donut and get ready for a hop, skip, and a jump through the annals of time.

GREAT FEATURE

Journeyman was the first game to offer multiple solutions to a game's central problem. Its outcome and the method of finding a solution depend on some of your early choices, and this of course makes the game replayable several times over. The puzzles in Journeyman are a tad linear in nature, but the visual treats you're given for solving problems are worth any lack of depth in the predicaments presented. The Journeyman Project is a visually impressive experience that even now has us in awe of its 3D photo-realistic screens. It's clear it was ahead of its time in many ways.

In Your Eye

As a card-carrying member of the protectorate, you have been implanted with a special device in your left eye that allows you to access various capabilities that will aid in your quest. The game's interface can be completely mouse controlled or augmented with keyboard commands for movement, but a mouse is a must regardless.

When moving about in Journeyman, each step is accomplished in a segmented way. That's to say that the movement is not fluid; it occurs a "chunk" at a time. Many of the screens—often animated—are worth the sacrifice, however. The biochip interface is always available, and access to mapping or time travel is just a click away.

A Game in a Game in a Game

The Journeyman Project incorporates over 30 minutes of live video that doesn't fall flat with lousy acting. There's also several integrated mind and arcade challenges that add to the gaming experience, so if you thought it'd strictly be point and click, you'd better check the old cranium in for an oil change. Journeyman was designed on a Mac, for the Mac, and it shows. Navigating the interface is a breeze, and such mundane tasks as saving and loading games are colorfully presented in the custom interface. If you like the completely original soundtrack, you can pop the CD in any audio player and listen to the nine tracks in full digital splendor. Although it's been surpassed many times since its 1992 release, The Journeyman Project has only one technical problem, that being the slowness of the early versions, but this should not be a problem on high-end 030 or 040 machines.

GREAT FEATURE

Our one major complaint with Journeyman is in regard to its—what else?—copy protection. Granted that it isn't overly obtrusive—you just have to look up a couple of codes during the course of play. But what the heck were they thinking when they copy protected a 400MB game back when a 400MB hard drive cost about 800 bucks? Did they actually fear moving mobs of pirates with bandannas, eye patches, and gigabyte hard drives strapped to their hips? Why did they need copy protection at all? Sheesh, talk about annoying.

Journeyman Still Cuts It

The Journeyman Project is still a compelling and exciting game. Even three-and-a-half years after its first release, the rendered graphics, branching storyline, and innovative interface make it an example for some new games. This is one game that had a dramatic effect on CD-ROM gaming in general, and its effects are still reverberating.

Pros: Excellent rendered art. Great early integration of video. Branching storyline.

Cons: Off-disk copy protection. Older versions of game painfully slow.

System Requirements: 256-color monitor, Mac II or better, 5MB RAM, 440K hard disk space, CD-ROM drive.

THE JOURNEYMAN PROJECT	
Fun factor:	3.5
Look and feel:	4.5
Value:	3.5
Replayability:	4.0
Overall:	4.0

The Journeyman Project II: Buried in Time

Presto Studios/Sanctuary Woods

So you think all's well now that you've saved the world from being thrust back into the war and suffering of the old days, eh? Getting a little cocky since you solved Journeyman I? Well, Agent 5, the fun is just beginning, because someone has altered the fabric of time, a capital offense, and left you holding the smoking gun. Yep, the guys down at Presto Studios have come out of their two-and-a-half year hiatus with a three-CD sequel to the best-selling Journeyman Project. But did they overcome their previous problems with game speed? The answer is yes, in a big, big way.

Groundhog Day

As Agent 5, you have for some strange reason been set up to look like a criminal who's marauded through time changing the past to benefit yourself. You are apprehended and thrown in jail without even passing Go or collecting 200 dollars. But through a fluke you are able to escape to the past to get yourself a jumpsuit before the Temporal Protectorate catches up. The jumpsuit has a nifty cloaking device that enables you to do a Timothy Leary and drop out whenever being seen is not appropriate.

With nothing but the jumpsuit on your back, you must traverse history and unravel the plot. Only diligent time travel can unwrap the mysteries of why you were framed. Be prepared to jump to such diverse locales as Richard the Lion Hearted's castle, Leonardo da Vinci's workshop, a space station, and even Mayan ruins. Unlike The Journeyman Project, Buried in Time does not impose any penalty for time spent in a particular zone. So kick back and take as long as you'd

The Journeyman Project II: Buried in Time offers a new interface and some of the most incredible graphics available in gaming today.

like. As you jump from zone to zone, you must search for evidence that will clear your name.

A Step Beyond

Buried in Time relies heavily on rendered graphics, but the QuickTime movie format allows you to "flow" toward your destination. In 16-bit color it is amazingly clear. Also, you almost always have the option to look from side to side and even up and down, so full visual inspection of any area is a treat, not an annoyance. The full-scrolling graphics in Buried in Time are amongst the best we've seen, and the method in which they've been melded seamlessly into gameplay results in quick, fluid movement. Buried in Time also incorporates live-action video into the rendered backdrops. The video is glitch free and adds greatly to the gaming experience.

GREAT FEATURE

Improved Speed and Interface

The game moves along very quickly on 040 and Power Macs. The only problem we came across was the need for swapping between the three CDs. This however, was usually a minor annoyance; it encumbered play only when we frequently jumped from zone to zone.

The interface has had a facelift, and it is quicker and more functional. Some nice features have been added, including better ergonomics and a larger display. The folks at Presto have definitely responded to the requests of users, and that's always good to see.

A Sequel Many Times Better Than the Original

The Journeyman Project II: Buried in Time is leaps and bounds ahead of the original game. Fluid QuickTime movement, a better interface, greatly increased speed, and a more complex story and world make BIT a great gaming experience. Although it comes on three CDs, it cannot be compared directly to Daedalus (reviewed later in this book). The visuals are different but equally impressive for both games. Buried in Time follows more closely in the footsteps of computer gaming, and it offers users a more hands-on and less passive experience. Buried in Time's puzzles, graphics, and amazing quality should make gamers eager for the next title from Presto Studios. But if it requires the kind of leap that Buried in Time took, they will probably have to wait for a while.

Pros: Improved interface. Amazing graphics. Lots of fun.

Cons: Needs fast machine with 16-bit color.

System Requirements: Thousands of colors, 68040 Mac or Power Mac, 8MB RAM, 4MB hard disk space, System 7.1 or later, double-speed CD-ROM.

THE JOURNEYMAN PROJECT II: BURIED IN TIME	
Fun factor:	5.0
Look and feel:	5.0
Value:	4.5
Replayability:	4.0
Overall:	5.0

Iron Helix

Drew Pictures

Iron Helix falls into the better-than-average category of early science fiction CD-ROM games. The game features good graphics, a high-tech interface, and game play and design that are a little lacking. Here's the plot in a nutshell:

Wretched quality control leads you, an underfunded scientist, to send valuable, unmanned probes to a cootie-ridden death ship to collect DNA samples that will provide access to video clues left by a dead crew. The clues, in turn, show you how to get out of the mess you're in and save the galaxy from immediate warfare with some testy otherworlders. The hitch is that a cranky on-board mobile security system known as the Defender would like nothing better than to eradicate your unarmed probes. Oh, and by the way, you have 90 minutes to complete your mission before war begins.

Clear enough? Good. Now let's take a look at the works behind the scenes.

The Works

Iron Helix contains some 1,500 animation sequences rendered in brooding 3D. Due to the performance limitations of CD-ROMs, the animation window needs to be small enough to allow the animation to play at a workable speed. The game's designers solved the tiny-window problem by incorporating the animation screen into a larger control panel. From this panel you not only view the animated on-board action but also get feedback regarding your probe and the Defender's location, and control simple game functions such as Pause, Save, and Quit.

Shut Up and Listen!

The game begins and ends with a video briefing from Admiral Arboc, a somewhat testy woman whose dominatrix appearance and attitude might be a source of either irritation or titillation. Sandwiched between these encounters, the

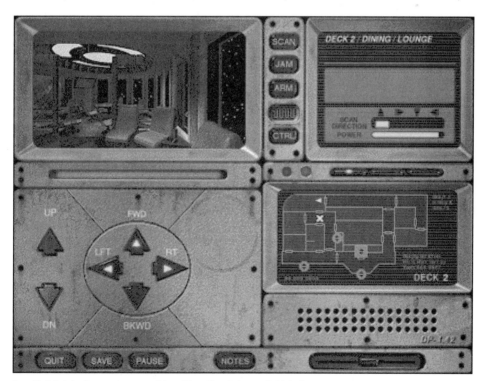

Iron Helix's interface comes complete with coffee stains and drink rings.

game proceeds in four phases: the search for the proper DNA strands; the hunt for video clues that detail various ways to defeat the Defender and disable the ship; the death of the Defender; and finally, the swan song of the death ship. You must complete each phase before proceeding to the next. To maximize performance, the phases of the game are laid out sequentially on the CD-ROM for faster access to the proper animation sequences. Although this is a good way to work around the speed restrictions associated with CD-ROM, it does tend to make subsequent playings of the game predictable.

The game has five levels of difficulty, and the difference between the levels is most often related to the varying intelligence and speed of the Defender and the availability of DNA strands and video clues. Although the enhanced degrees of difficulty are challenging at first, sophisticated gamers might grow bored and find Iron Helix a permanent home on the shelf after only a few days in the CD-ROM player.

Past Its Prime

In its heyday, when there were few CD-ROM games on the market, Iron Helix was a decent cat-and-mouse space adventure. Fortunately, we have far more choices today than we had in the past. If you can find Iron Helix in a bargain bin somewhere, it's worth a couple of run-throughs. The graphics are very good, and the integration of video is impressive. And playing the game the first couple of times is still entertaining. Alas, for Iron Helix, there are too many good CD-ROM games available now for us to recommend spending more than a nominal fee for this old soldier.

Pros: Good graphics. Innovative interface. Good performance from the actors.

Cons: Game gets tedious after more than a couple of playings.

System Requirements: 8-bit 13-inch color monitor, Mac II or better, 5MB RAM, System 6.07 or higher, CD-ROM drive.

IRON HELIX	
Fun factor:	3.0
Look and feel:	4.0
Value:	3.0
Replayability:	1.5
Overall:	3.0

The C.H.A.O.S. Continuum
Creative Multimedia

This is a truly awful game, and we wouldn't even bother mentioning it except we see that it's still on the shelves of less-than-discerning software dealers. Our page count is too precious to spend more than a paragraph on The C.H.A.O.S. Continuum, so let's leave it at this: Don't buy this game. It stinks.

Pros: So bad that we could write this review in under two minutes.

Cons: See Pros.

System Requirements: Who cares?

RANT

THE C.H.A.O.S. CONTINUUM	
Fun factor:	1.0
Look and feel:	2.5*
Value:	1.0
Replayability:	1.0
Overall:	1.0
(Okay, some scenes look great.)	

Hell Cab
Time Warner Interactive Group

In this game, you play the part of a weary traveler who has arrived at New York's JFK airport with a little time to kill between connecting flights. Enter Raul Delgado, a representative of the devil who apparently drives a cab in his off hours. Raul stops you in the lobby and offers to take you sightseeing around the Big Apple. With little else to do, you proceed outside to accept Raul's invitation.

It must be your lucky day, because Raul assures you that you will be getting the special tour. With a reassuring grin, your driver asks you to sit back and relax as he shepherds you into Manhattan and to the Empire State Building. Things go swimmingly until Raul pulls up to the curb and tells you it's time to pay up. It shouldn't be a problem, you think. You stopped at the ATM in the airport and withdrew what seemed to be a reasonable amount of cash. But wouldn't you know it, you're a few dollars short. You apologize, you plead, you bully, but to no avail. The only way out is to accept Raul's offer of a deal, a signed agreement with the Evil One himself. Simply answer a few questions, scrawl your name on the dotted line, and prepare for a journey designed to test your moral mettle.

Three in One
The adventure is divided into three main parts: a trip to Nero's Rome, an excursion to the trenches of World War I, and finally, a stop in the Jurassic Age. The

Hell Cab can be a dangerous ride.

Empire State Building serves not only as the jumping-off point of your adventure but also as the terminus for each of the three segments. During your travels, you are presented with numerous moral and physical challenges (thinking puzzles and arcadelike actions). Your successes and failures are tracked by the Soul-O-Meter, a taxi meter that details both your remaining lives (you are given three at the outset) and the state of your soul. If you lose all of your lives or your soul, you die and must suffer eternal damnation because "you've been a very bad boy." For female players, I doubt that using your sex as an excuse will help in any significant way.

I'm in Heaven

If you've seen Pepe Moreno's Batman: Digital Justice, you're familiar with the quality of artwork you'll find in Hell Cab. For those who have somehow missed Batman, it should suffice to say that the graphics in the game are nothing short of breathtaking. Hell Cab is further enhanced by Jim Ludtke's eerie 3D animation sequences and Jeff Essex's outstanding musical score. And the performances by the cast are convincing and entertaining.

The game contains a number of little surprises that, while often adding nothing to the plot, are a delight to discover. The Empire State Building, for instance, contains a trove of wonderful QuickTime clips ranging from video clips from Freak Show, the remarkable project created by animator Ludtke and musical group The Residents, to episodes of the *Dead Sullivan Show*. Raul's cab also holds a number of goodies that are worth a poke and a prod.

Hell Cab's charm is not limited to its visual beauty or eccentric accessories. The game is designed to allow the plot to fork off in one direction or another depending on how you handle certain dilemmas. You can, for instance, be rewarded for maintaining a pure soul and finishing the first two scenarios in record time by being whisked back to JFK without a visit to the Jurassic Age.

The Dark Side

As is the case with many early CD-ROM games, Hell Cab can be interminably slow. Major transitions occur, such as when you meet an untimely end, and seem to take forever to transpire. Once you've met your maker, you must wait and wait and wait while the death scene plays itself out and the game loads the transition scene. Only after the transition scene is up and running do you have access to the File menu, where you can choose to restore a game. After electing to restore, you again wait and wait and wait while the game locates your saved position. Dying can be an exercise in frustration.

LOUSY
FEATURE

There are certain parts of Hell Cab that simply do not work as well as they could. One example is your interactions with the game's characters. Conversation is carried out between you and an on-screen character in a call-and-response format. An actor natters on for awhile and then, when he or she has finished, you click on an answer from one of the possibilities printed at the bottom of the screen. The game hints that the tone of your conversation will determine the forthcoming action. Not so. When addressing Nero, for instance, you can be rude or sycophantic, navigate every which way through dialog buttons, and still find yourself plopped down behind bars.

Also, certain puzzles are puzzles only in the broadest sense. Take the case of a particular cache of goodies in the WWI scenario. You know that you're missing something, but only after you point and click on an unlikely location are the items revealed. One minute they're not there; in the next you click, and poof! an array of large objects appears before your eyes. They're certainly large enough that you wouldn't have missed them with a cursory glance. Is this some kind of arcane magic? Nope, just a bad puzzle.

Purgatory Cab

Overall, Hell Cab is neither heaven nor hell. The game benefits and suffers from the syndrome that is all too common in today's CD-ROM adventures: an emphasis on the glitzy elements of graphics, animation, and sound, but too little concern for plot and game design, and a tendency to run up against the limitations of the technology.

To their credit, Pepe Moreno and crew have created a terrific-looking product that, unlike some of the current CD-ROM titles, attempts to provide the user with a playing experience that can be quite different with each new game. The frosting on this particular enterprise is the inclusion of a number of totally unnecessary but often delightful treats sprinkled throughout the adventure.

But they could have done more. Here was an opportunity to create a game that addressed the perils of moral choice in a refreshing and humorous way. Regrettably, although the concept was inspired, the execution fell short. We hope that the small tease for Hell Cab 2 contained within the Empire State Building becomes reality. Hell Cab 1 demonstrates a mastery of image and sound, and the technology, although still not perfect, is bound to improve. With just a bit more attention to narrative and design, this could become a heck of a game.

Pros: Fantastic graphics, sound, and animation. Hidden surprises. Nice performances from the actors.

Cons: Long delays in loading certain scenes. Not particularly interactive. Not all puzzles are truly puzzling. Protagonist can only be male.

System Requirements: 8-bit 13-inch color monitor, Mac II or better, 3MB RAM, System 6.07 or higher, CD-ROM drive.

HELL CAB	
Fun factor:	2.5
Look and feel:	4.0
Value:	2.5
Replayability:	2.0
Overall:	2.5

The Better Dead Ratification

ARTSector ONE

The Better Dead Ratification is the first offering from ARTSector ONE, and although the game includes some cool animations and graphics, there are some definite growing pains that are going to have to happen before the company releases its next title. This is one of those games that might have been a big hit in 1991 when cool animation and graphics were the rage. As it stands now, it behaves a little more like a beta than a finished product, although it certainly does have some redeeming qualities.

Commander Paine and the Quest for Bad Anagrams

You, as Commander Paine, learn quickly after fooling with a bar room television that you're being pulled from the present to enter into intergalactic battle against the Binwas. This race of creatures is lead by Mi Natas Phoule, whose name when run through an anagram program becomes I'm Satan Phoule. To defeat this foe, you'll have to become a cyborg and collect a series of holobible links. Fortunately, you're not alone, because there's some guy on the TV linking back to you from the future to help guide you through the quest.

Crrrash

For some reason, we had a lot of difficulty running this game. We tried it on a IIci, an LC 475, and a PowerMac 6100/66 with many a splendiferous crash and fizzle. This is too bad because some of the animation and graphics are kinda cool, and the premise, although farfetched, could be fun if contained in a more robust environment. The interface is not intuitive, and there are numerous problems with such things as saving games and finding hot spots on the screens. When searching for a particular spot on the screen, there is no cursor feedback to let you know whether you're in the right place or not, so you've got a greater chance of clicking on something that you don't want.

DANGER

A Word of Encouragement

We suspect that a little more beta testing would have caught some of these problems early on, and we certainly hope this is the case for any future releases from ARTSector ONE. Quite clearly these folks have some talent, and it'd be a shame to see another game limited because of bugginess. We cannot recommend The Better Dead Ratification in its present state; there's just too much of a chance that it won't work on your machine. Come on ARTSector ONE! Let's see you tie up these loose ends on your next project.

Pros: Some cool animation and art.

Cons: Buggy as all get out. Questionable interface.

System Requirements: 256-color monitor, 68030 or better Mac, 5MB RAM, System 7 or later.

THE BETTER DEAD RATIFICATION

Fun factor:	2.5
Look and feel:	2.0
Value:	2.0
Replayability:	2.5
Overall:	2.0

Star Trek: 25th Anniversary
MacPlay

Space, the final frontier. This is the review of the Star Trek compromise, on a six-month mission to port where so many have ported before. Yep, you got it: Spock, Uhura, Captain Kirk, Sulu, and the mandatory guy in the red shirt who will invariably bite the dust. Trekkers everywhere will rejoice that a graphical game with their favorite crew of aging interstellar explorers has reached the Mac. Unfortunately, this is a crude port from the DOS galaxy, and its interface will not please the Macintosh crowd. Of course we're talking about Star Trek here, so perhaps it'll be loved no matter what its quality.

Damn It, Jim! I'm a Doctor, Not a Mac Game!

Star Trek: 25th Anniversary is certainly true to its television roots and includes all the characters, color, and feel of the original series, which changed television and movie history. You'd have to have been living under a rock for the last 25 years to not be even somewhat familiar with the Trekker revolution. Star Trek 25 has two basic areas of play: on the bridge of the *Enterprise* and on a planet's surface. The bridge is where the ship-to-ship combat and navigation take place. The game progresses from mission to mission, often with a spot of space combat followed by a jaunt with the landing party (and don't forget to take the guy in the red shirt; he really does get smushed).

**LOUSY
FEATURE**

From the bridge you can control such equipment as weapons, shields, and engines and get the lowdown on the ship's condition. The navigation is the method of copy protection MacPlay has chosen to employ. If you do not have the map to figure out which sector to warp to, you usually end up in a nasty Kobayashi Maru scenario, which for those who aren't versed in these things, is a face-to-face battle with three Klingon War Birds. This isn't a winnable situation, so you'll need to lug the old manual around if you're going to play this game.

Captain! I Canna Give You Any More Power!!

The interface is very strange and uses a mouse driver that looks and behaves as if it had come from the old Apple II. Interacting with characters on the bridge involves clicking on the appropriate areas, but once a conversation is engaged, you're sometimes obligated to follow it through to the end of the dialogue. There isn't much in the way of flexibility, either, and what you see is what you get—their way or the Milky Way. Our next gripe is the ghastly graphics.

As we've mentioned before in this book, upgrade the graphics when you port, people! These graphics contain exactly one quarter the number of pixels the Mac is capable of displaying. They provide a very disappointing visual experience that reminds one of playing games on an old Vic 20.

LOUSY FEATURE

Scotty, Beam Me Up. Please.

This is a reasonably fun game, but the totally archaic interface makes basic maneuvers a chore, and beyond the desire to see the next screen and any references to the old Star Trek series, there's really not much to keep you coming back. The CD-ROM version, with the real characters' voices, offers more appeal than the disk game, but that's little consolation for a bad port. However, if you can see your way to looking past the interface and graphical problems, the underlying game can be fairly entertaining.

Pros: Solving the puzzles is fun if you can get over the graphics. Space combat can be fun.

Cons: Miserable interface. Poor graphics.

System Requirements: 256-color monitor, 68030 or better, 1.5MB RAM, 8.5MB hard disk space, CD-ROM drive.

STAR TREK: 25TH ANNIVERSARY	
Fun factor:	3.0
Look and feel:	2.0
Value:	2.5
Replayability:	3.0
Overall:	2.5

Rebel Assault
LucasArts

CD

Over the years, the folks at LucasArts have dabbled in the Mac market with titles like Pipe Dream and the Indiana Jones series, but they've never really brought the meat of their lineup over for Apple users to enjoy. The first indication that LucasArts was going to dive headlong into Mac gaming came with the announcement of Rebel Assault for the Mac, an action CD-ROM game based on the Star Wars saga. Mac gaming enthusiasts beamed with eager anticipation when they discovered this popular DOS game was on its way. But has it lived up to all the hoopla?

Space Opera

Rebel Assault begins with a spectacular cinematic opening sequence complete with Star Wars Fighters and a rocky ride through an asteroid field. In fact, these scenes are so stunning you begin to think the game might actually resemble the intro. The game is divided into 15 individual scenarios, and you must be successful in each one in order to advance to the next. These action segments are interspersed with cinematic story sequences that keep you abreast of the plot. You begin as a rookie pilot and can choose to take on either a female or male persona. The dialogue from that point forward is tailored to the gender of your character. The first challenge involves honing your piloting skills as you race through Beggar's Canyon with a two-ship escort, followed by a turkey shoot in the desert to help develop necessary survival skills. Each successive level is protected through a pass code system, so you must compete the task in one to get the password to the next, unless of course you are reading this book, in which case we're including them for your gaming enjoyment. Cheater!

Defective Perspective

**LOUSY
FEATURE**

The problem with Rebel Assault lies in perspective. Many of the action sequences are seen from outside the craft you're operating. For example, when flying through Beggar's Canyon the view is from behind the craft, and this makes judging distance very difficult. In the desert run, you're forced to line up targets from a bizarre overhead viewpoint that makes any enjoyment of the proceedings a joke. When on foot and shooting at the enemy, the controls have to be operated from a viewpoint that gives a complete view of the surroundings but limits aiming and depth perception considerably. Thank goodness some of the segments use a first-person-perspective approach that lets you view the world from the cockpit, thus making control over events considerably easier.

Movie Time

Where Rebel Assault really shines is in its cinematic sequences. There are plenty of great voice-overs and animations that definitely add to the aura of a Star Wars production. In fact, we think it's almost worth getting this game just for the storyline and cinematic scene.

The graphics are superb, and for those who are limited by a slow CPU, there are options to adjust screen size and interlace the graphics (drawing every other line). This makes Rebel Assault playable on most machines, although we recommend at least an 040 and a double-speed CD-ROM drive for seamless action.

All Graphics and No Playability Make Luke a Dull Boy

Rebel Assault behaves like a bridge product between the LucasArts games of old and the hot new titles like Dark Forces and X-Wing, and while watching the movielike story segments with great animation can hold your attention for a while, it doesn't cut the cake after about the third time through. This game is a port from DOS, but the graphics are certainly very acceptable. The real problems come from the confusing choices of perspective when muddling through the action portions of

A view of the cockpit just before diving in for a trench run on the Death Star in Rebel Assault.

the game, and having to complete the storyline in a sequential manner while fever-
ishly copying down pass codes for further levels. In the end, Rebel Assault is both a
crummy and an excellent game, and it therefore falls into the realm of the average.

Tip
• Type in these cheat codes to move to whatever level you choose:

Easy Mode	Normal Mode	Hard Mode
2. BOSSK	2. BOTHAN	2. BORDOK
3. ENGRET	3. HERGLIC	3. SKYNX
4. RALRRA	4. LEENI	4. DEFEL
5. FRIJA	5. THRAWN	5. JEDGAR
6. LAFRA	6. LWYLL	6. MADINE
7. DERLIN	7. MAZZIC	7. TARKIN
8. MOLTOK	8. ULPA	8. MOTHMA
9. MORAG	9. MORRT	9. GLAYYD
10. TANTISS	10. MUFTAK	10. OTTEGA
11. OSWAFL	11. RASKAR	11. RISHII
12. KLAATY	12. JHOFF	12. IRZINA
13. IRENEZ	13. ITHOR	13. KARRDE
14. LIANNIA	14. UMWAK	14. VONZEL
15. PAKKA	15. ORLOK	15. OSSUS
Ending. NORVAL	Ending. NKLLON	Ending. MALANI

TIP

Pros: Great animated sequences. Runs well on most Macs. Good story for an action game.

Cons: Little replay value. Action sequences difficult to control. Some odd perspectives during gameplay.

System Requirements: 256-color monitor, LC III or better, 2.4MB RAM, 500K hard disk space, System 7 or later, CD-ROM drive.

REBEL ASSAULT	
Fun factor:	3.5
Look and feel:	3.0
Value:	3.5
Replayability:	2.0
Overall:	3.0

Super Wing Commander
Origin

Over the years, three DOS games have consistently topped Mac gamers' most wanted list: X-Wing, Wolfenstein 3-D, and Wing Commander. For oh-so-many years, these great games have been out of our reach. Fortunately, Wolfenstein has now arrived, while X-Wing will soon grace the Mac, and lo and behold Origin Systems has seen fit to combine the Wing Commander experience into one conglomerate game entitled Super Wing Commander. The DOS platform has seen Wing Commander I, II, and III, Privateer, and Wing Commander Academy cross its screens, all with great success. It's certainly good to see such an influential title come over to the Apple; undoubtedly the arrival of the Power Mac must have played a role in this. Perhaps this is the start of a new era, one in which the world's top game companies will stop ignoring the Mac and maybe even, heaven forbid, produce a game on the Mac first.

Kool Kilrathi Kutthroats

Super Wing Commander centers around an intergalactic conflict between humans and the catlike Kilrathi. These Kilrathi creatures are really, really mean—if they even catch a glimpse of a human they automatically switch into disembowelment mode. They want to destroy the human race. Geez, when are we gonna get a break here? At the point we join the story, the war's been raging for 20 years and both sides have taken heavy losses. One battle could turn the war's tide; this is where you sharpen your claws and jump into the fray. With a fresh pilot's license and an attitude toward ruthless felines, you just might be the person to save humanity. There's a special leather slave outfit waiting for you in the salt mines of Kilrath if you don't succeed, so buckle up and prepare for battle.

As you pilot various craft through battles, you gain experience, better spaceships, and a great deal of pride. Although there's an underlying storyline that you follow by chatting with characters in the bases and ports you visit, the real meat of Super Wing Commander is in the area of space combat. As you're fighting with the Kilrathi, you can exchange pleasantries with one another, and sometimes this can even work to your advantage if you can ignite a Kilrathi pilot's rage over what you say about his wife. There's the usual assortment of missiles and goodies to earn and then launch, and don't forget that you'll often have a copilot along.

Mommy, Why Do Those Graphics Look Like That?

The graphics in Super Wing Commander are right out of the rest of the WC series, and have a decidedly low-resolution feel. But when you've played WC on other machines for so many years, you really come to expect these kind of graphics in this game. It's like expecting *Life* magazine to have lots of glossy pictures; it just wouldn't be the same without them. The close-up screens employed for interactions with the game's characters are actually fairly well done, and the added speech is incorporated flawlessly, with nary an errant lip movement. We did have to turn off the super cheesy background music to save ourselves from going completely insane. That stuff sounds like it was created on an Apple II back in 1978.

The combat graphics are crude, and on slower machines most players will find themselves wildly overcompensating when attempting to line up the enemy fighters. Version 1.0.2 cleans up most of that, especially on Power Macs. One of

LOUSY FEATURE

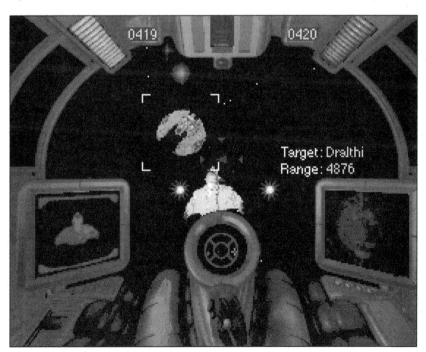

Super Wing Commander is similar to its DOS counterparts in every way, including graphics.

the features we really enjoyed when in combat situations was the banter between yourself and the copilot or a Kilrathi. When someone addresses you, their mug appears on a monitor and fully digitized speech flows like honey. You'll get everything from encouragement from your wing man to a verbal kick in the teeth from an enemy. And not all the enemies are anonymous, so over time you can develop a nice hatred for someone. Although the combat controls were not exactly the smoothest we've used, they were acceptable, and the built-in support for the ThrustMaster stick is a nice touch.

Extensions Manager Needed

DANGER

Super Wing Commander is a colossal drain on system resources. You're probably going to have to turn off all nonessential extensions and inits just to make it run, and those low on memory will sacrifice the music right off the bat. (No loss there.) If you're going to rush out and buy Super Wing Commander, we recommend that you have a fast 040 or Power Mac and more than 8MB of RAM.

This Is Wing Commander

Some reviewers have suggested that Super Wing Commander doesn't cut it on the Mac. They say the graphics are too blocky, the sound too cheesy, and the control response too clunky. But hey, this *is* Wing Commander, and the basic play of version 1.0.2 is very similar to most of the wildly popular Wing Commander games for DOS. It's also fun to play. And most of the storyline animations are very impressive and are cool to watch again and again despite the graphical resolution. For best results, we recommend you get the patch to version 1.0.2 from your favorite online service or the enclosed CD-ROM. Once you get over the shortcomings, it's easy to get hooked. After all, there's a reason why the Wing Commander games are among the most popular games of all time.

Pros: Famous game. Good storyline. Great transition scenes. Can become addictive.

Cons: Old graphics technology. Takes mucho resources. Crummy music.

System Requirements: 256-color monitor, 25MHz-68030 processor or better, 4MB RAM, 11MB hard disk space, System 7 or later, double-speed CD-ROM drive.

SUPER WING COMMANDER	
Fun factor:	3.5
Look and feel:	3.0
Value:	4.0
Replayability:	4.0
Overall:	3.5

The Daedalus Encounter
Virgin/Mechadeus

Ever since the release of Spaceship Warlock, there's been plenty of talk about interactive movies and how playing computer games will eventually be like playing personalized movies. For the most part, this hasn't really happened yet, but The Daedalus Encounter takes us a huge step closer to that dream. More often with large CD-ROM games, we're seeing big stars being recruited to act in these interactive dramas, making new games ever more like real movie productions in terms of content as well as price. It was rumored that the production costs of Wing Commander III with Mark Hammel ran into the millions, and there's no doubt most new games mean big budgets and big risks for game designers. Shipping on three CD-ROM disks, Daedalus was the largest CD-ROM game ever released for the Mac, but just since we've been writing this book, Journeyman Project II has also come out on three CDs. The stakes keep getting higher, but the results are ever more spectacular.

A Bad Day at the Office

The Daedalus Encounter begins with the most spectacular opening sequence these eyes have ever been privy to. This is simply a MUST SEE. The game begins in 2135 with you and your pals, Ariel Matheson and Zack Smith, patrolling a lonely sector of space during the war with the Vakkar. The Vakkar are a nasty bunch of creatures bent on the elimination of—what else?—humanity. Today they are particularly bent on your elimination. In several brilliant flashes of light, the Vakkar fighters close in on your interceptor, and before you can say head-on collision the three of you must jettison from the ship. Unfortunately, you have too close a call and your body is damaged beyond repair. Thank goodness for modern technology, because your friends manage to get you to a medical facility that puts your brain in a box to keep you alive until someone figures out how to transplant a human brain.

GREAT FEATURE

Some weeks later, you awaken from your sleep to find that the war is over and Ariel and Zack have kidnapped you and your life support systems so that you can cruise around with them looking for salvageable space debris from the war. When you come across a drifting Vakkar freighter, you decide to go in for a look by way of a remote-controlled probe. Thus the story begins. From here on it's a combination of awesome video, animated sequences, and puzzle solving on the wildest ride in the universe.

The Daedalus Encounter has some of the most awesome video, graphics, and sound we've seen in a game.

True Lies, Wayne's World, The Daedalus Encounter

What do these three titles have in common? Tia Carrere, that's what. The beautiful and sassy starlet from these hit movies has made the move to computer gaming along with comedian Christian Bocher. The acting in Daedalus is outstanding, with fully believable dialogue, props, and storyline to pull you in and keep you glued to the screen. And that screen is no postage stamp either; in many instances it's full-screen or one-third size. There is no degradation or skipping of the video playback. Daedalus truly shows that Hollywood and computers are coming closer together every day.

Integrated Video, Animation, Rendered Art, Whoa!

GREAT
FEATURE

Why the heck are we babbling? Simply put, Daedalus is the most breathtaking combination of the above elements we've ever seen. Everything fits together so well you forget you're looking at a computer screen. The characters' video presentation is so brilliant and lifelike we found ourselves playing certain segments of the game over and over again. The segments of spaceship battles are more impressive than the original *Star Wars* movie. Heck, the included trailer for the game is so action-packed that some of the people we showed it to wanted to know where they could rent the movie! Mechadeus has somehow perfected a way to stream full-motion video and graphics off the CD without any breakup or stutters. At least that was the case on the Power Mac 6100 with double-speed Apple CD-ROM drive that we used. The glitch was that we had to change the discs at certain points in the story, but the delay was minimal and continuity certainly wasn't lost.

Yeah, But Can You Play It?

The two drawbacks of The Daedalus Encounter are its fairly linear storyline and the interactivity of your character. Basically, you engage in gameplay by moving around and solving puzzles, but you spend a fair chunk of your time with this game watching the glorious animation and video play out. We'd normally call this a major drawback, but Daedalus is so good that we consider it a minor distraction. When you are moving through the game you interact strictly with the mouse, and the robot you reside in has several visual, laser, and scanning systems that often give you something to point and click on. Can you play it? Who cares? The game is too awesome for that to matter.

A New Horizon

The Daedalus Encounter breaks all the rules for interactive computer games. It comes on three CDs; it's acted beautifully; the story's compelling; and the technical wizardry is like nothing we've ever seen. Tia Carrere and Christian Bocher put in excellent performances and prove that actors and computer games can come together to achieve impressive results.

Warning: This game requires major computing power, especially RAM, to run well.

DANGER

Pros: Awesome video and graphics. Great story. Incredible ground-breaking game.

Cons: Needs horsepower. Linear storyline.

System Requirements: 256-color monitor, 68040 or Power Mac, 8MB RAM, up to 18.5MB hard disk space, System 7 or later, double-speed or faster CD-ROM drive (game is optimized for faster CD-ROM drives).

THE DAEDALUS ENCOUNTER	
Fun factor:	4.5
Look and feel:	5.0
Value:	4.5
Replayability:	3.5
Overall:	4.5

10

First-Person-
Perspective
Shoot-'Em-Ups

Remember PacMan? Of course you do. In it you control a small yellow critter gobbling its way around a maze in an attempt to avoid the rapidly approaching blue meanies. After chewing up a special power charge, you turn the tables and become hunter rather than hunted.

This is the general idea behind First-Person-Perspective Shoot-'Em-Ups (FPPSEU). But instead of monitoring the action from above, you're right down there in the thick of it—unsure of what horror lurks around the next corner. The power charges of old are translated into exotic tools of destruction and robust shields. And rather than barren, 2D, carbon copy mazes, these games invariably feature 3D labyrinthine levels containing ever-deadlier weapons, personal body armor, secret rooms, and healing kits.

As these games are kill-or-be-killed exercises, they all carry gauges, graphs, and other devices to indicate just how much more abuse your battle-weary body can absorb. These indicators range from the sterile high-tech meters found in Dark Forces to the bleeding visage of DOOM II's Space Marine.

These games have no socially redeeming value. Oh sure, the stories may place you in the position of Savior Who Represents All That Is Good, but to triumph over the bad guys you must let the psychopath within run free. The object of these games is short and perhaps not so sweet: kill or be killed.

Wolfenstein 3D

id Software
Published by MacPlay

CD

Wolfenstein 3D was one of those legendary games on the PC that Mac gamers tuned into other-platformed worlds salivated over. The story was that this game from id Software was very fast, featured nonstop action, and was tons of fun. After a two-year wait, Mac users were finally allowed to find out for themselves. As it turns out, the story was true.

Shoot to Kill

Wolf is the First-Person-Perspective Shoot-'Em-Up at its most marvelously basic. You begin the game with a revolver clutched in both hands. Ahead is a metal sliding door. In the far right corner is a blue clip of ammunition for the revolver. Using the mouse, keyboard, or a joystick, you move to the corner, walk over the ammo, and it's yours. Back to the door, where a press of the Space Bar causes the door to slide back and—wouldn't you just know it—nothing but Nazis.

FPPSEU CHRONOLOGY

DOS and Windows users have scads of FPPSEUs to choose from, yet these games are still in relatively short supply on the Mac.

Keeping a chronology of these games' appearances is a more taxing proposition than you'd imagine. Many of the popular DOS games of the past few years are only now being ported to the Mac. Because of this delay, it's possible to lose track of which games came when and what they added to the genre. Here's how the major players shake out:

1988: The Colony (Mac)
Wire-frame, black-and-white graphics. All corridors are at right angles. Single weapon. Plot.

1992: Wolfenstein 3D (PC)
Color graphics. Secret rooms. Overhead map. Cheat codes. All corridors are at right angles. Plug-in game files for adding new levels. Background music. Multiple weapons. Minimal plot.

1993: Pathways into Darkness (Mac)
First color Mac FPPSEU. Overhead map. Contoured corridors not at right angles. Lighting effects. Stereo sound effects. Texture mapping. Multiple weapons. Plot.

1994: DOOM (PC)
Multitiered levels (areas may have ledges or pits that are above or below you). Overhead map. Cheat codes. Secret rooms. Networking. Contoured corridors not at right angles. Plug-in game files for adding new levels. Lighting effects. Texture mapping. Background music. Multiple weapons. Minimal plot.

1994: DOOM II (PC)
Same as DOOM, except includes modem support.

1994: Wolfenstein 3D (Mac)
Same as Wolfenstein 3D for PC except Power Mac native.

1994: Sensory Overload (Mac)
No multitiered levels. Secret rooms. Overhead map. No networking. Background music. Lighting effects. Stereo sound effects. Texture mapping. Multiple weapons. Power Mac native. Minimal plot.

1994: Marathon (Mac)
Multitiered levels. Necessary to aim up or down to shoot baddies on different tiers. Secret rooms. Networking. Contoured corridors not at right angles. Plug-in game files for adding new levels. Background music. Lighting effects. Stereo sound effects. Texture mapping. Multiple weapons. Ability to save movies of your battles. Ability to send live audio over the network. Power Mac native. Plot.

1995: Dark Forces (PC and Mac)
Multitiered levels. Secret rooms. Overhead map. Cheat codes. No networking. Contoured corridors not at right angles. Background music. Lighting effects. Stereo sound effects. Texture mapping. Multiple weapons. Plug-in game files for adding new levels. Power Mac native. Plot.

1995: DOOM II (Mac)
Same as DOOM II for PC except Power Mac native.

And that's about it. There's no nagging plot line or puzzle solving to get in the way. Just dash around the various levels collecting treasure, ammo, progressively nastier weapons, healing kits, and extra lives, and kill anything that moves. This anything-that-moves category includes single-shot brown shirts, the tougher rifle-bearing guards, the quick-as-lightning SS troopers, guard dogs, Nazi zombies who fire as they salute, and the extremely tough Super Nazis featuring Der Fuhrer himself.

GREAT FEATURE

The graphics are somewhat basic but effective. No texturing is used on the floors or ceilings; all corridors are at 90-degree angles; and your enemies are cartoonish. The soundtrack is quite good and varies from military cadences a la *The Great Escape* to blazing guitar rock. Performance is just ducky on 040 Macs, but not as good on 030 Macs—movement there tends to be jerky, which can inhibit your ability to draw a bead on that goose-stepping zombie. Fortunately, those with these slower Macs can speed up the action by selecting a smaller window size—a technique used in nearly every FPPSEU on the market.

LOUSY FEATURE

Players with muscle-bound Macs suffer the opposite problem—Wolf runs too fast on Power Macs. Although the game includes a Speed Governor to keep performance from shooting through the roof, even with the governor engaged, things move a tad too quickly, and small adjustments in aiming become difficult. Without the governor, the game plays like an impossibly fast Keystone Cops movie.

Wolfenstein 3D packs quite a punch.

A Warning

Wolf is not going to be everyone's cup of tea. Parents may object to the level of violence, which is not nearly so graphic as the violence found in such console games as Mortal Kombat, but violent nonetheless. Anyone sensitive to Nazi themes and symbolism will likewise wish to avoid Wolfenstein. German crosses and pictures of Adolph Hitler litter the landscape. Because the display of Nazi symbols is forbidden in Germany, the game is banned in that country and the shareware version of the game is not carried on such online services as CompuServe that maintain German accounts.

DANGER

If the level of violence and the theme don't trouble you, Wolfenstein 3D is worth a look—particularly if your Mac is robust enough to handle its moderate demands. Though the game doesn't exhibit the kind of complexity and compelling action found in such later games as Marathon and DOOM II, it's still a heck of a ride.

Tips:

• You open secret doors by pressing the Open Door key. To quickly locate secret passages (without cheating, that is), try pressing the Open Door key on the run—no need to stop and press, stop and press.

TIP

• Type these cheat codes into the game as you play for a dishonest reward:

IDDQD   Invincibility.

BURGER   Maximum ammunition for all weapons.

WOWZERS   For bullet-based weapons, supplies 999 rounds.

LEDOUX   Supplies all weapons, invincibility, all keys, and limitless ammo.

SEGER   Supplies both keys.

MCCALL   Moves you to the next level.

Pros: Fierce action that scrolls smoothly on fast Macs.

Cons: Level of violence or Nazi theme may offend some players.

System Requirements: 68030 or better (68040 recommended), 4MB RAM, 2.5MB hard disk space, System 6.07 or higher.

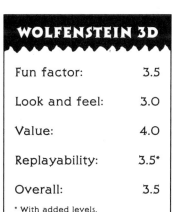

WOLFENSTEIN 3D	
Fun factor:	3.5
Look and feel:	3.0
Value:	4.0
Replayability:	3.5*
Overall:	3.5
* With added levels.	

CD

Pathways Into Darkness
Bungie Software

The release of Wolfenstein 3D for DOS computers really put a damper on the Mac's reputation as a major games machine. After all, was there anything comparable available for the Mac? Bungie Software, a small company based in Chicago, noticed this disparity and decided to buckle down and write some software that could fully exploit the Mac's graphical and sound capabilities while still keeping the user enthralled with game play. The deliverance from humiliation at the hands of DOS users came in the form of a new first-person-perspective game entitled Pathways Into Darkness. This game destroyed the notion of the Mac as a dog-slow machine with no good games, and in the process laid the foundation for all other games of this nature. Without it would we have seen Marathon? Or would id Software and LucasArts have taken a stab at the Mac without Pathways to prove the existence of a market for such games? Whatever the answers, Pathways Into Darkness was a huge success with ultra-compelling action that probably landed some diehard users in emergency rooms with anxiety attacks.

Strange Sleep

A huge alien craft crashed into the Yucatan Peninsula sixty-four million years ago and destroyed the dinosaurs. The craft contained an immortal creature that lay in slumber and dreamt weird dreams. Really weird dreams. The worst part is that these dreams somehow became reality, thus creating a huge maze of caverns in the bedrock. These caverns are populated by creatures that want nothing more than to ruin your day in the most deadly manner. It kind of makes you wonder why anyone would want to risk descending into the caverns, doesn't it?

Well, that's just why we're here, to crunch up that old alien by traversing the many levels of the caverns in order to plant a nuclear device just close enough to say I love you. Unfortunately, you've been separated from the rest of your commando group and begin the game with only a knife, digital watch, flashlight, and your iron will. (MacGyver eat your heart out!) And you'd better pack a lunch because there's over four million square feet of terrain to cover. As you wander through the ruins, you'll come across plenty of weapons and strange artifacts that will aid considerably in your quest. But if possible, save your ammo as there may be more monsters dwelling around the next corner.

TIP

Into the Darkness

Once you've equipped yourself with a gun and become familiar with the interface, the fun really begins. Pathways is a creepy experience, with 3D texture-mapped graphics and a stunning attention to lighting detail. The flashlight you

Pathways Into Darkness pioneered first-person-perspective games on the Mac. It still stands as an example of excellence.

carry only illuminates about 25 feet, so as you move forward, objects in the distance come into dim view. This effect provides an ambivalent desire to see what's around each corner. On one hand, you're hoping there's a new gun lying somewhere in the shadows. On the other hand, you know that a nasty creature known as a Headless is probably waiting to take a shot at you. We actually found ourselves moving our heads to peer around corners and straining our eyes to see further into the darkness. The realism of this feature cannot be overstated, and the name Pathways Into Darkness could not be more appropriate. There are 30 levels to complete and each is packed with a wide variety of super-annoying creatures.

GREAT FEATURE

All users will greatly appreciate the auto-mapping feature, and once mapped, most levels are stored forever. You can only save the game on red runes (symbols on the floor), which is somewhat of a drag, but usually there are a couple of runes on every level. There's also a wide variety of weapons to be found scattered about. These range from grenade launchers to sub-machine guns, and of course, there's a nice sprinkling of unconventional items that will help vanquish foes. One item of particular visual interest is the infrared goggle set. These little puppies increase your vision by about two-thirds, enabling better distance vision down those long corridors. What's most impressive is that the infrared goggle

effect was pioneered on Pathways and now shows up in other titles such as Dark Forces. However, we still find the red "shimmering" effect of the Pathways goggles to be superior to that created by any challenger.

One of the crystals you'll pick up enables conversation with some of the dead soldiers that litter the maze, and the information they give can be invaluable in your search through these darkened corridors of cold stone. Travel between levels is accomplished by ladders located in various rooms. There's also the odd teleporter to zip you to other locations. But be careful; some teleporters offer only one-way travel and can leave you trapped in nasty situations.

It's Like Being There!

When Pathways into Darkness came out, it surpassed the Wolfenstein games in the area of resolution. Although most people had to play Pathways in low-resolution mode (which is still pretty good) to increase performance, those who had the horsepower could cruise along in breathtaking high-resolution splendor. No one else had any home computer game that could rival the pixel count offered by Pathways. For the most part, the speed of the game is a function of the speed of your machine, although anyone with a Power Mac will be able to run with a large screen and all the bells and whistles humming along. For those with older machines, the screen is fully resizable and game play on a one-quarter screen is still surprisingly compelling. So if you have an original LC, don't worry.

The only aspect of game control that can be a bit tricky is learning to dodge correctly. However, a little practice can make this second nature. In the 3D sound category, Pathways still reigns supreme. The whoosh of a bone whipping past your head from right to left often alerts you to the whereabouts of monsters. This is a feature you'll come to depend on, and Bungie should be commended for creating such an impressive sound environment. In order to enjoy the active panning stereo sound in Pathways you must have Sound Manager 3.0 and headphones or external speakers.

To Sum It Up: One of the Best!

Pathways Into Darkness from Bungie Software is simply one of the best games ever made for the Macintosh line of computers. The learning curve is perfect, and Pathways should be challenging enough for everyone. Graphics, color, animation, sound, and playability make this game a must have for all serious (and not so serious) Mac gamers. So strap on those infrared goggles and put a fresh clip in the old AK-47; there's a Headless out there with your name on it.

Pros: Great 3D perspective. Very crisp graphics. Best use of 3D sound available. A blast to play (no pun intended).

Cons: Slow on older machines (we recommend anything faster than an LC).

System Requirements: 256-color monitor, Mac II or better, 2MB RAM, 4MB hard disk space.

PATHWAYS INTO DARKNESS	
Fun factor:	5.0
Look and feel:	4.5
Value:	5.0
Replayability:	3.5
Overall:	4.5

Sensory Overload
Reality Bytes

Sensory Overload's spin on the popular FPPSEU has its main character awakening in the hospital of the Biotex Research Labs to a room filled with dead guys who all wear white shirts, brown pants, and large red blood stains across their midsections. The sound of gunfire is heard in the distance, and there is an awful stench about the place. Your alter ego is an undercover CIA agent who is investigating Biotex's AlphaChannel project and who possesses many of the instincts and skills necessary to wantonly obliterate unfriendly humans. The latter take the form of the nefarious Dr. Craven and his band of buffed henchmen.

CD

The game requires you to run around various levels of the lab; search many tiny rooms for ammo, MedKits, and weapons; annihilate innumerable ruffians; disable deadly security systems; and finally expose and defuse the dangerous plot of the craven Dr. Craven.

Face the Face

Sensory Overload's interface and controls are laid out logically. Gunlike weapons are displayed on the left side of the screen and held with the left hand. Lobbed weapons, flares, and the right fist are relegated to the screen's upper right border. To choose any of these weapons, either click on them with the mouse or use a keyboard shortcut. To get an overview of the action, apply a single keystroke to toggle the Automap window on or off.

Players who like to fling their characters about or blast the baddies via the mouse are likely to be disappointed. In this game, the mouse is used solely to select items in the inventory and to click such objects in the main viewing screen as switches and buttons. All movement is controlled via the keyboard or with a supported game controller (Gravis GamePad, Gravis MouseStick II, ThrustMaster FCS, or CH Products's Flightstick Pro). Because we'd rather use the keyboard or a joystick than the mouse when gaming, we didn't find this to be bothersome. And it was a pleasure to find that, although the folks at Reality Bytes don't allow you to customize their keyboard controls directly, they do provide five keyboard layouts that should cover just about every player's requirements.

Reality Does Bite

If you haven't got the hint by now, let's make things clear: FPPSEUs demand more oomph from computers than just about any other kind of game. In order for these games to be played on a reasonable number of systems, programmers have to use all sort of tricks. Sensory Overload is no exception.

GREAT FEATURE

To begin with, you can turn off certain elements of the game that require more processing power and therefore can cause choppy movement when the processor is overloaded. These elements include game sounds, background music, and the display of floor and ceiling textures. For Macs that are considered dinosaurs by today's standards, such as the IIci and IIsi, there is even an Emergency Speed Option that temporarily turns off all texture mapping when the action gets particularly fast and furious. The game also provides nine different screen sizes and three levels of resolution. On slow Macs, the view window will have to be tiny and the graphics jagged, but at least overall movement can be maintained at a somewhat acceptable level.

Sensorily Underwhelmed

LOUSY FEATURE

The graphics are not up to the quality of most Macintosh games. Even in high-resolution mode, telltale jaggies are evident everywhere. When you shift to low-resolution mode, the graphics are nearly as jagged and blocky as—shudder—older PC games. In addition, the enemy terrorists look a lot like the strangely out-of-focus characters from that holier-than-thou puppet show *Davey and Goliath*. And although the furniture and bodies are 3D, their shapes are uninteresting and tend to be monotonous after you've see them on a number of levels.

Even on Power Macs, the movement of the bad guys is jerky and robotic. This can be a problem not only aesthetically but also strategically. For example, when you wait at an angle to plug a baddie as he emerges from a room, the evil one appears to turn from a side view to a frontal view in an instant rather than gradually. This allows him to squeeze off a shot long before he should be able to.

Good, Though

Despite these blemishes, there are things to like about Sensory Overload. Although the game relies heavily on quick reflexes, there are a few puzzles to chew on, some secret passageways to discover, and an element of strategic planning required to survive the enemy's unrelenting firepower. And, of course,

It appears you have a bone to pick with Sensory Overload's Dr. Craven.

there's the fun factor: regardless of how often we prayed that the enemy was a little more in focus, we couldn't quite manage to suppress our heart rates while preparing to storm Weapons Lab B.

Reality Bytes has made a decent start with Sensory Overload, but it doesn't raise our blood pressures to dangerous levels, as do those two great FPPSEUs, Marathon and DOOM II. Mac purists will justifiably gripe about the graphics and motion, and mouse fiends will mourn the loss of their favorite controller. However, if you accept Sensory Overload for what it is—a second-tier, reasonably interesting FPPSEU—find it for a good price, and have a Mac powerful enough to run it, the game is worth a look.

Pros: An okay first-person-perspective 3D shoot-'em-up. Considerate interface and controls.

Cons: Jagged graphics and some clunky movement. Overabundance of rooms to explore.

System Requirements: 13-inch color monitor, 20MHz 68030 or faster, 2.5MB RAM (2.8 for music playback), 8MB hard disk space, System 6.07 (System 7 for music playback).

SENSORY OVERLOAD

Fun factor:	3.0
Look and feel:	3.0
Value:	3.0
Replayability:	2.0
Overall:	3.0

CD

Marathon
Bungie Software

Like distant tribal drums echoing across the Serengeti, Macintosh gamers had heard this incessant sound: *DOOM, DOOM, DOOM, DOOM, you're never gonna get it! DOOM, DOOM, DOOM, DOOM, you might as well forget it! DOOM, DOOM, DOOM, DOOM.*

For a time, this persistent hubbub caused many an insecure Apple loyalist to wonder about possibly having made a slight miscalculation in the platform department. Signs of this discomfort could be viewed on Mac gaming bulletin boards in message threads with titles like, *Where is MacDOOM?* and *Why no DOOM for Mac?* and *Should I Endure the Hellish Interface and Buy a PC Just for This Friggin' Game?*

There was little joy in Macville.

But then, like the first delicate shoots of March, encouraging messages began to pop up on these same electronic services: *Marathon is coming. Hold out for Marathon. A Mac first-person-perspective Shoot-'Em-Up guaranteed to make PC players envious is on its way.*

And so we waited.

After months of delay, the full version of Marathon was released to coincide with 1995's San Francisco Macworld Exposition. To celebrate, Bungie Software hosted a Kill-a-Thon at which Expo attendees blasted the bejeezus out of their companions over several networked Macs in the Bungie booth. Did Marathon live up to the early hype? Having witnessed the sweat pouring down the faces of frantic players and the number of people lined up to purchase the game—and having played the game ourselves—we'd have to answer in the affirmative. Mac players finally got a texture-mapped, 3D diversion that muffled the thrumming of those far-off drums.

The First Steps

The game opens as you arrive on the hangar deck of the interstellar colony ship *U.E.S.C. Marathon.* You are a nameless security officer who discovers that an alien race, known as the Phfor, has invaded the *Marathon* with the intention of enslaving its occupants. Also, a rogue computer named Durandal has annexed the ship's artificial intelligence system. This would simply be a minor annoyance if it weren't for the fact that Durandal is controlling the ship's teleportation systems and thinks that biffing you into the midst of the alien marauders is a complete hoot.

Ostensibly, your mission is to defeat the Phfor, return the *Marathon* to its rightful owners, and propel Durandal from the ship's computer system. But as with most games of this type, your real mission is to tear through the beautifully rendered winding corridors; gather a deadly inventory of weapons; figure out how to get from point A to point B; and annihilate just about anything that stands in your path.

Whereas Bungie's previous FPPSEU, Pathways Into Darkness, contained many of the aforementioned elements, it felt more like an adventure game. Playing it required tracking down particular items and solving puzzles in order to proceed through the levels. Although Marathon has its share of plot elements and brow-furrowing puzzles, this game relies more heavily on quick reflexes and dexterous digits.

The View From the Road

As the fine and slightly tart Marathon manual explains, "being naked in space stinks," so you are attired in the latest futuristic military garb, complete with a Cyberhead Helmet that acts as your interface to the game's world. This interface reflects some of the game's innovations and contains such elements as a View Screen, Shield Energy Display, and Weapons Manifest. These doodads are old news to seasoned FPPSEU players, but they're just the beginning.

Take the Oxygen Level Display, for example. Space adventures always seem to assume that there's plenty of clean fresh air about. But let's face it: a breathable atmosphere isn't standard equipment in a vacuum. Marathon addresses this condition by equipping the player's suit with an oxygen supply. Additionally, the game's designers must have considered that running and dodging are likely to deplete this same supply. One particularly tricky level of the game requires the player not only to slaughter a large number of baddies, recharge his shields, and navigate a vexing maze, but also to stop off at inconveniently placed oxygen pumps to top off the tank.

GREAT FEATURE

Marathon's interface also includes a motion detector. Having this early warning system may seem like so much pabulum to DOOM II players accustomed to slimy goons springing from behind darkened doorways, but it does allow the player to more carefully plan the next move. Given that much of the ship is shrouded in eerie darkness, this tool is almost a necessity. However, the detector indicates only that there is some bad action nearby. Whether taking out the enemy will require a left hook or the SPNKR-X17 Surface to Surface Rocket is left to the player to discover.

Not only are high-powered weapons tougher to obtain than they are in DOOM II, but Marathon also provides the player with more control over those weapons once they're in hand. The last time we aimed a Tech .50 Fusion Pistol at a beetle-bodied creep on a high ledge, we actually had to move our arms up as well as over. Marathon requires you to move your weapons on the x and y axes. Pabulum indeed.

Being able to move your weapon up and down opens up some intriguing possibilities. Let's say, for example, that you have your shields powered to the max and you point your M.75 Assault Rifle/Grenade Launcher at the floor and fire off a grenade. Yes, you take some damage, but you are also propelled up and backward. Now suppose there's a low and otherwise inaccessible ledge behind you.... Grenade Hopping, as this technique is known to Marathon hipsters, is mentioned nowhere in the documentation, but it is a skill that one is expected to develop if all locations in the game—particularly the secret ones—are to be accessed.

MARATHON 2: DURANDAL

CD

Stop the presses!

Just prior to our chapter deadline, those rascals at Bungie announced that Marathon 2: Durandal will be shipping in the not-too-distant future. We don't have a load of information, but what we do have is worth mentioning. According to our super-secret inside sources at Bungie (oh heck, it's Bungie's media flak Doug "The Voice of the BOBs" Zartman who was kind enough to fax us the same press release everyone else on the planet received), Marathon 2 is on the way. Details are sketchy, and after the long shipping delay of the original Marathon, we're not about to say that the game will be released by the time you read this (although Doug claims it's well on its way). Here's what we do know:

Marathon 2 is a completely new adventure that takes us away from the confines of the original game's floating spacecraft and plops us down on an (presumably hostile) alien world. The latest chapter of the Marathon saga includes a wide-screen display (from the screen shots we've seen it looks a bit like the letterbox view found in those chic MTV videos), lush environmental sounds that change as your position changes, underwater and under-lava fighting, more-aggressive BOBs (the poor shmoes in Marathon 1 who became so much alien fodder), and dramatic lighting effects that shift according to surrounding conditions.

We expect that Marathon 2 will feature more of the fantastic FPPSEU action we've come to expect from Bungie. And we can hardly wait. It'll be great to break out our SPNKR-X17s again.

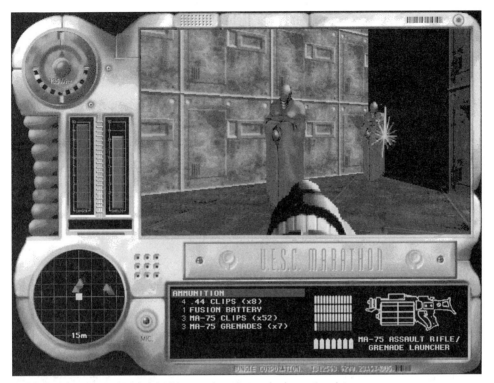

Is this Marathon cootie friend or foe? Best to shoot first and ask questions later.

Running a Marathon

In addition to the 26 levels in the single-player game, Marathon includes ten network scenarios. Within these scenarios, you can play in teams or as an independent warrior. The location of all network players can be shown on a map overview, and network games can go on as long as the power holds.

The game runs on LocalTalk, TokenTalk, and Ethernet networks. The latest update allows users to also run modem-to-modem via Apple Remote Access, but the current implementation is unbearably slow. As an extra treat, each copy of the game includes two installations: one for the full game, plus an extra network install so two people can play without having to purchase an additional copy.

Marathon is a remarkable effort, and we'd hate to think we're standing in the way of lead programmer Jason Jones's well-deserved purchase of a new Ferrari. But we do have one minor complaint to add to that of execrable performance in modem-to-modem play: When you switch into Full Screen mode, all on-screen indicators and gauges vanish—you're flying blind. Although you can quickly switch to a smaller view with a single keystroke, the less successful game Sensory Overload handled the problem more elegantly by shrinking these items and placing them along the edge of the screen. Bungie should explore this option.

But frankly, that's a tiny blemish in the big picture. Marathon is an absolutely enthralling and nerve-racking distraction as a single-player game, and it's the kind of networking experience that causes monthly productivity graphs to take a decided turn to the southeast. You must buy this game!

TIP

Tips

• To choose a level to begin the game, even a network game, hold down the Command and Option keys while pressing Begin Game.

• Learn to grenade hop as soon as possible.

• When you're standing on a transporter and don't want to transport, press the Escape key to abort transportation.

• Any BOB who says, "Thank God, it's you!" is no friend of yours.

Pros: Tremendous action, graphics, and network play. A terrific Mac first-person-perspective shoot-'em-up that contains a reasonable plot and enough puzzles to cause you to briefly cool your weapons.

Cons: Playing in Full Screen mode removes helpful indicators. Crummy modem-to-modem play.

System Requirements: 8-bit color monitor, 68020 or faster Macintosh, 12MB hard disk space, 3MB RAM, System 6.05 or later.

MARATHON	
Fun factor:	5.0
Look and feel:	4.5
Value:	5.0
Replayability:	4.5*
Overall:	5.0
* Networked.	

Dark Forces
LucasArts

DOS users have forever knocked the Mac because it lacked the fast-paced blockbuster titles that dominated the world of the command line interface (DOS machines). At some point, we have all confidently entered a computer debate with plenty of verbal justification for the Mac's supremacy only to hear a DOS user proclaim that X-Wing is not available on the Mac. In an instant, you know

Dark Forces proved that the Mac could handle those flashy DOS games, and do a better job of it as well.

those punishing words have dealt a death blow to your carefully structured arguments, and although you desperately respond by flinging forth information about the Mac's superior graphics and superlative interface, the battle is lost. After all, they have X-Wing. But this ancient argument has become moot thanks to Dark Forces, the Doom-like Star Wars action game that is destined to prove the Mac's legitimacy as a superior games machine once and for all.

Please Endorse, Luke

Dark Forces puts you in the shoes of a mercenary who must complete 14 increasingly difficult missions in an effort to aid the rebellion. The first mission introduces you to the basic control set by letting you blast your way through to a set of Death Star plans that you must take to a friendly ship. The remaining missions tend to run toward the mundane, with nearly all situations coming down to the find-a-key-open-a-door common denominator. If Dark Forces falls short in plot or puzzle complexity when compared to Marathon, it may be due to its greater emphasis on combat and tactical prowess. It is much more likely that you will find yourself debating which weapon to vaporize a storm trooper with than figuring out a secret code to open a special door.

R2, See What You Can Do With It

Anyone who has played DOOM or Marathon will have no difficulty adapting to the first-person-perspective movement and weaponry action in Dark Forces. In fact, the fluidity of motion is great on an LC 475 and nothing short of amazing on a Power Macintosh 6100/66. All of the controls can be changed to any keys you wish, and the game comes with sets for many of the joysticks currently available. Personally, we found the good old keyboard controls offered the best response and access. Dark Forces has incorporated fantastic scenery with sweeping vertical vistas that can force you to stop and look around to get your bearings. This is in stark contrast to Marathon, which largely takes place in more confined spaces. Suffice it to say, that if you thought the spaces in Marathon were big, prepare to be blown away.

**GREAT
FEATURE**

Stop, Rebel Scum!

Many of the sound bites in Dark Forces come directly out of the Star Wars vocabulary. This definitely helps set the mood, but it is a mixed blessing because of the corniness and downright inappropriate comments that emerge from the enemies' mouths. For example: when you come around a corner with a blaster pointed straight at the head of an enemy, you wouldn't expect him to say "you're not authorized to be in this sector" now, would you? Nope, a little cursing or begging for one's life would certainly seem more fitting. There also appears to be a lack of directional sound support despite the fact that there is a Panning Stereo Sound option in the preferences screen. For some reason, there seems to be little way for you to determine the enemy's location through sound. Ask anyone who's played Marathon the whole way through just how important that is. Dark Forces makes you turn around to see the location of the enemy that is shooting at you from behind rather than letting the stereo speakers supply that information. Once you are used to counting on the sound of the enemy (as you would if the game were real) it can be very hard to go back to a less realistic game.

**LOUSY
FEATURE**

The music is another issue that many will no doubt disagree on due to its repetitive nature and rather odd mood changes. Although the music is well orchestrated and can be presented in 16-bit stereo, I found it difficult to enjoy gameplay with the standard Stars Wars theme repeating at regular intervals. Many people will likely opt to turn the music off.

A Brighter Future

Where Dark Forces really shines is in showing that the Mac can be an acceptable computer for games that were traditionally barred from its screen because of the intense graphical and interface overhead inherent in Mac software. This games cooks on any Power Macintosh and is no slouch even on the slow 040 machines. Those with Power Macs will be thrilled to learn that Dark Forces plays in a high-res mode that delivers the kind of quality graphics Mac users have universally come to expect from their games.

Sweet Revenge

Although Dark Forces falls short in plot and doesn't break any ground in the grand scope of computer gaming, it does prove that the Mac is, and can be, an awesome gaming machine capable of defeating any Pentium-based VGA system. So the next time you get into a debate over which computer is better, just let the Mac bashers know that they can eat their hearts out. Because hey, the Mac can handle Dark Forces in high resolution. Can their machines? Sweet revenge.

Tips

TIP

• Type these cheat codes into the game as you play for a dishonest reward:

LAOZ	This shrinks enemies to 50% of their size.
LAPOSTAL	Gives all weapons and full ammo.
LAMAXOUT	This will, well, max out everything.
LARANDY	Supercharge weapons.
LAIMLAME	Invincibility.
LAUNLOCK	Gives all the equipment.
LACDS	Improves map so you can see enemies.
LAREDLITE	Stops enemies in their tracks.
LANTFH	Use your PDA to teleport yourself.
LAPOGO	Lets you walk up cliffs and on high ledges.
LASKIP	Skips to next level.
LADATA	Gives you your x, y, z coordinates.
LABUG	Insect Mode lets you fit in very small holes.
LASECBASE	Go to Mission #1;
LATALAY	Go to Mission #2;
LASEWERS	Go to Mission #3;
LATESTBASE	Go to Mission #4;
LAGROMAS	Go to Mission #5;
LADTENTION	Go to Mission #6;
LARAMSHED	Go to Mission #7;
LAROBOTICS	Go to Mission #8;
LANARSHADA	Go to Mission #9;
LAJABSHIP	Go to Mission #10;
LAIMPCITY	Go to Mission #11;
LAFUELSTAT	Go to Mission #12;
LAEXECUTOR	Go to Mission #13;
LAARC	Go to Mission #14.

Pros: Fantastic graphics and speed on Power Macs. Smooth game play. Intense action.

Cons: No save-game feature. Needs at least 68040 Mac and 8MB RAM to run. Music repetitive and sometimes inappropriate.

System Requirements: 256-color monitor, 68040 or PowerPC, , 8MB RAM, 5MB or 13MB hard disk space (depending on installation selected), System 7.1 or later, CD-ROM drive.

DARK FORCES	
Fun factor:	4.5
Look and feel:	5.0
Value:	4.5
Replayability:	3.5
Overall:	4.5

DOOM II

id Software
Distributed by GT Interactive

To gamers tied strictly to the Macintosh, the words id Software probably don't mean much. But id virtually *owns* the PC game market. Any game programmed or produced by id is a Very Big Deal to PC players. With the release of Wolfenstein 3D and DOOM II, id is now a Reasonably Big Deal with Mac players as well. And with good reason. The company's games may not have much substance, but for stimulation of the adrenal gland, few games on the market can compete with id's.

Hell on Earth

DOOM, a game we may never see on the Mac, and DOOM II are two fierce FPPSEUs that pit you against countless demons from that town across the River Styx. If you bother to read DOOM II's backstory in the manual, you'll discover that you play a Space Marine attempting to liberate an earthly space port from these hardboiled foes. But forget the backstory. All you really need to know is that every sentient soul in this dark world is your enemy, and you must kill, kill, kill or wind up dead, dead, dead.

As with all other FPPSEUs, you begin the game with just enough firepower to get you to the next, more deadly firearm. In this case, you are issued a mean left uppercut and a revolver. Have no fear that you'll be under-armed for long. By the end of the first level, you should have a shotgun, rocket launcher, and chain saw in your possession, provided you find all the secret rooms, of course.

Chain saw? Right. Using this labor-saving device as a weapon illustrates DOOM II's lack of subtlety in the violence department. This game is definitely not for the squeamish. When you hit the machine gun wielding former commando with a shotgun blast, for example, the top of his head flies off in a shower of blood.

DANGER

The violence is ameliorated to an extent by the roughness of the graphics. Although DOOM II for the Mac is a great game and features higher graphic resolution than the PC version, you can still discern its origins in the blocky graphics that are the hallmark of PC games. This may be just fine for those players with weak stomachs as the effect of turning a band of imps inside out with a well-placed rocket is not nearly so horrific as it might be with high-resolution graphics.

Just Like the Real Thing (Sorta)

DOOM II is extremely faithful to the PC version, even down to the cheat codes and DOS-like F-key commands. Mac users will be pleased to know that they too can enjoy the networked DeathMatch and Cooperative modes so beloved by their PC cousins. In these modes you're able to work with or against your pals over a network or head-to-head using a null-modem. You can send preconfigured messages, too.

**GREAT
FEATURE**

One area where the Mac version falls short of the PC version of DOOM II is in the implementation of music. Serious PC gamers load their machines with sound cards that produce stunning sound effects and music. These cards are not

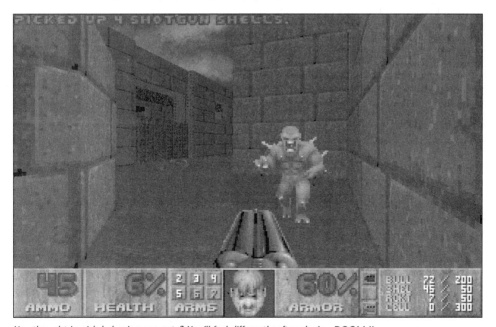

You thought impish behavior was cute? You'll feel differently after playing DOOM II.

available to Mac users, and their music is instead piped through QuickTime using the sounds contained in the QuickTime Musical Instruments file. Although these sounds are much more convincing than the wheezy tones generated by the Mac's four-voice synthesizer of old, they just don't have the presence or fidelity of the sounds delivered by PC sound cards. Using external speakers or headphones improves things markedly but fails to raise performance levels to the PC standard. Music aside, the sound effects on both versions of the game are the same and are equally chilling.

Performance is zippy as all get-out on a Power Mac, but gamers with 040 processors should be prepared to make adjustments in resolution and screen size to make the game playable. Folks with accelerators in their older Macs should be aware that 32-bit mode must be enabled for the game to work.

Point and Pulverize

DOOM and DOOM II followed Pathways into Darkness's lead and included lighting effects and texture mapping. To understand the effectiveness of these graphic devices, you need only look back at Wolfenstein 3D. In that earlier game, every room was brightly lit and the walls had a monotonous sameness about them. DOOM II is a completely different world, one shrouded in uneven darkness and containing blood-sprayed walls that can roil and churn in unsettling ways. This gloom creates a wonderfully tense atmosphere.

DOOM and DOOM II also include multitiered levels. This means that beasties can lurk above or below you within a room. Although this effect adds a nice depth to the game environment, it's not fully implemented. In the id games, there's no need to aim up or down as you must in Bungie's Marathon. Rather, simply point your weapon in the direction of your intended victim and fire. As long as they're lined up with the gun, they're meat.

This isn't necessarily a bad thing. It keeps the controls simple and allows you to concentrate on the task at hand: killing everything in sight. But if pressed, we'd have to admit that we prefer the more realistic approach taken by Marathon.

A Heck of a Lot of Fun

We've been waiting a long time for a Mac version of this game to appear, and we couldn't be more happy to report that DOOM II was worth the wait. The graphics are quite good; the sound effects are superb; network mode is huge fun; and the action is nothing short of heart busting. If you're a fan of FPPSEUs, prepare to have a bloody good time.

Tips

• You open secret doors by pressing the Open Door key. To quickly locate secret passages (without cheating, that is), try pressing the Open Door key on the run; there's no need to stop and press, stop and press.

• Type these cheat codes into the game as you play for a dishonest reward:

IDCLIP   Walk through walls.

IDKFA   Full armor and keys.

IDDT   Reveals all areas on the map.

IDCLEV   Transport to the level of your choice (try 31 or 32 for a treat).

IDDQD   Invincible.

Pros: Intense action. Wonderfully atmospheric. Dangerously addictive.

Cons: Level of violence may offend some players.

System Requirements: 68040 Mac, 8MB RAM (12MB recommended), 17.2MB hard disk space for full installation, System 7.1 or later.

DOOM II	
Fun factor:	4.5
Look and feel:	4.0
Value:	4.0
Replayability:	4.5*
Overall:	4.5

* With added levels or networked.

11 Conquest Games

In creating this book, we found that there are roughly ten categories of computer games, and that within each of these is at least one title that could be described as a blockbuster. Although not every title was initially created for the Mac, the conquest genre boasts such megahits as Civilization, Spaceward Ho!, and the Warlords duo. These games share a theme that involves the building of an empire, be it military, economic, or cultural, and an effort to crush all challengers bent on the same task. Many players like to classify these games as "god games" because of the omniscient position the user is able to enjoy as he or she dictates the course of history within the realm of a software-generated universe. Perhaps the allure of being omnipotent is the bait that draws people into spending mind-boggling amounts of time building empires of bits and bytes that exist tenuously in their computer's random access memories. Of course the reasons for the widespread appeal of these games could very well lie in the fact that we cannot rule our own bank books let alone become Napoleonic conquerors bent on world domination. Ruling a society with iron-fisted domination used to be a fantasy confined to the fanciful realm encountered just before the onset of sleep.

Ruling the World

Conquest games have enabled your average Joe or Jane to be Alexander the Great, Genghis Khan, and Erwin Rommel without having to undergo the tedium of recruiting angry, pitchfork-wielding militia.

When asked to list their all-time favorite games in informal surveys, Mac gamers often mention such titles as Strategic Conquest, Civilization, and even the oldie but goody, Balance of Power. These are merely variations on the ancient premise of conquest on a grand scale. As long as humanity exists, there will be an innate drive to conquer, dominate, and generally hog the remote control, which for most can only be fulfilled vicariously through these great programs.

CD

Empire Deluxe
New World Computing

Snappy titles on computer game boxes often belie the true nature of their contents. How many times have you scanned the shelves and seen an eye-catching box with neon lettering declaring "MacFudgecicle! Game of the Year!" without having any clue as to what sort of entertainment lies on the enclosed magnetic disks. Empire Deluxe is one title that says it all. This baby involves building a military empire through the conquering of cities, both neutral and enemy, by land, air, and sea. New World Computing has attached the moniker "deluxe" and endeavors to supply a few new twists to the old theme with the inclusion of new units, more flexibility in play, and most notably, head-to-head play over a modem or network with other Macs or even a PC.

GREAT
FEATURE

Conquest Is King

The object of Empire Deluxe is simple: starting from just one city, you must build a military empire large enough to crush all opposition. The more cities you have, the more fighting units you can produce. The weapons at your disposal include infantry, armor, battleships, cruisers, bombers, fighters, subs, transports, and destroyers. Many games of this nature have you facing off against one enemy, a sort of megalithic evil entity that you can come to despise with every fiber of your existence. Empire Deluxe differs by providing up to six opponents (either human or computer), each of which wants nothing less than to pillage and burn every last one of your cities while drinking your finest champagne.

Seek and Destroy

The initial portion of the game involves mostly exploration punctuated by the occasional capturing of a neutral city. Eventually, however, you will bump into a foe and the spaghetti will hit the fan in large quantities. Once contact with another player is made, the chemistry of the game changes dramatically, forcing you to put down the potato chips and seriously become concerned with military objectives. Victory in Empire Deluxe comes by eliminating all of the other players in the game, and we can tell you from personal experience that there are few things as satisfying as crushing an opponent's last city with an amphibious assault while singing "My Way" in an obnoxious manner.

Empire comes with a great map editor, 40 preset scenarios, and a random map generator, thus making it infinitely replayable. There is also the benefit of a handicapping system that allows advantage adjustments in one-third increments of production output and battle outcome. This evens the playing field for beginner and expert alike and makes computer opponents fully configurable. However, because of the turn-based method of game play, only one player moves at a time, making for very slow play, especially on large maps. We have been involved in a game in which each half of a turn took 20 minutes, and large games can easily take 500 turns if things are evenly matched. You'd better make sure you have several months of supplies on hand before tackling a large Empire Deluxe game. We find that large games are best played by modem over a period of weeks or months, allowing for such basic needs as eating and washing.

DANGER

The DOS Game Cometh

Although Empire Deluxe is a port from the DOS (actually Windows) world, the graphics are crisp and the interface utilizes the Mac's capabilities to the fullest. Along with the usual menu commands and mouse controls, a single keystroke interface has been included so that many tasks can be performed with the touch of one key. New World Computing should be commended for making sure the Mac's identity was not lost in the porting of this game. However, we cannot for the life of us understand why the Windows version of Empire Deluxe employs no copy protection while the Mac version (using the same manual) has a key word lookup every time the game is booted. Are Windows users less likely to pirate than Mac users?

RANT

Networkin' It!

There's nothing quite like a game that allows you to revel in the triumph over another human, and Empire Deluxe enables nearly every permutation and combination of humans (and various levels of intelligent computer opponents) to engage in play. The real kicker is that one of the six possible players can be some-one on a Windows machine. For example, there can be three people connected on AppleTalk, one computer opponent, and a Windows user connected over modem. Network play is most impressive, working flawlessly even between plat-forms. The other feature New World Computing included was a "play by mail" feature that allows you to take advantage of e-mail or regular snail mail to com-plete a game by swapping saved game files. We think you'd better have a great deal of patience to be playing by this method; it conjures up memories of Mr. French from *Family Affair* playing his excruciatingly slow chess game by mail.

Empire Deluxe, Fit for a King

Empire Deluxe is a great addition to the family of conquest games and takes the genre to new heights with the inclusion of seamless network and multiplatform modem play. This game is for anyone who would like to hone their world-domination skills.

Pros: Seamless modem and network play. Editor allows for unlimited variety. Excellent handicap-ping system. Nicely done port from Windows.

Cons: Annoying copy protection. Annoying music (but can be turned off).

System Requirements: All Mac models newer than Mac Classic, 2MB RAM, 4MB for color and System 6.07 or higher, 4MB hard disk space, System 6.07 or higher.

EMPIRE DELUXE	
Fun Factor	4.0
Look and Feel	3.5
Value	3.5
Replayability	4.5
Overall	3.5
(Key word protection lowers rating by 1/2)	

Civilization

Microprose

As one of the most prolific and successful game writers ever, it's a shame Sid Meier hasn't developed his software on the Mac. This however, is something most Mac owners can overlook with relative ease, because let's face it, this guy writes awesome games whether they were coded on a Commodore Vic 20 or a Cray super computer. In 1991, the not-so-wonderful world of DOS was exposed to Civilization, a game so insidiously addictive that daytime talk shows were exploring every aspect of the game's effects. Mac owners were dying to get a look at the game after watching Oprah dissect the emotional problems of a woman who became so addicted to Civilization that she saw the outline of Elvis in a con-tinental land mass. Mac aficionados had only to wait for Earth to revolve around the sun to taste the sweet elixir of complete power that's provided by creating a society from the ground up. December, 1992, marked the release of Mac Civilization, the grand-daddy of world empire games.

To Walk, You First Must Crawl

After enduring a cheesy opening sequence packed with shabby graphics and clunky music, you are able to set the game's parameters to your satisfaction. There are five levels of difficulty to choose from, and the layout of the world can be either that of Earth or a customized landscape created by selecting three of nine choices of terrain characteristics. The only thing left to do before getting your feet wet is to name the tribe you will be leading out of the planet's stone age. There are 14 titles to choose from, but we suspect that most will prefer to name their peoples the Foxy Fungi or some other such moniker to avoid wallowing in the mundane. Once the opening parameters have been set, you must begin the arduous task of building your civilization into a glorious spectacle of power and wonderment. Of course, you are just as likely to build a civilization that will be made to submit to a superior culture, but hey, you have to try. Despite the obviously ported screen art, the graphics are better on the Mac than on the original DOS program, and thankfully, the interface was redesigned with Mac users in mind.

Fertilizing the Embryo

The first action to be taken is that of building a city. Finding a suitable area with crop potential, mining prospects, and decent proximity to the ocean should be your foremost consideration. This will enable your first city to grow and produce units to protect itself and explore the surrounding country. Every unit or city improvement takes a certain amount of surplus resources to build. In other words, if your city does not have enough to feed its own population, you can forget that shiny new cavalry division you've been wanting. In the beginning, it is important to build some military units to protect your investment, but a new batch of settlers to build roads and found new cities should not be lagging too far behind. Of course, Civilization is not just about building up masses of units and expanding recklessly; after all, there are detailed cultural and scientific aspects of game play that cannot be swept under the rug. For a city to become economically viable and thus able to support distant military units, it must have an infrastructure for storing food, educating and entertaining its people, and protecting itself. This means building roads, granaries, irrigation systems, temples, marketplaces, and many other things to keep up with the torrid pace imposed by industrial and economic evolution.

Besides building a solid military and municipal infrastructure, you must consider positioning resources to benefit your technological development. Without technology, a civilization is destined to become piles of rubble for use in the construction of its conqueror's roads. There are a huge number of technological advances that will give you everything from the ability to ride horses to sending several nuclear weapons to annihilate a pesky adversary. Constructing universities and libraries and keeping the population happy will aid in making discoveries in an expedient fashion.

Howdy, Neighbor!

Eventually you will run into another culture and will be asked to have a chitchat with an emissary empowered to hash out necessary agreements. Civilization gives you the choice of making peace or war with these competitors, thus adding a wrinkle of diplomacy to intercultural dynamics. You can choose to spit on their shoes and begin a blood bath of a war or you can coax them into a trust position by bargaining away technology. Of course, as in real life, treaties are made to be broken, and when the time is right you may refute any agreement and send your minions on to victory—or defeat as the case may be. Of course you can always opt to sign a peace treaty and agree to be mutual enemies against some other culture in an effort to speed their exit from the game.

LOUSY FEATURE

Unfortunately, there is no network or modem play with this game, which is a crying shame, because although the AI is superior in Civilization, a human is always far more cunning in negotiations and more unpredictable in matters involving espionage and battle than a 68040 can be.

Buy an Alarm

DANGER

Civilization could be the most time-sucking game we have ever seen, and one can only speculate how many marriages have succumbed to its addictive nature. There are several detailed books on the market dealing with the intricate workings of building a society from scratch in this great game. It's incredibly easy to play, but yet so complex in nature that reading the manual eventually becomes mandatory. Most players are drawn to the manual to garner an edge in game play, perhaps by exploiting some nuance of city life to make their scientists more productive and happy. Civilization can end in any one of five ways. You can give up and quit, retire from the game and retain your score, be destroyed by the enemy, or conquer the entire world yourself. The only other road to completion is for one of the civilizations to manage to get a spaceship to the star Alpha Centauri. The latter represents a level of technological expertise that says "you've made it" and deserve to win the game by nerding your opponents to death.

In Civilization, nuclear weapons eventually become possible. In this case, Leningrad is in the process of being nuked as Kiev shows the signs of a previous blast.

The Never-Ending Game

With each attempt at world domination being affected by such a huge number or variables, Civilization is one of the most open-ended games we have laid eyes on. Its highly addictive nature is legendary, and the Mac version only contributes to the great fun and challenge Sid Meier has been able to provide computer gamers everywhere.

Pros: Better graphics than on the PC version. Complete, well-written manual. Highly addictive.

Cons: Slow animation on older Macs. Key word copy protection. No network or modem play.

System Requirements: 4MB RAM, 5.4MB hard disk space, System 6.07 or higher.

CIVILIZATION	
Fun factor:	4.5
Look and feel:	3.5
Value:	5.0
Replayability:	5.0
Overall:	4.5

Populous I & II
Electronic Arts

Certainly computer gamers enjoy slaying evil gnomes, vaporizing gigantic space cooties, and taking high-performance air fighters for jogs around the Middle East, but there are times when these diversions just aren't empowering enough. When those occasional megalomaniacal moments arise, there's nothing quite like strapping on the sandals and toga, adorning the old coconut with a wreath of olive branches, and taking on the role of Most Grand and Exalted. Mac users can now sample these almighty pleasures thanks to Electronic Arts's ports of the venerable god games Populous and Populous II, heretofore known as Populous I and II. These games hearken back to the days before gods were concerned with such pedestrian matters as interurban transportation, genetic mutation, and agribusiness. In this era of old time religion, these all-too-human deities were solely interested in carrying on in unseemly ways with their ethereal colleagues and mucking about in the affairs of those too puny to retaliate.

It's Greek to Us

You take on the role of a Greek god who must challenge other computer-generated gods for the title of Lord God of Big Cheesedom. The two games set up this god business in different ways—Populous I represents the opposition only as evil, but the sequel contains 32 discrete gods who must be opposed.

Students of mythology realize that when gods and gods-in-training do battle they rarely bother to sully themselves by actually getting off their holy heinies to smite their adversaries. Instead, they pick a load of earthbound Joes and Janes who have assembled an image of their Most Hallowed Benefactor out of mud and dung and pit them against an equally partisan group from across the swamp. The gods then kick back with a crucible or two of wine and watch as the little folks below kick, bite, and mightily clobber their neighbors with tree branches.

The View From On High

The two sides look remarkably similar. The only difference, in fact—other than kind hearts and pure souls—is that good prefers blue garments to evil's red. In the main view of the game, objects on land—such as the good and evil followers and their settlements—are displayed as nearly indiscernible dots. Below this overview is a close-up view detailing a small portion of the land. Just to the left of the close-up window is the Mana Bar. This indicator shows how much power you have to influence events. At the inception of each new world, powers are limited to raising and lowering the landscape. This power is vital to success, because the lemminglike worshipers (also known as Walkers) won't settle down,

A heavenly hotfoot is just one of the many acts of the gods you can inflict in Populous I and II.

raise crops, build forts, and make more Walkers unless the land is nicely flattened out. You'd like to encourage these activities because Mana—and thus power—increases as more good Walkers and settlements appear. This power can also be employed to add lumps and valleys to the opposition's real estate. As each side's Mana increases, gods earn the right to issue earthquakes, columns of fire, tidal waves, and plagues upon the opposition. Of course, while you are happily muddying your hands in landscaping efforts, the evil ones are likewise settling down, subduing the land, and designing an assault on their enemy (you). Although god-given disasters are likely to slow down the enemy, to expunge these critters entirely one must address the issue more directly. In other words, the good guys must be sent across the border to kick some evil butt. Unfortunately, flinging the feeble Walkers hither and thither isn't the most effective way to accomplish this end.

This is where the Papal Magnet comes in handy. When touched by the Papal Magnet, the said Walker becomes a Leader whom all the other Walkers blindly follow if called upon to do so. Once a Leader has been established, the Papal Magnet can be moved into the enemy's camp and the Walkers directed to forget about settling down and to march toward the Leader, who, in turn, marches toward the Magnet. If any of the enemy are encountered along the way, the Walkers and the Leader engage them in battle.

Each world is won when all the evil followers and their settlements have been wiped from the map. Points are awarded for such things as population and enemy Leaders killed. The score for a particular round determines which world will appear next—a high score causes the game to skip through a few intermediate levels in order to present something a little more challenging. There are 500 levels in Populous I and 1,000 rounds in the sequel.

Your Own Olympus

Populous II includes a number of enhancements not found in its predecessor that greatly speed up population growth and the game's pace.

GREAT FEATURE

We can also be thankful that Populous II's interface is more Maclike and consistent than that of Populous I—an ungainly port. Of course, no one is going to think for a moment that Populous II was created specifically for the Mac—it's that chunky graphics thing again—but at least all the options for the second iteration of the game are in the menu bar rather than scattered between the menu and a couple of on-screen buttons.

We enjoyed both games and, in the upper levels, found them to be quite formidable. Whether they will be successful among other Mac users depends upon the expectations they bring to the game. One drawback of these games coming to the Mac at such a late date is that conquering games and world simulations such as Civilization and the Maxis sims have made such amazing strides in recent years that these earlier efforts look somewhat primitive in comparison. But if players can accept them for what they are—worthy forbears from a simpler time—Populous I and II might occupy a corner of your own gaming Olympus.

Pros: Entertaining and challenging. Many levels.

Cons: Populous I has an insultingly lumpy interface and graphics.

System Requirements: 68020 or better, 2MB RAM for System 6, 4MB for System 7, 715K hard disk space, System 6.07 or higher.

POPULOUS	
Fun factor:	3.0
Look and feel:	1.5
Value:	3.5
Replayability:	3.0
Overall:	3.0

POPULOUS II	
Fun factor:	3.5
Look and feel:	3.0
Value:	3.5
Replayability:	3.0
Overall:	3.5

Strategic Conquest
Delta Tao Software

Strategic Conquest, by Peter Merrill, dates back to the very dawn of AppleTalk and was probably the genesis of conquest-style games on the Mac. The game gathered legions of followers who were compelled by its ease of use, chesslike complexity, and innovative network feature that enabled two humans to go head-to-head in battles of epic proportions. This is the first commercial game we can think of that utilized the Mac's infant networking software to add the human intangible to game play. It wasn't uncommon to see a couple of Mac owners connecting their 512K Macs together for a day of intense empire building and conflict that would usually end with the ingestion of several bags of corn chips and two severely distended abdomens. The original publisher of SC was PBI software, which first released the game in 1985. After a run of a couple years, and a couple of updates, SC seemingly disappeared forever into the software void that hungrily swallows unsupported programs. This game didn't die however, and although there are probably many reasons for this, we can think of three big ones. First, the software was relatively robust, and the original game from 1985 still worked on a IIsi with System 6.07. Second, the game had developed a cult of fans that continued to play it, talk about it, and wish it would come back. Third, this great company called Delta Tao realized the game was a gem, purchased the rights, made it System 7 compatible, and re-released it for all to enjoy.

General, the World Is Yours
The above words adorned the original box and clearly set the tone for the game inside. The premise is that of pure empire building from the get go. Starting with one city on a random map, you must choose to develop one of eight different units: one ground, two air, and five sea vessels. Only the immediate squares around the starting city are visible, while the rest of the map lies in quiet blackness awaiting cautious exploration by fighter jets or armies. As the world gets explored, neutral cities will be encountered and can be captured by attacking with an army from an adjacent square. If the invasion is successful, you can start the new city creating more juicy instruments of war. The world is generally a jumble of islands and bodies of water of varying sizes and dimensions; the early production of transports is very important. Of course, and this always has to happen, you are never, ever, alone. There is someone—either a computer of varying intelligence or a human—out there also gobbling up precious cities while producing a force he or she hopes will be enough to sufficiently humiliate you and your family.

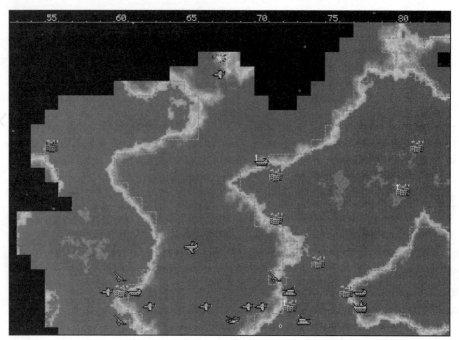

Forces gather for an amphibious assault on enemy ground. Version 4.0 of Strategic Conquest includes helicopters and artillery for ranged attack.

The game is played on a turn-by-turn basis. This works fairly well, and the player not moving can watch any combat action on-screen as it happens. Many of the mundane components of play, such as setting a destination for new units, can be automated to make a turn faster so that you can pass a turn before your opponent can make it back from the bathroom. This enables cities at the edge of the world to automatically send their production to the front lines to likely be destroyed in the next turn.

Escalation

GREAT FEATURE

Generally speaking, when the two combatants finally meet, both have had a chance to build up strong forces and lay claim to a sizable chunk of real estate while sharpening their egos for a victory dance. In fact, many games end up nearly equally, and the strategy and tactics of each player definitely factors into the outcome. If two players have very similar situations, the game could drag on indefinitely. However, Mr. Merrill made sure this wouldn't happen by incorporating a feature that no other similar game has. Nukes. Right from the onset of the game, you are given the ability to build aircraft called bombers which are (in the beginning) able to destroy all enemy units in whichever square they detonate over. A bomber is itself destroyed in this act. The bombers' power is amplified considerably as the game progresses because the blast radius increases every 25 turns. In a long game, this ever-increasing blast radius makes for highly destructive bombers that can wipe out entire islands and all the units and cities on them. Several carefully placed bombers late in a game can turn the tide decisively. The inclusion of this feature does not detract at all from the early game play because highly destructive bombers are only available after the game has progressed at length and a winner has not emerged through conventional means.

In the Top Ten Still

Strategic Conquest still rates on many gamers' top ten lists and is a classic that will likely live long into the future, much to the chagrin of many a spouse. Version 4.0 will be out by the time this book is and will include new helicopter and artillery units, as well as brand new graphics and sound. The artillery piece is perhaps the most radical change because it allows for ranged ground attacks or defense of important cities. Version 4.0 will definitely be another hit and carry on in the great tradition of this classic game.

Pros: Infinitely replayable. Easy to learn. Network play. A classic.

Cons: No modem play.

System Requirements: 2MB RAM for System 6, 4MB for System 7, 715K hard disk space, System 6.07 or higher.

STRATEGIC CONQUEST	
Fun factor:	4.0
Look and feel:	4.0
Value:	4.5
Replayability:	4.5
Overall:	4.5

Warlords II
Strategic Studies Group (SSG)

CD

SSG has long been known for their award-winning war games such as Carriers at War and the now legendary string of titles in the Battlefront series. Despite their success in this area, SSG has occasionally taken the time to stray into various other pockets of entertainment software for the good of game players everywhere. For evidence of where SSG has traveled, we can look at the Warlords duo, first released in the DOS realm but soon converted to Mac. These games share a rather bizarre theme that fuses dungeons and dragons with a smidgen of empire building and a heaping helping of medieval tomfoolery. They can be described as King-Arthur-meets-General-Patton flying a white fire-breathing dragon. It's an unorthodox twist of premise but yet one that also seems so obvious it's a wonder it hasn't been used in the past. So saddle up your giant mosquito, don your lucky Amulet of Death, and prepare to enter the mythical world of Warlords.

To War Is Human

GREAT FEATURE

In Warlords, victory comes when your armies destroy all your opponents. You can choose to face off against up to seven competitors, which can be any combination of humans and/or computers. It should be noted that the AI has been drastically improved in Warlords II, thus making single-player games an intellectual challenge. A quick glance at Warlords leads one to expect a rehash of concepts exploited in other conquest games. You know the routine: Start with one city, capture some more, build up your forces, kick some butt, have a nice day, etc. Warlords is pleasantly different, however, and augments this concept by introducing special units called Heroes that have unique abilities which enable them to search the ruins that dot the countryside for artifacts of varying descriptions. These artifacts can provide flight, extra movement, or any number of other abilities to aid in exploration or battle. Perhaps the most endearing quality of this game is the fantastic variety of creatures and objects that can be developed for use against your enemies. This diverse assortment is not only pleasing to the eye but also tugs at the sense of fantasy many of us try hard to repress in our day-to-day lives. We're not saying that to play Warlords you must don a horned helmet and call yourself Zontar, but the game is more enjoyable if the mythical themes are not cast off.

There's More Than One Way to Skin an Orc

Warlords II includes six preset campaigns along with a random map generator to allow for infinite replayability and control to adjust the percentages

This rather imposing messenger brings various greetings, from a pat on the back to a warning of total carnage.

of hills, water, and forest in your kingdom to be. You are also supplied the option of beginning with a "blacked-out" map which must be explored in order for you to know where everything and everyone is. In short, the game is very customizable and permits for the tweaking of most aspects of play to allow for a game style that can conform to everyone's obsessive compulsive side. Even diplomatic relations can be utilized to create tenuous alliances that make the Middle East look like Disneyland. We do wonder why SSG didn't see fit to include a scenario editor for Warlords II as they did on the PC version. But SSG has been a leader in game development on the Mac, so perhaps we shouldn't gripe. The color and graphics are excellent. The movement of the pieces themselves is clunky, as is to be expected with this kind of game. The interface and on-screen movement of pieces certainly does not detract from the fun in any way.

RANT

If You Can't Join 'Em, Beat 'Em

Aside from the lack of network or modem play and the absent game editor, Warlords II is an excellent and refreshing diversion from other conquest games. This is another of the breed that is capable of swallowing an average-size human whole and not regurgitating for a fortnight. We can only hope there will be a Warlords III for all to enjoy and lose 186 hours of their lives to.

DANGER

WARLORDS II	
Fun factor:	3.5
Look and feel:	4.0
Value:	3.5
Replayability:	4.0
Overall:	4.0

Pros: More variety in units. Great color and interface. Random map generator.

Cons: No modem play. Need to read manual to understand game completely.

System Requirements: 256-color 68030 or better (game is Power Mac-native), 8MB hard disk space, 4MB RAM, System 7 or later.

Castles: Siege and Conquest
MacPlay

Think back, way back. To a time when Saddam Hussein was a friend of the U.S. and Michael Jordan was known only as a basketball player. It was 1987, and a now defunct company by the name of Mindscape had released a pair of innovative games using a technique called Cinemaware, which in many ways was a precursor to the "interactive movie" games available today. One half of this pair was a game called Defender of the Crown, which was based on life in medieval England and on the movies that depicted this period. The goal of the game was to become King of England through force and espionage while engaging in a '40s-style movie storyline. Although Defender was innovative and enjoyable, it was crippled by the 800K disk limit (most Macs didn't have hard drives then) and the black-and-white, nine-inch screen that made the graphics crisp but lifeless. Fast forward to 1994, when MacPlay released Castles: Siege & Conquest. Although one's immediate thoughts turn to its similarities with Defender of the Crown, this is definitely a different game and one that's a cut above.

Who's Running the Country?

You're in 14th century France during the Hundred Years War, and the race is on to see who will sit on the throne recently vacated (through death) by King Charles. How does one go about that? Only the Pope can appoint the king, and there are a few other lords like yourself vying for the monarch's chair. Only through careful handling of the available resources and battle savvy can you rise to the highest nonreligious post in the French homeland. The quest begins with one piece of a jigsawed map of over 40 segments of land, with no castle and only one natural resource to call on. It will take careful administrative, political, and military management to achieve ultimate success.

TIP

It's best to start out by capturing some neighboring territories before your competitors can get their grubby hands on them. These early conquests will be relatively effortless, and will give your troops much-needed morale and will supply your realm with natural resources such as timber, iron, and gold. As events progress, the full extent of managing your personal empire becomes annoyingly clear when you have to deal with subplots of thievery, espionage, and diplomacy in the midst of recruiting a new group of archers. If you haven't been bled dry by the Pope's incessant griping for indulgences, you must build castles to protect your valuable territories from an aggressive, back-stabbing, pond scum enemy. Construction of a castle is achieved by either selecting a prefab job, or designing your own. The latter should be reserved for budding architects and those extremely gifted in spatial relations.

This Land Is My Land

GREAT FEATURE

The management of the political, administrative, and military aspects of Castles is achieved through an excellent Mac interface that combines several ways to perform most tasks. This kind of interface is highly commendable and allows users to devise their own methods rather than conform to a rigid control set. The left side of the screen has the three areas laid out in a wonderfully crisp group of "boards" that flip over when tasks are being performed. The color and graphics are stunning, and MacPlay has even included QuickTime movies from a couple of old movies of the genre to add to the experience. The cinematic sequences are in black and white and appear in the middle of the screen when something happens to warrant their usage. The battle sequences are fought in a 3D close-up view, complete with toy soldierlike archers, infantry, knights, and catapults. If the bells and whistles aren't to your liking, the music, movies, plots, graphic battles, and sound effects can all be toggled off. The manual is excellent and explains all aspects of game play thoroughly and clearly. It is not absolutely necessary to read the manual to play the game. However, as with all games of this nature, it is best to read it to understand the subtle nuances of Castles.

It's Good to Be the King

Castles is certainly a thorough look at the life of lords in the period of the Hundred Years War. To win you must become proficient in various "real life" aspects of the game as well as have a little luck. The game is visually stunning and offers complex, deep game play and excitement for anyone who loves strategy. For those of us that played the old Defender of the Crown and missed it, this is the answer times ten!

CASTLES	
Fun Factor	4.0
Look and Feel	4.5
Value	4.0
Replayability	3.5
Overall	4.0

Pros: Better graphics than on the PC version. Complete, well-written manual. Great interface. Cool movie clips.

Cons: Slow on anything lower than a 68040.

System Requirements: 256-color Mac, 2MB RAM, 6MB hard disk space for minimum install, 16MB for full, System 6.07 or higher.

DANGER

Space Conquest Games

The infinite realm of space has become somewhat of an interplanetary Mecca to which game designers have steadily gravitated (no pun intended) in their quest to create original software. The limitations imposed by our intimate knowledge of good old terra firma make earth bound games a tad dry after a while. The vast unknown emptiness of space helps provide a suitable backdrop for producing believable games capable of doing what a good conquering game should. This, of course, is to rob the youth and life force from unsuspecting souls sucked into tournaments of seven consecutive games of Crush Thy Enemy. Today's software owes a great deal to extinct games like Reach for the Stars and Galactic Frontiers, which emerged from the Mac's primordial sludge to inspire others to carry the dream further. Even though for some the dream may be somewhat of a nightmare, this select group of games has received a great deal of player support.

Pax Imperia
Changeling Software

In 1992, a small company by the name of Changeling Software launched their flagship program into the seas of the competitive Mac gaming market. The product was Pax Imperia. Spaceward Ho!, the competition in this particular niche, had already achieved cult status, and it was thus a smidgen challenging for Changeling to win over the Ho! heads. Pax was a particularly ambitious project that promised users complete control over the military, economic, and cultural aspects of intergalactic domination. Of course, a game can attempt to encompass a large number of variables within its framework in more ways than one. The game publisher might open a special college where a complete and thorough four-year degree program can be offered so that every nuance of the game can be exploited by the users. Or it can ingeniously incorporate all the variables with a mind-bogglingly simple interface that even a monkey could learn in five minutes. The later of these two is, as one might expect, a much trickier undertaking than say, writing a large manual, which is what many game developers do. Pax Imperia supplies both a more detailed environment and easier controls to make it the master of this category.

Just the Pax, Ma'm

The object of Pax is to conquer the universe through whatever means available. This can involve espionage, armed conflict, and even trade embargoes against some or all of your foes. Pax however, is not a game one can just dive into and start playing while watching *Star Trek* reruns. Almost immediately after pulling off the shrink-wrap and booting the game, you are faced with a multitude of decisions. These are so imposing that it makes your decision not to purchase that Magic Eight Ball seem like a big mistake. Before you can even consider building a weapon of mass destruction, you must decide on the number of opponents, size of the galaxy, style of empire, level of play, and even an advisory council to help make those oh-so-tough rulings. Once into the meat and potatoes of the game, the rather trivial issue of your home planet's atmosphere comes into consideration. Depending on what species you are, some of the air on certain planets will be unacceptable, making your colonies' existence there difficult if not prohibitively costly. This program is the War and Peace of computer games, forcing

VAPORWARE

Vaporware. The name brings to mind images of rosy-cheeked cherubs floating down from Elysium with golden floppy disks clutched in their chubby little hands.

Of course, vaporware is anything but heavenly. This rather derogatory term is applied to products that, although they are announced with great fanfare, either experience months and years of delays before they are released or never make it to market at all.

Vaporware exists for a number of reasons. For the big boys in the computer biz, vaporware is sometimes used as a technique to launch a preemptive strike on a competitor's product. For example, if MacroHard, Inc. has a wonderful new operating system in development and a smaller competitor has just released its operating system, it's to MacroHard's advantage to shout robustly to anyone who is forced to listen, "Hold on! Doorways 96 is just around the corner! Accept no substitutes!" If the plan works, users will wait and wait and wait for Doorways 96 while the smaller competitor slouches slowly toward Chapter 11.

RANT

In the Macintosh gaming business, this technique is rarely called for—after all, who's going to hold off from buying a perfectly reasonable arcade game just because a better cootie killer is in the wind? Vaporware games usually are the result of over-anxious marketing departments that want to sell, sell, sell, in order to generate cash, cash, cash, winning out over programmers who want their creations to work, work, work, on ever-changing platforms. But playing the vaporware game is dangerous business. Yes, it's a good idea to generate enthusiasm for a product in the marketplace, but if the delays are too extensive, the company's reputation can suffer irreparable damage—particularly if the game doesn't live up to expectations.

Our current award winner for vaporware of the decade goes to Pax Imperia 2.0. Now we're not only bringing this up because the folks at Changeling Software swore up and down that version 2.0 would be out in plenty of time for the release of the Fifth Edition of *The Macintosh Bible* and Chris, fool that he was, took their word for it and described Pax's wonderfully nonexistent networking features. No, we're singling out this program because not only has version 2.0 been delayed for years, but this is a repeat performance of Changeling's release of version 1.0. At that time, users were also up in arms about the constant delays.

Gee, people, haven't you learned anything in all these years? Please, you have a reasonable game, spend the money to hire an extra couple of programmers to complete the networking functions.

LOUSY FEATURE

anyone who wants to play it seriously to delve into the manual, which is appropriately titled Rules of Protocol. Pac's interface is Maclike, but it can be a tad quirky when it comes to moving ships and selecting planets or moons. The planets are so tiny on the screen that when they're densely packed, selecting a specific body can be an exercise in frustration.

The Solar System From Hell

DANGER

Pax does not disappoint in its promise to be incredibly flexible, interesting, and intricate. One could certainly spend an hour just exploring the solar system you are placed in at the outset of action. For example, each planet in a solar system is depicted as a dot moving in an orbit around a sun, and it can be brought into a closer view with a double-click. That planet, however, can have several moons, each with an atmosphere, minerals to be mined, and colony potential. This makes for a brain-numbing number of possibilities, and that's just for setting up colonies, which is perhaps only 10% of the game. Fortunately, the game's tempo can be adjusted through five levels of hustle and three levels of difficulty, otherwise you might need a personal companion to check your lucidity every couple of hours.

Deep Thoughts

Pax Imperia is a brave attempt to supply the ultimate space-empire conquering game. It's incredible depth will exclude those who want an easy experience with bells and whistles but will enthrall those left wanting more after defeating everyone at Spaceward Ho! Absolute control over everything from cultural events to mining to raids on enemy installations means this game is probably more like running a real empire than any of its contemporaries. Indeed, Pax Imperia provides insight into some of the complexities history's conquerors must have endured when toppling civilizations.

Pros: Absolute control over all aspects of the game. Good manual. Good support from Changeling.

DANGER

Cons: Sluggish on slower Macs. Might be too complex for some players. Screen can become too cluttered when looking at numerous planets.

System Requirements: 68020 or better, 2MB RAM for System 6, 4MB for System 7, 715K hard disk space, System 6.07 or higher.

PAX IMPERIA	
Fun factor:	3.0
Look and feel:	3.0
Value:	3.5
Replayability:	4.0
Overall:	3.0

Spaceward Ho!
Delta Tao

CD

Metal and money. This is what the world, or in this case galaxy, has come to. To survive out there you're gonna have to stockpile a mess of both while making sure that your space ship's technology is capable of stifling any nerdy opponent's attempt to wipe half a million people off the face of your planet. There's nothing worse then dragging oneself out of bed in the morning only to find that the planet you reside on has been completely destroyed by the amazing Timmer and that the fleet of Shadow destructor ships that were in orbit are now kitty kibble. Spaceward Ho! remains the leader in the space conquest category for reasons of simplicity, fun, and replayability. Version 4.0 is the latest incarnation of this now classic title, and incorporates just the right amount of new toys and inspiration to keep the concept fresh and fabulous.

If You Have What It Takes

The goal of Spaceward Ho! is to build an economic base sufficient to finance mining and weapons development so that you can expand and overtake as many planets as possible and ultimately get the galaxy under your thumb. Sounds complicated? Well, it could be, but it isn't. This game combines ease of use with enough complexity to ensure infinite replayability. At the outset, you decide how many opponents (computer or human) you'll face and the number of planets you'll attempt to pillage. Actually, you can shape the galaxy as if it were putty in your hands.

The first challenge for your noggin involves balancing the books to divide cash flow between various technical, mining, and terraforming activities. Just as in real life, there is never enough to go around, so it is crucial to allocate carefully, making sure to supply enough money for technical research. This area is of critical importance because the more technologically advanced a ship's weapons and shields are, the better they can crush your enemies. Your income must also support colonies on newly explored planets until they have the economic wherewithal to be self-sufficient. Mining planets' metal resources is crucial because not obtaining it means getting pelted by debris after a rather messy battle. Metal represents everything that is nonrenewable; if you use 500 units of metal to build a ship and it's subsequently destroyed, you have kissed 500 units of metal good-bye. In fact, if you run out of metal to produce space ships, you can kiss victory good-bye and watch the equivalent of Slim Pickins riding a doomsday bomb destroy your home planet.

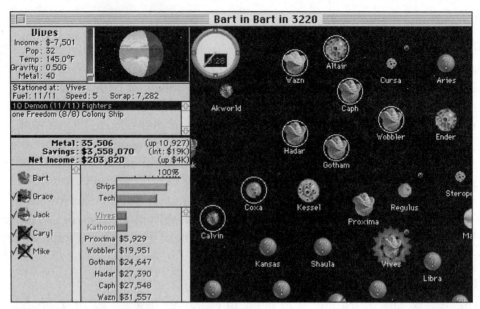

Spaceward Ho! has the distinction of having the most intuitive interface of the space conquest games. The planets are represented by friendly cartoonish graphics.

By the end of the game, metal is usually harder to find than a winning football team in Tampa Bay, and the combatants will resort to just about anything to hold on to a metal-rich planet. Spending money on terraforming worlds to make them hospitable to colonists (and ultimately more profitable) comes at the expense of mining operations or technical developments.

Yeeeeehaaa!

**GREAT
FEATURE**

The interface in the Ho! is truly a pleasure and was obviously designed for the Mac from day one. The allocation of monies is set with a convenient bar graph, and all functions in the game are attainable through pull-down menus or keyboard equivalents as well as by the old point-and-click method. The 256-color scheme is rich, and the graphics are pleasing to the eye as well as the funny bone. Digitized sound provides auditory confirmation when a ship is sent to a planet by furnishing a "Yee-Ha!" or a "Shucks" when you've had your butt kicked. Spaceward Ho! is networkable, and it can be played with virtually any combination of humans or computer opponents at a reasonable pace because the turns occur synchronously and the time limit for turn lengths is adjustable. Although this is a game made famous for its network play in offices and on such networks as Outland, it's still great to lay waste to some diabolical computer foes.

4.0 Glows—Spaceward Ho!

Version 4.0 incorporates just the right amount of new features to make the game fresh yet again. Now available in your arsenal are Dreadnought ships that can single-handedly wipe out established colonies in one fell swoop. Delta Tao has spruced up the alliance feature with the inclusion of a second level of alliance that allows a pact for acquaintances and an affiliation with your best buddies. There are also tankers, biological weapons (which are cheap to make but which use your populations for fuel), floating messages, and interface enhancements that will help keep Spaceward Ho! at the top of its form. One of the most player-requested features was a turn clock, so the folks at Delta Tao included it in 4.0.

**GREAT
FEATURE**

Ho! Ho! Ho!

Spaceward Ho! is chock-full of fun, strategy, and great graphics and sound that will continue to pull many into the darkness of gaming oblivion as they spend hour after hour chasing victory. And that victory is indeed sweet, because if you manage to defeat all your adversaries, you can give a permanent planet whatever name you choose. Version 4.0 of Ho! helps expand the already growing network and online gaming revolution.

SPACEWARD HO!	
Fun factor:	4.0
Look and feel:	4.5
Value:	4.5
Replayability:	4.5
Overall:	4.5

Pros: Charming manual. Great interface. Fun to play. Easy to learn. Network play; can be played on the Outland network through the Internet.

Cons: No modem play. Did I mention no modem play?

System Requirements: Mac Classic II or higher, 2.5MB RAM, 715K hard disk space, System 6.05 or higher.

TIP

Try logging into the game with the creators' names or playing the game on special days like Christmas.

Master of Orion

MicroProse/Take 2 Interactive Software

The newcomer on the space conquest scene is Master of Orion from Micro-Prose and Take 2 Interactive. Although this is really an older DOS game that won many an accolade as a top strategy game, it deserves to enter the Mac gaming scene as a freshman. Here is a game that's sold over a hundred thousand copies to the other guys, so it's gotta be good right? Unfortunately, we all know that success on one platform doesn't always translate to universal acceptance and success. However, with only a few reservations Master of Orion has been able to make the jump to the Mac while remaining a captivating and entertaining game.

The High Council Awaits

Master of Orion differs very little from the underlying premise of the other space conquest games we've looked at. You know the drill; conquer planets, mine resources, build ships, and generally blast the enemy into oblivion. Master of Orion places greater emphasis on alliances than its contemporaries however, and indeed victory comes only with election as the big cheese of the High Council. To attain the title of Master of the High Council a two-thirds vote majority is necessary, and this can be achieved either by owning two-thirds of the galaxy or through diplomatic savvy by convincing other races to follow your lead.

To get the ball rolling you must make decisions on the size of the galaxy (24–108 stars) as well as difficulty level and the number of opponents you will face. You can choose to have up to five enemies lurking in the stars, but unfortunately, modem and/or network play has not been incorporated into Master of Orion. Once the initial parameters have been established the business of building a strong empire begins in earnest. The same principles that govern Spaceward Ho! or Pax Imperia also apply to Master of Orion when it comes to over-expansion. Stretching the empire too thinly results in weak defenses and inadequate funding for technological research which is critical for developing strong spacecraft. There is a lot of technology in this game. Fifty levels in each of six categories, so get those university grants ready to go if you're going to keep up with the Joneses (or Alkari, as the case may be). Once your technology has begun to improve you can take advantage of the highly detailed space ship designer which is perhaps the best we've seen. With this attention to detail this is no doubt where budding engineers will spend many an hour.

**GREAT
FEATURE**

Manageable complexity

Master of Orion has a great variety in all areas of game play, but unlike Pax Imperia the vast amounts of information can be managed surprisingly well in the MoO universe. Although MoO was clearly not designed with the Mac in mind, and the graphics use one-quarter the number of pixels most Mac games use, the overall effect becomes acceptable quickly as you get sucked into the action. The biggest drawback of game play lies in the resolution of battles. Each battle must be fought to the bitter end every time, and although you can speed the action up, it would be nice to be able to just cut to the chase. This becomes especially important when fighting battles involving hundreds of ships.

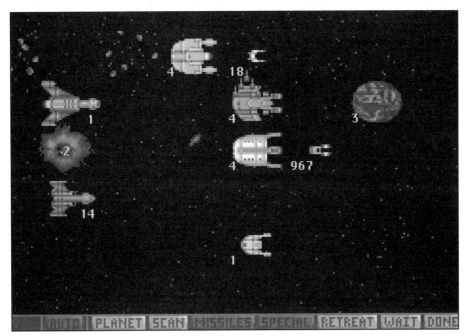

Despite the choppy DOS graphics, Master of Orion has an endearing quality that places it firmly in second place in the 'space conquest' wars.

Rule the Galaxy Through Espionage, Bloodshed, and Politics

With the inclusion of ten distinct races (each with its own strengths), multitudes of technological levels, and up to 108 star systems in a game Master of Orion proves to be just the right fit between the somewhat absurd complexity of Pax Imperia and the comical simplicity of Spaceward Ho! If Spaceward Ho! does not supply the necessary cerebral oomph you need in you conquest games then Master of Orion is certainly the place to go looking next. Despite the sub-par DOS graphics, Master of Orion is an excellent game and a welcome addition to the Mac games library.

Pros: Good manual, complex yet manageable game play, great ship design area.

Cons: No network play. Graphics are of DOS variety. Resolving battles can drag out.

System requirements: 68020 or higher, 256 colors, 4MB RAM, System 7.0 or higher, 12MB hard drive space, CD ROM drive.

MASTER OF ORION	
Fun factor:	3.5
Look and feel:	3.0
Value:	3.5
Replayability:	4.5
Overall:	3.5

12 | War Games

War and strategy board games have been popular for many years and have covered nearly every historical theater of war while evolving very complex rule sets. In the early '80s, game companies began to realize that many of the people playing these board games were the same folks who owned home computers. These players wanted to be able to sit down and control the outcome of the Battle of the Bulge without having to round up another player or struggle with terrain and movement charts.

It didn't take a great leap of logic to see that the computer environment lent itself beautifully to managing the incredible amount of data that needs to be manipulated in war gaming. Unfortunately, the limitations of early computers made initial attempts to translate war games to the computer screen fall flat. In time, though, these limitations were overcome with faster hardware and increased data storage.

The Mac was a relative latecomer to this genre, with only a handful of war games available in its first few years. The first was Dave and Barry Murry's classic The Ancient Art of War, released in 1985. It dealt specifically with the strategy and tactics of war (in a primitive sort of way) but had limited historical significance or accuracy. Still, it was a stunning example of the power of the Mac to produce complex war games and was such a big seller that it sparked a sequel, The Ancient Art of War at Sea. Game programming master Chris Crawford was responsible for another breakthrough title, Patton vs. Rommel, released in 1986, which dealt with a theoretical showdown between the two famous generals after D-Day. Mr. Crawford's incorporation of pictures, movies (before QuickTime), and animation were very impressive and made P vs. R the prototype of the modern Mac war game.

Ten years later, war gaming on the Mac is just now beginning to reach its potential, and some future releases we see coming down the pike will no doubt push the envelope further thanks to full networking, better graphics and animation, and superior artificial intelligence. There is also a greater number of quality simulator-type action war games that have permeated the Mac market, thus expanding the war gaming realm by creating an interest for those inclined toward a hands-on control theory. As the Battlefront series from SSG gives way to the company's new gaming system, and as Atomic's World at War series continues to be refined and expanded, we see new hope that the war game genre will have a better chance of keeping pace in the hectic realm of computer gaming.

Battlefront Series featuring
Panzer Battles
MacArthur's War
Rommel
Halls of Montezuma
Decisive Battles of the American Civil War, Volume III
Strategic Studies Group (SSG)

A Long Line of Conflict
Strategic Studies Group was one of the early birds in the computer war game derby. In fact, we consider their Battlefront gaming system to be the first bona fide attempt at creating a true war gaming environment on the Mac. Based in Australia, SSG has what few game companies possess: longevity. Although it dabbles in other areas of computer gaming, its forte has always been board-style war games. The heart and soul of this has proven to be the Battlefront series. This collection of hexagon-based board-style war games emphasizes strategy over glitz, with scenarios of the Civil War, WWII, and the Korean war. When it was first released, the Battlefront series was considered revolutionary, largely because of the artificial intelligence that drove the computer-governed opposition. Roger Keating of SSG is the mathematician mastermind behind the system that has provided a long line of games for IBM and Amiga machines as well as for the Mac.

Come One, Come All
SSG has released five board-style war games for the Mac: four Battlefront series games and one version of the similar Decisive Battles system. The latter system was designed for the Decisive Battles of the American Civil War series, of which only volume III made it to the Mac. Since all of these games are almost exactly the same in game play and controls, and share only minor variances in terrain, we will discuss the Battlefront system as a whole and then briefly review the premise of each of the five titles.

Battlefront Way of Life
Designed back in the mid to late eighties, the Battlefront system is the underlying engine that drives everything in the games, from artificial intelligence to the giving and carrying out of orders. It's certainly showing its age, and since SSG announced that MacArthur's War would be the last Battlefront game for the Mac, the company is rumored to be working on a thoroughly modern 32-bit system.

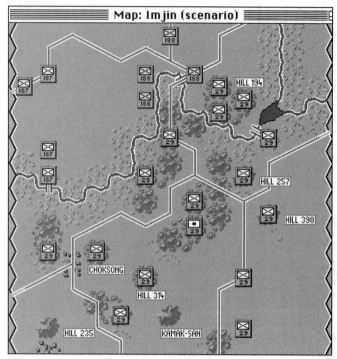

MacArthur's War is the last in SSG's legendary Battlefront series.

SSG will definitely need a new system to compete with the likes of Atomic Games and its increasingly popular V for Victory series. However, the current system is not without merit or its place on the software shelf; it can provide countless hours of excellent strategic gaming.

The Fundamentals

Game play is achieved through a turn system that has four turns for each day: AM, noon, PM, and night. There can be up to 25 days in a scenario and a maximum of 99 turns per game. Instructions are given from the Command Window, which lists information on topics ranging from weather and supply lines to regimental leadership ability. Learning the Battlefront system is certainly not as easy as one would hope, and reading the manual will be mandatory if you've never played the system before. However, the instructions are complete, and you are supplied not only with a generic Battlefront game system booklet but also with a scenario booklet (complete with tutorial) for whichever game you have purchased. They are all very good on historical detail. Several of the games include fantastic full-color maps of their battlegrounds, and these are excellent references to have on your wall. Suffice it to say that once you've spent about an hour reading the instructions and running through the tutorial you will be happily engaged in some serious combat. The biggest boon to a system like this is the obvious crossover between games. Once you've learned the system, you can comfortably play any game in the series without a manual.

The game board can be viewed in a number of modes, each of which provides a different set of information. Scenarios are decided by victory points awarded for holding specific predetermined objectives at various places in the game. The scoring can be viewed from turn to turn to keep you updated on your progress (or lack thereof).

Before starting the battle, you can enter the WarPlan mode and alter any of the game's parameters, from the number of enemy units to the administrative abilities of your generals. You can also alter the actual icons used in the game with WarPaint. WarPlan and WarPaint give you complete flexibility to create custom scenarios or modify existing ones. They allow for infinite replayability.

Commander in Chief?

The forces at your command are divisions, regiments, and battalions. You can have up to three divisions, which can each have four regiments, which in turn can have four battalions. Your line of command tends to be more realistic (and in a way more cumbersome) than in other games of this genre. There is more of a "fog of war" atmosphere because basically you are giving a group of four units a set of general instructions and you just have to hope they handle it well. There are virtually no specific individual unit commands to be had in the Battlefront system, but air support and artillery can be individually allocated. This creates a need for deeper strategic thought and less of the immediate tactical decision making required by games like those in the V for Victory series. This way of war gaming definitely has its appeal; it makes you think like a general would have to, being able to control only a portion of the action as orders are interpreted and acted upon by the individual units. You can find yourself agonizing over a battalion that let itself get cut off from supply lines even though you'd ordered the regiment to fall back.

Panzer Battles

Panzer Battles was the first Battlefront series release on the Mac. It focused on the savage tank fighting on the Russian front during WWII. There are six battles of various sizes: Minsk, Moscow, Kharkov, Prokhorova, Kanex, and Korsum.

MacArthur's War

SSG's MacArthur's War is the most recent labor in the Battlefront series. It deals with the Korean conflict from June, 1950, to April, 1951. There are eight different scenarios, starting with Across the 38th and ending with Imjin. This is said to be the last incarnation of this system for the Mac, and for some strange reason, the color version can be played only in 16 colors.

Rommel

Rommel revolves around the North African campaign of 1940–1943 made famous by Erwin Rommel, the Desert Fox. Scenarios consist of Syria, Sidi Rezegh, Malta, Cauldron, Alem El Halfa, Kasserine, Maknassy, and Tebourga Gap.

Halls of Montezuma

The Halls of Montezuma has perhaps the greatest variation in the Battlefront series. It focuses on U.S. Marine Corps battles that took place between 1847 in Mexico and 1968 in Vietnam. It's one of the few war games to have anything to do with the Vietnam war, which is usually avoided like the plague in this category. Scenarios include Mexico City, Belleau Wood, Iwo Jima, Okinawa, Pusan, Inchon, and Hue.

Decisive Battles of the American Civil War, Volume III

Although the Decisive Battles System is not exactly a clone of the Battlefront system, it is sufficiently similar that it can be grouped with SSG's other titles. Decisive Battles focuses on Civil War battles fought between May 5, 1864, and December 15, 1864. Scenarios include Wilderness, Spotsylvania, Cold Harbor, Atlanta, Franklin, and Nashville.

The Final Analysis

Over the years, SSG has shown extraordinary commitment to compatibility across the entire Mac line of computers. In fact, all these games include a folder of all the scenarios specifically for black-and-white machines. The Battlefront system has its pros and cons. The up side is that all the games absolutely cook on contemporary Macs; there's no waiting for a turn to finish with these babies. The down side of the compatibility issue is the lack of full-color support for the newer Macs. Granted that spectacular graphics and color have never been a hallmark of war/strategy games, but much more could be done to improve the graphics in this series. That aside, the graphics are surprisingly good (for 16 color), and the animation is smooth, although somewhat limited. A purist would say that's the way it should be. Your average gamer might be inclined to yawn. All in all, the Battlefront system is a decent experience in strategy gaming, and although there is little variation in form between games, each has its own terrain and units to make it unique.

Pros: Proven gaming system. Fast game play. Very compatible across Mac platform (black-and-white Macs supported). War-Plan and WarPaint editors make game infinitely playable. Good documentation (great color maps).

Cons: Graphics smooth but dated. Limited color support for some games. Steep initial learning curve.

System Requirements: Mac Plus or better, 1MB RAM for black and white, 2MB RAM for color, but for System 7: 2MB RAM for black and white, 4MB RAM for color, 1.5MB hard disk space, System 6.02 or higher.

BATTLEFRONT SERIES

Fun factor	3.0
Look and feel	3.0
Value	3.5
Replayability	3.5

PANZER BATTLES
Overall	3.5

MACARTHUR'S WAR
Overall	3.0

ROMMEL
Overall	3.5

HALLS OF MONTEZUMA
Overall	3.0

CIVIL WAR, VOLUME III
Overall	3.5

U-BOAT
Deadly Games

As your brow presses against the periscope, the tension on the bridge becomes palpable. Slowly you turn the scope, hoping to see the quarry you have stalked for 32 hours. The ship's batteries are nearly dead, and surfacing to recharge them would be suicide. Your only hope is to creep up on the destroyer with the remaining juice and hope you can calculate the torpedo's path accurately. Then you spot her. She's only 1,700 meters away, sitting ready for your torpedoes. You're about to give the order to fire when a shock rocks your ship. "They're shelling us, we're too close!" is heard in the confusion. The intercom crackles to life as your engineer reports that the torpedo tubes have been damaged and the bow is flooding. The first officer reports that the engines are out and the batteries are damaged beyond repair. You fill your lungs with the stale dank air of the U-BOAT as if you were taking your last breath.

The Daily Round

The object of U-BOAT is to command your sub on a series of patrols from the Baltic Sea to the eastern Mediterranean early in WWII. Each patrol is limited only by your fuel and armaments. The patrol ends whenever you return to base, so if you get into trouble and need to return to base during a patrol, when you reach the base the patrol is over. The next time you set sail it will be on a different patrol. Basically you are trying to accomplish what the real German U-Boat commanders were, to sink as many Allied ships as possible (this is measured in tonnage of sunken vessels) without getting yourself blown out of the water. Keeping in touch with your base (by radioing in your position) will inform you of Allied naval activity in your area.

Fortunately, U-BOAT doesn't require you to spend hours searching for vessels. Now it may not be overly realistic to come into contact with an Allied ship every day at sea, but it makes for a better, more playable game. You are supplied with a complete reference booklet that has pictures of the major ships to identify what you're up against when peering through the periscope. Patrol areas are marked out on a grid/sector system, and it is impossible to navigate without the manual. This allows for a measure of copy protection without its becoming overly obnoxious. However, PowerBook users won't appreciate having to carry around the manual, even if it is pamphlet-size. Quitting the game produces an automatic save so that you can pick up right where you left off. (And yes, this means you can't save games to keep yourself from getting into a tight spot, such as between two destroyers).

Easy Access

Your tour of duty as commander of the U-BOAT is served in five different areas aboard the ship. The bridge becomes like a second home, where only the conning tower and periscope views interrupt your view of the instruments. The bridge contains all the major controls to operate the sub—everything from fuel and battery gauges to charts, depth meters, and a compass. The remaining controls are in a movable window that allows easy access to them at all times. The rudder, radio, speed, firing, and depth controls reside in this window, as do the Attack Tabulator and the Report button. When the Report button is pressed, you get a verbal report from the chiefs of the different areas of the ship. When an area has been damaged, it's kinda cool to get immediate verbal confirmation that one of your engines has just failed.

GREAT FEATURE

Battle Sounds

The controls themselves are easy to use and generally respond quickly to your every whim. But when you get into a hairy situation in which there's plenty of

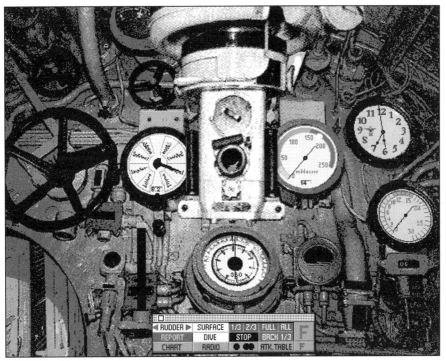

The main control screen of U-BOAT is constructed from actual digitized pictures of a U-BOAT.

sonar sound and reports being shouted, the command buttons tend to freeze up until all the noise has finished playing. This can be extremely frustrating when you want to fire your torpedoes and pull your periscope down all in one fell swoop rather than sit there taking a beating from a cruiser. It becomes a plus/minus situation because the sound slows down the action, but it is an integral part of the game. Every time you issue a command, you get verbal confirmation with digitized voices.

LOUSY FEATURE

U-BOAT is graphically similar to Bomber and M4 but is much cleaner and makes better use of color and detail. For example, it is easy to identify a ship on the horizon, and you will not have to spend hours searching for obscure little blips on the screen.

Cat and Mouse

For the Mac, U-BOAT is just what the doctor ordered. It provides very compelling game play, good graphics, and excellent sound to make a truly exciting campaign-style gaming experience. The makers of U-BOAT recommend that the base machine for this game be an LC III. But for quick responses in battle situations, we would recommend a 040 Mac. Where U-BOAT really shines, and the

THE APPEAL OF WAR GAMES

Chris: I guess I should admit right up front that I've never been big on war games. What's the attraction?

Bart: I wonder if a lot of people feel that way. After all, war games have been around since the dawn of home computers. The appeal of war games is probably due to several things. First, many people like to re-create famous battles and see what the outcome would be if they were in charge. Second, I suspect people want to relive the victories our culture has offered up in the past. Third, the computer is perfectly suited to handling the complicated calculations, die rolling, odds making, and rule sets that these games traditionally require.

Chris: Do tell.

Bart: The most popular war games are often those that deal with famous battles in which the Allies were victorious.

Chris: So you think people like to fight either romantic wars or those that the good guys (from our Northern American viewpoint) win.

Bart: Sure, notice the great preponderance of WWII games and scenarios available. Look at how there are comparatively *very* few that deal with Vietnam, a relative bad spot in American history. And conflicts in which we are generally uninterested parties, such as the Arab-Israeli wars, are rarely used. It's safe to say that people only want to be involved in victory situations that hit home.

only area where it wins out over WolfPack, is in atmosphere. This aspect of the game is excellent, and you'll really find yourself sweating it out while playing cat and mouse with the Allied ships. The day/night realism and constant background sound add greatly to the experience and pull you right into the game. Finally, hunting down and sinking a ship without getting pounded into the sea bottom with depth charges is a very satisfying feeling.

Pros: Plenty of action. Outstanding ambiance and atmosphere; great sound. Flexible patrol times are realistic. Compelling game play.

Cons: Needs a fast machine. Controls can temporarily freeze when multiple sounds play. Unplayable without map manual.

System Requirements: 13-inch monitor, 4MB RAM, 2.6MB hard disk space, System 6.07 or higher.

U-BOAT	
Fun factor	3.0
Look and feel	4.0
Value	3.0
Replayability	3.5
Overall	3.5

Chris: I think people can still relate to WWII. It had innocence and romance. WWI was just ugly and stupid. The Discovery Channel has made a living off WWII.

Bart: I hear you. The technology involved in WWII was much simpler than anything since. It was a simpler time, a prenuke time, when men were men and Ruskies were allies. I would expect that we will continue to see countless WWII war games.

Chris: How good is the AI on these things? Is it as good as playing a human?

Bart: The AI in some of the games is astounding. But accomplished war gamers still claim that they can always beat the computer, even when at a disadvantage. However, most armchair war gamers should be substantially challenged by today's war games.

Chris: So would you say that a major attraction to these games is the ability for someone to play without having to find another player?

Bart: Yep. The computer allows you to enjoy a game that would otherwise take tens of hours to set up and play. You can play at your leisure and without having to learn incredibly complex rule sets. And I mean incredibly complex. Squad Leader is legendary for complexity. There are rumors that several people have grown old and died trying to learn the movement modifiers for Squad Leader.

Chris: I guess I can see why some folk like these games, after all.

Bart: Someday the right game will come along and you'll be sweating it out in Normandy, just wait and see.

WolfPack
NovaLogic

Back in 1985, when some Mac gamers were wondering why they hadn't bought Amigas, a Mac version of the PC game GATO came along and everything suddenly seemed better. GATO was one of the first great games for the Mac that succeeded in doing a decent job of simulating the activities of GATO-class subs in the Pacific theater of operations. Just to give you an idea of how long ago this was, the system requirements on the side of the GATO box read, "Apple Macintosh 128K." Ultimately, GATO set the standard for submarine games on the Mac, and although there has subsequently been a continual (albeit slow) improvement in sub games for "the rest of us," they have been largely ignored. Enter WolfPack from NovaLogic, a fast-paced, graphically superior submarine simulator.

Different Port of Call

Nova Logic is primarily a DOS game company. We know from past experience that PC games appearing on the Mac are more often than not very average ports from the DOS versions. Clearly, however, Nova Logic learned from its predecessors' mistakes and realized that venturing into the Mac gaming arena while hoping VGA graphics would woo Mac users was not a clever idea. WolfPack is truly a Mac version of a PC game and not a cheesy imitation of one. For example, when booting WolfPack from the CD-ROM, you are treated to a spectacular five-minute movie of a submarine cruising a few feet under the surface of the ocean with destroyers in pursuit.

Operation Petticoat This Isn't

**GREAT
FEATURE**

WolfPack begins by giving you the option to watch a demo, construct your own mission, or play one of the 70 preset missions at your disposal. These missions are grouped into three sets of Easy, Medium, and Hard and range from submarine command to destroyer and freighter management. The inclusion of destroyer and freighter control makes this the first submarine game that deals with aspects of naval command as they pertain to the wolf pack. After choosing a scenario, you are transported to the bridge of your command vessel and are given a radio message explaining your mission's goals. Once you are familiar with your mission you can choose to either sit back and watch the action unfold or take control of the proceedings. This is achieved through the use of the Auto command button located on every ship's bridge. Use of this button lets you control as many or as few of the ships in your fleet as you wish. This makes it possible to jump in and supersede any captain's orders when you see fit. All ships are controlled by a computer captain who is described as either Relentless, Resourceful, Cautious, or By the Book. Each is thoroughly described in the manual so that attack strategies based on their individual personalities can be designed.

Score Card

The scoring system is based on a zero-sum approach, which means that no matter how many ships are on the surface, they add up to 50% of the ship points. Likewise, all the submarines also equal 50% of the total ship points. Confusing? Well, suffice it to say that if there are ten ships on the surface and five submarines, each submarine sunk will be worth twice what a surface ship is. That system accounts for 90% of the scoring, with total fleet damage accounting for the remaining 10%. In the event of a tie, the submarines always lose. The length of a game is determined by a time limit, although completion of mission goals and annihilation of the opponent will also end the scenario.

The Mouse That Roared

WolfPack's command interface can be accessed either by clicking appropriate areas on the screen or entering keyboard equivalents. Many of the keyboard

WolfPack has the best graphics of any submarine game yet released for the Mac.

commands require the simultaneous pressing of two keys, and we found that pointing and clicking was generally more efficient. All of the expected gauges are on the screen, including depth, speed, battery charge, fuel, and heading, as is access to torpedoes, depth charges, and deck guns. In fact, *all* the commands, as well as the maps and status reports are available from the main bridge screen, thus eliminating time-consuming switches between screens. And the controls are quick and responsive. Nova Logic should be commended for making every tidbit of necessary information so accessible.

GREAT FEATURE

Change of Attitude

WolfPack surpasses every previous Mac submarine game in graphic quality and color. Plumes of water tower in front of your periscope during enemy shelling and white-hot fire showers from torpedo-stricken freighters. But by far the coolest thing about the game play in WolfPack is the ability to really control a pack of subs, flipping from sub to sub, blasting away at convoys, and chalking up the tonnage. And hey, if you make a bad move and get scrunched by a depth charge, you can just switch to another ship. You actually have to think in terms of the well-being of the entire pack of subs, or convoy, to win the game. The ability to control various types of ships is certainly refreshing. Believe us, there's an interesting change of attitude when you're sitting on the bridge of a vulnerable freighter wondering if a submarine lies below rather than lining up a ship on the periscope.

The Inevitable Comparison

Although Sub Battle Simulator has recently been rereleased, it's really not in the same league as WolfPack, so for these reasons we will not include it in a comparison. This leaves only U-BOAT from Deadly Games to compete in this niche. When looking at speed, presentation, playability, graphics, and replayability, WolfPack is the hands-down winner. Inclusion of a scenario editor ensures infinite possibilities, and the two-player option will keep games fresh. Where WolfPack falls short of U-BOAT is in overall ambiance and realism. U-BOAT has that certain dramatic tension that makes you really feel like you're all alone when stalking a convoy and one mistake will snuff out your life. It will be difficult, however, for U-BOAT to compete against what is clearly a superior product that utilizes newer gaming technology. If you like this kind of game, you should have both. If you like lots of action, great graphics, and fast game play, WolfPack is your choice.

Pros: Great graphics. Scenario construction set keeps play fresh. All controls accessible through main screen. Great interface.

Cons: Manual could have included tutorial. CD-ROM should include digitized speech. No modem support.

System Requirements: 68020 and Color QuickDraw or better, 4MB RAM, 9.5MB hard disk space, System 6.07 or higher.

WOLFPACK	
Fun factor	4.0
Look and feel	4.5
Value	3.5
Replayability	3.5
Overall	4.0

Carriers at War I & II
Strategic Studies Group (SSG)

The battle for air supremacy in the Pacific theater is an aspect of WWII that has been left largely untapped by Mac war games. This seems odd when one considers that many of these pivotal Pacific naval and air battles were among the most intriguing and influential of the war. Fortunately, Carriers at War and its younger sibling CAW II, which have long been popular titles on DOS and Amiga machines, have been released for the Mac and have filled the void triumphantly.

The graphics in the Carriers at War series are pleasing, but you'll soon pass them over to get on with the battle.

Stop the Clock

CAW is a combined strategy and tactical war game that allows users as little or as much task force management as they choose. It covers nine WWII Pacific engagements ranging from Pearl Harbor to Santa Cruz. In each scenario, the user is given the choice of controlling either the Japanese or American forces, with the opposing side managed by the computer or another person (on the same machine). After selecting which side to control, you can allocate computer control over some or all of the task forces available to you. This enables you to work your way into the game slowly by taking responsibility for only a portion of total operations. The three basic parts of task force control are surface combat, navigation, and air power management. The last carries the greatest responsibility. It involves supervising the deployment of scout planes, combat air patrol (CAP) management, and air strike organization. CAW runs in five-minute increments. The game clock can be set to stop running for various reasons, including air strikes, ship spottings, and surface combat.

Battle Scenes

General task force navigation and attack strike orders are given on an immovable overview map that displays the entire area where the scenario takes place. The air-to-sea battle action can be displayed graphically if you wish. This is essentially a picture of a ship whose decks explode and smoke when hit. Attacking planes are depicted as postage stamp-size icons. A three-notch damage counter shows what condition the planes are in. An occasional smoking fighter

INTERVIEW: KEITH ZABALAOUI

Keith Zabalaoui is one of the three original designers of the V for Victory series, responsible for all non-AI programming, Macintosh implementation, and interface design. He is also the president of Atomic Games, a pioneer game company that has several exciting titles on the horizon.

Would you say that the war gaming genre has progressed at the same level as other types of computer games?

No. War gaming has definitely been left behind. I honestly think computer war games are harder to produce than most other games. Not because of the need for cutting edge technology but because there is so much information that needs to be manipulated and displayed to the user. An added drawback is that most war games are historical, so the designers and pro-

grammers are really working from a script, and woe be unto them if they change that script. There is a tremendous amount of design and research overhead that just isn't necessary with other types of games.

What kind of person plays war games. What's the appeal? It seems that war games that are successful tend to dwell on the romanticized wars, such as WWII and the Civil War. Do you think this is a factor in war game development?

For our games, so far, the demographics have been largely males over 30. These are usually people who grew up playing Avalon Hill and SPI games. In theory, I'd agree that the romantic wars are better subjects for war games, but Atomic has only done WWII, so I don't have numbers to back that up.

drifts across the sky above the featured ship. Although these screens accurately depict damage, the graphics themselves have no bearing on the outcome of the game, and we suspect that most players will opt for the quicker method of resolving battles once they've had their fill of graphical carnage.

LOUSY FEATURE

The other method of battle involves surface combat. If two convoys get close enough together, surface combat ensues. It is depicted with an overhead view of all the ships arranged into lanes. Each ship can be given one of two orders: to fire upon groups of enemy vessels, or to make a run for it and try to avoid the enemy's big guns. Surface combat is perhaps the weakest link of CAW and is also one of the more frustrating aspects of the game. This is due to the lack of simultaneous firing from both sides. It allows the side with the first salvo to pummel the opposition into the sea before it can get even a single shot away. It doesn't take a brain surgeon to realize that if two convoys meet, they will fire at each other simultaneously. CAW II did not fix this problem (why, we don't know), but

Where do you see war gaming going in the next five years?

I think the trend is toward "lite" war games that people can play in one sitting. I think we'll see historical accuracy and complexity being replaced by more animation and sound effects. To put it in a Hollywood reference frame, as seems popular today, I predict we're going to see more action/adventure and less documentary.

What's in the cards for Atomic? What will we see next?

At this very moment, Atomic is working on two projects: World at War: America Invades, and Beyond Squad Leader. We are also negotiating with several publishers for a couple of nonhistorical games.

What is the next major breakthrough we will see in war game technology?

I'm hoping you'll see it in Beyond Squad Leader. Without giving you a product description, our goal with BSL is to give you an electronic sandbox, if you will, so you can play Army Men. You'll actually be able to see the soldiers running on the field, the tanks firing, and the grenades exploding. This is much better than seeing little "cardboard" counters moving around.

Does the Mac have an edge in war gaming?

Everyone knows that the Macintosh is superior in most ways to the PC. This includes the development environments. That is why Atomic develops all of its games on the Mac and ports them to the PC. For the World at War series, we were usually able to test and release the games simultaneously on both platforms. The biggest problem we have is getting the DOS platform games to have the same features as the Mac platform games.

for the most part surface combat is an unlikely proposition that occurs very infrequently, making it more of a minor inconvenience then a major problem.

Quality
SSG made sure that the Mac version of CAW was redone from the ground up—not merely to avoid the look and feel of a port but also to ensure the quality Mac users expect. Their efforts were not in vain, because the interface is truly Mac-like and includes the expected complement of keyboard equivalents and pull-down menus consistent with an intuitive interface. The graphics and color are crisp and clean, and although they cannot be described as ground-breaking, they are superior to their DOS/Windows counterparts.

What Can CAW II Do for You?
On the surface, CAW II looks like a carbon copy of its older brother, but it contains eight new scenarios, including a 1939 prelude to war and a hypothetical

Japanese invasion as well as some minor changes to game play. The most notable of these changes is the inclusion of kamikaze planes in some of the later scenarios. SSG did not supply Mac users with a scenario editor, but CAW II allows users to import any scenario created on a DOS box, thus giving users a vast pre-existing supply of new challenges when the first eight are exhausted. Any Mac with System 7.5 will be able to read a DOS disk containing CAW scenarios.

1 + 1 = 1

Although CAW I & II are marketed as separate games, they are virtually the same game with different game sets. They are, however, excellent games, and if we were to purchase only one of them, CAW II would be our choice because of its ability to import DOS scenario creations.

Pros: Provides many variations in scenarios. Can play either side. Detailed.

Cons: Manual is for DOS computers. No scenario editor. Surface combat is not realistic.

System Requirements: Color Mac with 32-bit QuickDraw, 2MB RAM for System 6, 4MB RAM for System 7, 4.9MB hard disk space, System 6.07 or higher.

CARRIERS AT WAR I	
Fun factor	3.5
Look and feel	3.5
Value	3.0
Replayability	3.0
Overall	3.5

CARRIERS AT WAR II	
Fun factor	3.5
Look and feel	3.5
Value	4.0
Replayability	4.0
Overall	4.0

CD

Flight Commander II
Avalon Hill/Big Time Software

Big Time Software and Avalon Hill have provided us with one of the most unique and innovative war game titles to hit the market in recent years. Flight Commander II is neither a flight simulator nor a board-game-style variation on air warfare. Instead it's an interesting melding of styles into a tactical adventure of modern air warfare broken down into several large battles. Players without finely tuned reflexes will be glad to know that Flight Commander II does not need a ThrustMaster, or any joystick for that matter, to be played.

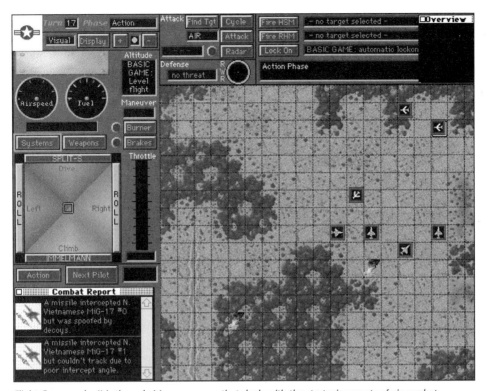

Flight Commander II is the only Mac war game that deals with the strategic aspects of air combat.

Fly the Not-So-Friendly Skies

You are initially given the choice of engaging in one of five campaigns, eleven scenarios, or two tutorials which together include the basics for air-to-air and air-to-ground combat. You then move to a briefing screen describing the overall situation, objectives, and available intelligence information. Following this, you must select the crew that will accompany you on your mission. The pilots on this roster are rated in several categories, including air-to-air and air-to-ground efficiency. The next stop is the armaments screen, where you can decide which weapons and accessories, such as targeting pods and missile jamming equipment, you will carry.

Once fully briefed and armed to the hilt, you are catapulted directly to flight. All the landing and takeoffs are computer controlled. We told you you didn't need reflexes, didn't we? The aircraft are presented in a zoomable overhead view, with the flight navigation and weapons controls surrounding this screen. The game is carried out on a turn-by-turn basis, and the aircraft can be controlled with the use of the flight stick on the screen. This is nothing like a flight sim and serves merely to set a course for the planes. However, there are also options to put your planes into advanced maneuvers such as high gravity turns and Immelmanns.

Splash One Bandit!

Flight Commander II is ultimately a very compelling strategic and tactical air conflict simulator, and the inclusion of great graphics and digitized sounds—such as the occasional radio chatter that crops up every once in a while—make it even more impressive. There is certainly nothing else like it on the market. Those who like to study classic air warfare will enjoy the complexity and tension a Flight Commander II game can generate. The addition of PBEM (play by e-mail) and a scenario editor make this game very replayable. However, the inclusion of manual-based copy protection is very annoying. It can become an excruciating hindrance to your game to be asked to identify a fighter aircraft nationality symbol found somewhere in the manual; an honest error in entering the proper information can result in your losing hours of game play. Persecuting the paying customer (however unintentionally) is no way to copy protect software. Still, we liked Flight Commander II and found that it earns its spot in the current crop of Mac war games.

RANT

Pros: Great graphics, sound, and animation. Fun head-to-head play. Intriguing marriage of conquest-style games with traditional hex-based war games.

Cons: No modem play. Limited use of naval operations.

System Requirements: 4MB RAM, 10MB hard disk space, System 7 or later.

FLIGHT COMMANDER II	
Fun factor	3.0
Look and feel	3.5
Value	3.0
Replayability	3.5
Overall	3.0

V for Victory Series featuring Utah Beach Velikiye Luki Market Garden Gold-Juno-Sword

Three Sixty/Atomic Games

A New Era

When Three Sixty and Atomic Games released the first of the V for Victory games, they ushered in a new era in Mac war gaming, one that was rich in color, depth, detail, and complexity. Atomic Games has now moved on to publishing their World at War series (which bares a striking resemblance to V4V) with Avalon Hill, and the V for Victory series has reached its end. Atomic did manage to release four segments in the V for Victory series: Utah Beach, Velikiye Luki, Market Garden, and Gold-Juno-Sword. Each of these dealt with several battles in a specific area of the European theater of operations during WWII. The engines that drive each of these games are very similar, and in fact all of the segments can be run from one game engine. It should be noted, however, that each of the V4V games is a stand-alone product; using it requires making no other purchases. In this review, we will look at these games by examining the underlying V for Victory engine and the game play it produces. This will be followed by a brief summary of the individual games and of any changes or improvements specific to each.

In the Beginning

The first decision at hand in the setup screen is to choose between Allied or Axis command for yourself and the computer. Heck, you can even set the computer to play both sides, which we wouldn't recommend unless you have a penchant for watching a silicon slug fest. Each of the V4V games has a number of scenarios to choose from, and it is during this selection that the weather conditions, accuracy of intelligence, and level of air support can be adjusted. The more fiddling you do with the options, the more uncertainty is introduced into the scenario, thus creating a greater challenge. There is a tutorial available in all the games, and while we recommend that novices follow it, we also advise that you double the time Atomic suggests it will take. In fact, when dealing with these manuals, double all the time you might think it would take to do something. The manuals in the V4V series are the opposite of those in the SSG Battlefront series. The V4V series has a strong reference manual, but lacks historical detail for the individual scenarios; vice versa for the Battlefront manuals.

The Guts and the Glory

V4V's game engine takes combat ratios, terrain, movement, and morale fully into account and spares the user the drudgery of looking up values in an endless array of charts. The entire series is played in an overhead view of a hexagonal grid, much like most other games in this category. Fortunately for novice gamers, many functions of managing your forces can be handed over to a Staff Assistant. This is basically a computerized helper that can be invoked when brain power is at a premium. Unfortunately, employing the SA is an all-or-nothing proposition; it can't be asked to handle just a few units or one flank, say. This probably won't impress ardent gamers, who will no doubt want complete control over their subordinates, even if they are computer driven. There are no less then 33 different types of units available, ranging from Soviet cavalry to SS police. The sheer variety of units will no doubt impress hardened war gamers, as will the high-quality graphics used to depict each encounter. Eight commands can be given to a unit, including probe, air attack, all-out assault, and entrench. The V4V scenarios allow air strikes and off-shore naval bombardment. Of course, air support is forever at the mercy of the weather, making for some frustrating moments when a fighter strike might come in handy.

Game play is divided up into four-hour turns, which are started at 0800 hours and rotate from there. Each turn is broken up into three phases: Planning, Execution, and After Action. The morning planning phase is distinctive in that it allows for extra administrative functions such as supply allocation and attachment of units to individual headquarters. After you are satisfied with your planning, the Execution phase plays out the turns simultaneously for both sides, taking care of movement and combat resolution. The After Action phase allows you to explore the various results of the fighting. At this time, victory points and scenario objectives can be examined to establish future strategy.

Don't I Know You?

Graphically, the V4V series is a leap ahead of previous offerings, and it looks good on both black-and-white and color machines. Each unit's piece is drawn differently, and in various scenarios the terrain changes accordingly with the weather. There are digitized sounds attached to many of the actions, and the battle sequences in the Action Phase range from diving aircraft to machine gun fire. The interface is very Mac-like, as it should be; all the V4V games were designed first on the Mac and then ported to DOS. Moving around on the screen is achieved with either keyboard or mouse commands, and the entire interface is intuitive enough that a game could be played without reading the 145-page manual. However, we don't recommend such foolish actions unless you're a direct descendent of General Patton.

Utah Beach

Utah Beach was the first in the V4V series. It thrust you into the role of a military strategist during the Normandy invasion of June, 1944. This initial offering was plagued by several nasty bugs. Despite this, it took war gaming on the Mac one level beyond SSG's Battlefront system and was the first to really accurately calculate all the variables and combat ratios needed by the ardent war gamer. Scenarios include Objective Carentan, SS Counterattack, Final Assault, and Race for Carteret.

Velikiye Luki

Velikiye Luki was the second installment in the V4V series. It dealt with the bitter fighting on the Russian Front in WWII. As German commander, you must rescue your encircled forces holding out at the ancient fortress town of Velikiye Luki, while protecting the Vitebsk-Leningrad railroad. This railroad is vital to the supply of Army Group North. As Russian commander, you must take Velikiye Luki and advance to the railroad to cut off and destroy the fascist invaders. By the time this game was released, Atomic had worked out many of the bugs seen in Utah Beach.

Market Garden

This game centered around the operation code-named Market Garden which was also the premise for the book and movie *A Bridge Too Far*. The Allies launched the largest air drop in history in an effort to secure the bridges across key rivers in Holland to help expedite the push to Berlin.

Gold-Juno-Sword

Gold-Juno-Sword examines a much overlooked aspect of D-Day, the Commonwealth invasion on the beaches of Gold, Juno, and Sword. Infantry and armor units of a combined British and Canadian landing force attempt to push southward and capture the city of Caen, the Axis transportation center of Normandy. By this final segment of the V4V series, supply handling, movement, and combat resolution have all been greatly improved. The AI is also greatly improved and is better both offensively and defensively. It will attempt to surround exposed units.

V-Day

All in all, the V for Victory series of games represents a major step forward in the Mac war gaming arena. It should be considered by all who have an interest in WWII games. The ability to gang all scenarios from all games into one folder and use them with the latest version of the game engine is a great feature. For those who are looking for more of the same, Avalon Hill is now publishing Atomic's games, and Operation Crusader and Stalingrad are the successors to the V4V series.

Pros: Nice 256-color graphics. Playable in black and white. Designed on Mac. Good interface. Extensive documentation. Highly sophisticated.

Cons: AI in early game sets average at best. No modem or network play. Early versions buggy.

System Requirements: Mac Plus or better, 2MB RAM for black and white, 3MB RAM for color, 3MB hard disk space, System 6.0.5 or higher.

V FOR VICTORY SERIES	
Fun factor	3.5
Look and feel	4.0
Value	3.0
Replayability	3.0
UTAH BEACH	
Overall	3.0
VELIKIYE LUKI	
Overall	3.5
MARKET GARDEN	
Overall	3.5
GOLD-JUNO-SWORD	
Overall	4.0

World at War Series featuring Operation Crusader Stalingrad
Avalon Hill/Atomic Games

More Fun!

Due to contractual difficulties, Atomic Games recently moved to Avalon Hill to produce a new series of war games under the World at War moniker. At first glance, the first two offerings in this lineup, Operation Crusader and Stalingrad, seem like games in the V4V series. They do represent a progression from that series, but these two offerings have become considerably more refined (especially Stalingrad). Certainly they can claim their own territory as V4V modules cannot run on the new system. Atomic Games has "grown up" and will continue to supply segments of the World at War series as well as produce Beyond Squad Leader, which is to be released in early 1996.

Look Ma, New Features!

The World at War games offer many new features, but the one that slaps you in the face the moment you open a game box is the breathtaking full-color manual. These manuals are by far the best we've seen for content, tutorial quality, and sheer beauty. Avalon Hill and Atomic need to be commended for this breakthrough. The graphics and art in the games has improved dramatically, so much so that the old V4V games seem primitive. The control sets have also been improved with better menus and tool bars, and the new Overview button displays the current scenario's entire playing area on the screen, allowing for a better grasp of the big picture. Some of the other important feature changes for Crusader and Stalingrad are as follows:

GREAT FEATURE

• The games can be played via electronic mail (PBEM), allowing two human opponents to compete on two different machines. PBEM files may be exchanged between opponents on Mac and MS-DOS computers.

• An HQ button displays all headquarters and their supply and organizational information.

• A new Leaders button displays information on German and Soviet leaders. You can assign specific leaders to specific units.

• A Frames button let you view your units in several different ways.

• A new Order of Battle button displays all of your headquarters that are drawing supplies directly from a supply source. Subordinate headquarters and attached units may be viewed by clicking on any displayed headquarters (Stalingrad).

• A more detailed Weather button (Stalingrad). Much more detailed and varied terrain.

• Armor can now transport infantry units.

• New types of artillery attacks: Counter Battery, Shoot 'n' Scoot, On-Call Fire Missions.

• New types of air operations. You can now supply units via air drop or air landing missions. Also, there are now air reconnaissance missions.

• Units now have to worry about the state of their supply lines.

Stalingrad is the most sophisticated and challenging board-style war game for the Mac. Its graphics and sound are light years ahead of early war gaming efforts.

CD

LOUSY FEATURE

Operation Crusader

Operation Crusader allows you to re-create a battle that took place in North Africa in November of 1941. In terms of features, it can be considered the transition game between the old V4V series and Stalingrad. The artificial intelligence is much improved. Operation Crusader's scenarios include Ducé's Finest, Fortress Tobruk, Hell Fire Pass, To the Rescue, Tobruk Relieved, and a campaign game. We should also point out that Operation Crusader has manual-based copy protection.

Stalingrad

Stalingrad covers a dramatic period of the conflict on the eastern front. You can lead the German army in a 1942 attempt to occupy Stalingrad or take command of the Soviet armies that were defending it. Scenarios in Stalingrad include To the Volga, A River Too Far, Mansteins Solution, Rattenkrieg, Winterwitter, Quiet Flows the Don, and Operation Uranus. Although Stalingrad's interface is similar to Operation Crusader's, the scope of battle is considerably larger and will challenge even the most ardent war gamer. Atomic deserves credit for dropping the manual-based copy protection in Stalingrad.

Sophistication

Operation Crusader and Stalingrad have proven to be sophisticated descendants of the V4V series of war games, and they offer up such an extensive array of new features that they have become far removed from Utah Beach, the first V4V game. These two games presently represent the pinnacle of board-style war games and should be on the shelf of any gamer with an interest in WWII and the strategy surrounding it. Crusader and Stalingrad are both highly detailed. If you're interested in reading more about them, look for Karen Kaye's reviews of them in the May, 1994, and April, 1995, issues of *Inside Mac Games* magazine, which are available on the CD-ROM in this book.

Pros: Nice-256 color graphics. Playable in black and white. Designed on Mac. Good interface. Extensive documentation. Highly sophisticated.

Cons: AI in early game sets average at best. No modem or network play. Early versions buggy.

System Requirements (Operation Crusader): Color Mac, 4MB RAM, 3.5MB hard disk space, System 7 or later.

System Requirements (Stalingrad): 68020 Mac or better (68030 recommended), 8MB RAM, 6.7MB hard disk space, System 7 or later.

OPERATION CRUSADER	
Fun factor	4.0
Look and feel	4.5
Value	4.0
Replayability	4.0
Overall	4.0

STALINGRAD	
Fun factor	4.5
Look and feel	5.0
Value	4.0
Replayability	4.0
Overall	4.5

Onslaught
Frontal Assaultware

CD

A couple of years ago, a few disgruntled war gamers decided to put an end to the drought of Mac war games and whip one up themselves. Frontal Assaultware was born, and Onslaught began its journey to store shelves. The folks at FA wanted to create a divisional-command-level game that was easy as well as fun to use for the average bloke. In many respects, they succeeded. Some war game purists might argue that Onslaught is not a true war game, despite its remarkable resemblance to both the V4V series and, to a lesser degree, the Battlefront

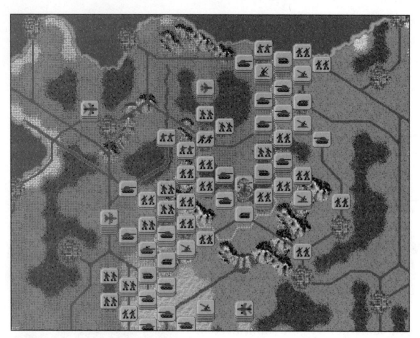

Onslaught is the perfect marriage of traditional hex-based war games and conquest-style games like Strategic Conquest.

series. However, trivial differences in gaming ideology and viewpoint should not be allowed to detract from what is a truly unique game.

No Game Is an Island

The goal of Onslaught is to build and command an army in the hopes of trampling the opposing player through strategic and tactical prowess. You are initially given a nice chunk of money with which to build your armies, and you put the armies together using 17 different unit types ranging from Marines to fighter bombers. These are then placed on a randomly generated portion of land that's divided in two, with each player staring down the throat of the other. The edges of the land mass are surrounded by clear blue water, thus enabling the odd sneaky amphibious assault. Once the troops have been piled up at the fronts during the build phase of the first turn, you can expect to witness fireworks aplenty. Although crushing enemy units should be uppermost in your mind when attacking, there is also the small matter of money, which you need to maintain your troops, equipment, and supply lines. Onslaught handles the monetary system by assigning dollar values to each city. An embattled city will not produce as much cash as a city far from the front lines, but one mustn't forget that each municipality means money in the bank and supplies for your troops. An opponent can meet defeat because of a financial squeeze.

Dig Those Stats

At first glance, Onslaught looks much like the other popular contemporary war games with its hex-based board, attractive color graphics and animation, and the individualized palettes that hide in the corners of the screen. The similarity basically ends there. The best way we can sum up Onslaught is to describe it as V for Victory meets Strategic Conquest. Individual units have great statistical detail, including strength, training, and even attack and defense thresholds. This enables the user to exhibit quite a bit of control and to fine tune certain battle situations. For example, if a unit is getting pummeled by repeated air strikes, you can bolster its strength by joining forces with a neighboring unit. Or you can adjust the defense threshold so that anything short of a nuke won't make your troops crack. Speaking of nukes, Onslaught has included them in the equation by making them only somewhat destructive. When a nuclear device is detonated in a hex, everything in that hex is destroyed forever, including its production capacity. Other hexes around ground zero are also affected. The decision to drop the big one carries large consequences for both sides.

A Refreshing Change of Pace

The interface is terrific, and we found ourselves able to play the game using only experimentation and no manual. Indeed, Onslaught has one of the more intuitive interfaces we've seen. The game also offers great head-to-head action and considerably more tactical detail then either Empire Deluxe or Strategic Conquest. And although it could be thought of as a conquest game, game play puts it more on the war game side of the spectrum. Because the computer offers up only average competition, we found head-to-head network play to be the most enjoyable combination, and we often threw in a few neutral computer countries to mix things up a bit instead of immediately butting heads. Onslaught is an excellent first attempt by Frontal Assaultware. If it's any indication of what's to come from this young company, we're in for a treat.

GREAT FEATURE

Pros: Great graphics, sound, and animation. Fun head-to-head play. Intriguing marriage of conquest-style games and traditional hex-based war games.

Cons: No modem play. Limited use of naval operations.

System Requirements: 68020 or better, 4MB RAM, 5MB hard disk space, System 7.1 or later.

ONSLAUGHT	
Fun factor	4.0
Look and feel	4.0
Value	3.5
Replayability	3.5
Overall	4.0

13 Flight Simulations

We would guess that a fair number of people play around with flight simulations for the same reason we do: they hate flying. We're not talking about the lost-baggage-and-nasty-little-meals inconvenience of the airline experience. We're referring to the cooped-up-in-a-metal-tube-hurtling-through-the-skies-at-an-unbelievable-altitude kind of terror faced by poltroons like ourselves. We gravitate toward flight sims for one reason only: control.

With a simulated mission up and running, no longer must we recall our silent suffering in the cheap seats as our fevered imaginations conjured up lurid pictures of the pilot and crew passed out over the controls with tiny, empty bottles of Old Crow clattering about on the floor of the cockpit. Thanks to the marvels of this modern age, we're the aviator who's passed out, not from the excesses of drink, but rather from the force of too many Gs slamming blood into our brains; we're the heroic warriors who chuckle in the face of angular little representations of flying machines that are bent on our destruction; we're the cocksure aces of the air who, when General Charles "Chuck" Yeager pops up on the screen to exhort us to "watch your six" boldly tell him to "can it" as we send our F-4s plummeting toward earth.

TERMINOLOGY

If you've read more than six pages of a Tom Clancy novel, you're aware that the military never met an acronym or bit of jargon it didn't lovingly embrace. Since the first use of advanced electronic systems in modern aircraft, the Pentagon's Department of Arcronymic Arcanity (pronounced *duh*) has, from all appearances, been burning the midnight oil.

If you have a desire to earn your wings on a modern Mac flight sim, you're going to be confronted with quite an array of terminology. In case you missed Defense Department Bulletin AAB-4438-59c, *Your Friend the F-18,* here's a rundown on the latest in flight sim jargon.

AGM: Air-to-Ground Missile
Keep reading, they're not all as easy as this one. It's a missile fired from an aircraft at a ground-based target. AGMs can be heat seeking, laser guided, radar tracking, or electro-optical.

AOA: Angle of Attack
Used to aid landing in low-visibility situations, this device activates when the landing gear is retracted and indicates if the airspeed and angle of descent are correct.

ARAD: Anti Radiation
A variety of air-to-ground radar that tracks ground-based radar sources.

CCIP: Continuously Calculated Impact Point
Once the pilot designates a target for free-falling bombs, this system calculates the precise moment to release the bombs and does so automatically—provided the pilot maintains the proper course and a reasonable angle (dropping bombs when the plane is upside down is a *bad* idea).

Chaff
Small pieces of metal released from a plane to confuse radar-tracking missiles.

Yes, we're the kind of people who buy every stinkin' Mac flight sim that comes on the market!

Um, Chris, the prose is getting a little purple here. We prefer not to use words such as stinkin' in a Macintosh Bible. *Could you tone it down a bit?—J.*

Sorry, I guess I got carried away.

And do you really believe this premise? As much as I appreciate the generosity of sharing your phobia with our readers, don't most people buy these games simply because the games are entertaining?—J.

ECM: Electronic Countermeasure
This device scrambles incoming radar signals, making it more difficult for radar-guided missiles to correctly track you.

EO: Electro-Optical
An optically-guided missile system. The pilot uses a camera contained within the missile to visually select a target. Once fired, the missile locks to that target and . . . KABOOM!

Flares
Small heat-producing flares can be released from a plane to confuse heat-seeking or infrared missiles.

FLIR: Forward-Looking Infrared
Tracks targets through infrared imaging. Useful for low-visibility missions.

HUD: Head-Up Display
A system for projecting such important data as airspeed, altitude, throttle setting, and magnetic heading onto the windshield of an aircraft. It helps pilots keep their eyes on the "road."

IFF: Identify Friend/Foe
An electronic system that allows a pilot to determine whether an airborne object appearing on radar is one of ours or one of theirs.

ILS: Instrument Landing System
Used for landing in low-visibility situations. AOA is an integral part of the ILS.

SAM: Surface-to-Air Missile
A pesky ground-based missile that tries to blow you out of the sky.

TACAN: Tactical Air Navigation
Provides information regarding bearing and distance to preset locations (known as waypoints).

Yeah, I guess so. But *I* buy them for the reasons I gave.

I'm sure that's true.—J.

Really.

Fine. Could we explain the jargon and move on to the reviews now?—J.

Okay.

~~~~~~

The Holy Trinity

Ask any experienced Mac pilot for a flight sim recommendation and you'll hear, "You mean *after* you get Hellcats, Hornet, and A-10?"

It's really that simple. If you have the slightest interest in computer flight, you must own these three games.

Hellcats Over the Pacific
Graphic Simulations

Prior to 1991, Macintosh flight sim fans had to content themselves with a weak diet of such games as Fokker Triplane, Red Baron, and the Microsoft Flight Simulator. The one decent flight sim of the day, Spectrum HoloByte's Falcon, offered the single faint glimmer of hope. Then, out of the blue, Eric Parker and Graphic Simulations unleashed Hellcats Over the Pacific with its mouthwatering frame rate and dynamic action. Hellcats became *the* flight-sim for the Mac. The battle was won with nary a shot fired.

Strap In
You pilot the F6F Hellcat, one of the meanest aircraft buzzing about the Pacific Theater. Introduced in the latter days of the war, the Hellcat soon became the dominant Allied air fighter—blasting Japanese Zeros from the skies and creating large holes in local real estate with well-placed bombs.

Compared to flying a modern-day jet fighter, flying the Hellcat is simplicity itself: grab the stick, adjust the flaps, race the throttle, shift the ailerons and rudder, locate the bogies on a simple radar screen, and pull the trigger. No need to concern yourself with heat-seeking missiles fired from ten miles out, complicated weapons systems, or flying low enough to escape radar detection. Just seat-of-the-pants flying.

The missions are also straightforward. Shoot down a couple of Zeros, blow a few chunks out of the enemy's runway, prevent suicide dive bombers from taking out your carrier, try to survive . . . you know, run-of-the-mill stuff.

Look Around
By today's standards, the Hellcats graphics are a little lean and boxy. Colors tend to be anything but subtle—the ocean is navy blue, the earth is dirt-brown and

Rough landing ahead! You'd better make sure your Hellcat's tray tables are in their full upright position.

grass-green, the sky is, well, sky blue. The smoothly scrolling terrain is made up of geometric shapes. Yet despite the sparse surroundings, Hellcats doesn't look cheap. Motion is realistic and the splashdowns are good enough to have been included in Parker's impressive follow-up flight sim A-10 Attack!

As we've more than hinted, Hellcats's strength is in its seamless action. Forget the strobing effect you're accustomed to in Falcon and Chuck Yeager's Air Combat. When banking sharply to starboard in pursuit of a troublesome Zero, we've caught ourselves leaning hard to the left—it's that good.

GREAT FEATURE

Those who are intimately familiar with actual aircraft of this era have justifiably complained that the performance of the simulated F6F has been significantly enhanced. In turning battles, for example, a real Hellcat wouldn't stand a chance against the zippy Zero. Although realism may be an attractive factor for some players, it's not high on our list of concerns. We're flying this thing for the purposes of entertainment rather than instruction, and we have no problem flying a juiced-up Hellcat. If you prefer instruction, look to A-10 Attack! for more realistic flight modeling.

Happy Landings

We could go on to tell you about the seven included missions and the eight additional missions contained in the Missions at Leyte Gulf add-on package. We could also mention that you can now get Hellcats bundled with Spectre and

Super Tetris on the MacBestsellers CD-ROM from Activision. But what's the point? You must own this game.

Pros: Smooth frame rate. Reasonable graphics. Great dogfighting action.

Cons: Fans of realism may find the Hellcat's performance optimistic.

System Requirements: 68020 or better, 2MB RAM, 840K hard disk space, System 6 or higher.

HELLCATS OVER THE PACIFIC	
Fun factor:	5.0
Look and feel:	4.0
Value:	5.0
Replayability:	4.0
Overall:	4.5

CD

F/A-18 Hornet
Graphic Simulations

Unlike the comparatively quaint Hellcat, the F/A-18 is a modern multimission jet fighter, and it carries all the goodies one would expect in a pricey bit of military hardware. These goodies include: two General Electric F404 engines; fly-by-wire; HUD; a radar system that employs four air-to-air and two air-to-ground modes; air-to-air weapons such as the M61A Vulcan cannon, the AIM-9 Sidewinder, and the AIM-120 AMRAAM missile; a variety of free-fall bombs and electro-optical missiles for air-to-ground attacks; defense mechanisms like chaff, flares, and ECM; TACAN, ILS, FLIR, RBGM (Real Beam Ground Mapping), and other assorted acronyms, each of which probably stands for something useful; and more lights and gauges than you could shake a ThrustMaster flight stick at.

Whew! One can surely imagine that an aircraft lugging about this kind of technology would require a healthy amount of training for prospective pilots. It does. Fortunately, that training is a simple Command-T away.

Flyin' and Shootin'

GREAT
FEATURE

The pilot in training is whisked off to the balmy environs of Hawaii, where you practice such skills as air base and carrier takeoffs and landings, navigation, and air-to-air and air-to-ground combat. During this period, although you are advised to follow a predetermined course of exercises to hone you skills, there is nothing that keeps you from, say, lobbing a Durandal antirunway bomb at Honolulu International or strafing the tourists on Waikiki. Naturally, if this sort of mischief took place during an actual mission, these untoward actions would result in a court martial and, in addition to blemishing your permanent record, would remove you from the active duty roster. But for now, anything goes. Once you're comfortable with flying, shooting, navigating, and dodging, you can elect to move from the tropical to the topical by choosing to fly through the dusty environs of Kuwait.

In order to earn a ticket home from this sandy conflict, you must successfully complete a tour of duty made up of seven missions spanning four levels of difficulty that are selected by the program from a pool of 28. Successful completion of a mission is defined as meeting the mission goals, returning to friendly territory alive (this doesn't mean that the plane needs to be in pristine condition or even recoverable), and not having destroyed any friendly property along the way. The missions cover everything from offensive and defensive strikes to escort duties to escapes from enemy bases. In each mission, enemy resistance comes in the form of surface-to-air missiles, antiaircraft fire, and skillfully piloted MiGs.

By the time you read this, Graphic Simulations will have released another set of missions, titled The Korean Conflict.

The Buzz on Hornet

Hornet sports the features found in the best of today's flight sims: network play (with AppleTalk and Apple Remote Access support); replay of the last mission, complete with multiple views; determination of the competence of your enemy and the lethalness of ground weapons; support for external controllers such as the Gravis MouseStick, Flightstick Pro, and the ThrustMaster system; support for multiple monitors; and the ability to make your aircraft more or less susceptible to enemy attack. Admittedly, this is a pretty powerful feature set, but all the features in the world don't mean diddly if the plane flies like a brick or the scenery strobes by. No worries here, though; Hornet feels and looks great. There is absolutely no problem with frame rate, the action is very fluid, and the updated graphics in version 2.0 are breathtaking. In addition to making the action smooth and the scenery splendid, Hornet's designers have taken pains to get the small things right. Everything from the interior of the cockpit to the inclusion of McDonnell Douglass's Hornet owners manual speaks to their attention to detail. In most cases, this pays off in a great gaming environment. At other times, one wishes things had been fudged a bit.

GREAT FEATURE

Take the cockpit, for instance. Rather than cram the necessary monitors, gauges, and indicators into an unrealistic single-screen view, the designers elected to provide the player with two views: the Cockpit View, which incorporates the canopy, HUD, and weapons and navigation screens; and the Look Down View,

Sure the Sharif doesn't like it, but rocking the casbah in an F/A-18 Hornet is just too tempting.

which contains the MultiPurpose Color Display (MPCD), engine and fuel displays, and analog gauges. Although this maintains the integrity of the Hornet's design, there are times when it's extremely inconvenient to take one's eyes off the road. The difficulty is compounded by the kind of simulation we're dealing with.

Modern Warfare

The F/A-18 Hornet is a modern jet fighter that operates under modern wartime conditions. Graphic Simulations has incorporated these conditions into its model and has produced a simulation that is very different from the dogfighting sims to which we've grown accustomed. In the good old analog days of flying by stick, we were allowed the luxury of engaging the enemy at a reasonable altitude and within sight of each other, machine to machine. This is no longer the case.

Today, most air fighters might as well carry bumper stickers on their tailpipes that state, "If you can read this, I'm dead." A modern mission is comprised of listening for the telltale radar targeting beep that indicates your enemy's presence, unleashing your missiles, and heading home for a warm supper.

The key to survival in an unprotected Hornet (one for which you haven't invoked any of the included cheats that make your fighter invulnerable to attack) is flying low and keeping an eye on the radar screen. Here's where the inconvenience of the Look Down View becomes readily apparent. In a low-altitude run when an electro-optical missile is required, the pilot has to switch views, hone in on the target using the missile's camera view in the MPCD, and hope that his hand has not strayed on the stick. At this point, one wonders if it wouldn't be easier to fly the real thing.

A pilot's first forays into Kuwait may reinforce this notion. Because the simulation is so complex and detailed, the initial learning curve can be a bit steep—there are numerous keyboard commands to memorize (having a flexible flight control system, such as the ThrustMaster package, will ameliorate this situation greatly). The player who chooses to fly without the benefit of cheating can reasonably expect to lose dozens of pilots before making the big breakthrough. Once that breakthrough comes, though, everything changes. It becomes clear that this is an exercise in strategy as much as of flight simulation. What previously seemed impossible is now only challenging. It's true that dogfight enthusiasts accustomed to drawing a visual bead on the enemy may be disappointed by this impersonal approach to warfare, but for those pilots willing to move into the modern age of air combat, Hornet provides an eye-opening and eminently flyable diversion. Highly recommended.

Tip

• To fly a particular mission, hold down the Option key while selecting Tour of Duty. Up pops a dialog box that instructs you to type in the mission number and type of aircraft you wish to fly (check out the CD-ROM for a list of missions and available aircraft).

TIP

Pros: Smooth frame rate. Terrific graphics and sound. Fierce action.

Cons: The Look Down view can be confusing at first.

System Requirements: 68020 or better, 4MB RAM, 12.4MB hard disk space, System 6 or higher.

F/A-18 HORNET	
Fun factor:	5.0
Look and feel:	5.0
Value:	5.0
Replayability:	5.0
Overall:	5.0

A-10 Attack!
ParSoft

As the name implies, this sim from Eric "Hellcats" Parker is modeled on the A-10A Thunderbolt II, which is known to the aviation-aware as the Warthog. A late '70s, ground-attack aircraft used extensively in the Gulf War, the A-10 carries the biggest durned gun this side of Arnold Schwarzenegger and enough ordnance to put a serious crimp in anyone's weekend plans.

"Whoa, Nelly!" those of you already inducted into the winged world may mutter, "*That* slow, ugly beast? Why would anyone want to fly a Hog?"

Admittedly, the A-10 is neither a sexy high-performance jet fighter nor a classic WWII dogfighter. The charm of the A-10 lies not in sleek lines and turn-on-a-dime performance. We must hearken instead to our childhood roots; flying a Hog is exhilarating because it's a blast to blow things to smithereens when you're up close and personal.

Hog Rolling

Compared with such high-tech flying machines as the F/A-18 Hornet, the A-10 is fairly stripped down. The plane possesses no active radar, just a simple flashing

A-10 Attack! is the first Macintosh flight simulation that allows you to manipulate cockpit controls with the mouse. This is a cool concept, but it's clumsy in the heat of battle.

light and alarm to indicate when someone in the vicinity is painting the skies with radar. The HUD is straightforward, offering three operational modes: Navigation, Pave Penny (for missile guidance), and CCIP (for bomb targeting). The plane comes complete with chaff, flares, and ECM. And, of course, you have the usual views: peek-out-the-window, weapons, tower, and external. A-10 Attack! also offers a terrific zoom mode that can't be found anywhere else in the Mac universe. But where the game gets complicated is in its weaponry.

This sucker carries a wide variety of armaments—ranging from simple iron bombs to laser-guided missiles and electro-optical weapons—loaded onto 11 separate stations. Besides trying to remember exactly what each weapon does and how best to deploy it, you have to recall where you put it, because you cannot cycle through the different weapons as you can with the F/A-18 Hornet. You beginning pilots will spend much of your time flipping on the Autopilot, switching into Look Down view, locating a particular weapon, and then activating it with an Option-click—yes, this is the first Mac flight sim that allows you to operate switches and knobs with the mouse—or with one of the function or keypad keys. Players hungry for promotion will quickly develop standardized placement of their weapons.

Operating the A-10 takes some adjustment of your expectations. To begin with, accurately dropping bombs, even while employing CCIP, isn't easy. When targeted from a distance, bombs invariably fall short or long. A-10 Attack!'s maker, ParSoft, claims that this is a true representation of bomb targeting on an A-10: you must get close to ensure a direct hit. Players doubting this claim (or simply lacking the patience to practice) are welcome to turn on the Easy Weapons Hits option. A-10 Attack! also includes environmental modeling that affects the performance of your aircraft. In other words, wind happens. Lining up on the runway, dropping the gear and flaps, and pulling back on the throttle just aren't good enough in this sim. Rather, you have to contend with the possibility of being blown all over tarnation just prior to touchdown.

This buffeting emphasizes the importance of realistically modeled rudders to an aircraft's performance. Unlike some simulated aircraft whose rudders simply rotate the nose of the aircraft left or right, the A-10 yaws like the real thing. This action not only adds a new dimension to aiming, landing, and banked turns but also finally justifies the purchase of those rudder pedals you've been lusting after.

GREAT FEATURE

As we mentioned, this is an Eric Parker product, so it goes without saying that motion is extremely fluid. Since Hellcats, Eric and crew have radically improved

INTERVIEW: ERIC PARKER

Eric Parker is the programming whiz behind ParSoft, the company responsible for two of the greatest flight simulations in computer gaming: Hellcats Over the Pacific and A-10 Attack!

Mr. Parker was kind enough to take a break from revolutionizing the computer gaming industry to grant us this exclusive interview.

Tell us a little about your early programming experience.

My first programming experience was on an HP-2000 timesharing system that my high school rented time on. I wrote a flight simulator in BASIC that let you fly the final approach to a runway. The shape of the runway was printed out once every second of flight time (using asterisks on a 300 baud thermal printer). At this point you were prompted for your throttle and control inputs for the next second of flight. Pretty low-tech.

What attracts you to flight sims?

I've always been interested in aircraft, and a flight simulator lets you have fun with airplanes without the down side of becoming dead. I especially like the double challenge of programming flight simulators. The first is to create as highly realistic an environment as you can. This means wind, visuals, object collisions, aerodynamics, and so forth. And it must be real-time. The second challenge is flying the airplane after you've succeeded. Like learning to do a snap roll,

or a hammer-head stall, or to trim a battle-damaged aircraft for a successful landing. The second challenge is more or less fun in direct relation to how good a job you do with the first.

Explain the basics behind your Virtual Battlefield Environment.

VBE is really just a buzzword for programming modularity. With VBE, we can enhance and upgrade our products in a convenient and powerful way. The plug-in nature of VBE modules enables easy distribution of bug fixes and patches. New missions and scenery can just as easily be created.

Give us your vision of the ultimate VBE setup.

A VBE module is nothing more than the collection of C++ objects and 3D database elements comprising a simulation. Hooked to the simulation is a user-interface application (like the present tactical map). I envision a series of user-interface applications connected to a series of VBE vehicle simulators controlled by a scenario object (the globe icons). A player could control AWACS aircraft and vector fighters to enemy positions with an air defense application. Another player could provide logistical support with a military air command application. On the other side, new vehicle simulators for F14, Apache, M1 Abrams, Nimitz-class carriers, and so forth can provide the pieces being controlled. Who knows where it all leads? But it will be fun trying to get there.

Aside from VBE and flight sims, are there any other kinds of programming that you'd like to do?

I like writing compilers. And of course rendering algorithms.

Why do flight Sims like A-10 look and behave so much better than DOS flight sims? Does the Mac have an advantage?

Some parts are easier, and others are harder. There is only one Macintosh manufacturer, and this greatly simplifies making your simulator compatible—you have to go through a lot of pain on the PC to make your sim work with most machines. However, the PC has a 320 x 200 resolution screen mode, which means there are only one-quarter as many pixels to draw. This is the main advantage of the PC, but it's also a disadvantage in that the result is not as good looking as what's displayed on the Mac's 640 x 480 screen. If you can keep frame rates up, then the Mac is going to look better, but it takes more work.

Where do you draw the line between realism and playability? And does the newer technology, such as faster Macs and joysticks with rudder controls, change the equation?

Realism is my stock in trade, as long as it's not boring and can be done effectively. An example of this in A-10 is starting the engines. The real plane's engine start procedures take about 90 seconds. I think most people would tire of this very quickly. On the other hand, I went all out on the flight model for the A-10. You really have to fly the thing. It would have been easier for players (and me!) if I'd done a flight model similar to the one most simulators use, but there is a greater sense of accomplishment when a player becomes proficient with A-10 and knows it's much closer to the real thing.

That's really where I draw the line. If I can feel pride as I get better at flying, and if I get excited about trying out a new tactic to defeat the enemy because I really don't know if it will work beforehand, then I know it's right.

Where do you see flight sims going in the future?

Personally, I will keep pushing for more and more realism. We'll have to get better input and display devices though, because you can only go so far with a mouse and keyboard.

What's in the works for ParSoft in the future?

VBE modules of course. But we'll also keep improving the graphics and simulation. I don't intend to provide the enemy with a stationary target.

the rendering of scenery; the landscapes are studded with more-realistic mountains and pitted with canyons. They even went to the trouble of including sun blinding and an accurate representation of the constellations you'd see on a nocturnal mission.

A-10 comes with four training missions for practicing takeoffs, landings, and air-to-ground and air-to-air attacks. For additional training, you're welcome to take on one of the two open-ended, quick-start missions—one with a variety of targets and another that's enemy-free, for those times when you feel like just tooling about. The real meat and potatoes of the action takes place during eight missions set in a Germany soon to be overrun by a reformed Communist threat.

Virtual Battlefield Environment

These eight missions give you your first hint that A-10 Attack! is more than merely a great flight sim. The game is only the first piece in a much larger enterprise called the Virtual Battlefield Environment (VBE). Here's the idea:

GREAT FEATURE

In real battles, you have a number of participants—some air-based, some floating on a body of water, others riding around in tanks and jeeps. Traditionally, Mac-based sims limited your participation to operating a single vehicle while the battle raged around you. Using VBE, it will be possible to jump from one vehicle to another. For example, you'll be able to take out a SAM site with your high-tech fighter, jump to the A-10 to blow up the fuel dump, jump to a submarine to sink a battle cruiser, and finally jump to a jeep back at the base in order to nip over to the Officer's Club for a well-deserved drink. Although the VBE concept is familiar to war gamers accustomed to planning campaigns, the exciting difference here is that you actually will get to pilot the plane, fire the torpedo, and pull the trigger (and, with a little luck, live to tell the tale).

In VBE's current A-10 implementation, you can command several aircraft at the same time. Simply create a series of waypoints on the Tactical Map for the planes to follow, indicate how fast and at what altitude they should fly, and indicate the missions you'd like them to carry out. You could, for example, command an A-10 to take off, level out at 150 feet, travel southeast for 22.6 miles, make a sharp left turn, climb to 630 feet, take out a pesky AA site perched on a hill, fly west for 15.2 miles, bomb a destroyer, and return to base. During this mission, an automated F-16 could be taking care of the bogies above while you personally fly a second A-10 against a complement of tanks. As the battle progresses, it's possible to monitor the other planes by "visiting" them—watching their progress from a wing man's perspective. If visiting seems too passive, you can take over the controls of any of the A-10s.

Because the VBE engine is already contained in A-10, adding new vehicles, missions, and code is as simple as dropping additional VBE modules—much like Photoshop plug-ins—into the A-10 folder.

Squeals and Kinks

Considering the complexity of the planning components in this sim, it's a pity that more care wasn't taken in preparing the manual. The online tutorial suffices for walking you through the training missions, but vital information concerning waypoints—which are at the heart of many of the German missions—is woefully lacking. Although you can piece this puzzle together by studying aircraft with preset waypoints, an additional tutorial would help immensely.

LOUSY FEATURE

And we're a little disappointed that, at the time of this review, networking isn't up and running. We were told that networking would be implemented by the time you read this. Although we're sure that it will be worth waiting for, we're not going to hold our breaths. A-10 Attack! was released a full two years after an initial showing at Macworld Expo.

Finally, flight sim fanatics are braggarts at heart and love nothing better than dragging out old missions to show their friends. A-10 Attack! does not carry the mission replay feature found in CYAC and Hornet that allows you to replay every excruciating detail of previous missions. (Just between you and us, we're thrilled that ParSoft left this out. Watching someone else's mission is like looking at a slide show of your aunt's vacation in Kansas.)

Hog Wild

These complaints aside, without VBE, A-10 Attack! would be just a terrific flight sim. With VBE, A-10 Attack! represents a remarkable first step in a revolutionary Mac gaming technology. As far as we're concerned, this Hog is a blue ribbon winner.

Tips

TIP

• Look for the carousel, Tonka truck, and tunnel in the training missions.

• Be wary of flying too low in the training missions when traveling above the highways.

• If you're looking for the Big Headache, try ejecting while in the hangar.

• For those pesky radar-controlled AA sites around which you control multiple A-10s, consider using one of them as a suicide plane. Climb, climb, climb, above the radar site and dive, dive, dive, to knock it out.

Pros: Realistic Hog flying with typically swell Eric Parker-style interface and frame rate. Virtual Battlefield Environment could change the face of war gaming and flight sims.

Cons: Less-than-thorough manual and—at this time—unimplemented networking.

System Requirements: 13-inch color monitor, 68030 Macintosh, 4MB RAM, 11.4MB hard disk space, System 7 or later.

A-10 ATTACK!	
Fun factor:	5.0
Look and feel:	5.0
Value:	5.0
Replayability:	5.0
Overall:	5.0

The Rest of the Flight Sims

Microsoft Flight Simulator 4.0
Microsoft

RANT

If Bill Gates is compiling a list of why so many Macintosh users consider him to be The Great Satan, he may wish to add these words: Microsoft Flight Simulator 4.0 for the Macintosh.

Somewhere between MFS versions 4.0 and 5.0, it was determined by those in Redmond that as far as the Mac gaming market was concerned, the flight sim stops here. Full speed ahead for the PC, of course, but not for the Mac.

Far be it for us to suggest to the minions working for The Wealthiest Man on Earth that two can play this game or hint that Nisus and WordPerfect make lovely word processors and that ClarisWorks is the finest all-in-one package there is.

As for MFS 4.0?

Ppbbbbtttttttttttt.

Pros: Our big chance to bash Microsoft.

Cons: At the risk of repeating ourselves: Ppbbbbtttttttttttt.

System Requirements: Desperation.

MICROSOFT FLIGHT SIMULATOR 4.0	
Fun factor:	2.0
Look and feel:	1.0
Value:	2.0
Replayability:	2.0
Overall:	1.5

Chuck Yeager's Air Combat
Electronic Arts

CD

Air Combat is a very decent DOS port of a dogfight sim that mirrors General Yeager's career during three wars: World War II, Korea, and Vietnam. You can choose to fly any of six aircraft (WWII's P-51 Mustang and Focke-Wulf 190A, Korea's F-86 Sabre and MiG-15, and Vietnam's F-4 Phantom and MiG-21) and pick which side you'll pledge allegiance to. You can also select five modes under which to fly: Test Flight, Create Mission, Historic Mission, Campaign, and Head To Head. As a bonus, you determine the skill level of the opposing pilots—from Amateur to Excellent—in every mode except Campaign and Head To Head.

Should You Choose to Accept Them

Test Flight mode lets you hop aboard one of the six planes and take it for a spin without the distraction of other pilots attempting to blow you out of the sky. Test Flight's Location option places your plane on the runway, on a final approach to the runway, or at an altitude of 10,000 or 40,000 feet. It lets you practice such skills as taking off, landing, maneuvering, and spinning wildly out of control.

GREAT
FEATURE

When you Create a Mission, up pops a dialog box from which you choose one of the six aircraft at your command and then select, from a list of 17, the enemy aircraft. Options include three different opposing planes, with as many as five of each plane. You also select your altitude, whether you approach the enemy with a tactical advantage, disadvantage, or neutrally, and whether enemy flyers are chumps or champs. The resulting dialog box looks something like this: "There I was in my P-51 at 20,000 feet when I jumped five B-29s, three Yak-9s, and two MiG-17s. The guys in those planes were mediocre." As you can see from this example, you have the dubious pleasure of being vaporized by aircraft from any of the three eras.

Historic Missions consist of 16 or 17 missions, ranging from easy to difficult, for each of the three eras. Your aircraft is selected for you, as is the enemy's. Missions include everything from escorting bombers to strafing a slow-moving truck to snatching a MiG-15 and flying it to the enemy base in order to cash in on a $100,000 reward.

In Campaign mode, you really start to get serious. Select an era and a side, and listen up while the General gives you a rough idea of your assignment. After successfully completing each mission—by carrying out your assignment *and* getting home in one piece—your cumulative campaign stats are presented and then it's

It isn't the prettiest flight sim in the Mac world, but Chuck Yeager's Air Combat is chockfull of airborne action.

on to the next job. Once you've finished all the missions, a splash screen informs you that your tour of duty is at an end and it's time to go home for a well-deserved rest.

GREAT FEATURE

Last, but far from least, Head To Head mode is your opportunity to strut your stuff against a human adversary over a network. Oddly enough, the PC version of CYAC cannot be networked, yet on the Mac it's one of the most enjoyable network games going and the one really good reason to buy the sim. Simply arrange for an opponent to log on over AppleTalk, EtherTalk, or TokenTalk, agree via the chat line on the type of aircraft you will be flying, your altitudes and range, and have at it. The sim keeps a record of your aircraft kills and your rating—Rookie, Veteran, or Ace—based on those kills.

The Look

Air Combat uses the now-traditional method of representing objects outside the cockpit as geometric shapes. Grass is green, sky is blue, haze is represented by white lines on the horizon, and clouds are decidedly round and globular objects that float about obscuring your view. Plastered to the windscreen is your HUD (yes, we know the HUD is a fairly recent innovation, but you still have the option to display it in aircraft from all three eras).

The cockpit design is where the DOS-to-Mac port is most apparent. Overall, the look is strictly DOS; that is, it's fat and cartoonish. Far more disturbing than the aesthetics, the gauges are rendered in such a way that you can only get the vaguest sense of what they indicate. Pilots desiring an authentic WWII flying experience will find themselves at a disadvantage when flying with only the cockpit controls.

LOUSY FEATURE

The Feel

Air Combat, although exhibiting motion that is noticeably superior to that of Microsoft's Flight Simulator 4.0, is not up to the level of Hellcats, Hornet, or A-10. Although Air Combat responds as readily as these products, the animation frame rate is slower and lacks the competition's seamless fluidity.

Air Combat's planes are also harder to fly than these others, but that's not necessarily a bad thing. Try as you might, you will never, *ever*, be able to stall a Hellcat. Oh sure, you can climb and climb and eventually start falling back to earth, but the engine will never give out, and once you've got your nose pointed toward the horizon, you're back on track. Air Combat is, sometimes frustratingly so, more realistic. If you crank back on the stick during takeoff, dollars to doughnuts you'll stall out and find yourself in pieces on the runway. Not only that, but the stall function is tuned differently for each type of plane. The P-51, for instance, is fairly tolerant of steep climbs, while the FW-190 is extremely touchy. Pilots using joysticks should be especially careful. A tug on the stick that would send your Hellcat into a gentle climb will cause any plane in Chuck's air force to find the ground in a hurry.

The End

Is Air Combat entertaining? You betcha! Does it offer a variety of options that guarantee that we won't soon stick the box on the shelf? Darn tootin'! Is it cheap? With the new Electronic Arts CD-ROM bundle, it's practically being given away! Would we buy it just to play networked? Amen to that! Do we wish that the folks at Electronic Arts had supplied motion as smooth as that found in products made by Graphic Simulations and ParSoft? Why, sure! Is the program realistic? How would we know? We're not pilots. (And we bet you aren't either.) What we do know is that a sim with the number of features, the variety, and the responsiveness of Chuck Yeager's Air Combat is worth a test flight.

Pros: Great game for networked dogfighting. Lots of variety. Deeply discounted as part of the Electronic Arts bundle.

Cons: Frame rate and graphics don't approach those in Hellcats, Hornet, or A-10.

System Requirements: 68020 or better, 2MB RAM for black and white, 4MB RAM for color when running System 7, 2.8MB hard disk space for black and white, 4MB hard disk space for color, System 6.07 or higher.

CHUCK YEAGER'S AIR COMBAT	
Fun factor:	3.5
Look and feel:	3.0
Value:	4.0
Replayability:	4.0
Overall:	3.5

Out of the Sun
Domark

Released prior to A-10 Attack!, Out of the Sun (OOTS) was the first Mac flight sim that attempted to instill a measure of realism into flight models by presenting planes that didn't fly as if locked to rails. But they wobbled in flight, tended to be tail or nose-heavy, and were difficult to land. Many die-hard flight sim fanatics thought this kind of performance extremely frustrating and quickly abandoned the game for the friendlier aircraft found in Hellcats or Hornet. More persistent players found the OOTS interpretation to be a refreshing change from the all-too-controlled sims of the day.

As nonpilots who wouldn't know an accurate flight model if it dropped a two-ton iron bomb on our heads, we lean toward the latter view. Admittedly, OOTS is no Hornet or A-10, but given a speedy enough Mac—and we *do* mean Power Mac-speedy—OOTS is a worthwhile addition to a flight sim fan's collection.

All This and World War II?
OOTS is a WWII sim that features three historic scenarios: Midway, D-Day, and the battle of Kursk. Each battle is divided into six discreet missions that must be flown in succession. For example, you aren't allowed to take on the Japanese carrier Hiryu in Midway's Final Blow mission until you've successfully completed the previous five sorties. On each mission, you can fly for either the Allies or the Axis and, in most missions, can select from a variety of aircraft.

OOTS offers four levels of play—from Arcade, on which performance characteristics have been significantly enhanced, to Veteran, on which flight models are more realistic and the computer presents opponents that are more skillful.

If you get bored blowing up carriers at Midway, take a side trip to visit the world's most famous rubber monster.

The View From Above

The look of Out of the Sun is fairly typical of most Mac flight sims. You peer out of a cockpit that contains machine gun cross hairs; fuel, altitude, speed, and oil pressure gauges; flaps, gear, brake, dive brake, rudder, and artificial horizon indicators; a compass; and four red warning lights that glow when you've stalled, sustained engine or hydraulic damage, or are out of gas. And, oh yes, there is a woman's picture stuck to the dash (how a picture of Nicole, OOTS producer Bryan Walker's sweetie, ever got into the cockpit of a Russian plane is beyond us). To maintain realism, the cockpit contains no radar or HUD. The only compromise made in this regard is the fluorescent lettering just to the side of the compass that indicates how much ammo remains.

The 3D world below is made up of the usual geometric shapes that are occasionally dotted with rivers, trees, villages, air bases, vehicles, ships, and antiaircraft emplacements. Unlike those in many other Mac flight sims, all of these objects are real in the sense that if you hit a tree, you're meat. You can choose to display horizon and ground shading, the aforementioned objects, and smoke. There are also at least three Easter Eggs in the game (look for Godzilla in the obvious place). To get an overview of this world, press M to display a map that provides the positions of friends and foes. Views include the even-numbered clock views (2, 4, 6, and so forth), the heartily appreciated step views, which let you scan the horizon as well as look above and below as if you were swiveling your head; and outside, flyby, and munitions views. Each view allows for three levels of zoom.

LOUSY FEATURE

OOTS's graphics are not its strong suit. Although land-based objects are rendered well, it's tough to distinguish the good guys from the bad in a sky full of planes. Likewise, it's very difficult to tell where the sky ends and the earth begins—unlike most other Mac flight sims, OOTS does not supply many visual clues as to how close you're getting to the ground or sea. AA and machine gun fire looks decidedly cheap, as do the crashes.

Power Hungry

On our copies of the game, a sticker on the box covers the original System Requirements label. The old requirements read, "Minimum CPU: Mac 68030." Our guess is that after six seconds of testing on the speediest of 030 machines, someone at Domark shouted, "Stop the presses!" Although the new sticker reads, "Minimum CPU: Mac 68040," we'd suggest the addition of this parenthetical remark: ("But partner, it had better be a *fast* 68040, and you'd be wise to shut down most of your extensions and control panels, and while you're at it, have you thought about picking up a Power Mac? You'll *love* this on a Power Mac!")

Flight sims live and die on a single performance feature: frame rate. Fail to deliver adequate frame rate and players get extremely testy. If you happen to be one of the lucky few who own a top-end Power Mac, this is not going to be a major issue—frame rate, although not equal to that of Hellcats, Hornet, or A-10, is acceptable. Unfortunately, difficulties arise for owners of non-PowerPC Macs. Although performance on 040 machines is ducky when you're casually flitting about the skies taking on one or two enemy planes, things bog down quite a bit when you get into the serious stuff.

GREAT FEATURE

OOTS demands this kind of power because it has loads of action per pixel—the scope and complexity of these scenarios is quite impressive and is where OOTS's real strength lies. Rather than the typical one or two planes and a couple of trucks found in most other sims, expect scores of flying and driving objects and numerous installations.

Come Fly With Me

With its wide variety of wind-buffeted planes, Domark obviously went to great pains to create a realistic flying experience that the crustiest of computer pilots will find challenging. But while pursuing that goal, a feature or two that are now standard to most Mac flight sims was left by the wayside: no network mode and no way to bail out. We regret that we can't take up one of these birds against a human opponent.

Mission Complete

OOTS's creators strove to build a flight sim that was formidable but not intimidating, playable but not easy. OOTS, with its rich battle environments and complex flight modeling, has this and more going for it. The missions are engaging, and the action is fierce. Dogfights are tough, and seasoned pilots will find themselves smacking the dirt more often than they are accustomed to—which ain't necessarily a bad thing. Yes, these testy pilots will have to do without some of the niceties found in other Mac flight sims and will experience a measure of frustration when flying some of the more challenging planes, but these are not compelling enough reasons to shy away from OOTS. Check out the demo on our CD-ROM and see for yourself.

Pros: Complex battles and less-than-stable aircraft make for a challenging environment.

Cons: A real power hog that only works optimally on a Power Mac 7100 or better. Not networkable.

System Requirements: 256-color monitor, 68040 Macintosh or Power Mac, 5MB RAM (8MB recommended), 18MB hard disk space for floppy version, System 7 or later, CD-ROM player for CD-ROM version.

OUT OF THE SUN

Fun factor:	4.0
Look and feel:	3.0
Value:	3.5
Replayability:	4.0
Overall:	4.0

F-117A Stealth Fighter

MicroProse

F-117A Stealth Fighter is one of the most popular flight sims of all time for MS-DOS computers. Therefore it seemed only logical that it be ported over to a growing Mac market. After all, this was a game that could run on a 286, so the 030 and 040 Macs should have no problems with it, right? Wrong. Terribly, horribly, stupendously wrong. We want to say good things about companies that see fit to port to the Mac. Honestly, we do. But as disheartening as this may be, we must view F-117A as what it is, a port gone wrong.

Nice Idea

F-117A incorporates nine different world areas into flight operations, including Korea, Cuba, and the Persian Gulf. Each hot spot has its own set of missions, and all told there's plenty of action to keep your Stealth fighter in the air for countless hours. The level of conflict in a region has a direct influence on how you're going to carry out your missions. For example: a Cold War area needs to be treated carefully, with your points being amassed by not being detected by enemy radar, while a Conventional War situation is an anything-goes proposition. The missions themselves come in three flavors: air-to-air, strike, and training. The training missions take place in a "simulator," allowing a mission to be carried out without fear of enemy damage. Overall, the variety of missions is very impressive, and F-117A can easily boast of having the most scenarios of any flight simulator.

Briefing Room

Before taking on a mission, you must go to the briefing room, where you are given a primary and secondary target as well as a landing point to be used when the mission is completed. In the briefing room, you are treated to a great color map showing the safest route through enemy radar to your objectives. You can even get an idea of the effective range of enemy SAMs and radar facilities. Once assigned a mission, it's off to the armory, where you can equip your Stealth with the latest weaponry. Speaking of which, we found that most air-to-ground situations can be resolved using good old Maverick electro-optical guided missiles. This is the first area in which we found F-117A deviating from the realistic. After all, how likely can it be that one weapon reigns supreme for almost every mission while a huge arsenal is available? The other main knock on realism comes when facing off in air-to-air combat. Lobbing a few cannon shells in the general direction of the enemy is all it takes to buy them a one-way ticket to terra firma.

LOUSY FEATURE

Every weapon, flight technique, and important detail is laid out wonderfully in the 180-page manual, which is superior despite the fact that it deals with the DOS version of the game. There is, of course, an insert detailing the discrepancies between the versions, but such niceties as a Mac keyboard overlay were left out.

Ka-Chunk! Ka-Chunk!

Every detail of F-117A is very impressive until you climb into the cockpit for takeoff. The preflight animations actually look very much like Hornet 2.0 or A10-Attack! so we found ourselves getting quite excited waiting to see some

RANT

impressive graphics and extra-smooth flight. Wrong. Wrong, wrong, wrong. It's almost as if MicroProse had two separate teams working on this game, one for the preflight section and another for the actual flight model. The frame rate is so pathetic we found this game almost unplayable. Certainly when F-117A was under development, Hellcats was available and MicroProse could see what a success it was. You'd think they'd have said, "Hey, that game looks good, let's make ours better." Instead they made it 50 times worse, so that merely attempting to bank the Stealth results in a 20-degree "clunk" from one side to another. Frankly, we are amazed. Even on a fast 040, F-117A frame rate is terrible. Ancient games like Fokker Triplane and Falcon have smoother flight.

A Crying Shame

Most everything other than the actual flight characteristics of F-117A Stealth Fighter are indeed very impressive. But for a flight simulator, it's kind of important that the flight simulator part of the game work well. We actually looked forward to this game. Where did MicroProse go wrong? It's a crying shame.

Pros: Decent graphics. Plethora of missions in nine world arenas. Good manual.

Cons: Buggy at times. Horrendous flight characteristics and shoddy frame rate render game almost unplayable even on fast Macs.

System Requirements: Any desktop Mac, 2MB RAM, 1.3MB hard disk space.

F-117A STEALTH FIGHTER	
Fun factor:	2.0
Look and feel:	1.5
Value:	2.0
Replayability:	2.0
Overall:	2.0

Flying Nightmares

Domark

CD

Flying Nightmares is a landmark game for a couple of reasons. It was the initial Mac game offering from the longtime DOS games company Domark. More importantly, it was the first game to be optimized for the Power Mac. Certainly Domark took a big RISC in doing this.

Acronyms From Hell

You are the commander of a UN-sanctioned rapid deployment force (RDF) poised for the invasion of East Timor in Southeast Asia. Your job is to take the island by landing marines against a numerically superior enemy while supporting them with Harrier jump jets (the same kind of jet that appeared in the movie

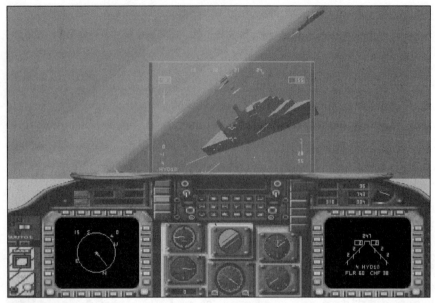

Flying Nightmares was the first Power Mac-native game. However, the difficult flight characteristics of the Harrier and the DOS interface and graphics make it a game for fanatics only.

True Lies). The first part of the game plays rather a lot like a traditional war game and involves laying down a battle plan using the Tactical Amphibious Warfare Data System (TAWADS). This system provides you with information on both friendly and enemy forces.

And You Thought Chewing Gum and Walking Was Hard

The second part of Flying Nightmares is the actual flight simulator, which puts you in the cockpit of a Harrier jump jet right on the deck of the *USS Tawara*. Fortunately, the *Tawara* has a simulator below deck, so you can hone your skills before battle. And believe us, you'll need to. These babies are very, very difficult to get a handle on, and mastering hovering and basic maneuvers without inducing death will take hours of play. These jets do not feel the way other games have led us to believe jets should feel. They're heavier and less maneuverable. We liken it to driving a minivan after scooting around in a Mazda Miata for a day. Once learned, however, Harrier jockeying will make almost anyone a better flight simulator pilot.

Mix and Match

The graphics in the splash screens for everything from the command center to the weapons area are strictly DOS in nature. Very shoddy for us Mac users. However, the TAWADS graphics are sort of a hybrid of Mac and SVGA graphics that we were able to accept fairly readily. The actual flight simulator graphics, while nowhere near the level of Hornet or A10-Attack!, were decent enough to keep our interest when learning to fly the darned Harrier. The animation and flight characteristics are a bit of a mixed bag that depend on how deep your pockets were when you purchased your beloved Mac. Those with Power Macs will enjoy butter-smooth animation, with fantastic frame rates all around. However, those with 040s will barely be enthused, while 030 users will be crying for a refund. Of course, the screen can be set to one of three sizes, but the smallest is just too tiny to get any enjoyment out of Harrier flight. The biggest drawback we saw in the graphics engine for flight lies in the lack of fine detail and the deficiency of landmarks to help establish altitude visually. Many a time we found ourselves splashing into the ocean while fiddling with the controls because there was no verbal or visual clues that we were plummeting to the earth (other than the not-so-obvious altitude gauge).

LOUSY FEATURE

Falls Short

We haven't seen flight simulators that feature Harrier jump jets since Miles Computing delivered Harrier Strike Mission I & II back in the mid-'80s, and it's good to see another games company picking up the mantel and incorporating new technology and ideas. But the lack of a decent Mac interface and the incorporation of screen after screen of super-low-res DOS graphics really take away from the enjoyment a game like this should offer. Despite these shortcomings, Flying Nightmares was a decent first attempt at bringing games to the Mac market, and Domark has proved that it can learn from its mistakes (witness Out of the Sun). For those really needing a piloting challenge and strategic fix, Flying Nightmares will provide many hours of challenge. However, if a happy-go-lucky flight/fighter simulation is what you're looking for, perhaps you should look elsewhere.

Pros: First Power Mac game. Strategy and action melded well. Realistic and challenging flight model.

Cons: Poor Mac interface. Poor performance on 030 Macs (PPC recommended). Graphics in flight simulator spartan. Harrier difficult to master.

System Requirements: 68020 or better (we recommend a PPC), 4MB RAM (8MB recommended), 3.5MB hard disk space, System 7 or later.

FLYING NIGHTMARES	
Fun factor:	3.0
Look and feel:	3.0
Value:	3.5
Replayability:	3.0
Overall:	3.0

Falcon MC
Spectrum HoloByte

In 1987, Spectrum HoloByte released Falcon, the fighter simulation that has been proven to possess the greatest longevity of any comparable game. Falcon continues to linger on store shelves in the form of Falcon MC (Mac Color), a game that in many respects has remained faithful to its predecessor. Despite being a little long in the tooth and grossly outclassed by the likes of A-10 Attack! and Hornet 2.0, Falcon MC remains a very playable fighter simulation, most notably for those with systems not endowed with the horsepower required by recent titles. Actually, this game could be played head-to-head with one player on a Power Mac and one on an old SE (with Falcon 2.X) quite comfortably. Undoubtedly there have been back room whispers that this game should be put out to pasture, but we felt it appropriate to have a closer look at the forerunner of today's fighter simulators.

Bandit Inbound!

Falcon MC puts you into an arena 80 by 80 nautical miles that's dotted with everything from nuclear power plants and SAM sites to hovercraft, T-80 battle tanks, and MiG-29s. Before you can be hoisted high in victorious jubilation, you must successfully complete 12 preset missions. This requires considerable skill, even for experienced flight sim jocks. After recruiting yourself as a new pilot and selecting a call sign, you're set to leap into the cockpit. But before you start strapping on your gravity suit and top gun sun glasses, you must choose from three starting points: Head-to-Head, Campaign, and Instant Action. The latter of these allows you to "jump" a MiG-29 and get a couple of kills under the ol' belt to build up your self-confidence. The 12 missions incorporate what you'd expect in this kind of game, including shooting down MiGs, blowing up bridges, and disabling SAM sites. Each mission can be individually selected, and you're not locked into playing them in order. After all, some days are dogfighting days and some days are fly-at-mach-one-to-destroy-a-nuclear-power-plant-with-a-Maverick-video-guided-missile days.

Flying with Falcon

Falcon's control set is similar to that in any of the newer flight sims. Due to its age, it only takes direct advantage of the Gravis MouseStick. However, many sticks now come complete with preexisting Falcon sets, and if you happen to have a MouseStick lying around, you can use this second stick as a throttle. Falcon's frame rate is more than acceptable on most machines, including Power Macs, and although it's not one of the best flight sims, we definitely found it

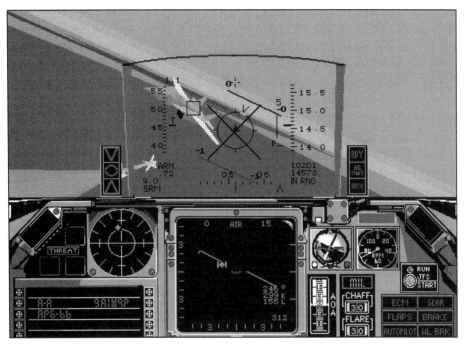

A MiG-29 comes zipping by the left side of the F-16 while a missile is released. Despite its age, Falcon MC from Spectrum HoloByte still packs a flight sim punch.

playable. It includes the usual assortment of air-to-air and air-to-ground missiles and bombs, and those of us who spend our spare time with these games won't even have to crack the manual to be experts on the various armaments available. Despite the aging system, the flight dynamics are fairly realistic, with redouts and blackouts and a turn rate that is severely restricted at speeds over 700 mph.

Two Bit 4-Bit?

Falcon MC was touted as the major upgrade that would finally bring color to Falcon on the Mac. In many ways the improvements didn't meet expectations. The color is only 4-bit (16 color) video, and by the time MC was released in 1992, most machines being sold were capable of 8-bit (256 color) video. This, coupled with unchanged graphics, took much of the punch out of what otherwise could have been an impressive upgrade. Falcon has always incorporated digitized sound, including important messages from AWACS surveillance planes and audio feedback from within the F-16 when fuel is low or damage has occurred. It's surprising that we haven't seen more of the recent flight sims incorporate radio messages into game play. After all, if an eight-year-old program has it, it should be standard. There's nothing like hearing your wing man

GREAT FEATURE

say, "Splash one MiG!" or having your base verbally verify the completion of mission objectives.

Still a Contender

Falcon MC hit the scene after Hellcats of the Pacific came out, and it most certainly wasn't able to match the animation fluidity of Hellcats. Falcon was subsequently stung by the release of Hornet, a vastly superior fighter simulation that was like nothing seen before. It became clear that Falcon would be a secondary game from that point forward. It is a low-overhead game however, and it can still be played on almost any Mac (choose Falcon 2.X for black and white) with decent performance. Best of all, Falcon is still fun to play and has a couple of features not seen in the flashier games, making a tour of duty in your F-16 an enjoyable one.

Pros: Good manual. Plays on all Macs. Head-to-head modem/network play. Staying power.

Cons: Only 4-bit color. Average graphics by today's standards. Limited screen size (12-inch monitor).

System Requirements: 68020 Mac or better, 32-bit QuickDraw, 4MB RAM for color, 2.3MB hard disk space, System 6.05 or higher.

FALCON MC	
Fun factor:	3.0
Look and feel:	3.0
Value:	2.5
Replayability:	3.0
Overall:	3.0

14 | Hardware

In the last decade, Mac gaming labored under several serious deficiencies. Perhaps none are as baffling as the complete lack of those nifty bits of molded plastic called joysticks. Without such an animal, the Mac as a game machine was painfully crushed by all other platforms, many of which were versatile enough to accept the old Atari-style connections, which are still the home video gaming standard. Even for a dyed-in-the-wool Mac head, it requires an enormous leap of imaginative faith to transmogrify a mouse into the flight stick of an F-16.

Apple's now legendary the-Mac-is-not-a-toy stance must share some of the blame with the Mac's tiny nine-inch black-and-white screen for the early days' pathetic gaming lineup. But time and time again when established game publishers are asked why they don't take the Mac plunge, they begin to shudder at the complexities of programming a machine with a high- resolution, CPU-sucking graphical interface. Only with the release of the PowerPC Macs have the performance hurdles been cleared. We Mac users demand high-quality graphics and animation, and the 680x0 line of CPUs just didn't have the gusto to manage the same fluidity of motion and responsiveness seen in many of its DOS counterparts. But Mac users have never enjoyed a greater selection of gaming peripherals than they do at present. Add to this the raw horsepower of the RISC-based PPC chips and we've got the potential to make the Mac the premier computer gaming platform. If the last two years is any indication, there will be little difference in the availability of gaming peripherals between the two major computing worlds.

Game Controllers

Yes, the Mac is a mighty cool computer and the mouse is a darned fine input device. But for serious gaming, the keyboard and mouse just don't have what it takes to control a madly spiraling A-10 or a darting space fighter. To get a handle on these vehicles, you need a game controller.

These add-on ADB devices range from inexpensive gamepads and two-button entry-level joysticks to bank-account-depleting three-piece weapon control systems. Whether your game controller needs are simple or complex, we're sure you'll find something here that fills the bill.

MouseStick II
Mac GamePad
Advanced Gravis

My, my, how things change in this fast-paced world. Just a few short years ago, Advanced Gravis ruled the Macintosh game controller world with its Mouse-Stick II and GamePad. These then-state-of-the-art ADB devices were the pride and joy of every serious Mac gamer.

But time moves along, and today's blue plate special is destined to become tomorrow's leftovers. Although hardly ready for retirement, these Gravis products are no longer the be-all and end-all of game accessories.

THE ULTIMATE GAMING MACHINE

No game book would be complete without mention of what we'd consider the ultimate gaming machine. Keep in mind that technology is constantly progressing at a rapid pace, so some of what we suggest may already be out of date when you read this. Here's what we think you really, really need if you want to take a trip to Mac gaming Nirvana:

• The fastest Mac available. No whining about how much it costs or the fact that you have to eat and pay the rent, just the fastest Mac available.

• RAM and lots of it. Jammed to the limit down the throat of your machine. If you can't afford a metric ton of RAM, then we consider 16 MB to be the minimum needed to even come close to "ultimate."

• A quad-speed CD-ROM drive. Sure, there's not much performance benefit over a double-speed drive, but this *is* Nirvana we're talking about.

• A Virtual Pilot™ from CH Products, complete with rudder pedals. And don't forget the complete ThrustMaster system.

• Gigabyte upon gigabyte of fast hard drives. This is partly to house the humongous amounts of games you own and partly so that you can copy your CD-ROM games over to a hard disk for better performance.

• A Flightstick Pro, Jetstick, ChoiceStick, and any other stick you can get your hands on. You can never have enough input devices (of course chaining them all together at once will not only create serious havoc on your Mac but could also overload the power capacity of the ADB port and blow your Mac sky-high).

• A 28.8 modem for Internet and online gaming fun.

• Multiple 20-inch monitors with enough 32-bit accelerated video cards to drive them, thus ensuring your ability to enjoy Hornet in the multiple-monitor mode.

• External speakers with a sub woofer; the greater the wattage, the better.

• A trackball and a programmable mouse.

• You'll definitely need an extended keyboard for games that rely heavily on key commands.

• Let's not forget a comfortable, supportive chair. You can even include some soft cushions.

• Finally, you probably would want to have a DOS card in your machine to play those good DOS games that haven't already been made better on the Mac.

We don't even want to think about what all of this would cost. But if you have the gumption to be gaming on the high side, the ultimate machine awaits.

MouseStick II

The MouseStick II is a five-button joystick featuring a trigger button, two buttons located on the top of the stick, and two large buttons on the left side of the large base. The grip is covered with soft black rubber and is narrow enough to be used by children as well as adults. You can adjust the stick's tension with a large wheel planted in the base.

Preconfigured game sets for the MouseStick II are easy to come by. Advanced Gravis includes a number of them with the software, and because the MouseStick was something of a standard for a number of years, game sets are often included with new games. You will also find a number of user-created sets online.

Although completely serviceable, the MouseStick II is starting to show its age. Look for Advanced Gravis' new all-in-one game controller, the Firebird.

GREAT FEATURE

If you can't get a preconfigured set, don't fret—it's easy to configure the stick. Simply open a control panel and assign keystrokes to the buttons and one of three kinds of cursor movement to the stick: auto center to window or monitor (useful for flight sims in which you want the cursor to spring back to the middle of the screen); glide control (moves the cursor in the direction of the stick but doesn't spring back to the middle when you let go); and four- and eight-direction keystroke movement (assigns cursor keys to the stick for those games that allow only keyboard control). We wish the MouseStick II control panel could be opened from within a game for automatic linking of game sets, but as Bart's Prime Minister might comment in his inimitable French-Canadian way, "C'est la vie."

Sticky Feeling

LOUSY FEATURE

By today's standards, the MouseStick II feels a little cheap. Even after adjusting the tension control wheel to its most rigid setting, the stick exhibits too much play. And although we appreciate the luxury of having five buttons to work with, we would like the buttons all to be accessible with one hand. Finally, a number of users have reported that, over time, the springs break on their MouseStick IIs. Players who like to apply a lot of English to their game controllers may wish to look into sturdier units.

Mac GamePad

The Mac GamePad, on the other hand, is built solidly enough that your dog could probably gnaw on it with no ill effect. *[Chris, sorry to interrupt, but our attorneys have advised us that telling the readers to allow their pets to chew on a piece of hardware could result not only in serious injury to the hardware and pet in question but also in a nasty lawsuit. I must state clearly that under no circumstances should the Mac GamePad be used for anything other than its stated purpose.—J.]*

Oh, yeah, as if anyone would be so stupid as to. … *Bart!* Take that thing out of your mouth this instant! Yes, right now! Geez, man.

Bart: Well, we've gotta be accurate.

Chris: I know that, but now look what's happened. I was right in the middle of a perfectly serious review of the Mac GamePad. …

Bart: Except for the dog comment.

It's colorful, it's sturdy, it's cheap. If you need a low-cost controller without a lot of bells and whistles, check out the Advanced Gravis GamePad.

Chris: … and then you and Jeremy jump in and ruin the whole thing. Not only is the review hosed, but now we've broken into dialog, and you know as well as I do that the production people are going to throw a fit when they see this.

Bart: Sorry. Boy, I bet Advanced Gravis is gonna be POed too. Maybe you could mention at the end of the review that both of these products have been priced to compete with entry-level controllers and that even though they're not the most modern units around, they're still worth having for the right price.

Chris: That's true enough, but. …

Bart: And you could also say that Advanced Gravis has a cool new controller called the Firebird coming out that will feature loads of buttons, a hardier stick, and the ability to hook PC rudder pedals up to it. Then go on to explain that it wasn't out in time for us to look at, but it should be ready by the time this book hits the shelves.

Chris: And after all this, how am I supposed to break out of the dialog and end the GamePad review?

Bart: Well, since this is partly my fault, I'll give you a hand:

Folks, the GamePad is a Nintendo-style controller that features an eight-direction control pad and four buttons that can be configured to move the cursor and fire keystrokes. If you want to use the control pad for a mini-joystick, Advanced Gravis includes a handle that can be screwed into the center of the pad. The software is functional and easy to use. Like the MouseStick II, the GamePad includes a pass-through ADB connector so you don't have to give up one of your valuable ADB ports. It doesn't cost a lot and is sometimes bundled with game software. We think it's a perfectly reasonable game controller, it just isn't our number-one favorite.

Jeremy: Fellas, this has gone on far too long. Would you please get to the ratings!?

Chris: Okey-dokey, boss.

Bart: Right away, sir.

Chris: (whispered to Bart) Now look what you've done!

Bart: Oh, shut up.

Jeremy: Ahem!

Pros: Inexpensive five-button joystick. Many games come with preconfigured sets.

Cons: Not as sturdy as modern joysticks.

System Requirements: ADB-equipped Macintosh, hard disk recommended, System 6.07 or higher.

MOUSESTICK II	
Feel:	3.0
Configurability:	3.5
Value:	4.0
Construction:	3.0
Overall:	3.0

MAC GAMEPAD	
Feel:	4.0
Configurability:	3.5
Value:	4.0
Construction:	4.0
Overall:	3.5

Pros: Solidly built. Many games come with preconfigured sets. Inexpensive.

Cons: Not as many buttons as modern gamepads.

System Requirements: ADB-equipped Macintosh, hard disk recommended, System 6.07 or higher.

JoyStick
Batwing
MacALLY

MacALLY also has a pair of game controllers: the how's-this-for-an-obvious-name JoyStick, and the aptly titled gamepad, Batwing.

JoyStick

This two-button ADB jobbie carries one of the more innovative features of any joystick we examined—four suction cups attached to the base. If you've never used a joystick before, this may seem like no great shakes, but think about it for a second. One of the major design problems inherent with joysticks is that the base must be large enough to keep the unit from toppling over when you make that desperate right turn. Thus, most joysticks have these enormous, clunky bases that, despite your best efforts, still tend to fall on your desktop and are much too large to hold comfortably in your lap. MacALLY had addressed the problem admirably with these little suckers.

The stick itself is one of the most comfortable we've tried. It features a nicely contoured grip and large rounded buttons. The JoyStick's action, although not as tight as some others, felt smooth and solid.

Thanks to the included suction cups, the MacALLY Joy-Stick sports a more streamlined base than other joysticks.

Batwing

After opening the box and taking a gander at this contraption, we couldn't help but wonder whether MacALLY had discovered some hidden vault full of plastic spinoffs from the first Batman movie. This eight-button controller looks that much like a bat. The illustration on the box makes it look even more so with its dark purple shading. Unfortunately, the unit we received was along more albino lines: computer-platinum with light blue buttons and a purple movement pad.

POW! BLAM! KAPLOOEY!
It's the alien-killing, pinball-plunging, weapons-selecting Batwing!

The Batwing is set up in the traditional Nintendo and Sega style—four buttons on the right wing, two buttons in the middle, two buttons on the back, and an eight-direction movement pad on the left. Although it's thicker than either the Gravis GamePad or the bundled ChoiceStick gamepad, it doesn't feel overly bulky.

The Software

The software for both units is set up along the same lines as the Gravis products—assign keystrokes to the buttons and different glide and centering options to the stick. There are a couple of crucial differences, though.

GREAT
FEATURE

On the MacALLY JoyStick, it's possible to assign three separate actions to each button. For example, a single pull of the trigger fires the gun, a double-click drops a bomb, and a triple-click ejects the pilot. Up to five modifier keys can be simultaneously triggered. You might, for instance, fire Command-Shift-Option-Control-Caps Lock-D. This is very convenient and quickly becomes natural.

The Batwing software allows for the same kind of multilevel setting for seven of the buttons. The eighth button, Select, is used to toggle the movement pad between mouse and keystroke emulation.

Here's the Beef

This is all good, but we have a few problems with the MacALLY products:

**LOUSY
FEATURE**

One: Neither of the controllers are "application aware." So? So every time you want to play a game using one of these babies, you have to open the application, select a new game set, and then start the game. So? So it's inconvenient if you play a lot of different games.

And we play a *lot* of games.

Two: The ADB cables are too short. We understand that these things were intended to be placed in the chain between your keyboard and mouse—MacALLY provides an ADB Y-cable just for this purpose. But folks, please, allow us to take advantage of that extra ADB port way over there on the base of the Apple monitor or on the back of the Mac if we feel like it. How much can an extra couple of feet of cable cost?

Three: No contact or warranty information in the manual or on the box. We hope that MacALLY will be more forthcoming about their whereabouts in the near future. (Hint to MacALLY: Almost everyone has a modem now. Try online support if you don't have enough people to handle the phones.)

Here's the Scoop

The JoyStick is solid, comfortable, and, for a two-button joystick, fairly flexible with the software's multiclick option. And although we have no idea how robust they'll be over time, we like the suction cups a lot. The Batwing falls somewhere between the GamePad and ChoiceStick (reviewed later) as our Nintendo-like controller of choice; there are good options for the buttons, but it's not as cool as ChoiceStick when it comes to mousing around. We really, really, really wish that these things had longer cables and were application-aware, but we imagine these are problems that can be corrected with a few late nights of programming and a more generous cable specification. When these changes are implemented, we'll be happy to change our fair-to-middlin' opinion to two strong thumbs-up.

Pros: Entry-level two-button joystick with a flexible multiclick feature. Cool suction cups. Smooth action.

Cons: Software is not application-aware. ADB cable is too short.

System Requirements: ADB-equipped Macintosh, 600K RAM, hard disk recommended, System 6.08 or higher.

JOYSTICK	
Feel:	3.5
Configurability:	3.5
Value:	3.5
Construction:	3.0
Overall:	3.5

Pros: Multiclick option. Lots of buttons. Mouse/keyboard emulation switch for movement pad.

Cons: Software is not application-aware. ADB cable is too short.

System Requirements: ADB-equipped Macintosh, 600K RAM, hard disk recommended, System 6.08 or higher.

BATWING	
Feel:	3.5
Configurability:	4.0
Value:	4.0
Construction:	3.0
Overall:	3.5

ChoiceStick
Kernel Productions

How's this for a brilliant idea: Forget designing a sturdy joystick or gamepad for the Mac; there are loads of game controllers in the world—why reinvent the wheel? Instead, spend your time creating a little black box that operates as a link between the Mac and the heavy-duty game controllers already available for home entertainment systems. Can we hear a deafening round of applause for this idea, ladies and gentlemen? We said, can you please give it up for the little black box concept?

Like most really good ideas, this one seems so patently obvious that it's surprising no one came up with it until now. But come up with it Kernel Productions did, and once you've seen it implemented, you'll realize what a doozy of an idea it is.

The Box

As we said, the ChoiceStick is not a stick at all, but rather a small black box about the size of two decks of playing cards placed side by side. On one end are a pair of ADB connectors and on the other two 9-pin game controller connectors. As

It may not look like much, but ChoiceStick's little black box may be the answer to your prayers.

should be obvious, you use one of the ADB ports to connect your Mac to the ChoiceStick. The other acts as a pass-through port for connecting your keyboard or mouse. The two 9-pin connectors are for attaching game controllers designed to work with Sega Genesis and Master Systems or the Atari 2600 and 7800. You can buy these controllers separately or pick up one of the ChoiceStick bundles that includes an extremely sturdy six-button Sega style gamepad or joystick.

The Cool Software

The real workhorse of the product is the ChoiceStick software. This control panel and collection of extensions activates the ChoiceStick on startup and keeps track of which application is currently active. As is typical with most game controller software, the ChoiceStick programs are application-aware—when you switch applications, the software reconfigures the controller button assignments for the new program.

The ChoiceStick comes with over 140 preconfigured game setups (and no, we're not talking about just the big commercial hits; someone at Kernel spent a lot of time creating configurations for popular shareware games as well). But if you don't find your favorite game on the list, creating a new set is a snap. Simply start the game, press the ChoiceStick hot key combination, and assign keystrokes or mouse movements to the buttons on your controller. Alternatively, you can create new controller configurations directly from the ChoiceStick control panel.

GREAT FEATURE

This software lets you to do more than simply mimic mouse clicks and keystrokes with your controller. Among other things, you can also assign locking, adjustable, auto repeat functions to the controller buttons (in which case a single press of a button will fire that button at a user-determined rate until you press the button again) and can set how far and with what degree of acceleration a joystick will move the cursor across the screen. Although this kind of configuration sounds daunting, for the most part, setting up the controllers is a breeze. The software is extremely intuitive and easy to use.

What It's Good For

The ChoiceStick's only limitation is the kind of controllers you can attach to it. Although we were able to make perfectly reasonable control sets for our Hornets and A-10s, standard Sega joysticks don't come with ergonomic, button-studded sticks, as do the ThrustMaster and Flightstick Pro controllers (both reviewed later). For this reason alone, we wouldn't use the ChoiceStick as our number-one flight sim controller. But doggone if we don't use the ChoiceStick for everything else—Chris even uses it with Microsoft Word.

Because we won't feel we've done a thorough job if we don't crab about something, we will mention that we'd be happier if the ChoiceStick came with hardcopy documentation. The online documentation is very thorough, but it's about 60 pages long and in DOCMaker format, which does not provide for double-

LOUSY FEATURE

sided printing. We've heard that by the time you read this a paper manual may be included with the ChoiceStick.

ChoiceStick Is Our Choice

We can not stress enough just how wonderful the ChoiceStick is. The concept and design is elegant; the software is intuitive and nicely put together; you can attach kid-proof game controllers that won't break after marathon Marathon sessions; and best of all, the thing works like a charm. We think we've fallen in love.

Pros: Powerful yet easy to use software. Allows you to attach robust game controllers to your Mac. Tons of included game configurations. The best game control device for all games except flight simulations.

Cons: No hard-copy documentation.

System Requirements: ADB-equipped Macintosh, 2MB hard disk space, System 7 or later.

CHOICESTICK	
Feel:	*
Configurability:	4.5
Value:	5.0
Construction:	5.0
Overall:	4.5
* Depends on attached controller.	

Jetstick
CH Products

As input devices become more complexly designed, it'd be nice to have something that harkened back to a simpler time, one when we didn't know what to do with the second button on a joystick and action only occurred in two dimensions. Have no fear; we can all journey back to that simpler era with the Jetstick from CH Products, a joystick that proves that low cost does not have to mean low quality.

Better Than They Used to Make 'Em

The Jetstick is described by CH products as a low-end, novice joystick that offers quality performance at a low price. We were so impressed with this device that it became our joystick of choice for several games despite the fact that we have access to every available stick. The solid construction and feel of the stick harkens back to the ThrustMaster with its molded hand grip. The Jetstick also comes with software for configuring its two buttons. It may sound silly to be flapping our jaws about programming a measly two buttons, but you'd be surprised how handy it can be to have button #2 launch a salvo of constipation pellets at the planet Fiber. And for those gamers who don't want to spend hundreds of dollars on peripherals, the ability to configure buttons becomes a boon of

TRACKBALLS

Many folks with cramped hands (or desks) have found salvation in trackballs, which can be a superior alternative to the click-and-drag workaday world of novelty mousepads and tangled cords. Trackballs can have another purpose in the grand scheme though, one that involves strategic defense, plasma photons, and dive bombers. Indeed, the good ol' trackball certainly does have a place within the realm of computer gaming. After all, many of the coin suckers in shopping malls used the roller as a primary alien zapper. What would Centipede, Missile Command, or even some of the old football games be without the kind of maneuvering only a trackball can deliver?

Contemporary Classics Made for the Ball
We don't have to look very far to find some great games that would be hard to imagine without TB control. Apeiron, Patriot Command, and Arashi are just a few of the fabulous titles crying out for a spinning trackball and a quick trigger finger. And longtime online guru Kent Filmore swears trackballs give him superior control in flight sims.

Eight Ball, Corner Pocket
With the plethora of trackballs on the market, we suggest you shop around and get a feel for one before laying out any cash. We prefer the Kensington TurboMouse and the CH Products TrackBall Pro, both of which have application-aware programmable buttons and variable sensitivity settings.

---

great proportions. The Jetstick software is easy to use and comes in the form of a control panel. It will feel familiar to any regular Mac user.

Big Stick, Small Click

The Jetstick excels as a low-end gaming device. It makes little sound when the buttons are depressed—which will no doubt be greatly appreciated by housemates everywhere—and delivers solid, reliable performance. For anyone who needs a novice input device for the weekend shoot-'em-up, the Jetstick will stick.

Pros: Easy to use. Nice feel. Low price. Buttons configurable. Configured buttons are application-aware.

Cons: For entry-level gaming. (But is this a con?)

System Requirements: Any Mac with ADB port.

JETSTICK

Feel:	3.5
Configurability:	4.0
Value:	3.5
Construction:	4.0
Overall:	3.5

Flightstick Pro
CH Products

The premiere joystick from CH Products wins extra points for being the most peculiar looking piece of plastic on any computer desk. This strangely shaped black grip that some have described as an egg on a joystick initially called forth waves of skepticism within us, but it took only a squeeze of the trigger to realize this was a solid product. Still, one could say that CH Products took a stylistic risk, if not a page from a sci-fi novel, when laying down the blueprints on this baby.

Feelin' Groovy

After putting the Flightstick Pro through its paces, we felt very strongly that it had the best feel of all the sticks. The relative weight, the wide base (which prevents sliding), the form-fitted grip, and the incredibly smooth action all contributed to this conclusion. We can't say enough about the smoothness and solid feel the stick returns to your hand, and it turns out the awkward-looking head of the stick is anything but. There are three buttons and an eight-way hat switch on the oval shape at the head of the stick, and each of these is readily and comfortably accessible to the thumb at a moment's notice. The trigger is set low-profile

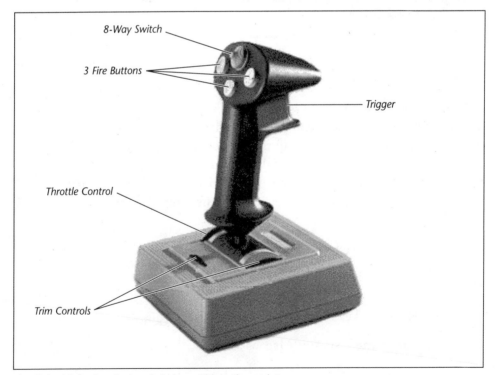

The Flightstick Pro has the best feel of any stick on the market.

and gives a solid response. A throttle wheel for power adjustments rests on the left side of the base. Southpaws will be thrilled to hear that the Flightstick Pro is designed specifically so that either lefties or right-handers can operate it without a hitch. The only catch is the placement of that throttle wheel. But when one considers that many sticks are right handed, this is a minor complaint.

Ready to Run

This stick's name belies the multiple personality it harbors in its fully configurable and application-aware software. Flightstick Pro's software is intuitive, and each of the buttons and the hat switch on the stick can be set to perform any combination of keyboard or mouse commands. However, custom programming of buttons is rarely needed due to the tremendous selection of preconfigured game sets. The Flightstick Pro comes with sets for nearly every Mac game on the market, and new titles are shipping with their own Flightstick sets already embedded in them. The stick can be programmed to run in three separate manners: absolute, keyboard mapping, and relative. Keyboard mapping would be most acceptable for a game like Hornet, in which there's plenty of finger work required on the keyboard. Absolute is essentially the equivalent of a mouse. The relative mode responds to the speed of the stick movement input, and it can allow for movement acceleration.

GREAT FEATURE

All Things to All People

The Flightstick is probably the best all-around stick on the market. It supplies enough extra control to make flight sims better yet still remains flexible enough to be used in a shoot-em-up. The awesomely smooth action provides a comforting resistance that is very easy to adjust to, and the quasi-grotesque shape of the stick soon becomes comfortable. The Flightstick Pro is the best choice for someone who doesn't want to spend the money on a complete ThrustMaster set but wants a hat switch, throttle control, and full configurability.

Pros: Best feel of all the sticks. Incredibly smooth action. Good software. Preset controls for most games. Good construction.

Cons: No auto calibration. Throttle inconveniently located for southpaws.

System Requirements: Any Mac with ADB port.

FLIGHTSTICK PRO	
Feel:	5.0
Configurability:	4.5
Value:	3.5
Construction:	4.0
Overall:	4.5

ThrustMaster Flight, Weapons, and Rudder Control System

ThrustMaster

Mac gamers had reason to rejoice in early 1994 when the ThrustMaster people announced complete Macintosh support for their most coveted group of products, the complete Flight Control System. This equipment is what dreams are made of. Just imagine little Mac boys and girls saying their prayers and trying to be good so that Santa will convince companies like ThrustMaster to support "the computer for the rest of us." And now the dream is a reality. No longer must we have one hand on the key board and the other on a joystick. Nay! We now can enjoy separate joystick and weapon/throttle controls, not to mention heavy-duty rudder pedals that will put callouses on our footsies. Indeed, possessing the ThrustMaster system propels the gamer ever closer to flight sim virtual reality.

Three Are One

The ThrustMaster system consists of three separate pieces. The Flight Control System (FCS) is a copy of the flightstick in an F-4 Phantom fighter. The Weapons Control System (WCS) is like the system found in an F-15. The Rudder Control System (RCS) is simply a heavy-duty set of foot pedals that control the rudder action of the plane. These components are joined together with 15-pin connectors, with the marriage to the Mac made through a standard ADB connection from the FCS to the keyboard. The connector has a pass-through port that enables other ADB devices, such as a mouse or trackball, to be connected with the ThrustMaster system. The system also comes with configuration software that lets each button or rudder motion be programmed to do anything you want.

ThrustMaster Flight Control System

The only piece of the trio that can be used solo is the FCS. This form-fitting piece of molded hard plastic is the starting point and centerpiece of the complete system. The FCS is essentially a joystick, but with some decidedly special features, among them an eight-way hat switch for the thumb and four buttons, including the trigger, along its shaft. Each of these buttons conforms exquisitely to one of your fingers. There are three positions, including the hat switch, for your thumb. The hat is usually used for changing the viewing perspective of the pilot; it enables you to "look" around the cockpit without ever removing your

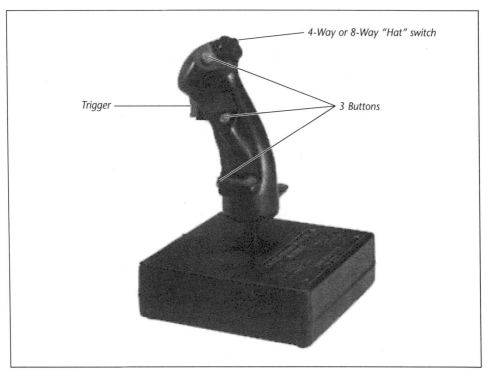

The ThrustMaster control system is a must for hard-core flight sim fans.

hand from the stick. Quite simply, there's nothing like this system, and once you've used it for piloting Hornet or Hellcats, they'll probably have to drag you kicking and screaming to set you back to a two-button joystick.

ThrustMaster Weapons Control System

The second piece of the ThrustMaster puzzle is fitted for the left hand and is usually used for weapons control and throttle operations. The stick is only able to move forward and back (like a throttle), but it provides a beautiful silky-smooth response while conforming to the natural shape of the hand. The WCS is equipped with six buttons laid out between where the thumb and fingers rest, and there is a three-way rocker switch for the shaft of the thumb that is used for modifying the other six buttons. With the rocker switch as a modifier, there's a grand total of 18 buttons at your disposal on the WCS. When used in combination with the FCS, there is very little reason you'd ever to need take your hands off the controls to complete an entire mission.

ThrustMaster Rudder Control System

The ultimate flight simulator system cannot be considered complete until a set of rudder pedals sits under the desk. These actually serve only one purpose: to let you manage the rudders of the aircraft without taking your hands off the controls. Rudders are important for aiming and can allow for tighter turning, which can be of critical importance when staring down a Frank in Leyte Gulf. Of course, the rudders can be programmed for other actions, but unless you find it easier to accomplish tasks with your feet than your hands, it's probably best not to. The RCS is constructed of a very sturdy (and heavy) combination of plastic and metal that will stand up to almost any abuse your feet can throw at it. If you do get the RCS, you'll really have to put your foot down to keep yourself from playing flight sims 24 hours a day.

Software

If we have any gripes at all with the ThrustMaster system, it lies in the software. Although it is incredibly powerful and allows for programming of any function into the controls, it could be a little more intuitive. This is a minor complaint, however, as most games come complete with ThrustMaster's settings (sometimes several of them) that completely circumvent the need for programming the controls. Perhaps the strongest feature of the software is its ability to be application-aware and load the appropriate set of controls for whatever game currently occupies the RAM.

The Price of Paradise

We found the construction and reliability of the ThrustMaster equipment to be very good, and we've never heard any complaints other than minor grumbling about the weight of the FCS and WCS. ThrustMaster also updates their software and game sets from time to time, but the basic software comes complete with a large list of preset settings for most of the popular games. Perhaps the biggest hurdle to using the complete ThrustMaster set lies in the cost of its components. As we write this, the complete ThrustMaster set runs around $300, but for those who want just the great feel of the F-16 stick on the FCS, they can take the plunge for about a third of that.

Serious Hardware for Serious Gaming

The ThrustMaster system really shines when used with the breed of game it was designed for—flight sims. However, there are uses for it in almost any game, and its many programmable buttons have changed forever the way we look at gaming input devices. The flight experience is unquestionably heightened with this system, and we recommend it for anyone, but it should be considered essential for those whose gaming passion lies in flight simulator games.

Pros: Sturdy. Very realistic. Great feel. Programmable Software.

Cons: Software could be more intuitive. Pieces could be heavier.

System Requirements: Mac with ADB port, System 7.

THRUSTMASTER SYSTEMS	
Feel:	4.5
Configurability:	4.5
Value:	3.5
Construction:	4.0
Overall:	4.5

Other Add-Ons

Haven't spent enough money yet? Read on.

DOS Compatibility Card

Apple Computer

It's no secret. There are a jillion times more games for PCs than there are for Macs. It's also no secret that compared to Macintosh games, the graphics and sound of these PC products is decidedly inferior. But you needn't take our word for it. If you have a Power Macintosh 6100 or Performa 6100, you can find out for yourself with what may be the ultimate hardware add-on, the DOS Compatibility Card (DCC).

Yes, Mac users can now find out for themselves what all the PC hubbub is about without actually having to suffer the humiliation of placing DOS boxes on their desks. The DCC, a circuit board containing an Intel 486 DX2/66 processor, is safely tucked away in the 6100's Processor Direct Slot. No one need ever know that you have a PC in your Mac.

Memories Are Made of This

The DCC carries a single 72-pin SIMM socket for installing up to 32 MB of RAM. As originally configured, the card contains no RAM of its own and must share the Mac's RAM. The card only recognizes physical RAM, and therefore Virtual Memory and RAM Doubler cannot be used with shared memory (although you can use these schemes if the DCC is using its own RAM). Once you've assigned a block of RAM to the card, that RAM can no longer be used by the Mac.

POWERBOOK GAMING

Chris hasn't changed his tune since his admonition in the 5th edition of the *Macintosh Bible* that the perfect PowerBook game should be lean and mean. As you may recall, he stated:

• no 256-color requirements

• no look-in-the-manual copy protection

• no CD-ROM required

• no games that require more than a couple of megabytes of RAM or hard disk space.

That covers the software. But perhaps a more important question is, what should you look for in a PowerBook intended for heavy game abuse? Glad you asked.

Plenty of Oomph
As we remarked earlier, games push your computer's processor to its limits. Therefore, a PowerBook that you intend to use for serious gaming will have a processor with plenty of get-up-and-go. A 68040 or PowerPC-based PowerBook is necessary for games such as flight simulators and first-person-perspective shoot-'em-ups that demand peak performance. 68030 PowerBooks are fine for brain games and arcade diversions, but they just can't hack it on the studlier stuff.

An ADB Port
The trackball and trackpad are not precision instruments; they make lousy game controllers. Before you buy, look for that all-important ADB port on the back of the Power-Book (nope, you won't find it on the bargain-basement PowerBook 150). Along with extra batteries and the external power supply, every PowerBook gamer should carry a

If you intend to play games with this card (and honestly, what other reason could you possibly have for owning it?) it's a good idea to give the card its own RAM. This speeds things up significantly and makes your Mac operating environment more manageable. For reasonable performance, you should install at least 8 MB of RAM—16 MB if you can afford it.

Highlights

In what we perceive to be a mixed blessing, the card behaves just like a PC. If you're running DOS, there's the ugly command line interface. If you have Windows installed, say howdy to the Mac's bastard cousin. Software installation is just as confusing and awkward as it is on the real thing, and just like PC users, you'll have an opportunity to spend hours and hours configuring the software.

gamepad controller. But be warned: some game controllers demand more power from the ADB port than can be consistently delivered under battery power. Use the controller only when the PowerBook is plugged into a power outlet.

Screen Resolution of 640 x 480
Certain games will not work in resolutions less than this.

A Modem
Well how else are you going to link up to your favorite online gaming service or download the latest DOOM II cheater?

An Active-Matrix Color Screen, a Huge Hard Disk, and Loads of RAM
We understand that if you're serious about PowerBook gaming, you'll ignore our software rules and try to jam the latest full-color, RAM-hogging shoot-'em-up on your machine. But unless you own the high-priced spread, you'll be sorely disappointed by the performance of these games.

Of course, it's difficult to justify spending several thousand dollars on a portable game machine. But let's face it, most of the work that people do on the road—word processing, contact management, telecommunications—can be easily handled by the puniest of processors and in black and white. People don't buy high-end PowerBooks because they need them. People buy them because they're cool.

So forget about what other people think. Buying a tricked-out PowerBook to play Hornet on transcontinental flights is no less honorable than picking one up to impress trade show sales reps.

The card comes with a SoundBlaster chip set that plays via the Mac's internal speaker and sound output port. For the few DOS games we tried with the card, the SoundBlaster worked flawlessly. A connector for plugging a PC-style joystick into the card is also supplied. DOS and Windows are included.

Lowlights

The key word in the name DOS Compatibility Card is "compatibility." Yes, with the DCC installed you could slap an "Intel Inside" sticker on the outside of your Mac, but it wouldn't really be a PC through and through.

DANGER

For example, the card doesn't recognize non-Apple CD-ROM drives. The reason is that the DCC doesn't employ standard PC SCSI drivers but instead uses its own sorta-kinda SCSI driver emulator designed exclusively for Apple CD-ROM drives. Unless third-party CD-ROM drive vendors come up with their own sorta-kinda driver emulators, you'll have to stick with the Apple brand. Apple's imitative driver also prevents you from using both an internal and external CD-ROM drive.

The other major problem with the card has nothing to do with the card itself or with Apple. The other major problem is DOS.

RANT

If you've never worked with this demonic operating system before, you'll soon begin to appreciate why Windows users are so grateful for their second-rate graphic interface. For those of us who grew up on the Macintosh, installing and working with DOS is a nightmare, plain and simple. If you can avoid installing DOS and Windows yourself by getting the DCC preinstalled on your 6100, do so.

But Is It PC?

We checked out the board with a few of the most popular and processor-intensive games for the PC and found that they ran quite nicely. Of course we found—as we expect you will—that we spent far too much time mucking with the config.sys file (don't ask) to get to that point. But from what we understand, this is all part of the requisite DOS hazing and you shouldn't take it personally.

The DCC costs around $700 without RAM. Figure another $350 for an 8MB SIMM. While $1,050 may seem like a good price for a fully operational PC, keep in mind that although Apple has made Macs more competitively priced in the last few years, you can still buy a comparable PC for less money than a Mac. For a little more than that same $1,050, you can buy a real PC system with monitor and CD-ROM drive.

Is It Worth It?

Right now this question is a little tough to answer. By the time you read this, the next generation of PCI Power Macintoshes will be available and the DCC may be slated for Apple's old-and-in-the-way list. At just over a thousand bucks for an operational system, we think the DCC is a little pricey. We hope that by the time this book sees print the DCC will be cheaper or there will be a less expensive and more powerful alternative for the latest Macs. We like the PC-on-a-card concept and hope that the DCC is not just an aberration. As much as we hate to admit it, playing PC games on a Mac is a gas.

Pros: You can play all those PC games you missed over the years.

Cons: Works only with the Mac 6100s. Optimal system is expensive. DOS.

System Requirements: Power Macintosh or Performa 6100.

Speakers

Okay, you've bought the fastest Mac you can afford; you've installed megabyte upon megabyte of RAM; your monitor is big enough to put the projection TV down at Joe's Bar to shame; you've plugged in the latest 6X CD-ROM player; and you have every joystick and rudder pedal known to man. Are you finally ready for a little serious fun?

Not yet. You're missing the one item that guarantees aural gratification: external speakers.

What's the point of having the latest and greatest shoot-'em-up when it sounds like you're blasting those beetle-headed creeps with a pop gun? The sad but true fact is that the Mac's internal speaker is incapable of producing the kind of sound necessary for a Satisfying Gaming Experience. For the true SGE, you need a decent pair of personal stereo speakers—with a subwoofer if you can dig up the dough. Here's what to look for when you go shopping:

Great Sound

Well, *duh!* you're probably saying. But here's the thing: No matter how many bells and whistles a speaker system may have, if it sounds terrible, what's the point? Sound quality should be the paramount consideration. Listen to a lot of speakers before you buy. And check the specs if you can find them. Home stereo speakers have a range from around 20 to 20,000 Hz. The closer you get to this range, the happier you'll be.

Shielding

Shielding keeps the magnets in the speakers from causing your monitor to appear as if it's ingested a psychedelic substance. All speakers intended for computer use are shielded.

Balance and Tone Controls

Personal computer speakers usually feature execrable bass response. Using separate bass and treble controls can improve the sound enormously.

A Headphone Jack on the Front of the Speaker

How many times have you found yourself playing games late into the night? You may be having a blast, but your family and neighbors probably don't appreciate hearing alien cries of anguish at two in the morning. For the sake of politeness, you'll want to use headphones, and you'll want them to be easy to plug in.

An Extra Input Jack

One for your Mac and one for an external source, such as a CD player.

3

Branching Out

Computer gaming no longer means sitting alone in a dark-ened room, facing unfeeling digital opponents. Now, thanks to networking and online services, games have once again become a social pastime.

CHAPTER 15: Network Games

CHAPTER 16: Online Gaming

15 | Network Games

For years, computer gaming was a solitary practice. The few games that allowed for two-player input were limited to action games that forced players to share the cramped confines of a common keyboard. Because experienced gamers understood that playing a computer game against a living, breathing opponent was the ultimate challenge, they grudgingly suffered this inconvenience.

But a vastly superior alternative emerged: networking. No, we don't mean attending cocktail parties with industry leaders. Networking is a way of connecting two or more computers at remote locations in order to share information in real time. As you can imagine, this technological breakthrough had an astounding effect on computer gamers. Instead of flying computer-generated missions with silicon opponents, players could now vaporize that rat-in-human-form over in the accounting department. Computer gaming had become personal in a way that had been impossible with even the best programs.

Recently DOS and Windows software companies have been looking into networking their games. But PCs don't have the built-in networking Apple's machines have always enjoyed. In fact, PC gamers consider 1991 to be the dawn of the genre as this was when networks for PCs began to be priced within reach of the average user. Not surprisingly, they ignore the fact that Mac users were gaming on networks five full years before that.

Apple pioneered this technology with the introduction of AppleTalk in 1986. Soon all Macs had this tool, and head-to-head network games began to sprout up in both the commercial and shareware realms. The first such product was Maze Wars Plus, a 1986 network game that was years ahead of its time. It allowed for play over AppleTalk or modem connection at 1200 or—hold on to your hat— even 2400 baud! But the astounding part of the MW+ story lies in the fact that the networking actually worked, and worked well—a claim few games of the time could make. The shareware arena had its very own hot network game called Nettrek, which can be found floating about in cyberspace to this day (although few contemporary Macs will run this interplanetary starship shoot-em-up).

Meet the Future, Face to Face

Increasingly, Mac game titles are including some sort of network play—be it through a serial cable, a modem, or AppleTalk. Modern games such as Chuck Yeager's Air Combat and Marathon, which are terrific single-player games, include networking elements that add a wonderful depth and dimension to the games.

It isn't difficult to imagine games of the future that will allow two players at remote locations to work together in a 3D world solving virtual murders or going 12 rounds in an online Madison Square Garden. With the introduction of cross-platform capabilities and ever-faster computers, the future looks bright indeed.

Minotaur (The Labyrinths of Crete)

Bungie Software

Bungie Software launched into the Mac games market with Minotaur (The Labyrinths of Crete), a complicated yet easy to play network game that combined elements of classic network games like Nettrek with the fantasy intrigue of dungeons and dragons. While not producing the first-person-perspective thrill of their second title, Pathways into Darkness, Minotaur proves to be one of the most endearing and replayable network games available. It also stands alone in the network arena as the only commercial game that must be played with other flesh-and-blood opponents as it contains no real single-player mode. Bungie partially circumvents this by shipping Minotaur in a two-pack that

GREAT FEATURE

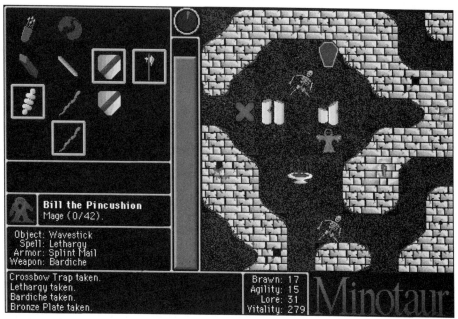

Bungie Software's Minotaur supplies one of the best network gaming experiences, but it does not offer a computer opponent.

comes complete with two disks (necessary for network play), documentation, and quick-reference cards for two.

Hack, Slash, and Zap!

The object of Minotaur is to vanquish all characters in a maze through the use of spells, potions, magic items, armor, and weapons. First you must create a character (you have 60 points to divide between brawn, agility, and lore) and begin the game with nothing but the clothes on your back. Then you must wander about the maze and collect all the items possible before meeting up with another person. Getting a decent weapon and armor should be a priority. But not to worry; there are more than 65 different items and weapons to be found scattered about the maze. These items are classified into four groups—Items, Spells, Armor, and Weapons—and a healthy number of each kind will go a long way in battle. The only other living creatures in the maze (other than people) are the Stalkers. These are spiderlike creatures that can't be destroyed but that will inflict considerable damage to those they come in contact with. There's a time limit on the game, and if no clear winner is decided before the clock runs down, it's Armageddon time, and we can assure you that this is nothing like Miller time. Armageddon places all the surviving characters in a small room with no way to get out except to kill or be killed.

2D or Not 2D

Minotaur is played from an overhead view, and only a fraction of the maze can be seen at any one time. Your character is always in the center of the screen and as he/she moves about, the maze moves accordingly. This passé 2D environment is actually wonderfully suited to this game, and it is supported by cool art and rich, full color. Controlling your character can only be achieved with keyboard commands; we recommend you keep the quick- reference card close at hand until you get the hang of the interface. Minotaur can have up to seven players competing in one maze over a network. But don't worry if you only have six computers in your network; a seventh person can dial in remotely and connect to the group via modem. All aspects of the network operations work flawlessly and easily.

A Minor Annoyance

Overall, Minotaur nicely fills a niche in the Mac gaming world by offering a true network experience at a reasonable price. The only drawback is the inability to enjoy the game when playing alone, which is due to the lack of a real computer opponent. However, this is a minor annoyance, and Minotaur's ultra compelling multiplayer action will keep it on networks for years to come.

TIP

Tips

• Do you really want to invoke the Stave of Ultimate Doom?

• Use the feather of levitation to pass over walls when gathering items.

Pros: It's easy to learn the interface. The game is easy to play yet complex. Flawless modem and network support.

Cons: Isn't really playable as a one-player game. Movement of characters is a tad clunky.

System Requirements: Mac Plus or better, 1MB RAM for black and white, 2MB RAM for color, 900K hard disk space, System 6.05 or higher.

MINOTAUR	
Fun factor:	4.0
Look and feel:	3.5
Value:	3.5
Replayability:	4.0
Overall:	4.0

Spectre
Activision

Spectre Supreme
Spectre VR
Velocity

In the early 90s, previously speedy office networks suddenly slowed to a crawl. Network administrators across the land plied through their servers and drives in a vain attempt to discover the problem. Was it some nefarious virus? An errant control panel?

Hardly. It was the networkable cybertank game Spectre. This game was so popular and so devastating to network speed that playing it on office networks during business hours was allegedly banned in companies across the nation.

Three Generations

Since 1991, there have been three renditions of the game: the original Spectre, Spectre Supreme, and Spectre VR. Each of these games is networkable. They vary in a number of ways, among them: the quality of the graphics; the variety of weapons and enemies; the number of network scenarios; and the inclusion of QuickTime movies in Spectre VR. You can not network different versions of the game.

Each game places you at the controls of a futuristic tank, a Spectre. When you are playing in nonnetworked mode, your mission is to scurry around a large gridded matrix collecting flags. To grab the flags, simply drive over them. Each level is complete when all its flags are cleared.

Admittedly, this process would soon become tiresome were it not for the game's inclusion of a large contingent of nasties whose sole desire is to chase you about the matrix and mash your precious tank through various malicious means.

These enemies are comprised of fairly-harmless-when-not-arrayed-in-packs Rovers and heavily shielded Warrior robots. In the later versions of the game, you also do battle with Radar and Optically Cloaked Robots, chain saw-like Slicers, Smart Acid Pools, and flying Hunter Killers.

To beat back this aggressive hardware, your tank is equipped with a cannon and, in later levels, grenades. Spectre Supreme and VR add Smart Missiles, Seekers, Scattershot, and Proximity Mines to their arsenals. Although you carry no defensive weaponry, your tank is outfitted with shields that allow it to take a

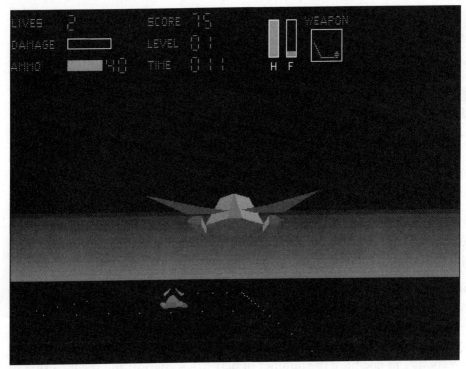

Spectre VR's flying tank floats above the hostile matrix.

certain amount of punishment before it is completely vaporized. You replenish supplies of ammunition and shields by driving over the Ammo Dumps scattered over the matrix.

Along with the Ammo Dumps, the matrix contains other treats. You will find Invulnerability Shields that protect your tank from cannon shots aimed from the front. Additional shields are added to the sides and back of the tank as you roll over more orange squares. New to Spectre VR, the Anti Grav Packs (appearing as light blue squares) briefly bestow the power of flight to your Spectre. Flight is especially handy on those levels on which the matrix contains Flow Fields and Force Fields. As long as your Spectre is earthbound, the arrow-shaped Flow Fields force it to travel in the direction they point. Force Fields are lines over which your Spectre cannot flow. A winged Spectre easily floats over these fields.

In addition to travel on and above the matrix, you can zip from one location to another by engaging Hyperspace. Launching into Hyperspace is equivalent to hitting the panic button: You're surrounded by baddies and are taking a horrible licking; you need to go somewhere—anywhere—that is less hostile. Hyperspace zips you away from your present position and plops you down randomly in another spot.

Spectre Supreme and VR add paired Transporters, which lack this random element and move you quickly from one Transporter to the other as you drive through them. Additionally, you can journey beneath the surface by entering a Submergence device. This is a dark blue portal that sends your tank to the relative safety—Slicers are still just as nasty below as above—of Spectre's underground. To return to the level playing field, you must locate and employ an Emergence device.

Jacked In

Although the Spectres are great single-player action shoot-'em-ups, they really shine as network games. In multiplayer mode, you can play with up to eight others over an AppleTalk network. Each player must own a copy of Spectre, complete with unique serial number. The games include a number of multiplayer scenarios that run the gamut from the cooperative Base Raid, in which two teams attempt to capture each other's flag, to the anarchistic Arena, in which your goal is to blast everyone in sight. Spectre Supreme adds such scenarios as Cyber Soccer and Bumper Tanks. VR includes flight-based enhancements for many of the network games found in Spectre Supreme.

VR the Vorld

Every version of Spectre, from the original to the current VR, has allowed you to customize your tank's capabilities to a limited extent: you are provided with 15 points to be distributed to speed, shields, and ammo. But until the inclusion of John Lindal's VRchitect, there was no way to tinker with other aspects of the game. VRchitect has changed all that. Although customization options for your tank are still limited to the 15-point system, virtually every other part of the game—difficulty, number of levels, colors, music, availability of weapons, placement of obstacles, lethalness of enemies—is editable. This is a wonderfully powerful tool. Our only niggling complaint is that you are not allowed to create a matrix from scratch; you must load a preexisting matrix.

GREAT FEATURE

In Spectre VR, the additions of flight, QuickTime movies, and more-complex shapes take their toll on game speed. Whereas Spectre Supreme rolled smoothly on a 68030, VR tends to jerk and become unresponsive when the enhancements are turned on. To effectively run Spectre VR, you need an 040 Mac.

SETTING UP A NETWORK AT HOME

If you're networked at your place of business and the boss isn't too watchful, you're in fat city—you can play network games until your eyes fall out.

But what about the home user? The Macintosh has been around long enough that people are purchasing their second or third computers. When it's time to trade up, rather than dumping your machine via the classifieds, you might want to think about turning your old hardware into one of the ultimate gaming accessories—a networked Mac.

Here's how to set up a friendly little LocalTalk network in your home sweet home:

• Pick up some PhoneNet connectors either through mail order or at your local computer shop. If you plan to connect two Macs and a printer, buy a less expensive three-pack. A brand name three pack can be had for under $60.

• Plug the connectors into the printer port of each Mac and the serial port of the printer. Chain them together this way: The first connector is terminated (jam the little plastic doohickey into the other hole) and goes into Mac #1's printer port, the second connector goes into your printer's serial port, and the third connector goes into Mac #2's printer port, again with the terminator in place (PhoneNet connectors should be terminated at each end of the chain). Link the cables from Mac #1 to the printer, and then the printer to Mac #2.

• If you're still wallowing around in System 6, join the rest of the world and buy a copy of System 7. That's where all the cool networking goodies reside.

The following instructions apply to both Macs and will leave your Macintosh wide open for snooping. If you want a more secure machine, consult the system software manual or Apple Guide.

• Open the chooser and turn on AppleShare.

• Open the Sharing Setup control panel and enter a user name, a password (this is optional), and a name for the Mac.

• Click the Start button under File Sharing and close the Sharing Setup control panel.

• Open the Users & Groups control panel to find two icons—one with your name and another labeled <Guest>.

• Double-click the icon with your name and check all three boxes under File Sharing. If you wish to maintain a separate identity on the different machines, choose New User from the File menu and give yourself a name different from the one on your companion Mac. For example: King Godhead of Gaming for Mac #1 and Mister Fuh Fuh on Mac #2.

• Jump back to the Finder, highlight the folders or disks you want to share, and select Sharing from the File menu. When the dialog box appears, check every box you see.

You're nearly there!

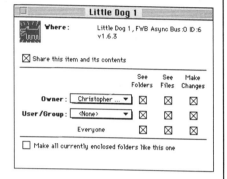

• Now, open the Chooser, select the Apple-Share icon, and double-click on the name of the Mac you want to share. Up pops a dialog box asking for your name and password. Type in the name the other Mac expects to see and, if you required a password, type it in exactly as you entered it in the Sharing Setup control panel (the password is case-sensitive). In the future, if you want to connect automatically on startup, check the Save My Name and Password box.

• Close the Chooser and you're done.

Supremely Missed

Unfortunately, you can no longer purchase Spectre Supreme. The original Spectre is available in Activision's MacBestsellers bundle, and VR is, of course, still being sold by Velocity. But Spectre Supreme carried the best feature/performance balance of the lot. The original is darned speedy but lacks the cool new weapons and enemies of Supreme and VR. And VR, although full of new enhancements, doesn't run smoothly on anything but the fastest 040s (at the time of this writing there is no native version of Spectre for Power Macs). Even if you turn off all of VR's enhancements, it still runs less smoothly than Supreme.

One other regret: Spectre does not dumb down to operate only as fast as the least powerful Mac on the network. *Huh?* This means that if you are running a IIci and your opponent is behind the wheel of a Quadra 750, you will not be able to fire or maneuver as quickly as your buddy. So here's a hint: If you have the chance, dash into the boss's office and use the high-powered hardware.

TIP

Despite these drawbacks, the Spectres still offer some of the best fun you can have on a network. If you're looking for fast, furious, and not-too-frilly action, pick up Spectre in the MacBestsellers bundle (hey, you'll get the wonderful Hell-cats Over the Pacific and Super Tetris thrown in). And although we think that Spectre Supreme is still the supreme Spectre, Spectre VR is a terrific game if your hardware is up to the challenge.

Tips

• Type God in any of the Spectres to get an otherwise unavailable overview of the playing field.

• In Spectre Supreme or VR, shooting a spinner through a transporter and then driving through it will immediately move you up five levels.

TIP

Pros: Simple controls. Fast action. Variety of network games. Great single-player game as well. VRchitect allows you to customize Spectre VR games.

Cons: Spectre VR is slow on less-than-speedy Macs. No more Spectre Supreme.

System Requirements: As fast a Mac as you can find, 1.4MB RAM for Spectre, 6MB RAM for Spectre VR under System 7, 700K hard disk space for Spectre, 6MB hard disk space for Spectre VR.

SPECTRE SPECTRE SUPREME SPECTRE VR	
Fun factor:	4.5
Look and feel:	4.0
Value:	4.0
Replayability:	4.0
Overall:	4.0

CD

Super Maze Wars

Callisto

Following in the venerable shoes of Maze Wars+, Super Maze Wars zips you into head-to-head combat with up to eight computer or human opponents. The action can best be described as Spectre in a maze. You'll be doing the locomotion in an armored MazeCruiser while cohabiting with other battle-hardened maze dwellers who want nothing more than to vaporize you with a ButtKicker™ missile. The objectives of the six preset scenarios range from survive-if-you-can to get-the-gold-and-kill-your-buddies-along-the-way, making for a reasonable amount of variation in gameplay. You can also adjust the requirements for victory and the number of computer and human opponents. And there are seven separate mazes to use as the battle field. Of course, Super Maze Wars can be

NETWORKED MACINTOSH GAMES

Game	Company	Network Options	Number of Players	Messaging	Individual Copies
Links Pro	Access	AppleTalk, ARA	8	Chat	Yes
Minotaur	Bungie Software	AppleTalk, null modem	7*	Chat	Yes
Marathon	Bungie Software	AppleTalk, ARA	8	Audio via Mic	2 Installs Per Copy
Super Maze Wars	Callisto	AppleTalk	8	No	Yes
Pararena	Casady & Greene	AppleTalk	2	No	2 Installs Per Copy
Spaceward Ho!	Delta Tao	AppleTalk	20	Preset/Chat	No
Strategic Conquest	Delta Tao	AppleTalk	2	No	No
Oxyd	Dongleware	AppleTalk, modem-modem, null modem	2	Chat	Yes
Power Poker	Electronic Arts	AppleTalk, ARA	10	Chat	No
Chuck Yeager's Air Combat	Electronic Arts	AppleTalk, null modem	2	Pre-Game	Yes
Onslaught	Frontal Assaultware	AppleTalk	2	No	Yes
F/A-18 Hornet	Graphic Simulations	AppleTalk, ARA	4	Pre-Game	Yes
Checkmate	MacPlay	Modem-modem, null modem	2	Chat	Yes
Battle Chess	MacPlay	Modem-modem, null modem	2	No	Yes
Robosport	Maxis	AppleTalk, modem-modem, null modem	4	No	No
Empire Deluxe	New World Computing	AppleTalk, modem-modem, null modem	6*	Chat	Yes
WordTris	Spectrum HoloByte	AppleTalk, null modem	2	No	Yes
Super Tetris	Spectrum HoloByte	AppleTalk, null modem	2	No	Yes
Falcon MC	Spectrum HoloByte	AppleTalk, modem-modem, null modem	2	Chat	Yes
Spectre Supreme/VR	Velocity	AppleTalk	8	Pre-Game/Preset	Yes
Spectre	Velocity	AppleTalk	6	No	Yes

* Among the players, one can be connected via modem.

Network Games Key

AppleTalk: We use AppleTalk to denote both LocalTalk and Ethernet networks. Ethernet is quite a bit faster than a LocalTalk network, but it also requires more expensive hardware.

ARA: (Apple Remote Access) This is a commercial product sold by Apple that allows you to access a remote Macintosh over phone lines.

Modem-modem: This is a non-ARA modem connection. The player who initiates the call enters the remote Macintosh's number into a Dialing dialog box. The player who receives the call sets the game to Auto-answer.

Null modem: Two Macs are connected together with an ImageWriter cable via the modem or printer port of each Mac.

Messaging

Pre-Game: You can send typed messages prior to playing the game. This is used primarily so that players can agree on the different game options.

Preset: The game includes prewritten messages that you can send to other players.

Chat: You can swap typed messages across the network at any time during the game.

Audio via mic: With a microphone hooked up to your Mac, you can scream curses at your opponents over the net.

Individual Copies

To work across a network, most games require a unique serial number for each player's copy of the game. Marathon and Pararena allow two people to play the networked version of the game with a single copy. The copy that is designated as the network version cannot be played in single-player mode.

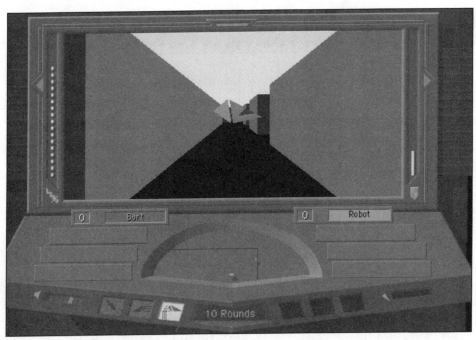

An enemy MazeCruiser makes a run for it in Super Maze Wars, a multiplayer bonanza.

played against the computer, but the real fun comes when you're facing off against your friends in a nail-biting shoot out.

One Step at a Time

GREAT FEATURE

The visuals are crisp, clear, and colorful if not outstanding. And while the motion of the craft is smooth, it maneuvers only in segments; if you move it forward, it's going to move forward one space, no more, no less. It's kind of like playing on a giant snap-to grid, which may frustrate those gamers accustomed to inching along walls while creeping up on distracted opponents. However, this is a small annoyance and is of no consequence when moving rapidly through a maze. The network play is fantastic, leaving no trace of degradation in speed or responsiveness, even if there are six people cruising the network. The controls can be fully configured with minimal effort, and the display is highly ergonomic, with a 180-degree radar smack in the center of the screen for tracking friend and foe alike. Connecting over AppleTalk is also a breeze, and we found ourselves settling into the various scenarios without even so much as cursing the network or smashing equipment in frustration (well okay, Bart did smash the equipment a little).

A-maze-ing

Super Maze Wars is what a networking game should be, and although it's well-endowed with graphics and sound, these are not exactly cutting edge and were probably scaled down to ensure acceptable frame rates on slower machines. If you love the human component and enjoy first-person-perspective maze games, this is for you.

Pros: Great network play. Smooth graphics. Allows up to six opponents.

Cons: Movement of MazeCruiser can be annoying.

System Requirements: Any Mac with 256 colors, 2MB RAM, 4MB RAM for system 7, 704K hard disk space, System 6.07 or higher.

SUPER MAZE WARS	
Fun factor:	3.5
Look and feel:	3.0
Value:	3.0
Replayability:	3.0
Overall:	3.5

Full Metal Mac
SoftWars

If you've ever played the Avalon Hill classic Squad Leader, you're aware that games involving squad-level combat tend to have extremely complicated rule sets involving everything from morale to whether the squad commander shaved with a blade that morning. This may be why we haven't seen a squad-level combat game on the Mac before Full Metal Mac. This is an aging title, and by the time you read this, new titles like Beyond Squad Leader from Avalon Hill and Atomic Games will be on the shelves pushing war gamers, as well as CPUs, to their limits. However, if you love this kind of game but can't afford elitist hardware, you may want to consider Full Metal Mac as a simple yet enjoyable simulator that really shines in head-to-head network action.

Simple Yet Complex

The object of Full Metal Mac is to lead a squad of 10 to 20 men in an attempt to capture the enemy's flag, which lies somewhere in the ruins of a war-weary hamlet. Your squad is equipped with M-16 rifles, fragmentation grenades, smoke grenades, and numerous other goodies designed specifically for this kind of street-to-street fighting. The dispersal of men and supplies must be handled carefully, and you'd better hope your radio operator can make the connection to call in the crucial mortar fire on the enemy line. You maneuver each soldier in your squad foot by foot (*Or in Bart's case, as a courtesy to his Canadianism, meter by meter—J.*) toward the enemy objective, knowing that with every step a sniper could punch a hole in a chest, or an unwitting combatant could have a leg removed by a land mine. Control is largely mouse work, and most players will find themselves doing the old click and drag to move soldiers, although keyboard equivalents are available.

All of the elements are here: learnable game play, simple interface, and tense strategy. Despite this, it seemed to us that FMM fell flat on its shell casings when played against the computer. The AI is just too good; it allows no mistakes, ever. In fact, if we didn't know better, we'd say the computer stacks its side with extra weapons, or is getting some extra intelligence. A novice playing a few rounds against the computer would be likely to fall into the deep ugly pit of frustration and despair, and the FMM disks might get placed in storage beside the old Apple II software. But we found that it's the human component that makes this game worthwhile, and that's why we placed FMM with the network games in this chapter rather then with the war games.

Graphics? What Graphics?

If you're starting to think that this is an awesome state-of-the-art game, we'd better back up and take a look at the graphics. Frankly, they stink. They look cold, plain, and primitive, as if they'd come straight out of 1978. It almost makes you want to get out the old leisure suit and spin up some Barry Gibb (well, not really). To get a small sample of the bland taste these visuals can leave in the mouth, you need look no further then the squad members' icons, which are small circles. Whoa! Doom II move over! Now many will argue that flashy graphics are only skin-deep decorative devices and that the true measure of a great game is in its belly. In part, we agree. And that's why we still consider FMM to be worthy of booting up on a rainy afternoon for some head-to-head action.

In hundreds of games played with everything from a PowerBook 100 to an LC 475, Full Metal Mac never failed to connect and run smoothly with minimal networking headaches. For those who love flashy graphics and sound, the uninspiring visuals of FMM may suck the life right out of you. But if you can overcome the inadequacies and find a human opponent, it has some intangibles that make it a truly enjoyable game.

Pros: Flawless network play. Head-to-head play is surprisingly fun.

Cons: Terrible graphics. Very difficult computer opponent.

System Requirements: Mac Plus or better, 2MB RAM, 599K hard disk space, System 6.05 or higher.

FULL METAL MAC	
Fun factor:	3.0
Look and feel:	2.0
Value:	3.0
Replayability:	3.0
Overall:	3.0

Bolo 0.99.6
Stuart Cheshire

Bolo is a graphical, networked, real-time, multiplayer tank battle game. Although it has elements of shoot-'em-up action, when played with groups of 12 to 16 people for hours on end, it tends to become a game of strategy. According to Mr. Cheshire, "You have to play it to understand." This pretty much sums it up for one of the most successful network games ever to grace a computer screen. Developed in 1987, Bolo was a pioneering shareware title that incorporated full multiplayer networking on a grand scale. Still playable on almost every Mac, and with new versions hitting the Net at regular intervals, Bolo will no doubt continue to reign as King of the shareware network games for years to come.

Bolololololo

The basic theme of Bolo is conquest, but this involves many details, ranging from the harvesting of resources to the building of such infrastructure components as roadways and walls. You are a tank that roams around a two-dimensional overhead map composed of trees, water, rubble, walls, swamps, and roads. The two most critical pieces on the map are pill boxes and bases, the former of which will launch a formidable salvo of gunfire at any foreign tank that wanders too close for comfort. The battles for control of these items can become

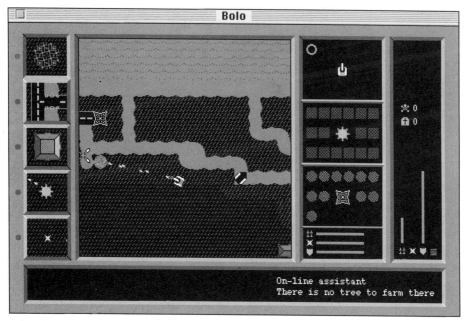

Bolo is the granddaddy of shareware network games, and commands a large worldwide following.

extremely bloody, and the strategic complexity of an offensive can rival that of dedicated war games. In fact, multiplayer games with more then 10 players usually result in teams spending many hours locked in battles for territory, bases, and pill boxes while they chop down trees for the materials needed to construct defensive positions. The tanks have a finite amount of fuel and ammunition, which can be replenished at bases. But bases are not endless reservoirs of materials and must themselves be tended to. Bolo is a classic example of a game that is very simple to pick up and play, but takes time and energy to become intimate with its nuances. The game includes mines, naval transports, rules for both deep and shallow water, and armor allowances. If you have access to a network and several people to play this game, you'd better get in the habit of setting a timer to prevent losing a job or, worse, a marriage.

Internet and Network Bolo

The most impressive feature of Bolo is its robust performance on almost all Macs and over the various networks it can latch on to. Bolo can be networked via a serial/modem port, AppleTalk network, or over the Internet, all with surprisingly minimal pain and suffering. The opening splash screen prompts you to choose what kind of a connection you wish to engage in, and within a few clicks of the mouse you're up and running. Not to worry for those lonesome souls with one machine though, because there are two single-player modes, including a tutorial, for first-time players. Although AppleTalk Remote Access did work with earlier versions of Bolo, Stuart Cheshire advises us that this will not be the case with future versions. Network play features full messaging and options for forming alliances, as well as the ability to look into the thought patterns of the auto pilot (if you are using it).

Color Bolo

Recent incarnations of Bolo have provided some improvements over early versions, such as better graphics, sound, and color, and some other minor adjustments, including the ability to toggle the gun sight on and off. The menus in Bolo are a plethora of options and even go so far as to include an option for people who suffer from green-red color blindness. Bolo's controls are keyboard-based and are fully configurable. This makes it easy for folks with preset keyboard systems to set things up to their liking.

The King of Shareware Networks

Bolo is the granddaddy of networkable shareware games, and it will no doubt continue to be a popular diversion both in office networks and in cyberspace. The melded themes of conquest and cooperation are time tested and continue to draw incredible interest from around the globe. We like this game so much, in fact, that the CD-ROM that comes with this book includes an entire folder chockfull of Bolo paraphernalia and documentation (and, of course, the latest version of Bolo) for hours of intense strategic fun.

Pros: Extensive networking support. Simple to play yet complex. Can be played over the Internet for little or no cost. Runs on almost all Macs.

Cons: Only fun as a multiplayer game.

System Requirements: Mac Plus or better, 1MB RAM for black and white, 2MB RAM for color, 900K hard disk space, System 6.05 or higher.

BOLO 0.99.6	
Fun factor:	3.0
Look and feel:	3.0
Value:	4.5
Replayability:	4.0
Overall:	3.5

Pararena
Casady & Greene

Pararena is another john calhoun creation (see the Glider review for more on calhoun). This two-player, one-on-one-basketball-in-a-bowl-shaped-arena-while-riding-a-hoverboard game takes place in the far reaches of outer space, where you and an opponent vie for the title of Champion of the Universe.

Your job is to secure a ball that is whirling around the inside of the bowl, skim up to your goal, and toss the ball through the small hole that represents the goal. Meanwhile, your opponent is also scrambling for the ball with the intention of scoring a goal of his own. Imagine wearing roller skates while playing hoops in an empty swimming pool.

Because of the sloped floor and the hoverboards, inertia plays a big part in the game. Give your opponent a serious enough bump and he or she will be launched into the wild black yonder. Of course, the force of your collision could very well propel you into the outer reaches as well, so you have to be careful.

Gaining control over your player is the toughest part of the game. Although you can move and shoot with the mouse, you also need the extra oomph that a press of the B, N, or M keys provide. For those times when you're whipping around the arena too quickly, a quick stab at the space bar will provide the necessary brakes.

Better With Two
Although Pararena is a perfectly reasonable game for a single player, like most games, it's much more fun over a network. There's something gratifying in knowing that the creep who just bumped you into orbit wasn't some unfeeling

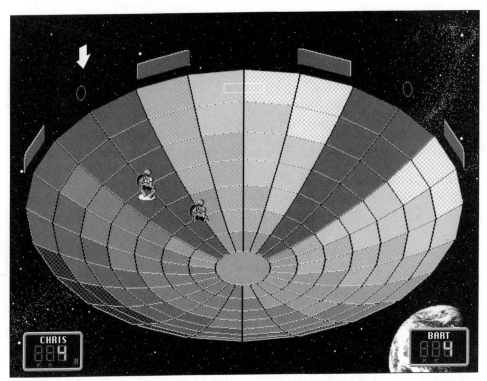

You shoot, you score! in John Calhoun's networkable Pararena.

bit of code but a former friend who is gonna take a licking as soon as you climb back into the arena.

It takes some time getting used to the odd gravity and slope of the playing field, and it's humiliating to have little computer-generated figures running circles around you. Knowing that the person at the other end of the network controlling that bumbling figures is having just as hard a time as you is oddly comforting.

Thanks, John

Pararena was released in 1992, so don't expect lushly rendered graphics and stereo background music. The graphics and sound are fine, but they're definitely dated. Yet despite its age, the game runs flawlessly on the latest Macs and sprints right along even over LocalTalk. Best of all, two players can play the game with a single copy. *We wish everyone producing networked games was this generous.* (Okay, thanks to Bungie as well. Marathon also allows two people to play from one copy).

**GREAT
FEATURE**

Pararena isn't easy to find in the stores or mail order houses, but fortunately Casady & Greene still sells most of their older products directly. Many of

C & G's games are deeply discounted and can be had for next to a song. If you're looking for an inexpensive networking diversion, give Casady & Greene a call at 800-359-4920. And tell 'em we sent you.

Pros: Fast action over the network. Two people can play with one copy of the game. Inexpensive. Supports black and white.

Cons: Controls are hard to master.

System Requirements: Mac Plus or better, 1MB RAM, 1MB hard disk space, System 6.02 or higher.

PARARENA

Fun factor:	3.5
Look and feel:	3.0
Value:	4.0
Replayability:	3.5
Overall:	3.5

16 } Online Gaming

Once you've exhausted your supply of office network and modem-to-modem opponents, it's time to expand to the world at large through the means of online communications.

Online gaming differs from network gaming in a number of respects. To begin with, most of your online playmates will be strangers, folks who are connected to the same service and who are also looking for a little entertainment. And, except for Internet games such as MUDs, you generally have to pay to play. Payment may come in the form of regular connect-time charges for commercial services such as GEnie and CompuServe, or as flat rates for such dedicated gaming services as Sim-Net/OMNI Games and Outland. Finally, the quality of the gaming experience depends on modem—rather than network—speed.

We took a gander at the major online commercial services to see what games are being offered. In addition, we looked at two new dedicated gaming services. And last, but hardly least, what would an overview of online gaming be without a roll in the MUDs?

Commercial Services

In addition to supplying a cozy e-mail address and a place to download the latest shareware and bug fixes, online commercial services provide a number of games for those people who like to play in real time. Some games, such as CompuServe's Island of Kesmai, can be played alone or with others, and some, such as GEnie's Air Warrior, are strictly intended for multiple players.

CompuServe

Online Games

As with most commercial online services, CompuServe provides more gaming services to PC users than to those of us who prefer the Macintosh. All is not lost, however. CompuServe does offer text-based adventures such as Island of Kesmai and British Legends and a conquer-the-galaxy game called MegaWars.

In addition, you can enter the Modem-to-Modem forum (Go MTMGAMES) and use CompuServe to connect to other modem players around the world. Because this service is mainly enjoyed by PC users, the interface will seem archaic by Mac standards; it includes lots of backslashes and command line garbage. This service is surcharged.

Although CompuServe's offerings are better than most—it offers wider access to the Internet, where text adventure gaming is virtually free, and less expensive dedicated modem-to-modem services such as OMNI Games that employ reasonable Macintosh front ends—CompuServe's Macintosh online gaming services are hardly compelling. We'd like to see more Mac gaming on CompuServe, but given the service's past record, we're not going to hold our breath.

Forums

The one good reason for Mac gamers to belong to CompuServe is the Macintosh Entertainment Forum (Go MACFUN).

The strength of this forum is not so much in the timeliness of its shareware and demos—AOL and eWorld invariably beat CompuServe to the punch when it comes to getting the latest games—but rather in the knowledge and helpfulness of the forum's members. In general, members tend to be more experienced than those found on AOL.

The Flight Simulations area (Section 13), in particular, is outstanding. Discussion Leader Christopher Perez and the section's regulars are experts on all things related to Mac flight sims. One warning: These people take flight sims *very* seriously. The regulars go so far as to adopt online call signs. Polite dweebs (the nickname for inexperienced sim pilots) will receive loads of help and support from forum members. But those with strong opinions should be prepared to back them up. Some members can get mighty cantankerous if they suspect that hot air is the only thing keeping you afloat.

GREAT
FEATURE

GEnie

Online Games

GEnie has the usual contingent of single-player diversions such as trivia games and text adventures, but it is by far the leader in multiplayer online games for the Mac or, for that matter, any machine. For some strange reason, this aging, offbeat, and outclassed service has continually featured an awesome lineup of multiplayer games ranging from cosmic soap operas to fighter plane extravaganzas. In fact, GEnie was the first service to commit an entire online multiplayer game to the Macintosh computer, the now-defunct maze shoot-'em-up entitled A-MAZE-ING. When it comes to ease of use, we can only scoff at GEnie's pathetic command line interface. However, there is some redemption in the fact that there are now a couple of GUI packages available for navigating the service. The multiplayer games area can be reached by typing GAMES at any prompt and downloading. The front end software for the online games is usually free, although actual game play is charged at the regular GEnie connection rates.

GREAT
FEATURE

The current flagship multiplayer/multiplatform game on any service is the timeless classic Air Warrior. It enables you to hop into a P-51D Mustang and engage in historic WWII battles, or sit in the tail gunner's seat of a B-17 during a bombing raid in which your plane is piloted by a complete stranger from another country. The most astounding thing about Air Warrior is its relatively smooth playability even when connected at 2400 bps, which is the only available connection option for many GEnie users because of the archaic access system GEnie relies on. There's a new version of Air Warrior (currently in beta) that should bring Mac front end graphics more in line with the high-quality SVGA screens DOS users enjoy, and that should add some other needed features, including a built-in tutorial. New software or not, this game is a blast from start to finish, and you may find yourself flying a Hellcat into the heat of battle or operating a ground-based AA battery every time you boot your machine. Air

Air Warrior is still one of most popular online multiplayer games around. It runs well despite GEnie's many 2400 baud connection sites.

Warrior is a world in and of itself. We found that it carries a high addiction liability and may be justification enough for belonging to GEnie.

Orb Wars is the second multi-player GEnie game that can be used with a graphical front end program. It's somewhat less popular than the other titles and can best be described as a niche game for those who enjoy the wizards-and-warlocks type of game. It does offer decent graphics and game play, which involves teams of wizards facing off in dungeon-like surroundings in a magical frenzy to the death. Spell casting is the name of the game, and we found it necessary to have reams of spell charts and such at the fingertips to learn the game and fend off frustration. The competition is largely made up of hard-core Orb Wars fans. Beginners won't even get the chance to utter the words "double, double toil and trouble" before the game is over and they're asking "when shall we three meet again?"

RANT

There are 12 multiplayer online games on GEnie, and only two of them have graphical Mac front ends. Now this wouldn't be so hard to swallow if we hadn't come across numerous games with front ends for DOS, Amiga, and Atari computers. But no Mac versions! WHAT!?! Do the people who manage these games honestly believe that there are more Atari home computers on the market than Macs? What planet are these people from?

The other multiplayer online games on GEnie that are Mac friendly are text based and therefore rely, to varying degrees, on players' imaginations. Despite the lack of front end software, some of these games have become very popular and have legions of dedicated fans clogging cyberspace while chalking up hundreds of hours of game play. Federation II is a prime example of this phenomena. It can best be described as a combination of Spaceward Ho!, Zork, and a soap opera. Conjures up interesting imagery, doesn't it?

The Hundred Years War is another text-based game. It revolves around the management of land and warfare in feudal Europe. Stellar Emperor puts you in a futuristic universe where intergalactic domination is the name of the game.

Forums

The main gaming chat area on GEnie is Scorpia's round table, which can be reached by typing SCORPIA at any prompt. Although this is the place to go for many gamers, it's not the place to go for Mac gamers. In fact, if you were cruising through the message boards, you'd be hard pressed to notice the Mac even existed. To top it off, the vibes we get from the management suggest that if you're a Mac user, you're a second-class citizen. The icing on the cake for this round table is the strange lack of current Mac game updates and shareware material in the Scorpia libraries, and there seems to be little interest in improving a glaring lack of support for the Mac. Fortunately GEnie has its own smaller Macintosh gaming area. This message board lies buried in the Mac round table (which can be reached by typing MAC), and although not huge, it usually contains some refreshingly cerebral Macintosh game talk and offers the best messaging system of any online service.

LOUSY FEATURE

America Online

Online Games

When we inquired about online Macintosh games on America Online we received this response:

"There is currently no Macintosh version of Neverwinter Nights, MasterWord or the Casino. This does not mean, however, that those who are 'Intel impaired' cannot access these games.

"Put simply, you need something that will allow you to RUN IBM compatible software."

And there you have it. There are no Macintosh online games on one of the biggest online communications companies in the world because millions of Mac users are *Intel impaired.* Excuse us as we raise our collective voice.

HEY AOL! WAKE THE HECK UP! THERE ARE TRUCKLOADS OF MAC USERS OUT HERE WHO LIKE TO PLAY ONLINE GAMES. WHILE YOU'RE TAKING A SHORT BREATHER BETWEEN COMPANY BUYOUTS, DO YOU THINK YOU COULD HIRE ONE OR TWO MAC PROGRAMMERS TO BUILD A COUPLE OF ONLINE MAC GAMES? WE BOUGHT A MACINTOSH BECAUSE WE THINK IT'S A SUPERIOR PLATFORM. IF WE WANTED TO EMULATE PCS, WE WOULD HAVE BOUGHT ONE OF THE LOUSY THINGS IN THE FIRST PLACE!

RANT

Forums

America Online's value for gamers lies in the quantity of its freeware and shareware games and in the support from members of the gaming industry that it makes available. Everyone who is anyone has an AOL account (unlike CompuServe, where game publishers are not given free accounts unless the publisher promotes CompuServe through the inclusion of advertisements in the game package). With a little legwork, you can find most shareware and commercial game developers on this service.

Unfortunately, it's extremely difficult to glean information from AOL's message sections because of the way messages—sometimes hundreds of them—are clumped together in vast folders. CompuServe's messaging is vastly superior to AOL's (and by extension, to eWorld's, which uses AOL's interface as a model).

eWorld

Online Games

Unfortunately, eWorld has been slow on the draw to incorporate multiplayer graphical online games despite its early claims to the contrary. The gaming that is offered is well managed and supported, but it involves sitting in chat rooms exchanging text. There are trivia and D&D games, and even a name-that-tune game (which requires the downloading of sound files). Now we admit that this can be fun, but given a choice between that and fighting a dragon to a fiery death in 256 colors, which would you pick? Presently eWorld offers eight games of this nature, and they have no surcharge attached to their use other than the normal eWorld connection rates. We can hope that eWorld will get with the program and learn what GEnie learned long ago: Great games bring users in droves.

Forums

The main gaming forum on eWorld is Inside Games, which uses eWorld's current Mac-only status to ensure that Mac games get the exposure they deserve. Inside Games also offers a publisher's forum in which a number of game companies stand ready to answer your questions while keeping the libraries full of the latest and greatest demo and shareware software available. In fact, Inside Games seems to get some of the demos ahead of the other services fairly frequently. Unfortunately, the messaging system in Inside Games, and in eWorld in general, is similar to that of AOL, thus making navigation of the message boards an exercise in futility. Alas, nothing is perfect.

Gaming Networks

There are an increasing number of dedicated game services cropping up all over the world, and the Mac has not been left out of the derby. Indeed, the Mac's built-in networking has made it an excellent machine for this sort of activity. Several dedicated networks covering all kinds of online gaming are currently available through the Internet and direct phone connections.

Sim-Net/OMNI Games

CD

Sim-Net/OMNI Games is one of a pair of online services dedicated to offering an electronic meeting place to those who enjoy networkable commercial games. Through the use of Apple Remote Access (ARA), the Mac's built-in networking capabilities, and a program called First Class Client, users can come together through the Internet (or direct phone connection) and compete in their favorite games. Any game that works with ARA can be used over this service; it gives you the ability to play games like F/A-18 Hornet or Links Pro head-to-head with a complete stranger while never leaving the comfy seat in front of your computer.

The service also offers message boards, mail services, and chat rooms for discussing strategies or gloating over narrow victories (which Bart has never been known to do). Getting online can be achieved via direct phone connection (this can be very expensive) or over the Internet with IPRemote (much cheaper). Sim-Net recommends a bare minimum 14.4 bps modem—28.8 bps if you can afford it. It seems that it won't be long before 28.8 bps is the standard modem speed and that that blazingly fast 9600 bps modem you coveted is given dinosaur status. We found that a 14.4 bps modem coupled with a contemporary Mac is more than enough to play all currently available games at impressive speeds. In

Sim-Net (formerly OMNI Games) offers a way for people to face off in popular network games such as F/A-18 Hornet or Links Pro.

fact, we were very impressed with the overall performance achieved with this setup. The only crimping factor is the need for at least 8 MB of RAM, preferably more, to handle the demands of First Class Client, ARA, and the individual game software simultaneously. Sim-Net is priced at a monthly flat rate for unlimited usage. This makes it very attractive for real online junkies who like head-to-head action.

GameNet

GameNet is the younger cousin of Sim-Net/OMNI games, and although the two companies are not related in the true sense, the family resemblance is remarkable. GameNet also uses ARA and First Class Client software, and offers virtually the same services as Sim-Net, including network game connections, chat rooms, e-mail, and messaging. Connection to GameNet can be handled over the Internet as well as with direct phone access. Sounds familiar, doesn't it? What separates these two companies? Not much. Sim-Net has been around longer, but to be honest, they're both good. Both have excellent support staffs that are friendly and helpful, and both offer free trial periods to give you the opportunity to check things out. Sim-Net and GameNet product demos are available on the CD that comes with this book, and we recommend you try them both before making any online head-to-head decisions.

CD

MARK PAYNE OF OMNI GAMES/SIM-NET

Mark Payne is the cofounder of OMNI Games/Sim-Net, a games network that allows networkable games such as Links Pro to be played among opponents from all over the world.

Tell us a little about yourself and Sim-Net/OMNI games.

My partner Ken Green and I developed the concept of creating an online network devoted to Macintosh interactive games in June of 1994. We decided to put together a small online service called OMNI Games to be used as a test case by which we could better assess the growth potential of this new enterprise. On July 1, 1995, the name OMNI Games will be forever changed to Sim-Net Corporation. Sim-Net will be targeting a world-wide market by allowing access to our online network via the Internet. Members can play interactive games like F/A-18 Hornet, Chuck Yeager's Air Combat, PowerPOKER, Bolo, Links Pro Golf, and soon we hope to be playing DOOM and A-10!

What sort of potential do you see for this kind of service on the Internet?

Sim-Net expects to achieve a membership base of approximately 50,000 Macintosh users within five years. Sim-Net will not only be the first Macintosh interactive network available on the Internet, it will retain unique qualities that no other service can duplicate. The members themselves control the general operations through input received and distributed. The system management approach is like no other network service in operation today.

Describe basically how it works: the kind of client software we need, access charges, minimum modem speed for reasonable play, whether it's Mac only or also for PCs.

Macintosh users who would like to try out the interactive game environment are welcome to log in as a guest and play for free. Guests are allowed to play in 30-minute intervals but are prohibited from entering tournaments; and some other features are not accessible to them until they become full members. If accessing through the Internet (PPP or SLIP accounts), the guest user will only pay access charges due to their Internet provider. In most cases, guest users can access the Internet for as little as $30 per month (unlimited access—no hourly charges—check with your local Internet provider for rates). The recommended modem speed is 14.4; anything less will not do the games justice. At this time, all approved games play well over 14.4 modem connections. Sim-Net will be accessible through the use of Apple Remote Access Software (ARA Client), and via the Internet using IPRemote.

Specifically which games are you currently offering? Any plans for MUD-like games?

Sim-Net allows almost all ARA and AppleTalk games to play over our service. We don't restrict the types of games played. Members can play any network games they like. Our biggest draw by far has been F/A-18 Hornet from Graphic Simulations. This game offers four-way participation in a flight simulation over ARA and two-way participation over the Internet. We hold tournaments and rank pilots based on their abilities. Links Pro Golf allows up to eight participants to play golf in real time, and Mac Doom will be yet another addition to our games. The list goes on and on. If the membership wants to play MUD games, then we will incorporate the changes in the system as necessary. Again, the membership controls the content.

Do you feel that networkable and online games are the future of gaming on all platforms?

In short, yes! We have recognized that there is far more value in a game when it can be played against a real live person. In the past, the network features have been afterthoughts rather than preplanned. This causes serious problems with the graphics used today in game production. Thus the game needs to be written first around the network capabilities. Packet transmissions need to be minimized to allow for real-time

game play. With the introduction of Mac Doom, I think that there is a time and place coming where Mac users will be doing battle against PC users. Sim-Net is going to be there to make that possible.

What is the next big step for online gaming?

The next big step we see is the ability to communicate with your opponent. This includes text, voice, and video. All of these things are on the way.

Will hardware dictate the future of online gaming?

Yes and no. From our experience so far, hardware is less important than it first seems. The user's equipment will need to be somewhat game-ready out of the box (which is one of the reasons we are a Macintosh network). Sound and graphic capabilities are extremely important, but it has been our experience that members with low-end machines can still participate and have a great time, though of course, the better the hardware, the more realistic the game.

CD

Outland

Outland is a unique graphical multiplayer game network for Macintosh users. It is accessible through the Internet or by direct connection with a modem. Outland differs from other services in one critical aspect: all of its games are included in the software package and require no further downloading. Outland's software is an even split between two-player and multiplayer games, and some of the games allow for computer players to fill out the player rosters. Outland currently offers Spaceward Ho! 4.0, Chess, Reversi, Hearts, Backgammon, Galley (a pirate ship action game), Backstab, and a graphical BBS for subscribers. The games are always being expanded and updated. In fact, by the time you read this there will be two new titles including a game reminiscent of Risk entitled Conquest and a multiplayer diversion called Assassin, which is rumored to follow in the footsteps of Maxis's RoboSport.

Outland has fantastic graphics and a user-friendly intuitive interface complete with some ongoing animation. It's a nice touch. The network itself is fairly stable, and in months of play we were bounced off only a couple of times. More often than not, this was due to out Internet carriers. We found the staff at Outland to be very helpful. They're available through an 800 number or by e-mail. And if you're having problems online, there's always someone there to help out.

GREAT FEATURE

Spaceward Ho! 4.0 is by far the most popular game on Outland. At any given time there's a game to be joined, and people are always mulling around the chat areas looking for gaming partners.

You can connect to Outland if your Mac has Internet access using MacTCP, if you have a Unix, Delphi, or other account that can Telnet, or if you dial the Outland modems directly. Connecting is very simple and involves less setup than Sim-Net and GameNet do, but then the nature of the games available is very different as well. If you're looking for a very inexpensive, straightforward, and diverse online gaming network for the Mac, there is nothing else like Outland. Although other services offer excellent fast-paced action from the current hot

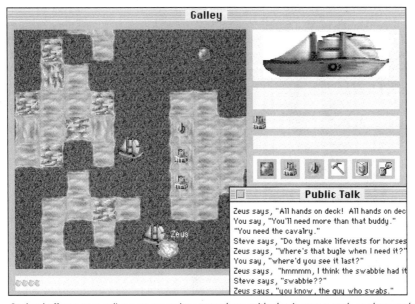

Outland offers a true online games service atmosphere, with classic games such as chess and multiplayer action in games like Galley.

networkable games, Outland has its own more subdued attitude and broader appeal for all kinds of gamers.

MacF.I.B.S.

If you love to play backgammon and the idea of facing off against opponents worldwide makes your palms sweaty, you're in luck. Californian Paul Ferguson has given us MacF.I.B.S., a freeware gem that enables graphical Internet multi-player backgammon. MacF.I.B.S. is an acronym for the Macintosh version of the First Internet Backgammon Server and it lets players engage in competitive backgammon matches in real time. The F.I.B.S. server is located in Gothenburg Sweden and runs on a Sun SPARC workstation. You'll need Mac TCP/PPP software and Internet access. No fees are applicable other than the cost of your Internet connection, and there are always players hanging around waiting for the chance to double on you.

You begin your life on the server with a score of 1500.00 and decide your fate with the quality of your play. If you continue to lose match after match, your score will drop and you will find yourself in therapy attempting to regain what remains of a shattered backgammon ego.

The game board window can be set to either a large or small setting. The smaller window allows you to note the chatter and the comings and goings of other players. MacF.I.B.S. is an excellent way to play backgammon against a vast array

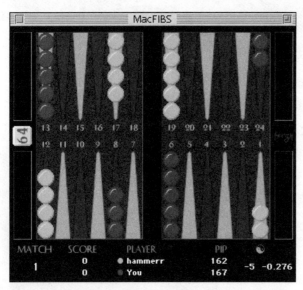

of opponents for only the cost of your Internet connection. If you're connected to the Net, you have no excuse for not giving Mac-F.I.B.S. a look, unless it's an irrational fear of dice.

MacF.I.B.S. is a backgammon server based in Sweden that allows players from around the world to have a game or two at any time of day.

MUDs

MUDs may be the most notorious online games. Multi-User Dimensions (the D can also stand for Domain, Dialog, or Dungeon) are text-based virtual worlds accessible through the Internet and certain commercial services. Unlike traditional single-player text adventures that rely solely on computer-generated personalities, these worlds are also populated by human beings who interact with you in real time.

You can think of MUDs as online costume dramas. Each participant adopts or is assigned a character that becomes his or her online personality. Such a personality may differ wildly from that of the real person typing at the other end of the line. The sultry enchantress you find so enticing could very well be a large male construction worker. The allure of MUDs is fantasy. They provide a unique opportunity to become anyone you desire.

MUDs can be roughly divided into two main categories: game-oriented hack-and-slash Combat MUDs and the more social and less structured TinyMUDs.

MUD Wrestling

Combat MUDs are an extension of the Dungeons and Dragons games of the '70s. Based on the original 1978 game MUD1, these MUDs pit you, in the guise of elf, enchanter, samurai warrior, or other fantastic character, against a variety of monsters and unsavory beings. The idea is to quest about—either alone or as part of a group—and gain power and experience through puzzle solving, combat, and the acquisition of treasure and magical items.

The two major kinds of Combat MUDs are LP MUDs and DikuMUDs. LPs tend to be oriented toward quest and adventure, and DikuMUDs focus more on combat.

A Little MUDdy

TinyMUDers, on the other hand, rarely slap each other about. And TinyMUDs, comprised of such subdivisions as MUSHes (Multi-User Shared Hallucinations), MUCKs, and MOOs, are not as goal-oriented as Combat MUDs. Although there are tasks to perform and vast areas to explore, TinyMUDs are mostly social centers based in fantastic virtual lands. In many TinyMUDs you can drop in and out of character more easily than you can in Combat MUDs.

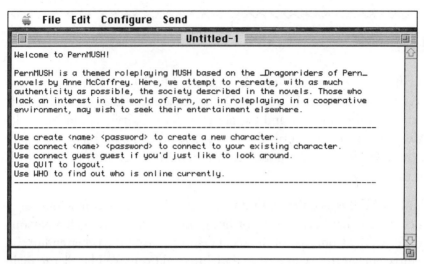

PernMush is one of the more serious TinyMUDs. Its participants are expected to remain in character and know the ins and outs of the Pern fantasy stories.

Although many TinyMUDs embrace the medieval charms of dragons, knights, and gnomes, other worlds are also represented. Current TinyMUDs employ such themes as Star Trek, Star Wars, gothic horror, and Frank Herbert's Dune series. There's even a genre of MUDs in which you must adopt the character of an anthropomorphic furry creature. Yes, they're called FurryMUDs.

How MUDs Work

Most MUDs are free to the extent that you access them over the Internet and, in most cases, pay no additional fees for connecting to them. Of course, any charges for connect time to your Internet provider do apply.

Because MUDs require a dedicated Internet connection and a fair amount of memory and storage, these lands are usually contained within a large workstation at a university or corporate site. MUDs are created and maintained by people known as system Gods. The Gods are assisted by Wizards (also known as Implementors on DikuMUDs). These computer-savvy folks have special powers—such as the ability to create new areas and objects in the MUDs—that are unavailable to regular users. In addition to maintaining the MUDs, some Wizards act as guides and, occasionally, police for participants who find it difficult to play by the rules.

How to Sign Up

If you're running a SLIP connection from your Mac, you'll want to use a client program rather than arcane UNIX commands to access MUDs. We've included a copy of MUDDweller, a popular Macintosh client program, on our CD-ROM. MUDDweller allows you to connect to MUDs with a friendly graphic user interface. Without a SLIP connection, you'll have to use the old-fashioned method and telnet to MUD sites.

CD

To log on to a MUD, you must obtain the TCP/IP address and port number for it. You can find these addresses on-line in different newsgroups and ftp sites (see MUD Information). While you're there, download the latest MUD FAQ (Frequently Asked Questions) to learn more about commands, rules, and netiquette.

Once connected to the MUD, you'll be asked to create a name and password for yourself. While you're waiting for approval to join as a proper character, many MUDs allow you to stroll about as a guest. During this guest period, it's a good idea to type HELP in order to obtain a list of the rules and commands for that particular MUD.

Rules of behavior vary depending on the kind of MUD you're visiting. For example, player killing may be allowed (encouraged?) on a hard-core DikuMUD while the same action could get you banned from a TinyMUD. Visiting a new MUD is a bit like entering a foreign city: if you respect the local customs and don't make a nuisance of yourself, you should get along just fine.

You travel about in a MUD using the same direction commands found in text adventure games: N (north), SW (southwest), and D (down), for example. Commands for communicating with other people can vary from MUD to MUD. Again, read its help file to familiarize yourself with a particular MUD's command set.

One last bit of advice: MUDs can contain hundreds and hundreds of rooms. Stock up on such map-making supplies as pencils and graph paper.

The Controversy

Generally, MUDs have received less-than-glowing publicity in the popular press. We've all heard the horror stories of people who become addicted to their fantasy lives and stay connected to MUDs for days on end while ignoring such comparatively mundane responsibilities as work, school, and in-the-flesh social interaction. As horrific as these stories sound, we suspect that they are less common than tabloid TV shows would have us believe.

True, there is potential for addiction. Fantasy is a strong drug. Add to it an environment in which others actively encourage these fantasies and it's possible that those who don't know "when to say when" will find themselves hopelessly

DANGER

MUD INFORMATION

Because MUDs are considered nonessential by many of their host sites, they occasionally disappear or move to other, friendlier sites. Lists of current MUDs can be found across the Internet. A few sources for MUD information are:

Newsgroups

```
rec.games.mud.announce
alt.mud
rec.games.mud.tiny
rec.games.mud.diku
rec.games.mud.misc
```
(Check here for the latest MUD FAQ.)

FTP Sites

```
avatar.snc.edu
ftp.matg.okstate.edu
b63062.student.cwru.edu:/pub/mudlist/
```

World Wide Web

```
http://www.ccs.neu.edu/home/lpb/muddex.html
http://www.cis.upenn.edu/~lwl/mudinfo.html
```

wrapped up in a MUD. But let's face it, there are also people who spend every cent they make on clothes for teddy bears or who become progressively more wretched while watching *The Brady Bunch* marathons on television. Addictive personalities can be found in all walks of life.

The other aspect of MUDs that some outsiders find objectionable is known in MUDding as TinySex. This occurs when people meet, slip off into private areas, and exchange sexually explicit messages. These exchanges are intended to be between consenting adults and must be agreed upon by all parties. Users engaging in cybersexual harassment are swiftly banned from most MUDs.

Those participating in TinySex should be reminded that the folks they communicate with may not resemble, or even be the same sex as the persons they purport to be. Additionally, there have been reports of individuals who have taken part in TinySex encounters discovering transcripts of their encounters elsewhere on the Net. In such cases, although you are protected by your alias, all your friends on the MUD who know you as, say, Korn the Chowderhead, may gain a deeper insight into your personality than you would like them to have. These instances are rare, but they do demonstrate that the cyberpartner you find so fascinating may, "in real life," be just another jerk.

The Dirt on MUDs

For those who have Internet access, enjoy bouts of shared fantasy, and find interacting with others rewarding, MUDs can be the most engrossing gaming experience in computerdom. Those rare individuals who take fantasy a little too seriously may find that MUDding becomes more a hindrance to life than a boon. If this kind of fantasy role playing sounds like your cup of tea, and you're mature enough to handle the responsibility, it may be time to get down and dirty.

BART AND CHRIS' TOP TEN LIST

All players have games that hold a special place in their hearts. And we're no different. Since we've splattered our opinions all over the rest of the book we thought we might as well list our most beloved games. Below are alphabetical lists of our personal favorites—some new and some very old.

Because gaming is so subjective we fully expect that your list varies wildly from ours (heck, we don't have a single game in common on our two lists).

Bart:	Chris:
Balance of Power	A-10 Attack!
Dark Castle	Crystal Caliburn
Dark Forces	F/A-18 Hornet
GATO	Ishido
Maelstrom	JauntTrooper Mission: THUNDERBOLT
Might and Magic Series	Leather Goddesses of Phobos
Minotaur	Lunar Rescue
Pathways Into Darkness	Marathon
SimCity	MYST
Strategic Conquest	The Colony

Appendix

~~~~~~

Game Sources

Key

AL: AppleLink
AOL: America Online
BBS: Bulletin board system
CIS: CompuServe
eWorld: eWorld
GE: GEnie

Access Software

4750 Wiley Post Way, Building #1, Suite 200
Salt Lake City, UT 84116
800/800-4880, 801/359-2900
fax: 801/596-9128
AOL: Linkspro1; CIS: 72662,61

Activision

11601 Wilshire Boulevard, Suite 300
Los Angles, CA 90025
800/477-3650, 310/479-5644
fax: 310/479-4005
CIS: go gambpub

Advanced Gravis

3750 North Fraser Way, Suite 101
Burnaby, British Columbia, Canada V5J 5E9
800/663-8558, 604/431-5020
fax: 604/431-5155
BBS: 604/431-5927
CIS: macdven; Internet: tech@gravis.com

Alliance Interactive Software, Inc.

1859 North Pine Island Road, #103
Plantation, FL 33322
305/424-9054
fax: 305/423-4289

Ambrosia Software

PO Box 23140
Rochester, NY 14692
716/325-1910
fax: 716/325-3665
AOL: AmbrosiaSW; CIS: 74777,1147;
    eWorld: AmbrosiaSW; GE: AmbrosiaSW;
    Internet: AmbrosiaSW@aol.com

American Laser Games

4801 Lincon Road N.E.
Albuquerque, NM 87109
800/863-4263, 505/880-1718
fax: 505/880-1557

Amtex Software

PO Box 572
Belleville, Ontario, Canada K8N 5B2
800/810-7345, 613/967-7900
fax: 613/967-7902

Apple Computer
1 Infinite Loop
Cupertino, CA 95014-2084
408/996-1010
eWorld: APPLEWDSG

ARTSector One
360 Hunyadi Avenue
Fairfield, CT 06430
203/338-0192
fax: 203/338-0201

The Avalon Game Company
4517 Harford Road
Baltimore, MD 21214
410/254-9200
fax: 410/254-0991
AOL: AHGames; CIS: 72662,1207

Berkeley Systems
2095 Rose Street
Berkeley, CA 94709
510/540-5535
fax: 510/540-5115
AL: D0346; AOL: BrklySystm;
   CIS: go macbven

Brøderbund Software, Inc.
PO Box 6121
Novato, CA 94948-6121
800/521-6263, 415/382-4400
fax: 415/382-4419

Bungie Software
1935 S. Halsted Street, Suite 204
Chicago, Il 60608
312/563-6200
fax: 312/563-0545
AL: BUNGIE; AOL: Bungie1;
   eWorld: Bungiecorp;
   Internet: Bungie1@aol.com

Callisto Corporation
182 West Central Street
Natick, MA 01760
508/665-0707
AL: callisto; CIS: 71302,3374;
   eWorld: Callisto1;
   Internet: Callisto1@aol.com

Casady & Greene
22734 Portola Drive
Salinas, CA 93908-1119
800/359-4920, 408/484-9228
fax: 408/484-9218
AL: d0063; AOL: Casadygree

CH Products
970 Park Center Drive
Vista, CA 92083
619/598-2518
fax: 619/598-2524
AOL: CHproducts; CIS: go chproducts;
   GE: CH.Products

Changeling Software
596 Elm Street
Windson, Locks, CT 06096-1603
800/769-2768, 203/844-6157
AL: Changeling; AOL: Changlings;
   CIS: gamcpub;
   Internet: Changelings@aol.com

Cogix Corporation
3030 Bridgeway, #305
Sausalito, CA 94965
415/289-5710
fax: 415/332-5443

Creative Multimedia
514 NW 11th Avenue, Suite 203
Portland, OR 97209
503/241-1530
BBS 503/241-1573
CIS: 71333,3143;
   Internet: 71333,3143@compuserve.com

CyberDreams Entertainment

21243 Ventura Boulevard, Suite 230
Woodland Hills, CA 91364
818/223-9990
CIS: 72662,120

CyberFlix

4 Market Square
Knoxville, TN 37902
615/546-1157
fax: 615/546-0866
AOL: Cyberflix; eWorld: Cflix

Deadly Games

PO Box 676
Bridgehampton, NY 11932-0676
516/537-6060
fax: 516/537-3299
AOL: Deadly G; CIS: 74431,2470;
   eWorld: Deadlygame

Delta Tao Software

760 Harvard Avenue
Sunnyvale, CA 94087
800/827-9316, 408/730-9336
fax: 408/730-9337
AOL: deltav

Digital Eclipse

5515 Doyle Street, Suite 1
Emeryville, CA 94608
510/547-6104
fax: 510/547-6104
Internet: AndrewA@Sirius.com

Discis Knowledge Research, Inc.

90 Sheppard Avenue East, 7th Floor
Toronto, Ontario, Canada M2N 3A1
800/567-4321, 416/250-6537
fax: 416/250-6540
Internet: Discis@goodmedia.com

Domark

1900 South Norfolk Street, Suite 110
San Mateo, CA 94403
800/695-GAME, 415/513-8929
fax: 415/571-0437
Internet: info@Domark.com

Dongleware Publishing

35 Howard Street
Cambridge, MA 02139
800/228-6993, 617/497-1130

Drew Pictures

246 1st Street, Suite 402
San Francisco, CA 94105
415/247-7600

Eccentric Software

PO Box 2777
Seattle, WA 98111-2777
800/436-6758, 206/628-2687
fax: 206/628-2681
CIS: 73677,1537;
   Internet: xcentric@aol.com

Electronic Arts

1450 Fashion Island Boulevard
San Mateo, CA 94404
800/245-4525, 415/571-7171

Focus Enhancements

800 West Cummings Park
Woburn, MA 01801
800/538-8865, 617/938-8088
fax: 617/938-7741

Frontal Assaultware, Inc.

48 Grove Street, Suite 203
Somerville, MA 02144
617/623-6006
fax: 617/623-6466
AOL: FAI; Internet: FAI@shore.net

GameNet

212/254-5300

Graphic Simulations
15400 Knoll Trail Drive, Suite 104
Dallas, TX 75248
800/850-4723, 214/386-7575
fax: 214/386-7875
AOL: Graphsim; eWorld: Graphsim;
    Internet: Graphsim@aol.com

Great Game Products
8804 Chalon Drive
Bethesda, MA 20817

GT Interactive Software
16 East 40th Street
New York, NY 10016
303/522-1844

Intracorp Capstone
501 Brickell Key Drive, 6th Floor
Miami, FL 33131
800/468-7226, 305/373-7700
fax: 305/577-9875

HyperBole Studios
2225 4th Avenue, 2nd Floor
Seattle, WA 98121
206/441-8334
fax: 206/441-9134
AL: HYPERBOLE.SD; AOL: HB Studios;
    CIS: 70471,1635

Kernel Productions
24 Kensington Lane
Newark, DE 19713
302/456-3026
fax: 302/456-3124
AL: KERNEL.PROD; AOL: KernelPup

LucasArts
PO Box 10307
San Rafael, CA 94912
800/STAR-WARS, 415/507-4545
fax: 415/507-0300
BBS 415/507-0400
AOL: LucasArts; CIS: go gamapub;
    Internet: LucasArts@aol.com

MACE Group
2550 Corporate Place, #C 101
Monterey Park, CA 91754
800/644-1132, 213/780-6110
fax: 213/780-3250

MacPlay
17922 Fitch Avenue
Irvine, CA 92714
714/553-3251
fax: 714/252-2820
BBS: 714/252-2822
AOL: Interplay; CIS: 76702,1342

Maxis
2121 North California, Suite 600
Walnut Creek, CA 94596
800/336-2947, 510/254-9700
fax: 510/253-3736
BBS: 510/254-3869
AL: d4459; CIS: gambpub

MegaCorp International, Inc.
1257 Worcester Road, Suite #280
Framingham, MA 01701

Merit Studios
13707 Gamma
Dallas, TX 75244
214/385-2353
fax: 214/385-8205

Microleague/SAI Sports Associates
PO Box 4547
Lancaster, PA 17604-4547
800/334-2722, 717/872-6567

MicroProse
180 Lakefront Drive
Hunt Valley, MD 21030
800/879-7529, 410/771-1151
fax: 410/771-1174
BBS: 410/785-1841
AOL: MicroProse; CIS: 76004,2223

MicroQue, Inc.
5211 Greenpine Drive
Murray, UT 84123
801/263-1883
fax: 801/263-2886

Microsoft Corporation
One Microsoft Way
Redmond, WA 98052-6399
800/426-9400, 206/882-8080
fax: 206/936-7329

New World Computing, Inc.
PO Box 4302
Hollywood, CA 90078
800/325-8898, 818/889-5650
fax: 818/889-5682
AOL: Newworld; CIS: gamdpub;
  GE: Newworld

NovaLogic, Inc.
26010 Mureau Road, Suite 200
Calabasas, CA 91302
818/878-0325

Omni Games/SimNet
408/295-GAME
AOL: Klarkent;
  Internet: Iceman@aimnet.com

Origin Systems, Inc.
5918 West Courtyard Drive
Austin, TX 78730
512/434-4263
fax: 512/794-8959

Outland
405 El Camino Real, #224
Menlo Park, CA 94025
800/PLAY-OUT, 415/328-5659
fax: 415/851-5882
Internet: info@outland.com

ParSoft International
101 West Renner Road, Suite 430
Richardson, TX 75082
214/479-1340
fax: 214/479-0853
AOL: Parsoft; Internet: Parsoft@aol.com

PlayMaker, Inc.
19 Overshot Court
Phoenix, MD 21131-1851
800/324-7774
fax: 410/667-8429
AOL: PlayMaker; CIS: go macbven;
  eWorld: PlayMaker

Presto Studios/Quadra Interactive
PO Box 188033
Carlsbad, CA 92009-9793
619/931-4755

Psygnosis
675 Massachusetts Avenue
Cambridge, MA 02139
800/438-7794, 617/497-7794
fax: 617/497-6759

Reactor
445 West Erie
Chicago, IL 60610
312/573-0800

ReadySoft
3375 14th Avenue, Units 7 & 8
Markham, Ontario, Canada L3R 0H2
905/475-4801
fax: 905/475-4802

Reality Bytes, Inc.
One Kendall Square, Building 400
Cambridge, MA 02139
617/621-2500
fax: 617/621-2581
eWorld: RealBytes;
  Internet: RBYTES@netcom.com

Sanctuary Woods
1825 S. Grany Street
San Mateo, CA 94402
800/943-3664, 415/286-6110,
   415/286-6000

Sierra On-Line
PO Box 485
Coarsegold, CA 93614
800/SIERRA-5, 209/683-4468
fax: 209/683-3633
BBS: 209/683-4463
AOL: Sierra; CIS: 76004,2143

Spectrum HoloByte
2490 Mariner Square Loop
Alameda, CA 94501
800/695-4263, 510/522-1164
fax: 510/522-9357
BBS: 510/522-8909
AOL: Sholobyte; CIS: 76004,2144

SSG
3186 Hyde Park Place
Pensacola, FL 32503-5846
904/469-8880
fax: 904/469-8885
AL: AUST0161; CIS: 72040,34; GE: SSG

SSI/WizardWorks
Minneapolis, MN 55447
612/559-5301

StarPlay Productions, Inc.
PO Box 217
Greeley, CO 80632
800/203-2503, 303/339-7016
fax: 303/447-2739
CIS: 94031,155

Synergy Interactive Corporation
333 S. Hope Street, Suite 2500
Los Angeles, CA 90071
213/687-2905
fax: 213/687-2946
Internet: syncorp@netcom.com

ThrustMaster, Inc.
10150 SW Nimbus Avenue
Portland, OR 97223-4337
503/639-3200
fax: 503/620-8094
AOL: Thrustmaster; CIS: 76520,3325;
   Internet: thustmaster@checksix.com

Time Warner Interactive Group
2210 Olive Avenue
Burbank, CA 91506
800/593-6334
AOL: DukeofROM;
   Internet: dukeofrom@aol.com

Varcon Systems, Inc.
10509 San Diego Mission Road, Suite K
San Diego, CA 92108
619/563-6700
fax: 619/563-1986
AL: varcon; AOL: Varcon; CIS: 76350,3036

Velocity, Inc.
4 Embarcadero Center, Suite 3100
San Francisco, CA 94111
415/776-8000
fax: 415/776-8099
CIS: 76670,2202;
   Internet: 76670,2202@compuserve.com

Virgin Interactive
18061 Fitch Avenue
Irvine, CA 92714
800/833-1999, 714/833-1999

Virtual Vegas, Inc.
800/575-3766 (orders)

Online Services

AppleLink
Apple Online Services
1 Infinite Loop, MS: 41-D
Cupertino, CA 95014
408/974-3309

America Online
8619 Westwood Center Drive
Vienna, VA 22182-2285
800/827-6364
BBS: 800/827-5808

CompuServe
PO Box 20212
5000 Arlington Centre Boulevard
Columbus, OH 43220
800/848-8199, 614/457-8600
fax: 614/457-0348

eWorld
PO Box 4493
Bridgeton, MO 63044-9718
800/775-4556

GEnie
401 N. Washington Street
Rockville, MD 20850
800/638-9636

Publications

As much as we'd like to believe that we are the ultimate authorities on Macintosh gaming, we don't have the opportunity to update this book once a month to bring you the latest news on the subject. For late-breaking news in print, check out the following:

Inside Mac Games

We both write for IMG, so naturally we're a little biased; but even taking our bias into account, we can honestly say that IMG is the best and most current source for information on Macintosh gaming. Published ten times a year, IMG is a CD-ROM-based magazine that features reviews, interviews, game previews, editorials, and a great collection of shareware and game demos. The cost for a year's subscription is $59. Online demos of the magazine can be found on all the major online services and on the Internet.

Mac Home Journal

Although MHJ devotes a fair amount of space to its game reviews, we think they're a bit wimpy. We like a little vinegar with our sugar.

MacSense

Winner of the *MacUser* 1995 Shareware Award for Best Electronic Publication, this online Canadian journal should have some great game reviews just as soon as Bart starts contributing them. The rest of the magazine is worth a read as well.

MacUser

Disclaimer: Chris is a contributing editor for *MacUser* and really likes his job. That said, *MacUser* now includes a column titled The Game Room written by Mac guru and sometimes-Elvis Costello-impersonator Bob LeVitus. Further Disclaimer: Chris is Bob's partner in the magazine's Help Folder column. Bob prefers gentle criticism to the sledgehammer we occasionally apply, but his reviews are invariably on target and well balanced. Roman "The Man" Loyola provides a monthly sidebar on gaming tips.

MacWEEK

MacWEEK also devotes a number of pages to games in one of its December issues. More comprehensive than *Macworld's*, the *MacWEEK* roundup is fine enough to warrant stealing the issue from your boss's office.

Macworld

If you're looking for a good wrap-up of the year's best games, check out contributing editor Steven Levy's Macintosh Game Hall of Fame article in each January issue of *Macworld*. Steven nails 'em every time (and we give him bonus points for declaring Mission: THUNDERBOLT best adventure game a few years back). Because of the time-bending nature of magazine dating, this issue appears in plenty of time for December holiday shopping.

XYZZYnews

Published by IMG contributor Eileen Mullin, *XYZZYnews* is a bi-monthy online magazine devoted to interactive fiction. Included in *XYZZYnews* are interviews with game designers, reviews, editorials, hints and tips, and pointers for locating the latest interactive fiction games online. Subscriptions are $21 a year (six issues), or you can download the magazine via FTP (the repository from which you can upload or download software) from ftp.gmd.de. Published in text and Acrobat formats. Highly recommended.

Inside Mac Games
3862 Grace Lane
Glenview, IL 60025
800/339-0636 (orders), 708/486-0636
fax: 708/486-0647
AOL: IMGames; CIS: 71554,2761;
  eWorld: Tuncer;
  Internet: Tuncer@mcs.com

Mac Home Journal
544 2nd Street
San Francisco, CA 94107
415/957-1911

MacSense
3 Greynam Court
Nepean, Ontario, Canada K2G 5T1
613/228-3268
AOL: MacSenseEd; eWorld: MacSenseEd.
  (Include the period.)

MacUser
950 Tower Lane, 18th Floor
Foster City, CA 94404
415/378-5600
eWorld: MACUSER; WWW:
  http://www.macuser.ziff.com/~macuser/;
  ZiffNet/Mac via CIS: GO ZMC:MACUSER

MacWEEK
301 Howard Street, 15th Floor
San Francisco, CA 94105
415/243-3500
fax: 415/243-3651
ZiffNet/Mac via CIS: GO ZMC:MACWEEK

Macworld
501 2nd Street
San Francisco, CA 94107
415/243-0505
fax: 415/442-0766
AL: Macworld1; AOL: MACWORLD; CIS:
  70370,702; eWorld: MACWORLD

XYZZYnews
160 West 24th Street, #7C
New York, NY 10011
Internet: eileen@interport.net

~~~~~~

Shareware

"Wow!" you probably exclaimed when you launched our enclosed CD-ROM, "Look at all the free stuff!"

Sorry to burst your bubble, but much of that software is anything but free—it's shareware.

It's called shareware for a simple reason. The authors agree to share the fruit of their hard labor with the understanding that if you like what they've created, you'll send them the reasonable fee they've requested. What could be more fair? You get the opportunity to test-drive a professional piece of software with no money down. If you like it, you pay for it. If you don't, throw it away with a clean conscience.

There are a couple of very good reasons for paying shareware fees:

- **Here's an opportunity to directly support a creative effort.**
Your money's not going to pay for fancy, wasteful packaging. Nor will it under-write someone's jaunt to Barbados or brass fixtures in the executive washroom. Nine times out of ten, the person who wrote the game you love so dearly opens the envelope containing your check or answers the phone when you call to register. That person may use the money to buy lunch or pay the rent.

- **Your shareware payment encourages talented people to continue to produce great products.**
Listen, if you don't think folks like Andrew Welch and Tuan Huynh could be making buckets of money working at some large database-mill, you've got another think coming. It's simple: To get, you gotta give.

- **Pride of ownership.**
It's tough to break into the commercial software business. Many talented authors start out by producing shareware (some prefer to stay there. Check out our interview with Andrew Welch) and then move into the commercial world. When author X creates THE NEXT BIG COMMERCIAL THING, you'll be able to boast to your friends, "Oh yeah, I knew her when she was doing shareware. Here, let me show you the registration card she sent me."

- **It will make you feel good.**
Forget the boasting. Sending in your shareware fees demonstrates that you are an honorable person. This realization should give you an all-over cozy feeling.

There is no greater reward.

INTERVIEW: ANDREW WELCH ON SHAREWARE

Some of the finest Macintosh arcade games are designed and published by Ambrosia Software, the shareware game company created by programmer Andrew Welch. We checked in with Andrew regarding his thoughts on shareware versus commercial distribution.

Your games are of very high quality and surpass commercial standards in many instances. Why distribute your products as shareware rather than going the commercial route?

Commercial software distribution—putting a box on a shelf—is a dated concept in my opinion. Software publishers are attempting to sell software as if it were a toaster or other household appliance.

The problem is that this is essentially retrofitting an old paradigm onto an entirely new animal. For example, when you buy a software package, you aren't buying the software. In fact, in many cases you're not even buying the manuals, box, or disks that the software comes on. What you are buying is a license to use the software. Software ain't toasters folks.

The legal enforceability of these "shrink wrap" licenses is questionable because— among other reasons—the person buying the product doesn't have a chance to read over the license they are "agreeing" to at the point of purchase. Try walking into a software store and ripping a package open in front of your friendly neighborhood soft-

ware salesman so you can read the license agreement. They won't appreciate it.

Beyond the legal issues, as we all well know, software gets pirated no matter where it originally came from. Whether it is a shareware product that people download from an online service or a box they pick up at a store, the ease with which people can copy software leads to it being passed around like a social disease.

Just as water naturally flows downhill, software naturally gets copied—there are fundamental truths in human nature as well as in physics. Commercial software publishers have tried such dams as copy protection, serial numbers, or manual lookups, but I view these as short-term solutions used—and used validly I might add—to extend the viability of commercial software distribution.

We're trying to ride the tide rather than fight it. Will commercial software distribution collapse on itself? Definitely not. However, I do feel that there will be a gradual shift towards electronic software distribution in the future. We're already seeing it happen: Take a look at what database giant Oracle has done. Their new product is available only electronically.

This is happening now because there is a critical mass of people connected to various electronic information services. If you're looking for an address book product, would you rather search online for products that fit your needs—and try them first to ensure this is the case—or buy a product from a store based on the box it comes in? It's akin to asking someone to buy a car without test-driving it, or a shoe before trying it on.

What has been somewhat lacking until recently is quality software products available as shareware. We're working to change that, and it is working because consumers realize that they're getting a quality product for one-half to one-third of the price they'd pay for the box and distribution overhead used with commercial distribution methods.

Will you stay in the shareware realm in the long term?

Absolutely. This is a company based on a vision. If we're right, we'll hopefully be one of the pioneers. If we're wrong, we'll have to take a few arrows and rethink our focus. For now, however, I'm happy to report that things are indeed working.

The shareware games you distribute are not truncated in any way. They allow the user to experience the game in its final version with only a shareware message separating the unregistered user from the paying

customer. Some companies prefer to give the user only a taste of the game, with more features added after registration. Do you feel that you lose business from this practice?

Here you're walking the line between a demo product and a true shareware product. I view this distribution method as a hybrid between electronic distribution and traditional commercial software distribution.

At the present moment, this dual-headed method is likely the best approach—in monetary terms—and I feel it definitely makes sense for games that come in the form of missions such as DOOM. However, this just turns electronic distribution into glorified but effective advertising. You can test drive the car, but you can't take it over 20 mph or honk the horn.

If we come up with a game that is mission-based, we might go with this type of software distribution. However, my preference is to end up being either ahead of our time or naively foolish by distributing our full products online.

You've added the registration splash-screen to the latest revisions of your products. Has this helped to encourage people to register their soft-

ware? How about the ability to register with a credit card via telephone?

The answer is a profound yes in both cases.
Our belief is that people all have hundreds
of things more important in their life than
remembering to pay for a software product
they already have. Therefore, we shift the
burden away from the user and make it as
easy as possible for them to pay.

Our registration system serves three purposes. First, it explains what shareware is.
This is basic, however shareware distribution is a unique enough concept that I feel
it is a bit short-sighted to gloss over
explaining what it is from the get-go.

Second, it reminds the user that they still
haven't paid for the product. Our true purpose isn't to annoy users into paying—after
all, when was the last time you were
annoyed into buying *anything* from a pushy
salesman? Rather, we simply want to
remind people that they haven't paid for
our product, and need to do so if they
choose to keep it.

Third, it provides a simple and painless way
for people to register our products. Users
can register by calling our 800 number,
faxing in their registration, sending their
registration in via e-mail, or by using tradition US mail.

This all certainly does cause more regis-
trations to come our way. The reason is
simple: it mirrors the reality of the situation
by making it as easy as possible for people
to pay.

What are the most important things
one can do to become a successful
shareware author?

First and foremost is to create a quality
product. I hear many people complaining
about their lack of success in the shareware
market. Then I look at their products and
understand why they haven't done well.
Few people are going to give you money
because they like your smile; deliver something worthwhile.

Product support is also an important issue.
People expect it, and for a product as complicated as modern computer software, I
agree with them 100 percent. We offer
support forums on America Online, eWorld,
CompuServe, and GEnie. We also offer
technical support via e-mail, fax, telephone,
and, of course, regular old pony-mail.

If you want to approach shareware writing
as a hobby, there's nothing wrong with
that. But few part-time businesses turn into
successful enterprises.

JOE WILLIAMS ON COPY-PROTECTION

We hate copy protection—absolutely hate it. Thankfully, it has nearly disappeared from the gaming market (now if we could just get it out of MIDI software). In an attempt to drive that last nail into the copy protection coffin, we offer this interview with Delta Tao's president, Joe Williams.

Your stand on copy-protection is fairly well known around the industry and a bit notorious. Care to restate it here?

Copy-protection is evil.

How has your view been received in the business?

Most publishers hate it (copy protection), but they won't come out in public and say so. Copy-protection is like killing stray puppies—if you think it's a good idea, you don't want to talk about it. It's awfully unpopular with the masses.

What about the argument that companies lose countless sales to piracy and that unless companies copy-protect their products, they won't make enough money to A) stay in business or B) devote the kind of resources necessary to create their next mega-blockbuster.

Yeah, right. There are companies that lose sales to piracy—they make software that isn't as good as it sounds. People pirate their software, try it, and throw it away. With copy-protection they can stick some of their customers with the sale (Also, ironi-cally, people are much more forgiving with software they paid money for. They want to justify their purchase decision). Piracy leads to a lot of sales for us. People try our software, see how good it is, and buy it for the support and documentation.

Mega-blockbusters suck. I just played Wing Commander 3 (for the PC). Hidden inside there is a pretty good spaceship shoot-em-up, but the four CDs-worth of live-action movies are painful. Nothing is as boring as watching stupid 10-second film clips over and over. "Interactive" games are a joke.

Market forces will determine which games get produced. If a game costs more than it will make, it probably shouldn't be written.

What about network games?

We believe in the "Monopoly theory" of network games. When you purchase a board game, only one copy is necessary for as many people to play in a game together as the game supports. On the other hand, duplicating the game so they can each take it home is illegal. Nothing is more annoying than getting a "network game" only to find that you'll have to buy several more copies to actually play it with your friends.

Do you approve of such non-intrusive copy-protection as serial number entry, or one time lookup?

No, they're still bad. Still, if somebody's going to kick you in the shins, it's better they do it just once.

Index

~~~~~~

3 in Three, 177–178
3D Sound, 318
4D Boxing, 124–125
7th Guest, The 265–266

A

A-10 Attack!, 400–406, 484
A-Train, 210, 224–227, 232
Access Software
    Links Pro, 116–121
Activision, 12, 54–55, 108, 192, 257, 259, 451
    Infocom, 54–55
        Purchase of Infocom, 10, 12
    Paparazzi! Tales of Tinseltown, 259–262
    Return to Zork, 257–259
    Sargon V, 108–109
    Shanghai II, The Dragon's Eye, 192–193
    Spectre, 451–456
    Zork Anthology, 546–55
ADB, 422
Advanced Dungeons and Dragons Series,
    Collector's Edition, 270–272
Advanced Gravis, 422, 424–425
    Firebird, 425
    GamePad, 422, 424–426
    MouseStick II, 422, 424
ADVENT, 11–12
adventure games, 241–284
Air Warrior, 469
Alexander the Great, 336
Ali, Mohammed, 124
Alice, 278, 280
Alice in Wonderland, 278
Alliance Software
    Sub Battle Simulator, 64–66
Alone in the Dark, 266–268
Ambrosia Software, 23, 28–29, 33, 196
    see also Welch, Andrew
    Apeiron, 23–25
    Chiral, 196–197
    Maelstrom, 33–34
    Swoop, 28–30
America Online, 471–472, 491
American Laser Games
    Mad Dog McCree, 41–43
Amtex Software Corporation, 45
    Eight Ball Deluxe, 45–48
    Tristan, 45

Ancient Art of War, 362
Andreas, Glenn, 174
Anyone for Cards?, 89, 91
Apeiron, 22–25
Apple Computer, 3–8, 60, 439–442
    DOS Compatibility Card, 439–442
Apple II, 4, 211
AppleLink, 491
Appleton, Bill, 147
Arashi, 26–28
arcade games, 133–172
ARTSector ONE
    The Better Dead Ratification, 298–299
Astro Chase 3D, 152–155
Avalon Hill,
    Flight Commander II, 378–380

B

Backgammon, 478
Balance of Power, 484
basketball, 122–123
Battle Chess, 108–108
Battlefront Series, 363–367
    Decisive Battles of the American Civil War, 366
    Halls of Montezuma, 366
    MacArthur's War, 365–366
    Panzer Battles, 365
    Rommel, 366
Batwing, 427–430
Bentley, Tom, 222
Berkeley Systems
    Lunatic Fringe, 38–39
Better Dead Ratification, The 298–299
Blackjack for Macintosh, 83–84
Blackjack Trainer, 83–85
Blaze, 30–32
Blobbo, 174–175
Bluth, Don, 41
board games, 98–101
Bocher, Christian, 308
Bolo, 461–463
boxing, 124–125
brain games, 173–208
Braun, Jeff, 210–212
BreakThru, 202–203
Bremer, Michael, 222
bridge games, 94–97
BridgeMaster, 95–96

Brøderbund, 136, 210, 242, 246
  Prince of Persia I & II, 136–139
  Myst, 242–252
Brown, James, 231
Buckland, Patrick, 18
BugByte, Inc.
  Minefield, 193–195
Bungie Software, 316, 322, 324, 448
  Marathon, 322–326
  Marathon 2: Durandal, 324
  Minotaur, 448–450
  Pathways Into Darkness, 316–319
Bush, George 209

C

Caesar's Palace, 77–80
Calcutris, 201
calhoun, john, 20, 160, 166, 463
  Glypha III, 20–21
  Pararena, 463–465
Callisto, 193, 195, 205, 456
  Super Maze Wars, 456–459
  Super Mines, 193–195
Canadian Football League, 128
Capstone, 77, 89, 95
  Anyone for Cards?, 89–91
  BridgeMaster, 95–96
  Trump Castle II, 77–80
card games, 89–93
Carmen San Diego Rules the World, 211
Carrere, Tia, 308
Carriers at War I & II, 374–378
Carroll, Lewis, 278
Casady & Greene, 18, 157–160, 164, 166,
    463–465
  Crystal Crazy, 157–159
  Crystal Quest, 157–159
  Glider Pro, 166–168
  Pararena, 463–465
  Sky Shadow, 18–20
  Spaceway 2000, 160–161
  Zone Warrior, 164–166
Casino Buddy, 80–82
Casino Master Gold, 80–82
Castles: Siege and Conquest, 349–351
CD-ROM arcade games, 147–152
cellular automata, 215
centipede-style games, 21–25
Centron Software Technologies, 69, 80
  Casino Master Gold, 80–82
  Puzzle Master, 69–72
CH Products, 432–435
  Flightstick Pro, 434–435
  Jetstick, 432–433

Chamberlin, Steve
  Tetris Max, 199
Changeling Software, 36, 352
  Pax Imperia, 352, 354
  Space Madness, 36–37
C.H.A.O.S. Continuum, The 295
cheat codes,
  Dark Forces, 329
  DOOM II, 333
  Rebel Assault, 303
  Wolfenstein 3D, 315
CheckMate, 109–110
Cheshire, Stuart,
  Bolo, 461–463
chess games, 106–112
Chessmaster 3000, 110–111
Chiral, 196–197
  see also Welch, Andrew
ChoiceStick, 430–432
Chuck Yeager's Air Combat, 407–410
Civilization, 338–341
classic games, 13–66
ClockWerx, 205–207
Club Racquetball, 126–128
Cogito, 178–179
Cogix
  Crossword Wizard, 69, 71–72
Cold War, 197
Color MacCheese, 60
Colony, The 484
Commodore 64, 210, 2111
  joke at the expense of the, 198
  Will Wright uses, 210, 211
CompuServe, 468–469, 491
ConJelCo,
  Blackjack Trainer, 83–85
conquest games, 335–359
contacting us, xx
copy protection, 498
Costello, Elvis, 492
Cotter, Tim, 60
Cowtris, 201
Crawford, Chris, 9, 362
  interview, 5–7
  pizza preference, 112
Creative Multimedia
  The C.H.A.O.S. Continuum, 295
credentials, xvii
Crossword Wizard, 69, 71–72
Crowther, Willie, 11
Crumb, R., 179
Crystal Caliburn, 48–51, 484
Crystal Crazy, 157–159
Crystal Quest, 157–159

Cyan, 242–252
  see also Miller, Rand and Robyn
  Cosmic Osmo, 242
  Myst, 242–245, 252
  Spelunx and the Caves of Mr. Seudo, 242
  The Manhole, 242
CyberFlix, 147–152
  Jump Raven, 150–152
  Lunicus, 147–149
Cyclone, 25–26

D

Daedalus Encounter, The, 307–309
Dark Castle, 10, 58–62, 484
Dark Forces, 326–330, 484
Darwin's Dilemma, 179–180
Darwin, Charles, 179
Davey and Goliath
  the wretched cartoon, 320
Deadly Games
  U-BOAT, 367–370
Defender, 14, 15
Defender-style games, 14–19
DejaVu, 10
Delirium, 17–18
Deliverance, 139–141, 177
Delta Tao Software, 58–61, 92, 345–347,
    355–357, 498
  Beyond Dark Castle, 61
  Color MacCheese, 60
  Cotter, Tim, 60
  Dark Castle, 58–62
  Eric's Ultimate Solitaire, 60, 92–93
  Spaceware Ho!, 60, 355–357
  Strategic Conquest, 345–347
  Williams, Joe, 60, 498
Deluxe Bridge With Omar Sharif, 94–95
Diamonds, 188–189
Digital Eclipse, 14–16
  Defender, 14–16, 17
  Joust, 14–16
  Robotron, 14–16
digital environments, 278–283
Discis Entertainment
  Jewels of the Oracle, 252–254
Domark, 410, 415
  Flying Nightmares, 415–417
  Out of the Sun, 410–413
Dongleware Publishing, 162–164, 184–186
  Oxyd & Oxyd Magnum!, 184–186
  Tubular Worlds, 162–164
DOOM II, 330–333
DOS Compatibility Card, 439–442
Dragon's Lair, 40–41

Drew Pictures, 292
  Iron Helix, 292–294
Dynamix, 62–63, 69, 190
  Stellar 7, 62–64
  Take•A•Break! Crosswords, 69–70, 72
  The Even More Incredible Machine, 190–191

E

Eat my Photons, 156–157
Eccentric Software
  Eat My Photons, 156–157
Eight Ball Deluxe, 45–48
El-Fish, 237–238
Electronic Arts, 9–10, 87, 116, 120, 124, 342,
    407
  4D Boxing, 124–125
  Chuck Yeager's Air Combat, 407–410
  PGA Tour Golf III, 116–121
  Populous I & II, 342–344
  Power Poker, 87–89
Ellington, Duke, 224
Empire Deluxe, 336–338
Epyx Software, 9, 66
Eric's Ultimate Solitaire, 60, 92–93
Essex, Jim, 296
Even More Incredible Machine, The 190–191
eWorld, 472–472, 491

F

F-117A Stealth Fighter, 413–415
F/A-18 Hornet, 396–399, 473, 484
  The Korean Conflict, 397
fable, the wholly untrue, 134–135
Faces, 200
Falcon MC, 418–420
Federation II, 471
Firefall Arcade, 21–23, 177
first-person-perspective shoot-'em-ups,
    311–333
  chronology, 313
Fishies, 237
Flashback, 144–146
Flight Commander II, 378–380
flight simulations, 391–420
  terminology, 392–393
Flightstick Pro, 320, 434–435
Flying Nightmares, 415–417
Focus Enhancement, 21, 177–184
  Deliverance, 139–141
  Firefall Arcade, 21–23
  Inline Greatest hits Game Pak, 177–184
Fool's Errand, 177
football games, 128–131
Foreman, George, 124

Frontal Assaultware
  Onslaught, 387–389
Fryar, Craig, 7
Fujita, Yoshikatsu, 45
Full Metal Mac, 459–460

G

Gadget, 278–280
Gaia, 222
Galactic Slimeweasels, 173
gambling, 76–89
game controllers, 422–439
  Batwing, 427–430
  ChoiceStick, 430–432
  Flightstick Pro, 434–435
  GamePad, 425–426
  Jetstick, 432–433
  JoyStick, 427–429
  MouseStick II, 424, 426
  ThrustMaster Systems, 436–439
  Trackballs, 433
game sources, 485–490
GamePad, 154, 319, 425–426
GameNet, 474
GameTek, 104
  Jeopardy, 104–105
Gates, Bill
  as the Great Satan, 406
GATO, 64, 371, 484
GEnie, 469–471, 491
Glenn Andreas Software
  Blobbo, 174–175
Glider Pro, 166–168
Glypha III, 20–21
Godzilla, 215
golf games, 116–121
Graphic Simulations, 394–399
  F/A-18 Hornet, 396–399
  Hellcats Over the Pacific, 394–396
  Missions at Leyte Gulf, 395
Great Game Products
  Micro•Bridge Companion, 96–97
GT Interactive
  DOOM II, 330–333

H

Haller, Ben, 39
Halvorsen, Patrick
  Slam Dunk!, 122–123
hardware, 421–443
  add-ons, 439–443
    DOS Compatibility Card, 439–442
    Speakers, 443
    Ultimate Gaming Machine, 423

Haslam, Fred, 211
Hell Cab, 295–298
Hellcats Over the Pacific, 394–396
  Missions at Leyte Gulf, 395
HemiRoids, 35
Henderson, Scott, 12
High Risk Ventures, 25–26
  Cyclone, 25–26
  Space Madness, 26
horror games, 265–268
Hoyle Classic Card Games, 89–92
Hundred Years War, The 471
hunting and gathering games, 254–264
Huynh, Tuan
  Delirium, 17–18
  Space Junkie, 17
HyperBole Studios, 280–283
  Quantum Gate, 282–283
  The Madness of Roland, 280–281
HyperCard, 244, 246

I

ICOM, 10
  DejaVu, 10
  Shadowgate, 10
  Uninvited, 10
icons, defined, xviii
id Software, 312, 330
  DOOM II, 330–333
  Wolfenstein 3D, 312–315
Infocom, 9, 10, 12, 55–57, 259
  Leather Goddesses of Phobos, 12, 54, 55, 484
  Planetfall, 12, 55
  Return to Zork, 257–259
  Zork, 12
Inline Design, 21, 139, 177–184
  3 in Three, 177–178
  Cogito, 178–179
  Darwin's Dilemma, 179–180
  Deliverance, 139–141
  Firefall Arcade, 21–23
  Greatest Hits Game Pak 177–184
  S.C.Out, 182–183
  Tesseræ, 183–184
  The Tinies, 181
Inside Mac Games, 492–493
Interactive Fiction, 10–12
  Programming Tools,
    Adventure Simulator, 12
    Inform, 12
    TADS, 12
  Sources, 12
Iron Helix, 292–294
Ishido, 175–177, 484

J

Jacks, Rodney and Brenda,
  Jewelbox, 199
JauntTrooper Mission: THUNDERBOLT,
  262–264, 484
Jeopardy, 104–105
Jetstick, 432–433
Jewelbox, 199
Jewels of the Oracle, 252–254
Jobs, Steve, 106
Johnson, Cliff, 177
Journeyman Project, The, 288–290
Journeyman Project II: Buried in Time, The,
  290–292
Joust, 14–15
JoyStick, 427–429
joysticks *see* game controllers
Judson, Jeremy
  editorial comments, xix, 392–393, 425, 426
Jump Raven, 147, 150–152

K

Kaneko, Kuniyoshi, 278
Kelly, Mike, 26, 37
Ken's House of Pancakes, xiii
Kepler's Books, xiii
Kernel Productions
  ChoiceStick, 430–432
Khan, Genghis, 336
King's Quest VII: The Princeless Bride, 254–257
Kite, Tom, 118
Klein, Eric, 7

L

L-Zone, 278–280
Leather Goddesses of Phobos, 12, 54, 55, 484
Lemmings, 204–205
LeVitus, Bob, 492
Levy, Steven, 493
Limbaugh, Rush, 168
Links Pro, 116–121, 473
LittleWing, 45–53
  Crystal Caliburn, 48–51
  Eight Ball Deluxe, 45–48
  Loony Labyrinth, 51–53
  Tristan, 45
Lockard, Brodie, 192
Lode Runner: The Legend Returns, 56–58
Lombardi, Vince, 115
Loony Labyrinth, 51–53
Lovelock, James, 222

Loyola, Roman "The Man," 492
LucasArts, 301–304, 326–330
  Dark Forces, 326–330
  Rebel Assault, 301–304
Ludtke, Jim, 296
Lunar Rescue, 484
Lunatic Fringe, 38–39
Lunicus, 147–149

M

Mac Games Evangelist, 6–8
Mac Home Journal, 492, 493
MacALLY, 427
  Batwing, 427–430
  JoyStick, 427–429
MacF.I.B.S., 478
Macintosh Bible, The, 353
Macman Pro, 30–32
MacMines, 193–1965
MacPlay, 73–80, 94, 98, 100–103, 106–108,
  142, 144, 152, 168, 175, 266, 300, 312,
  349
  Alone in the Dark, 266–268
  Astro Chase 3D, 152–155
  Battle Chess, 106–108
  Caesar's Palace, 77–78
  Castles: Siege and Conquest, 349–351
  CheckMate, 109–110
  Deluxe Bridge With Omar Sharif, 94–95
  Flashback, 144–146
  Ishido, 175–177, 484
  Mario's Game Gallery, 102–103
  Monopoly, 100–101
  Out of this World, 142–144
  Power Pete, 168–172
  Risk Deluxe, 98–99
  Scrabble, 73–76
  Star Trek: 25th Anniversary, 300–301
  Wolfenstein 3D, 312–315
MacSense, 492, 493
MacSoft
  Troubled Souls, 186–188
MacUser, 492, 493
MacWEEK, 492, 493
Macworld, 493
Mad Dog McCree, 41–43
Madness of Roland, The, 280–281
Maelstrom, 33–34, 484
Marathon, 322–326, 484
Marathon 2: Durandal, 324
Mario's Game Gallery, 102–103
Master of Orion, 357–359
Maven, 73–76

Maxis, 209–240
  see also Wright, Will
  A-Train, 224–227
    Healthy Disagreement Regarding, 227
  El-Fish, 237–238
  manuals, 222
  our top five list, 232
  SimAnt, 231–233
  SimCity 2000, 215–219
  SimCity CD-ROM, 214
  SimCity Classic, 213–216
  SimEarth, 221–223
  SimFarm, 234–236
  SimLife, 223–224
  SimTower, 228–231
  SimTown, 219–221
  Widget Workshop, 238–240
Maze Wars Plus, 10, 448
mean review, a really, 295
Mechner, Jordan, 136
MegaCorp
  JauntTrooper Mission: THUNDERBOLT,
    262–264
Merit Studios,
  Tom Landry Strategy Football, 130–131
Merrill, Peter, 345–346
MicroProse, 338, 357, 413
  Civilization, 338–341
  F-117A Stealth Fighter, 413–415
  Master of Orion, 357–359
Microsoft, 4, 406
  Microsoft Flight Simulator 4.0, 406
  necessary bashing of, 406
  Windows, 4
  Word, 57, 431
Microsoft Flight Simulator 4.0, 406
Micro•Bridge Companion, 96–97
Might & Magic III: Worlds of Xeen, 274–277
Miles Computing, 10
Miller, Rand and Robyn, 242
  interview, 246–251
  pizza preferences, 112
Milnes, Jon, 26
Milton Bradley Company, 73
Mindscape, 64
Minefield, 193–195
Minefield Deluxe, 194
Minotaur, 448–450, 484
Monopoly, 100–101
Moreno, Pepe, 296, 298
MouseStick II, 154, 319, 418, 422–426
MUDs, 479–483
Mullin, Eileen, 493
Murray, Bill, 148
Murry, Dave and Barry, 362
Myst, 242–252, 484
  see also Miller, Rand and Robyn
Myst II, 249–251
  see also Miller, Rand and Robyn

N

Nelson, Graham, 12
Nettrek, 448
network, 447–465
  Mac games list, 457
  setting up your Mac, 454–455
New World Computing, 275–277, 336–338
  Empire Deluxe, 336–338
  Might & Magic III Worlds of Xeen, 275–277
Nojima, Reiko, 45, 47, 52
Norman, Greg, 237
North, Ollie, 28
Nostradamus, xiii–xiv
NovaLogic
  WolfPack, 371–374

O

Oasis, The, 43–45
Oh No! More Lemmings, 204–205
Old Crow, 391
online gaming, 467–483
  America Online, 471–472
  CompuServe, 468–469
  eWorld, 472–473
  GameNet, 474
  GEnie, 469–471
    Air Warrior, 469
    Federation II, 471
    Orb Wars, 470
    Scorpia's Round Table, 471
    The Hundred Years War, 471
  MacF.I.B.S., 478
  MUDs, 479–483
  Outland, 476–478
  services, 491
  Sim-Net/OMNI Games, 473–474
Onslaught, 387–389
Orb Wars, 470
Origin Systems, 10, 304–306
  Super Wing Commander, 304–306
Out of the Sun, 410–413
Out of this World, 142–144
Outland, 356, 476–478
Ouzts, Todd, 87
Ovaltine, 127
Oxyd, 184–186
Oxyd Magnum!, 184–186

P

PacMan Games, 30–32
Pajitnov, Alexey, 202–203, 205, 207
Pangea Software, 22, 169
Paparazzi! Tales of Tinseltown, 259–262
Pararena, 463–465
Parker Brothers, 101
Parker, Eric,
    A-10 Attack!, 400–406
    Hellcats Over the Pacific, 394–396
    interview, 402–403
    pizza preference, 112
ParSoft, 400
    see also Parker, Eric
    A-10 Attack, 400–406
Pathways Into Darkness, 316–319, 484
Patton vs. Rommel, 362
Pax Imperia, 352–354
Payne, Mark
    see also SimNet/Omni Games
    interview, 475–476
    pizza preference, 112
Pelak, Robert, 12
Perez, Christopher, 469
Perot, Ross, 139
PGA Tour Golf III, 116–121
Pickens, Slim, 355
pinball games, 43–53
    see also LittleWing
    terminology, 44
pizza of the programmers, 112
Planetfall, 12, 55
PlayMaker,
    PlayMaker Football, 128–130
    Ultima III, 269–270
PlayMaker Football, 128–130
Plotkin, Andrew, 12
Populous I & II, 342–344
Power Pete, 168–172
Power Poker, 87–89
PowerBook Gaming, 440–441
Presto Studios, 288–292
    The Journeyman Project, 288–290
    The Journeyman Project II: Buried in Time, 290–292
Prince of Persia I & II, 136–139
Project STORM Team
    Arashi 1.1 26–28
Psygnosis
    Lemmings & Oh No! More Lemmings, 204–205
publications, 492–493
Puzzle Master, 69, 72
puzzling adventures, 242–254

Q

Quantum Gate, 282–283
Quest For Glory I, 272–274
questing games, 269–277

R

racquetball, 126
Raid on Bungeling Bay, 210, 211
    see also Wright, Will
Rassmusan, Billy, 166
ratings, xvii–xviii
Reactor
    Spaceship Warlock, 286–287
ReadySoft
    Dragon's Lair, 40–41
Reagan, Ronald, 13, 28, 64, 197
Reality Bytes
    Sensory Overload, 319–321
Rebel Assault, 301–304
Redburn, Kendall, 194
reissued games, 54–66
repetitive strain injury (RSI), 170–171
ResEdit, 62
Return to Zork, 257–259
Risk Deluxe, 98–99
Roach, Greg, 280, 281, 282
Robbin, Jeffrey, 160
Roberts, Michael, 13
Robotron, 14–16
Rommel, Erwin, 336
RSI *see* repetitive strain injury

S

S.C.Out, 182–183
Saenz, Mike, 286
Sargon V, 108–109
science fiction games, 285–309
Scrabble, 73–76
Sensory Overload, 319–321
Shadowgate, 10
Shanghai II, 192–193
shareware, 494–497
Sheppard Company, The
    Maven 73–76
Sheppard, Brian, 76
Shono, Haruhiko, 278–280
Sierra On-Line, 56–58, 89–92, 254–257, 272–274
    Hoyle Classic Card Games, 89–92
    King's Quest VII: The Princeless Bride, 254–257
    Load Runner: The Legend Returns, 56–58
    Quest for Glory I, 272–274

Silicon Beach Software, 9, 10, 64
   Dark Castle, 10
Sim-Net/OMNI Games, 473–474
   see also Payne, Mark
SimAnt, 231–233
SimCity, 210, 211–212, 484
SimCity 2000, 213, 214, 215, 216–217
SimCity Classic, 213–216
SimCity Enhanced CD-ROM, 214
SimEarth, 221–223
SimFarm, 234–236
SimLife, 223–224
SimTower, 228–231
SimTown, 219–221
Sky Shadow, 18–20
Slam Dunk!, 122–123
Smash Hit Racquetball, 126
Smith, Douglas, 56
Softstream International
   Blaze, 30–32
Software Toolworks, The
   Chessmaster 3000 110–111
SoftWars
   Full Metal Mac, 459–460
songs
   happy, 234
   homey, 43
SoundBlaster, 441
Space Ace, 41
space arcade games, 25–29, 32–39
space conquest games, 351–359
Spaceship Warlock, 286
Space Junkie, 17
Space Madness, 26, 36–37
Spaceship Warlock, 286–287
Spaceward Ho!, 60, 355–357
   see also Williams, Joe
Spaceway 2000, 160–161
speakers, 443
Spectre, 451–456
Spectre Supreme, 451–456
Spectre VR, 451–456
Spectrum HoloByte, 9, 197, 197–203, 205–207,
   418–420
   BreakThru, 202–203
   ClockWerx, 205–207
   Falcon MC, 418–420
   Tetris Gold, 197–202
      Faces, 200
      Super Tetris 201–202
      Tetris, 198
      Welltris, 198–200
      Wordtris 200
spell of unsightly warts, 269
Spin Doctor, 205, 206
sports games, 115–131

Spracklen, Dan and Kathe, 108
SSG *see* Strategic Studies Group
SSI
   Advanced D & D Series, The Collector's
      Edition 270–272
Stadler, Craig, 118
Star Trek: 25th Anniversary, 300–301
StarPlay Productions, 48–53
   Crystal Caliburn, 48–51
   Loony Labyrinth, 51–53
Stars Wars, 328
Stellar 7, 62–64
Strategic Conquest, 345–347, 484
Strategic Studies Group (SSG)
   Battlefront Series, 363–367
      Decisive Battles of the American Civil War,
         Volume III, 366
      Halls of Montezuma, 366
      MacArthur's War, 365–366
      Panzer Battles, 365
      Rommel, 366
   Carriers at War I & II, 375–379
   Warlords II, 347–349
Sub Battle Simulator, 64–66
Super Maze Wars, 456–459
Super Mines, 193–195
Super Tetris, 201–202
Super Wing Commander, 304–306
Swoop, 28–30
   see also Welch, Andrew
Synergy, Inc., 278–280
   Alice, 278–280
   Gadget, 278–280
   L-Zone, 278–280

T

Take•A•Break! Crosswords, 69–70, 72
Telarium, 9
Tesseræ, 183–184
Tetris, 197–200, 202
Tetris Gold, 197–202
Tetris Max, 199
Three Sixty/Atomic Games, 381–387
   see also Zabalaoui, Keith
   V for Victory Series, 381–384
      Gold-Juno-Sword, 383–3844
      Market Garden, 383
      Utah Beach, 383
      Velikiye Luki, 383
   World at War Series, 384–387
      Operation Crusader, 386–387
      Stalingrad, 386–387
ThrustMaster, 306, 319, 399, 436–439
   Flight Control System, 436–439
   Rudder Control System, 436–439
   Weapons Control System, 436–439

Time Warner Interactive Group
Hell Cab, 295–298
Tinies, The, 181
Tom Landry Strategy Football, 130–131
top ten list, our, 484
Torkelson, Cary
MacMines, 193–194, 195
Tower of Power, 52
trackballs, 433
traditional games, 67–111
Trebek, Alex, 104
Trilobyte/Virgin Games
The 7th Guest, 265–266
Tristan, 45
Troubled Souls, 186–188
Trump Castle II, 77–80
Tubular Worlds, 162–164
Tyson, Mike, 139

U

U-BOAT, 66, 367–370
Ueno, Koji, 279
Ultima III, 269–270
ultimate gaming machine, 423
Uninvited, 10
Urich, Robert, 58
his dog, 58

V

V for Victory Series, 381–384
Gold-Juno-Sword, 383–384
Market Garden, 383
Utah Beach, 383
Velikiye Luki, 383
vaporware, 353
Varcon Systems, 30, 80, 83, 188
Blackjack for Macintosh, 83–84
Casino Buddy, 80–82
Diamonds, 188–189
HemiRoids, 35
Macman Pro, 30–32
Velocity, 451–456
Spectre Supreme, 451–456
Spectre VR, 451–456
Virgin Games, 126–128, 307–309
Club Racquetball, 126–128
Daedalus Encounter, The, 307–309
Virtual Battlefield Environment, 404–405
Virtual Vegas Volume 1: Blackjack, 85–86
Virtual Vegas, Inc.
Virtual Vegas Volume 1: Blackjack, 85–86

W

Walker, Bryan, 411
war games, 361–389
Warlords II, 347–349
Welch, Andrew,
see also Ambrosia Software
Apeiron, 23–25
Chiral, 196–197
interview, 495–497
Maelstrom, 33–34
pizza preference, 112
Welltris, 198–200
Widget Workshop, 238–240
Williams, Joe
see also Delta Tao Software
interview, 60–61, 498
pizza preference, 112
Wolfenstein 3D, 312–315
WolfPack, 66, 371–374
Wolosenko, Ihor, 212
Woods, Don, 11
word games, 68–76
crossword puzzles, 68–72
scrabble games, 73–76
Wordtris, 200
World at War Series, 384–387
Operation Crusader, 386–387
Stalingrad, 386–387
Wozniak, Steve, 106
Wright, Will, 210, 212–213, 221
see also Maxis
interview, 211–212
pizza preference, 112

X

XYZZYnews, 493

Y

Yeager, Gen. Charles "Chuck," 391

Z

Zabalaoui, Keith,
interview, 376–377
pizza preference, 112
Zartman, Doug, 324
Zoeller, Fuzzy, 118
Zone Warrior, 164–166
Zork, 12, 54–55
Zork Anthology, 54–55

NOT ALL GAMES ARE CREATED EQUAL

Ever buy a Macintosh game and feel like you've been taken to the cleaners? What you need is Inside Mac Games (IMG), the only magazine solely devoted to Macintosh entertainment. Each issue is packed with in-depth game reviews of what's hot and what's not. Before you buy that next game, read the review in Inside Mac Games, try the demo, and take a look at the full-size screen shots before putting your hard-earned money down.

Inside Mac Games also gives you exclusive previews of the hottest soon-to-be released games, stunning color screen shots, QuickTime™ movies, insightful interviews, industry news, feature columns, hints, tips, and tricks, rumors, and special reports.

But hang on, there's more! Each CD-ROM issue of IMG is filled with the latest shareware games, commercial games demos, walkthroughs, bug fixers and updaters, and cheater programs. You get it all!

In addition to games, Inside Mac Games also provides reviews of the latest educational and edutainment software. So no matter what your interests are, IMG has something for the entire family. And best of all, IMG covers ONLY Macintosh entertainment. Finally, a computer entertainment magazine "for the rest of us!"

YES! I WANT TO SUBSCRIBE TO INSIDE MAC GAMES!

Get 10 issues on CD-ROM for just $59 ($79 outside the U.S.)

FULL NAME (please print clearly) _____   ADDRESS _____

CITY _____   STATE _____   ZIP _____

☐ PAYMENT ENCLOSED   ☐ VISA/MC   CARD# _____   EXP DATE _____

For faster service call toll free: 1-800-339-0636

Make all checks payable to: Inside Mac Games, 3862 Grace Lane, Glenview, IL 60025